Dear

many more conversations in the coming years. With all best wishes,

ANNUNCIATIONS

George

Annunciations:

Sacred Music for the Twenty-First Century

Edited by George Corbett

https://www.openbookpublishers.com

© 2019 George Corbett. Copyright of individual chapters is maintained by the chapters' authors.

This work is licensed under a Creative Commons Attribution 4.0 International license (CC BY 4.0). This license allows you to share, copy, distribute and transmit the text; to adapt the text and to make commercial use of the text providing attribution is made to the authors (but not in any way that suggests that they endorse you or your use of the work). Attribution should include the following information:

George Corbett (ed.), *Annunciations: Sacred Music for the Twenty-First Century*. Cambridge, UK: Open Book Publishers, 2019, https://doi.org/10.11647/OBP.0172

In order to access detailed and updated information on the license, please visit, https://www.openbookpublishers.com/product/994#copyright

Further details about CC BY licenses are available at, https://creativecommons.org/licenses/by/4.0/

For copyright details of all third-party materials, please see the lists of illustrations at the end of each chapter. Copyright of recorded material belongs to the University of St Andrews.

All external links were active at the time of publication unless otherwise stated and have been archived via the Internet Archive Wayback Machine at https://archive.org/web

Updated digital material and resources associated with this volume are available at https://www.openbookpublishers.com/product/994#resources

Every effort has been made to identify and contact copyright holders and any omission or error will be corrected if notification is made to the publisher.

ISBN Paperback: 978-1-78374-726-9
ISBN Hardback: 978-1-78374-727-6
ISBN Digital (PDF): 978-1-78374-728-3
ISBN Digital ebook (epub): 978-1-78374-729-0
ISBN Digital ebook (mobi): 978-1-78374-730-6
ISBN XML: 978-1-78374-731-3
DOI: 10.11647/OBP.0172

Cover image: Don Simone Camaldolese. Frontispiece from a Choir Book, ca. 1390. Ink on vellum, 59.4 x 44.8 cm. (irregular left edge). Brooklyn Museum, Brooklyn Museum Collection, X1015.

Cover design: Anna Gatti.

All paper used by Open Book Publishers is sourced from SFI (Sustainable Forestry Initiative) accredited mills and the waste is disposed of in an environmentally friendly way.

To the Cathedral Choir of St Albans Abbey

Contents

Acknowledgements	xi
Notes on the Contributors	xiii
Introduction *George Corbett*	1

Part I: Compositional and Theological Perspectives — 7

1. The Most Spiritual of the Arts: Music, Modernity, and the Search for the Sacred — 9
   James MacMillan

2. The Surrogate Priest: Reflecting on Vocation with Welsh Composer Paul Mealor — 17
   Margaret McKerron with Paul Mealor

3. Mary as a Model for Creative People: Establishing Theologian-Composer Partnerships with James MacMillan — 31
   George Corbett

4. When Gods Talk to Men: Reading Mary with the Annunciations of the Hebrew Bible and the Ancient Near East — 45
   Madhavi Nevader

5. Old Testament Typology: The Gospel Canticles in the Liturgy and Life of the Church — 57
   William P. Hyland

6.	Composing for a Non-Professional Chapel Choir: Challenges and Opportunities *Tom Wilkinson*	69

Part II: 'Annunciations' in the Hebrew Bible — 95

7.1.	'Where are you?': The Temptation of Adam and Eve (Genesis 3) *Margaret McKerron*	97
7.2.	Composer's Reflections *Anselm McDonnell*	111
	'Hinneni'	115
8.1.	Jacob Wrestling (Genesis 32.22-32) *Marian Kelsey*	127
8.2.	Composer's Reflections *Dominic de Grande*	141
	'Whilst falling asleep, Savta told me of Jacob'	145
9.1.	Setting Fire to Music: Theological and Aesthetic Approaches (Exodus 3) *Rebekah Dyer*	161
9.2.	Composer's Reflections *Kerensa Briggs*	173
	'Exodus III'	177
10.1.	A Dark Dream: God's Calling of Samuel and the Ministry of Eli (1 Samuel 3) *Caleb Froehlich*	189
10.2.	Composer's Reflections *Seán Doherty*	201
	'God Calls Samuel'	207
11.1.	Elijah's Silent Annunciation (1 Kings 19.8-15) *Mary Stevens*	217
11.2.	Composer's Reflections *Lisa Robertson*	229
	'The Silent Word Sounds'	233

	12.1.	Musical Arguments and Gender Performance (Song of Songs 3.6-11) *Kimberley Jane Anderson*	253
	12.2.	Composer's Reflections *Stuart Beatch*	265
		'The Annunciation of Solomon'	269

Part III: Programming and Performing Sacred Music — 277

	13.	Sacred Art Music in the Catholic Liturgy: Perspectives from the Roman Catholic Church in Scotland *Michael Ferguson*	279
	14.	Commissioning and Performing Sacred Music in the Anglican Church: A Perspective from Wells Cathedral *Matthew Owens*	297
	15.	Music at the Borders of the Sacred: Handel, Elgar and Poulenc *Michael Downes*	311
	16.	Sacred Music in Secular Spaces *Jonathan Arnold*	325
	17.	Music and Theology: Some Reflections on 'the Listener's Share' *Gavin Hopps*	337

Index — 353
Bibliography — 363

Acknowledgements

This volume grew out of a collaboration between the Institute for Theology, Imagination and the Arts (ITIA), in the University of St Andrews' School of Divinity; the University of St Andrews Music Centre; and St Salvator's Chapel Choir. I would like to thank the exceptional research community of ITIA: students on our MLitt in Theology and the Arts, our cohort of doctoral students, as well as staff and affiliated staff (former and current) generously supported this venture in numerous ways, from providing underpinning research to facilitating workshops. I would like to thank, in particular, Kathryn Wehr and Margaret McKerron for their invaluable help in co-ordinating the theologian-composer partnerships and the TheoArtistry Festival, and Rebekah Dyer for designing and maintaining the TheoArtistry website. Michael Downes (Director of Music), James MacMillan, and Tom Wilkinson (who directed St Salvator's Chapel Choir) grasped the potential of this project from its inception, and supported it throughout. St Salvator's Chapel Choir's speedy mastery of six new pieces of music was especially impressive to witness. I would also like to thank Jeremy Begbie, Chris Bragg, David Brown, Mark Elliott, Michael Ferguson, Stephen Holmes, Gavin Hopps, Sherrill Keefe, Rebekah Lamb, Ann Loades, Michael Partridge, John Perry, Bede Williams, and Judith Wolfe.

It has been a joy and privilege for me to work so closely on this project with the six theologians and six composers in the TheoArtistry partnerships, and with James MacMillan, who mentored the composers on the scheme. I would also like to thank my colleagues Gavin Hopps, William P. Hyland, and Madhavi Nevader, who shared the insights of their research with the theologians and composers, and the Austrian filmmaker David Boos, who produced a documentary, as well as two other short films, about the TheoArtistry collaborations. Twenty-two of the collaborators on this project have also contributed chapters to this volume, and I am deeply grateful to you all. I would like to thank the School of Divinity's Research Committee for funding a research assistant, and I am especially indebted to Margaret McKerron for her work on the volume. I would particularly like to highlight her role as visual editor, in preparing the volume's illustrations and innovative graphics, and in tirelessly securing copyright for each image.

In envisaging a volume that incorporates text, images, sound, musical scores, and links to video documentaries, I only ever had one publisher in mind: Open Book Publishers. I am very grateful to the team at OBP, and especially Alessandra Tosi, for collaborating on a volume which, I hope, showcases some of the possibilities of their pioneering publishing model. I am indebted to the peer reviewer for their support of the volume, to Rob Wilding and Lucy Barnes for their very helpful comments, meticulous copyediting, and for preparing the index, and to Luca Baffa for his expert typesetting and production of the final manuscript. I am also grateful to Michael Byce and the University of St Andrews Library, as well as the School of Divinity, for supporting open access, and co-funding the subvention grant. I would like to thank Anna Gatti for her design of the book's cover, and Monica Park and the Brooklyn Museum, New York, for permission to print the choir book frontispiece illustrated by Simone Camaldolese.

This project would not have got off the ground without the vision and support of its key funders: the University of St Andrews Research Policy Office, the School of Divinity, the University of St Andrews Music Centre, and the Russell Trust. I would like to thank, in particular, Laura Bates, Michael Downes, Mark Elliott and Stephen Holmes. I am also indebted to Kevin Nordby, who provided assistance, and kept my spirits up, in writing funding applications.

Finally, I would like to thank all those, starting with my parents, who gave me the opportunity of a musical formation within the British choral tradition. This volume is dedicated to the Cathedral Choir of St Albans Abbey, where I had the privilege of beginning this formation as a chorister under Barry Rose and Andrew Parnell.

Notes on the Contributors

Kimberley Jane Anderson is a PhD candidate in the Institute for Theology, Imagination and the Arts (ITIA), University of St Andrews. Her thesis explores the spiritually transformative potential of 'progressive' rock as experienced by fans, drawing on responses to a qualitative survey, her own, situated aesthetic analysis, and phenomenological accounts of imaginative experience.

Jonathan Arnold is Dean of Divinity at Magdalen College, Oxford. He is a former member of The Sixteen, author of *Sacred Music in Secular Society* (2014), and co-founder of Frideswide Voices.

Stuart Beatch studied music and composition at the University of Regina, the University of Alberta, and King's College, London. His music has been performed by ensembles across North America and the UK, including the BBC Singers, the National Youth Choir of Canada, Pro Coro Canada, the Chronos Vocal Ensemble, the Elysian Singers, musica intima, the Toronto Mendelssohn Choir, and the Choral Arts Initiative.

Kerensa Briggs is Composer in Residence at Godolphin & Latymer School, and previously studied composition at King's College, London, where she also held a choral scholarship. She won the 'National Centre for Early Music Young Composers Award' (2014), and her music has been recorded by Delphian Records for broadcast on BBC Radio 3 and BBC Radio Scotland.

George Corbett is Senior Lecturer in Theology and the Arts, University of St Andrews. He teaches and researches in theology and the arts, and in systematic and historical theology, and he is the author of *Dante and Epicurus: a Dualistic Vision of Secular and Spiritual Fulfilment* (2013), and co-editor, with Heather Webb, of *Vertical Readings in Dante's 'Comedy'*, 3 vols. (2015, 2016, 2017).

Dominic de Grande studied at the Royal Birmingham Conservatoire and the University of Cambridge, where he was awarded the Sir Arthur Bliss Prize for his portfolio of compositions. Specialising in contemporary classical and electronic music, he has composed the scores for award-winning documentaries and films, and has long-term partnerships with leading visual and video artists and choreographers.

Seán Doherty is Assistant Professor of Music at Dublin City University in the School of Theology, Philosophy, and Music, where he is active as a composer, musicologist, and performer. Originally from Derry, Northern Ireland, he read music at St John's College, Cambridge, and received his PhD at Trinity College, Dublin.

Michael Downes became the University of St Andrews' first full-time Director of Music in 2008, following a similar post at Fitzwilliam College, Cambridge. He conducts the St Andrews Chorus, Scotland's largest choral society, and is the founding artistic director of Byre Opera. His publications include the first full-length study of the music of Jonathan Harvey.

Rebekah Dyer is a theological researcher and creative practitioner based in Scotland. She graduated with a PhD in Theology, Imagination and the Arts from the University of St Andrews in 2018.

Michael Ferguson is Director of Music at St Mary's Metropolitan RC Cathedral, Edinburgh, and Teaching Fellow in Music, University of St Andrews. His academic research encompasses music and religion, community music-making, and the creative process. As a composer for film, his music has appeared on BBC, Channel 4, and at film festivals worldwide, and his choral music has been performed in the UK, Ireland and the USA.

Caleb Froehlich is a PhD candidate in the Institute for Theology, Imagination and the Arts (ITIA), University of St Andrews. His thesis examines how ostensibly non-religious art in the United States opened up or introduced young people to religion during the first half of the 1970s.

Gavin Hopps is Senior Lecturer in Literature and Theology, and Director of the Institute for Theology, Imagination and the Arts (ITIA), University of St Andrews. His particular interests are in Romantic writing and contemporary popular music, and he is the author of *Morrissey: The Pageant of His Bleeding Heart* (2009), editor of *Byron's Ghosts: The Spectral, the Spiritual and the Supernatural* (2013), and co-author, with David Brown, of *The Extravagance of Music* (2018).

William P. Hyland is Lecturer in Church History, University of St Andrews. He specializes in Medieval Church history, with a particular focus on monasticism and spirituality, and he is the author of *Custody of the Heart: Selected Spiritual Writings of Abbot Martin Veth, O.S.B.* (2001), and president of the editorial board of *Premonstratenisan Texts and Studies*.

Marian Kelsey recently completed a PhD in Hebrew Bible in the School of Divinity, University of St Andrews. Her research investigated the use of inner-biblical allusions and literary context in the book of Jonah.

James MacMillan is one of today's most successful composers, whose works are performed and broadcast around the world, and he is also internationally active as a conductor. He is Professor of Theology and Music, University of St Andrews, the founder of The Cumnock Tryst, and was awarded a knighthood for his services to music in 2015.

Anselm McDonnell is a PhD candidate in Music Composition at Queen's University Belfast. He is the winner of the International Kastalsky Choral Writing Competition (2018), and he has worked with ensembles including the CRASH Ensemble, C4 Conductors/Composers Collective, BBC Singers, BBC National Orchestra of Wales, and the Ulster Orchestra.

Margaret McKerron is a PhD candidate in the School of Divinity, University of St Andrews. Drawing on the work of Scottish theologians Thomas Erskine of Linlathen and Alexander John Scott, her research considers the relevance of personal relationships in theological education and hermeneutics.

Paul Mealor is an internationally acclaimed composer, and Professor of Composition at the University of Aberdeen. The first president of 'Ty Cerdd', Wales's National Centre for music making, and Vice-President of the Llangollen International Eisteddfod and the North Wales International Music Festival, he received the Glanville Jones Award, from the Welsh Music Guild, for his outstanding contribution to music in Wales (2013).

Madhavi Nevader is Lecturer in Hebrew Bible, University of St Andrews. Her main areas of research are the political theology of the Hebrew Bible and other ancient Near Eastern texts, as well as Prophecy and Israelite/Judahite religion.

Matthew Owens is recognised as one of the UK's leading choral conductors, choir trainers, and organists. He is Founder and Artistic Director of Cathedral Commissions, which commissions new works from pre-eminent British composers, and the innovative festival *new music wells* at Wells Cathedral, where he is Organist and Master of the Choristers. He is a published composer with Oxford University Press and Novello.

Lisa Robertson is a PhD candidate in Music Composition at the Royal Conservatoire of Scotland. Her music has been performed by the Czech Philharmonic Orchestra, Red Note Ensemble, and Karlovy Vary Symphony Orchestra, among others, and at the Sound Festival, West Cork Chamber Music Festival, Edinburgh Fringe Festival and on BBC Radio 3.

Mary Stevens was a cloistered, contemplative Carmelite nun for thirty-three years, before gaining an MLitt and PhD in Theology at the University of St Andrews. Her doctoral research considered the theology of consecrated life presented by Pope John Paul II's apostolic exhortation *Redemptionis Donum*, with particular reference to his theological anthropology, soteriology and sanjuanist spirituality.

Tom Wilkinson is Teaching Fellow in Performance, University of Edinburgh, and engaged in doctoral research on the music of J. S. Bach. From 2009–2018, he was University Organist and Director of Chapel Choirs, University of St Andrews; he will become University Organist and Associate Lecturer in Music from July 2019.

Introduction

George Corbett

In *Sacred Music in Secular Society*, Jonathan Arnold highlights a strange phenomenon: 'the seeming paradox that, in today's so-called secular society, sacred choral music is as powerful, compelling and popular as it has ever been'.[1] The explosion of new media through the internet and digital technology has created a new, broader audience for 'the creative art of Renaissance polyphony and its successors to the present day', a genre of sacred music that seems to have 'an enduring appeal for today's culture'.[2] Arnold suggests, moreover, that sacred choral music is thriving in Anglican worship: although attendance continues to decline in general, he cites the rise at religious services sung by professional choirs in British cathedrals over the last two decades.[3] In 2015, Pope Emeritus Benedict XVI, while acknowledging the tension in Catholic music-making following the Second Vatican Council, reaffirmed his conviction that 'great sacred music is a reality of theological stature and of permanent significance for the faith of the whole of Christianity, even if it is by no means necessary that it be

---

1 Jonathan Arnold, *Sacred Music in Secular Society* (Farnham: Ashgate, 2014), p. xiv. I would like to thank Edward Foley for inviting me to reflect on the TheoArtistry project in a special issue of *Religions*, and the journal's general editors for permission to reprint material here and in Chapter 3. For the original article, see George Corbett, 'TheoArtistry, and a Contemporary Perspective on Composing Sacred Choral Music', *Religions*, 9.1 (2018), 7, 1–18 (Special Issue: Music: Its Theologies and Spiritualities — A Global Perspective), https://doi.org/10.3390/rel9010007

2 Arnold, pp. xiv–xv. In the later twentieth and early twenty-first centuries, there has been a remarkable flowering of different kinds of Christian music both inside and outside denominational churches. Genres of contemporary music as diverse as Christian Pop, Christian Hip Hop, and Praise and Worship arguably have an equal right to be referred to as 'sacred music'. In this volume, nonetheless, the terms 'sacred music', 'sacred choral music', and 'sacred art music' are typically used to refer to the predominantly Western Christian tradition of classical choral music from Gregorian chant, through Renaissance polyphony, to the present.

3 See Arnold, p. xv. See also Alan Kreider, 'Introduction', in *Composing Music for Worship*, ed. by Stephen Darlington and Alan Kreider (Norwich: Canterbury Press, 2003), pp. 1–14; and Andrew Gant, *O Sing Unto the Lord: A History of English Church Music* (London: Profile Books, 2015): 'Tallis is not dead, because people are still using his music and doing what he did, in the places where he did it, and for the same reasons.' (p. 377). See also Jonathan Arnold's chapter in this volume.

performed always and everywhere'.[4] Whether in churches or in secular spaces, then, sacred music continues to be a significant part of many people's experience of, and theoretical reflection on, Christian faith and music today.

A foremost contemporary composer of sacred choral music for both secular performances and for Christian worship is James MacMillan.[5] In 2015, he was appointed as a part-time professor at the University of St Andrews, in the School of Divinity's Institute for Theology, Imagination and the Arts (ITIA). MacMillan sees music — with its special relationship to spirituality — as a medium which may lead the reintegration of theology and the other arts: 'The discussion, the dialogue, between theology and the arts', he comments, 'is not some peripheral thing that some have claimed it has been, but it actually might have been a very central thing in the development of the way that we think of our culture'.[6] Collaborating with MacMillan provided me with the stimulus for a new research project — 'Annunciations: Sacred Music for the Twenty-First Century' — that sought to contribute to the fostering of sacred choral music in the future, as well as to interrogate, more broadly, the relationship between theology and music.[7]

The project, undertaken between 2016–2018, aimed to re-engage composers with the creative inspiration that can come from an encounter with scripture, theology and Christian culture. While composers are typically educated in the *techne* of their craft at conservatoire or university, there has been a tendency in these contexts — as MacMillan highlights — to treat music as simply 'abstract', and to downplay the interrelation between music and the extra-musical. Commenting on the TheoArtistry Composers' Scheme, MacMillan wrote:

> It will be interesting to see if the next generation of composers will engage with theology, Christianity or the general search for the sacred. There has been a significant development in this kind of intellectual, academic and creative activity in the last twenty years or so. In the world of theology there is an understanding that the arts open a unique window on the divine.[8]

---

[4] For an English translation of Benedict XVI's speech, see Joseph Ratzinger, 'That Music, for Me, Is a Demonstration of the Truth of Christianity', trans. by Matthew Sherry (Chiesa.espresso.repubblica.it, 2015), http://chiesa.espresso.repubblica.it/articolo/1351089bdc4.html?eng=y. See, also, Michael Ferguson's chapter in this volume.

[5] MacMillan has also been a vocal public advocate for sacred choral music in Roman Catholic Liturgy, especially during the period leading up to and following Pope Benedict XVI's visit to Britain in 2010. For an account of MacMillan's approach to sacred music in relation to this context, see Michael Ferguson, 'Understanding the Tensions in Liturgical Music-Making in the Roman Catholic Church in Contemporary Scotland' (unpublished doctoral thesis, University of Edinburgh, 2015), and, also, Ferguson's chapter in this volume.

[6] See James MacMillan, 'The Power of the Arts to Communicate the Divine: TheoArtistry at St Andrews', https://www.youtube.com/watch?v=Ow5sumd_DrI

[7] I founded TheoArtistry in 2016 as a new dimension of the work of ITIA. TheoArtistry explores how ITIA's research at the interface between theology and the arts might inform directly the making, practice, performance, curatorship and reception of Christian art, and transform the role of the arts in theology, Church practice, and society at large.

[8] James MacMillan, 'A New Generation of Christian Artists', *Catholic Herald* (24 February 2017), p. 21.

For the TheoArtistry scheme, six composers were selected (from almost one hundred applicants) to collaborate with theologians in ITIA. This led to six new choral settings of 'annunciations' in the Hebrew Bible; six episodes in which God — in different ways — seems to communicate directly to humankind: God speaking to Adam and Eve (Genesis [Gen] 3); Jacob wrestling with God (Gen 32); Moses and the Burning Bush (Exodus 3); the threefold calling of Samuel (1 Samuel 3); Elijah and the 'sound of sheer silence' (1 Kings 19); and the Song of Songs 3.6-11.[9] In choosing the theme of 'annunciations', we were conscious that the 'word of the Lord' is arguably 'rare' once more in our contemporary culture; there seems to be, as in the time of the prophet Samuel, 'no frequent vision'. Nevertheless, people seem to be wrestling again with God (or something like God), whether rejecting or seeking, in organized religion or in a return to silence. We hoped, therefore, that our thematic focus on *how, when, why, through whom, to whom, in what ways* God communicates in the Old and New Testaments — and not on *what* God says (the content of God's revelation) — would be interesting and relevant to people today in reflecting on their experience, or lack of experience, of divine encounter.

For the project, we also sought to challenge what we perceived as an excessive formalism in musical performance. Historically Informed Performance (HIP), arguably the most influential development in classical music performance in the twentieth century, has privileged musical style over its content, with a claim to 'authenticity' based on the adoption of period instruments, pitch and performance practices. In the same period, developments in the recording industry have placed ever-greater emphasis on musicians' technical prowess, and on perfectionism in sound quality. These formal tendencies affect how we listen to, and appreciate, music. Prioritizing technically flawless and stylistically 'authentic' performances of well-worn, well-known pieces, risks turning music into just another cultural commodity, and the church or concert hall, into a museum. In advocating Theologically Informed Programming and Performance (TIPP), we sought to privilege, instead, the spiritual content of music: to show how an appreciation of the theological engagement or profound spirituality of composers can influence their music's performance and reception.[10] We developed

---

9   For a video documentary of the scheme, see 'TheoArtistry: Theologians and Composers in Creative Collaboration', dir. by David Boos, YouTube, 26 January 2018, https://www.youtube.com/watch?v=U2NoaJHcp2E. The soundtrack consists of extracts from the six new choral works composed through the scheme. See also the short introduction to the project: 'TheoArtistry: The Power of the Arts to Communicate the Divine', dir. by David Boos, YouTube, 21 February 2017, https://www.youtube.com/watch?v=Ow5sumd_DrI&t=1s

10 Admittedly, there is a noticeable trend in recordings of sacred choral music to pay attention to a liturgical season, gospel episode, or Christian theme; nonetheless, as with classical music as a whole, recordings of sacred music still tend to privilege a particular stylistic period, composer, performer or performance group often at the expense of attention to the spiritual or thematic content of the music. Jonathan Arnold explores this issue of performance context at some length in his *Sacred Music*, pp. 41–83. John Tavener recognizes the space for a kind of recording of his music that foregrounds its theological inspiration. See John Tavener and Mother Thelka, *Ikons*: *Meditations in Words and Music* (London: HarperCollins, 1994), which includes 'Meditations by Mother Thelka' and recorded music

and researched a programme (and new CD recording) that takes listeners on a musical journey through salvation history, exploring moments in the Old and New Testaments when God communicates to humankind.[11] The composers' six new settings of 'annunciations' in the Hebrew Bible are framed by moments of divine communication in the New Testament — including the songs of Mary, Zechariah, the Angels, and Simeon — as well as settings of *the* Annunciation: the Angel Gabriel announcing to the Virgin Mary that she will give birth to the Messiah.[12]

Most significantly, perhaps, the TheoArtistry project sought to experiment with collaborations between theologians and composers. MacMillan and his librettist, the poet Michael Symmons Roberts, highlight that the myth of the solitary, free-spirited, uncommitted artist is still with us.[13] The project sought to champion, by contrast, the immense power of collaboration for both theologians and composers. In doing so (as I discuss further in Chapter 3), we were particularly inspired by Jeremy Begbie's pioneering initiative, *Theology Through the Arts* (TTA). Foundational for creative collaboration between theologians and artists, Begbie's initiative also validates the process of collaboration itself as theologically significant, and worthy of critical reflection. Thus, in *Sounding the Depths: Theology Through the Arts*, Begbie collates the reflections of theologians and artists who worked together on four artworks: *Parthenogenesis* (a chamber opera); *Till Kingdom Come* (a play); *The Way of Life* (a cathedral sculpture); and *Easter Oratorio*.[14] These scholarly and artistic reflections demonstrate

---

by John Tavener. Tavener writes, 'The purpose of this book and CD is to try to give a hint of how it might be possible to reinstate the Sacred into the world of the imagination. Without this happening, I believe that art will continue to slither into a world of abstraction, into being purely self-referential, a sterile and meaningless activity of interest only to the artist and possibly "Brother Criticus". All great civilizations, except the present one, have understood this as a matter of course. We live in abnormal times; as André Malraux has said: "Either the twenty-first century will not exist at all, or it will be a holy century." It is up to each one of us to determine what will happen' (Tavener, 'Introduction', p. xi).

11 *Annunciations: Sacred Music for the 21st Century*, St Salvator's Chapel Choir and Sean Heath, cond. by Tom Wilkinson (Sanctiandree, SAND0006, 2018), https://stsalvatorschapelchoir.wp.st-andrews.ac.uk/recordings/. The programme order is as follows: 1. James MacMillan, 'Ave Maria' (2010); 2. James MacMillan, 'Canticle of Zachariah' (2007); 3. John Tavener, 'Annunciation' (1992); 4. Kenneth Leighton, 'Magnificat and Nunc Dimittis from the 2nd Service' (1971); 5. James MacMillan, 'A New Song' (1997); 6. Anselm McDonnell, 'Hinneni' (2017); 7. Dominic de Grande, 'Whilst falling asleep, Savta told me of Jacob' (2017); 8. Kerensa Briggs, 'Exodus III' (2017); 9. Seán Doherty, 'God Calls Samuel' (2017); 10. Lisa Robertson, 'The Silent Word Sounds' (2017); 11. Stuart Beatch, 'The Annunciation of Solomon' (2017); 12. James MacMillan, 'And lo, the angel of the Lord came upon them' (2009); 13. Benjamin Britten, 'Hymn to the Virgin' (1930); 14. Judith Bingham, 'The Annunciation' (2000); 15. James MacMillan, 'O Radiant Dawn' (2007).

12 In addition to this theological theme or journey, the recording also explores MacMillan's ongoing contributions to sacred music, particularly in the British choral tradition. Alongside five of MacMillan's own pieces, the recording includes works by two decisive influences on MacMillan (Benjamin Britten and Kenneth Leighton), by two significant contemporaries (John Tavener and Judith Bingham), and by the six 'next generation' composers mentored by MacMillan. Although this volume is self-standing, the recording ideally accompanies it.

13 Michael Symmons Roberts, 'Contemporary Poetry and Belief', in *The Oxford Handbook of Contemporary British and Irish Poetry*, ed. by Peter Robinson (Oxford: Oxford University Press, 2013), pp. 694–706 (p. 699). See also MacMillan, Chapter 1, in this volume, pp. 9–16.

14 See *Sounding the Depths: Theology Through the Arts*, ed. by Jeremy Begbie (London: SCM Press, 2002).

just how theologically and creatively productive such a process of collaboration can be. Part II of this volume similarly brings together the reflections of the six theologians and six composers involved in the project.

Finally, the project aimed to address the state of sacred music today, and to consider its future. The reflections of the six theologians and six composers are framed, therefore, by chapters setting out the compositional perspectives and theological framework underpinning the project (Part I), and by perspectives on the programming, performance and reception of sacred music in the twenty-first century (Part III).

In Part I, MacMillan provides the first of two compositional perspectives. MacMillan argues that the 'search for the sacred' has characterized modernism in music, and that a rootedness in tradition and religion leads to true creativity: 'the binding', in the poet David Jones's words, 'makes possible the freedom'. Paul Mealor then reflects with Margaret McKerron on his vocation as a composer, giving a fascinating insight into his own creative process. Both MacMillan and Mealor (in Chapters 1 and 2) discuss how they envisage the relationship between faith and music personally and, also, in terms of the recent, turbulent history of classical music. In Chapter 3, I analyse MacMillan's theology of music in relation to the project's theme of 'annunciations', and set out the flexible model for creative partnership between theologians and composers that we adopted for the TheoArtistry Composers' Scheme. In British choral music, musical settings of the New Testament proliferate but, with the exception of the psalms, there are relatively few settings of Old Testament passages. In Chapter 4, biblical scholar Madhavi Nevader reflects on 'annunciations', or moments of divine encounter, in the Ancient Near East, providing a context for the six passages of the Hebrew Bible explored by the theologians and composers. In Chapter 5, Church historian William P. Hyland explores the rich typological interpretations of Old Testament 'annunciations' through the Christian liturgy. The six composers were commissioned to write choral pieces approximately three minutes in length that would be performable by a good amateur choir, and Tom Wilkinson discussed with them how to balance technical demands in different areas of vocal writing. In Chapter 6, he presents these compositional guidelines, using musical examples from works by Benjamin Britten, Ralph Vaughan Williams, Kenneth Leighton, and MacMillan, as well as from the new choral pieces themselves.

Part II presents the six theologians' expositions of the scriptural episodes, (including visualizations and illustrations), alongside the six composers' reflections and musical scores. In preparing an Old Testament 'annunciation' for their composer-partner, the theologians may be seen to have taken three different approaches. The first was to reappraise a familiar scriptural passage through the lens of the artistic imagination, bringing out a new or hidden aspect that counters dominant interpretative paradigms. The second was to approach the passage with a particular question or personal interest. The third was to explore the semantic difficulties of representing God's presence. Whether challenging conventional readings of the Fall (Chapter 7) or the calling of

Samuel (Chapter 10), addressing contemporary questions about gender (Chapter 12) or faith in secular environments (Chapter 8) in dialogue with the Christian tradition, or meditating on divine communication through the word, senses, and silence (Chapters 9 and 11), the theologians' chapters open up new perspectives on these famous biblical episodes. The side-by-side reflections of the six composers reveal just how important they found this 'extra-musical' stimulus to be for their compositional process. The scores of the six new choral settings are also reprinted in full, with links to the audio recordings.

In Part III, Michael Ferguson and Matthew Owens consider the role and future of sacred music in Catholic and Anglican worship respectively. In Chapter 13, Ferguson emphasizes that, following the Second Vatican Council (1962–1965), sacred music in the Catholic Church in Scotland has been dominated by a liturgist and functional approach, with pastoral and practical considerations (such as congregational participation, and the lack of technical proficiency of musicians) leaving little room for the 'treasure' of sacred art music. He also cites, however, Joseph Ratzinger's critique of obscurantism in contemporary art music as a reason for its more generalized rejection. In the Anglican Church, the situation has been very different, with the cathedral foundations and college chapels still providing institutional support for extremely high levels of musicianship. The Church does not, however, typically fund new compositions. In Chapter 14, Owens reflects on his own commissioning projects at Wells Cathedral, which have led to many new choral works for the repertoire. In Chapter 15, Michael Downes interrogates the historical relationship between faith and music through the work of three composers — George Frideric Handel, Edward Elgar, and Francis Poulenc —, and the conflicted tension in their oratorios between the sacred and the secular. Jonathan Arnold, in Chapter 16, then analyses the appetite for sacred music in the ostensibly secular world of the twenty-first century. In Chapter 17, Gavin Hopps considers the 'listener's share', privileging, thereby, the audience as co-constitutors of music's meaning. Hopps argues that, if we take listeners' experiences seriously, sacred art music clearly is, for some, a mediator of the divine and the transcendent; on the other hand, again insisting on the effects of music on listeners, it is equally apparent that many other kinds of music are potential vehicles of transcendence. While contributing to the treasure of sacred choral music is a key endeavour of this volume, it seems salutary to conclude, nevertheless, with Hopps' openness to a variety of musical forms and idioms as potential mediators of profound religious experience.[15]

---

15   See also Gavin Hopps, 'Introduction', in *The Extravagance of Music*, ed. by David Brown and Gavin Hopps (New York: Springer, 2018), pp. 1–29.

PART I:
COMPOSITIONAL AND THEOLOGICAL PERSPECTIVES

1. The Most Spiritual of the Arts: Music, Modernity, and the Search for the Sacred

James MacMillan

My contribution to this volume is based on my work with students at the University of St Andrews, and on my observations of, and reactions to, the TheoArtistry Composers' Scheme and Festival which brought theologians and composers together.[1] As a composer with an interest in the theological reflections which underpin much of what I do, I try to account for this art form, which many, religious and non-religious alike, will refer to as 'the most spiritual of the arts'. I argue that the search for the sacred did not end with modernity in music and that, if anything, it has grown and become more complex.[2] I think some people regret asking me if it feels odd and lonely being a religious composer. This may be because I have a long answer for them, much of which considers other contemporary religious composers, like Arvo Pärt, John Tavener and Jonathan Harvey. But the story of twentieth, and now twenty-first century music, is the complicated and sometimes bewildering re-engagement of composers with metaphysical, spiritual and religious insights. Roger Scruton, in *Death-Devoted Heart*, claims that this outcome could be imputed to Richard Wagner and, in particular, *Tristan and Isolde*.[3] But music, though it may be, at times, the most abstract art form, does not come about in a vacuum. The other arts — specifically poetry — offer parallel lines of engagement.

---

1 See 'TheoArtistry: Theologians and Composers in Creative Collaboration', dir. by David Boos, https://www.youtube.com/watch?v=U2NoaJHcp2E. The TheoArtistry Festival was held in St Andrews, 5–6 March, 2018.
2 An earlier version of my reflections was first published by Standpoint Magazine in July/August 2016. I would like to thank Standpoint Magazine for permission to republish some of this material here.
3 Roger Scruton, *Death Devoted Heart: Sex and the Sacred in Wagner's Tristan and Isolde* (Oxford: Oxford University Press, 2004).

There are certain words associated in the public mind with modernism in the arts and, particularly, music. Modern music can sound wild and even savage. Like much else in the modern arts, contemporary music can open a door to the dark side of human nature and our thoughts, fears and experiences. Yet, it is also modern music that sparkles and bedazzles as generations of composers fall in love with new, bright instrumental colours and the experimental vividness of orchestration. And, in spite of the retreat of faith in Western society, composers over the last century or so have never given up on their search for the sacred. From Edward Elgar to Olivier Messiaen, or from Igor Stravinsky to Alfred Schnittke, one hears talk of transcendence and mystery.

Visionary mysticism, in particular, is currently in vogue in discussions about the arts. 'Spirituality' is held to be a positive factor by many, especially among the non-religious, or those who pride themselves on their unorthodoxy in religious matters. Music is described as the most spiritual art by those who proclaim their atheism and agnosticism. The word spirituality is used by many, covering everything from yoga and meditation to dabbling in religious exotica. For example, William Blake's visionary mysticism has become popular again in our own time. Its private mythology, narcissistic religion and gesture politics chime with the mishmash of sexual libertarianism and virtue-signalling at the heart of contemporary liberal culture. His work presaged our 'New Age'. Still, Carl G. Jung described Blake as having 'compiled a lot of half or undigested knowledge in his fantasies'.[4] In the face of his popularity, it might be this flaw that has alerted the wariness of others. It is worth exploring the scepticism that surrounds Blake and his influence, among perhaps more clearheaded and analytical artists, going right back to G. K. Chesterton and T. S. Eliot.

Chesterton regarded Blake as a mystic but, in his book, *William Blake*, he gives an account of why he thinks mystics go off-base — especially mystics of the modern world who seek to separate themselves from any traditional experience of visionary mysticism springing from Judeo-Christianity.[5] Chesterton suggests that this rudderlessness distinguishes them from the fundamental values of genuine mysticism.[6] Blake trusted and followed no tradition; he invented his own unseen world, leading in timeless gnostic fashion to obscurity and mystification. Blake's mysteriousness, in the negative sense, prompted Chesterton to define a true hallmark of true visionary mysticism — that it illuminates rather than obscures:

> A verbal accident has confused the mystical with the mysterious. Mysticism is generally felt vaguely to be itself vague — a thing of clouds and curtains, of darkness or concealing vapours, of bewildering conspiracies or impenetrable symbols. Some quacks have indeed dealt in such things: but no true mystic ever loved darkness rather than light. No pure mystic ever loved mere mystery. The mystic does not bring doubts or riddles: the

---

4   Carl. G. Jung, Letter to Piloo Nanavutty, 11 November 1948, in C. G. Jung, *Letters of C. G. Jung: Volume 1 of 2, 1906–1950*, ed. by Gerhard Adler and Aniela Jaffé, trans. by R. F. C. Hull (London: Routledge, 1973; repr. 1992), p. 513.
5   G. K. Chesterton, *William Blake* (New York: Cosimo Classics, 2005).
6   *Ibid.*, p. 4.

doubts and riddles exist already. [...] The man whose meaning remains mysterious fails, I think, as a mystic: and Blake [...] often fail[ed] in this way.⁷

Poets too have noticed the broader implications of modern mysticism in the literary arts. I have collaborated especially closely with the poet Michael Symmons Roberts. He highlights Seamus Heaney's reference to 'the big lightening, the emptying out' of religious language, and David Jones's vision of the English language 'littered with dying signs and symbols, specifically the signs and symbols associated with our Judeo-Christian past'.⁸ Symmons Roberts suggests that 'the resultant impoverishment hasn't just affected poets, but readers too, and this has been borne out by the now common struggles of English teachers in schools and universities to provide the biblical and historical literacy necessary to make sense of John Milton, John Donne, George Herbert, Eliot, and others'.⁹

Symmons Roberts argues that this 'emptying out' of religious language was the result of what might be described as 'The Enlightenment Project', which, for some of those involved, was 'meant to see off religion'.¹⁰ However, this has not happened. Symmons Roberts notes that 'many sociologists argue that it is secularism that is in retreat. Worldwide, the case is clear-cut. Christianity and Islam are growing very rapidly throughout the developing world, and a recent report placed the numbers of atheists worldwide at three per cent and falling'.¹¹ Yet this is, nonetheless, a powerful and well-heeled three per cent wielding clout over matters political, economic and cultural.

In *Post-Secular Philosophy*, Phillip Blond argues that 'secular minds are only now beginning to perceive that all is not as it should be; what was promised to them — self-liberation through the limitation of the world to human faculties — might after all be a form of self-mutilation'.¹² To this, Symmons Roberts adds:

> The myth of the uncommitted artist (free-spirited and unshackled from the burdens of political, religious, or personal commitment) was always an empty one. To be alive in the world is to have beliefs and commitments, and these extend at some level to politics and theology. But this myth has left us with a terror of the imagination in thrall to a belief. Surely this could limit the scope of the work, may even reduce it to a thin preconceived outworking of doctrine or argument? Yet this fear was always unfounded. The counter-examples are obvious, including great twentieth-century innovators such as Eliot, Jones, Auden, Moore, Berryman, and Bunting. [...] And there's an equivalent list in the

---

7   *Ibid.*, pp. 131–32.
8   Quoted in Michael Symmons Roberts, 'Contemporary Poetry and Belief', in *The Oxford Handbook of Contemporary British and Irish Poetry*, ed. by Peter Robinson (Oxford: Oxford University Press, 2013), pp. 694–706 (p. 696).
9   *Ibid.*
10 *Ibid.*
11 *Ibid.*
12 Philip Blond, 'Introduction: Theology before Philosophy', in *Post-Secular Philosophy: Between Philosophy and Theology* (London: Routledge, 1998), pp. 1–66 (p. 1). Cited in Symmons Roberts, 'Contemporary Poetry', p. 696.

other arts too (music's list would include Stravinsky, Schoenberg, Messiaen, Poulenc, Gubaidulina, Schnittke, Penderecki). The relationship between creative freedom and religious belief is far from limiting.[13]

I believe most of these writers and composers would argue that their religious faith was an imaginative liberation. Some, like Jones, have affirmed that this withering of religious faith and the resulting negative reduction of imaginative liberation represents a parching of our culture — a parching of truth and meaning, a drying up of historical associations and resonances leading to an inability for our culture to hold up 'valid signs'.[14]

The opposite of Jones's 'valid signs' would have to be 'invalid signs'. There is evidence that Eliot saw manifestations of these in what he perceived as the faulty, incoherent vision of Blake and his gnostic, romanticized heritage and legacy. As Symmons Roberts notes, Eliot disapproved of Blake's rejection of tradition, considering his obsession with inventing a religious worldview a distraction from the vocation of writing original poetry.[15] Eliot saw a strong framework as the means of avoiding the parching of the poetic flow, and as a structural conduit to a fuller and truer vision:

> [...] about Blake's supernatural territories [...] we cannot help commenting on a certain meanness of culture. They illustrate the crankiness, the eccentricity, which frequently affects writers outside of the Latin traditions [...]. And they are not essential to Blake's inspiration.
>
> Blake was endowed with a capacity for considerable understanding of human nature, with a remarkable and original sense of language and the music of language, and a gift of hallucinated vision. Had these been controlled by a respect for impersonal reason, for common sense, for the objectivity of science, it would have been better for him. What his genius required, and what it sadly lacked, was a framework of accepted and traditional ideas which would have prevented him from indulging in a philosophy of his own, and concentrated his attention upon the problems of the poet. Confusion of thought,

---

13 Symmons Roberts, 'Contemporary Poetry', p. 699. See also Michael Symmons Roberts, 'Freeing the Waters: Poetry in a Parched Culture', in *Necessary Steps: Poetry, Elegy, Walking, Spirit*, ed. by David Kennedy (Exeter: Shearsman Books, 2007), pp. 124–31 (pp. 128–29): 'There's a popular view, influenced by Romanticism, that only the pure, unfettered imagination can produce the great work. Poets should not be religious, or overtly political, or committed to anything much outside the poetry. Poets should be freewheeling, free-thinking free spirits. As if that meant anything.'

14 See David Jones, 'Preface' to *The Anathemata* (London: Faber & Faber, 1972), p. 15: 'The artist deals wholly in signs. His signs must be valid, that is valid for him and, normally, for the culture that has made him. But there is a time factor affecting these signs. If a requisite now-ness is not present, the sign, valid in itself, is apt to suffer a kind of invalidation.' See also Symmons Roberts, 'Freeing the Waters', pp. 125–26: 'If the language of poetry has become parched in our culture, parched of truth or meaning beyond the poem itself, parched of historical associations and resonances, parched of its potential to hold up, as David Jones would see it, "valid signs", then this is a particular crisis for religious poetry.'

15 T. S. Eliot, 'Blake', in *The Sacred Wood: Essays on Poetry and Criticism* (New York: Alrfred A. Knopf, 1921), pp. 137–43. Symmons Roberts writes: 'T. S. Eliot famously said of William Blake that since he worked within no tradition, he had to invent a religion and world view as well as to write original poetry.' (Symmons Roberts, 'Contemporary Poetry', p. 699).

emotion, and vision is what we find in such a work as *Also Sprach Zarathustra* […]. The concentration resulting from a framework of mythology and theology and philosophy is one of the reasons why Dante is a classic, and Blake only a poet of genius. The fault is perhaps not with Blake himself, but with the environment which failed to provide what such a poet needed.[16]

It is to this question of environment that we should now turn, because the very things disparaged by Eliot are held in highest regard by our own culture. The framework of theology and tradition held to be an essential grounding for Eliot is the focus of disdain and rejection according to our contemporary prejudices.

Let us take Elgar as an example. As John Butt writes, 'Elgar's Catholic upbringing tends to be underplayed in most writings on the composer, but it may nevertheless be one of the most significant sources of his compositional character'.[17] Since *The Dream of Gerontius*, commentators have fallen over themselves in an attempt to portray Elgar's Catholic faith as weak or insignificant. Charles McGuire notes that even his biographer, Jerrold Moore, follows the same tendency: 'It is therefore perhaps inevitable', Moore affirms, 'that, when he produced *The Dream of Gerontius*, a setting of a poem by a Roman Catholic Cardinal which explores various tenets of the Catholic faith, people should jump to the conclusion that his Catholicism underlay his whole life. But his faith was never that strong'.[18] McGuire explains this cultural anxiety about Elgar's Catholicism: 'The popular negating of Elgar's Catholicism both at his death and today serves an obvious end: it makes Elgar's music safer, more palatable for a British audience. In essence, it creates an avatar for Elgar as the "essentially English composer" beyond the reach of any of the complicating factors of partisan religion.'[19] However, as Stephen Hough argues:

> When he decided in 1899 to set Cardinal Newman's 'The Dream of Gerontius' to music, he was taking an enormous risk. It was his first major commission, and his career was all set to take off. So to choose this deeply Catholic text in a country where 'Papists' were a suspicious, despised and even ridiculed minority was to court disaster. Yet he went ahead, with total disregard for any possible censure or disfavour. So it's hard to believe that the words had no religious meaning for him at the time, especially as he was aware that his faith was an impediment to his career.[20]

If it is true that *The Dream of Gerontius* is the composer's masterwork, and a work of extraordinary vision, then it was a vision burnished with courage — foolhardiness

---

16   Eliot, 'Blake', pp. 142–43.
17   John Butt, 'Roman Catholicism and being musically English: Elgar's Church and Organ Music', in *The Cambridge Companion to Elgar*, ed. by Daniel M. Grimley and Julian Rushton (Cambridge: Cambridge University Press, 2004), pp. 106–19 (p. 107).
18   Cited in Charles Edward McGuire, 'Measure of a Man: Catechizing Elgar's Catholic Avatars, in *Edward Elgar and His World*, ed. by Byron Adams (Princeton, NJ: Princeton University Press, 2007), pp. 3–38 (p. 7).
19   *Ibid.*
20   Stephen Hough, 'Elgar and Religion', *BBC Radio 3: The Essay*, 5 June 2007, www.elgar.org/3gerontl.htm

even — and gained singularly through a particularly defined religious tradition and sensibility. This was the kind of framework regarded as vital and necessary by Eliot when he outlined the conditions required for outstanding visionary art and which had so eluded, or had been so self-consciously rejected by lesser seers like Blake and his romantic self-delusionists.

Elgar was to suffer for his courageous vision as performances of *The Dream of Gerontius* were banned as 'inappropriate' in Gloucester Cathedral for a decade after the premiere, and performances in Hereford and Worcester were only permitted with large sections bowdlerized, with much of the objectionable Catholic dimension removed.[21] This vehement reaction may have impacted greatly on the composer, even to the extent of him gradually losing his faith over the rest of his life. He may also have been seduced by the fame and praise which he found in the wake of his more secular instrumental works, which turned him into a national treasure. Indeed, he was to become Britain's official composer, being made a baronet, awarded the Order of Merit and appointed as Master of the King's Music. Proclaimed as 'quintessentially English', he became a totem of nationalism. Enjoying all that, why go back to the depredations of Catholic martyrdom?

Yet it was from this religion of martyrs and saints that Elgar drew the freedom to visualize a work of greatness. This is perhaps counterintuitive, since the etymology of *religio* implies a kind of binding. Symmons Roberts cites Jones's essay 'Art and Sacrament':

> The same root is in 'ligament', a binding which supports an organ and assures that organ its freedom of use as part of a body. And it is in this sense that I here use the word 'religious'. It refers to a binding, a securing. Like the ligament, it secures a freedom to function. The binding makes possible the freedom. Cut the ligament and there is atrophy — corpse rather than corpus. If this is true, then the word religion makes no sense unless we presuppose a freedom of some sort.[22]

This implies, as Symmons Roberts notes, that the visionary requires religion and theology: 'So perhaps to "free the waters" and help slake the thirst of a parched culture, poets and other artists *need* religion, *need* a theology. Now there's an unfashionable idea'.[23] An interesting and challenging idea indeed! How would that go down in today's citadels of metropolitan *bien pensant* culture? As Symmons Roberts continues, 'if David Jones is right, then that image of the free-spirited artist is, and always has been, an illusion. Freedom is not absence. The binding makes possible the freedom'.[24]

Indeed, major modernist composers of the last hundred years were, in different ways, profoundly religious men and women. Stravinsky was as conservative in his

---

21 Charles Edward McGuire and Steven E. Plank, *Historical Dictionary of English Music: ca. 1400–1958* (Plymouth, UK: Scarecrow Press, 2011), p. 112. See also: Anthony Boden, *Three Choirs: A History of the Festival — Gloucester, Hereford, Worcester* (Stroud: Alan Sutton, 1992), pp. 142–48 (p. 148).
22 David Jones, 'Art and Sacrament', in *Every Man an Artist: Readings in the Traditional Philosophy of Art*, ed. by Brian Keeble (Bloomington, IN: World Wisdom, 2005), pp. 141–69 (p. 152).
23 Symmons Roberts, 'Freeing the Waters', p. 128.
24 *Ibid.*, p. 129.

religion as he was revolutionary in his musical imagination, with a deep love of his Orthodox roots as well as the Catholicism he encountered in the West. He set the psalms, he set the Mass; he was a man of faith. Schoenberg, that other great polar figure of early twentieth-century modernism, was a mystic who reconverted to Judaism after he left Germany in the 1930s. His later work is infused with Jewish culture and theology, and he pondered deeply on the spiritual connections between music and silence. It is no surprise that John Cage chose to study with him. Cage found his own route to the sacred through the ideas, and indeed the religions, of the Far East. It is intriguing that his famous, or indeed notorious 4'33' (that is four minutes, 33 seconds of silence), a profound provocation to our listening culture and sensibilities or lack of them, can be traced back to ideas for a piece originally entitled Silent Prayer.[25]

The great French innovator and individualist, Messiaen, was famously Catholic, and every note of his unique contribution to music was shaped by a deep religious conviction and liturgical practice. Messiaen was a powerful influence on Pierre Boulez and Karlheinz Stockhausen (major figures of the post-war avant-garde) and therefore can be counted as one of the most impactful composers of modern times. Far from being an impediment to this, his Catholicism was the major factor behind it. Messiaen wrote one opera — *St Francis of Assisi* — but the most important French Catholic opera of the twentieth century was written by Francis Poulenc. His *Dialogues des Carmélites* appeared in 1956. Based on a true story from the beginnings of modern revolutionary violence — of sixteen Carmelite nuns guillotined in the terror of the French Revolution — it was an act of defiance on the part of the composer against the secular terror of that time and the secular orthodoxies of the modern world.[26] For a culture that had supposedly transcended such religious themes, the popularity of *Dialogues des Carmélites* is remarkable; it is probably the most successful modern opera of the last sixty years. As Mark Bosco argues: 'No other opera combines twentieth-century musical sensibilities with such profound theological themes on Catholic mysticism, martyrdom, and redemption'.[27] However, it is not just another avenue on the search for the sacred but a bold rebuttal of secular arrogances and certainties, and a beautiful proclamation of Catholic truths. Here, as Bosco highlights, 'traditional Catholicism becomes[s] intellectually compatible with all that was modern and progressive in French culture in the early part of the twentieth century'.[28] Poulenc's opera is 'at once a Catholic story of heroism and faith and yet speaks to the modern world, an opera for the post-war period of Europe in the 1950s and one resonant with our contemporary struggle with Christian faith and martyrdom'.[29]

---

25 See James Pritchett, *The Music of John Cage* (Cambridge: Cambridge University Press, 1993), p. 59: '"Silent Prayer," as it was thus described in 1948, is clearly the first glimmer of an idea that, four years later, would become 4' 33"; while "Silent Prayer" is not 4' 33" itself, it is its ancestor.'
26 Charles Osborne, 'Dialogues des Carmélites', in *The Opera Lover's Companion* (New Haven, CT: Yale University Press, 2004), pp. 310–12 (p. 311).
27 Mark Bosco, 'Georges Bernanos and Francis Poulenc: Catholic Convergences in *Dialogues of the Carmelites*', *Logos*, 12 (Spring 2009), pp. 17–39 (p. 17).
28 Bosco, p. 19.
29 *Ibid.*

There is a substantial list of composers in recent times whose work radiates profound religious resonance, covering a whole generation of post-Shostakovich modernists from behind the old Iron Curtain: Henryk Gorecki from Poland; Pärt from Estonia; Giya Kancheli from Georgia; Valentyn Silvestrov from Ukraine; Schnittke, Sofia Gubaidulina and Galina Ustvolskaya, all from Russia; again, figures who stood out and against the prevailing dead-hand orthodoxy of the day: state atheism. And, in Great Britain, after Benjamin Britten have come Harvey, Tavener and many others. Far from being a spent force, religion has proved to be a vibrant, animating principle in modern music and continues to promise much for the future. It could even be said that any discussion of modernity's mainstream in music would be incomplete without a serious reflection on the spiritual values, belief and practice at work in composers' minds.

But do these cultural 'spats' between the outlooks of Eliot and Blake, between Chesterton and the New Age, between orthodoxy and majoritarian scepticism, tussle with different types of transcendence? The search for spirituality seems ubiquitous these days. But in what sense can we call a spirituality made in our own image, to suit our own comforts, to fit our own schedules and agendas, transcendent of anything? Sometimes transcendence has to be fought for, as when Messiaen's music encounters the baffled sneers of its secular, super-rationalist modernist audience and critics, who are eventually won round and see the full glory of the composer's genius, and realize the music is the way it is, precisely because of its theology. When Elgar composed *The Dream of Gerontius*, he knew it would be met with immediate hostility and animosity. But in this work, he seemed to be preparing for the inevitable; he had to face up to an unavoidable spiritual challenge, which, for him, involved rejection and ridicule. The cleansing flames of public disapprobation, he would no doubt maintain, orientated him towards the cleansing flames of Purgatory itself, the very subject of the Newman poem he set. When people say they are baffled by what *The Dream of Gerontius* is all about, but are profoundly moved by the music, the transcendence, the revelation and the understanding has already begun in their souls.

The search for the sacred, therefore, seems as strong today in music as it ever was. Perhaps that search now — as it was with Elgar's *The Dream of Gerontius*; as it was with the theological rootedness of Messiaen's masterworks; as it was in Poulenc's glorious celebration of the mercy, sacrifice and redemption at the heart of Catholic teaching; as it was for any artist who has stood out and against the transient fashions and banalities of the cultural *bien pensant* — is the bravest, most radical and counter-cultural vision a creative person can have, in the attempt to re-sacralize the world around us.

2. The Surrogate Priest: Reflecting on Vocation with Welsh Composer Paul Mealor

Margaret McKerron with Paul Mealor[1]

'Music,' wrote Martin Luther, 'is the art of the prophets; it is the only other art, which like theology, can calm the agitations of the soul'.[2] 'Whether you wish to comfort the sad, to terrify the happy, to encourage the despairing, to [...] [influence] the emotions, inclinations, and affections that impel men to evil or good,' he reflected, '— what more effective means can you find than music?'[3] Luther's theological vision of music is counter-cultural to the more secular environment of contemporary music-making. As award-winning Welsh composer Paul Mealor comments, 'It is not an easy thing to stand up and say that you are a Christian in the twenty-first century — especially in the arts'. Mealor nevertheless feels that claiming his identity and vocation as a Christian *and* a composer is significant in understanding their mutual relevance in his own life and work. In this chapter, he shares — for the first time — how an unusual introduction to classical music, a near-death experience, and a longstanding love of Anglican liturgy dovetailed when he began to perceive that his calling to compose music was one of 'surrogate priesthood'. Through music, Mealor believes that a

---

1   The material for this chapter was gathered, arranged, and edited by Margaret McKerron. It is based upon original material developed by Paul Mealor for a presentation 'On Setting Religious Texts' for the Institute for Theology, Imagination, and the Arts (ITIA) research seminar (3 February 2017) as well as further conversations at the University of Aberdeen, Scotland.

2   Martin Luther, *The Life of Luther Written by Himself: Collected and Arranged by M. Michelet* (London: George Bell & Sons, 1904), p. 7.

3   Martin Luther, 'Preface to Georg Rhau's *Symphoniae Lucundae*,' in Martin Luther, *Luther's Works*, Vol. 53: Liturgy and Hymns, edited by Ulrich S. Leupold (Philadelphia, PA: Fortress Press, 1965), p. 323.

composer may offer listeners the opportunity to encounter the divine: whether by communicating a sense of God's transcendence, or being; or by creating space for responses of praise, yearning, lament, or even anger. Through music, moreover, a composer may comfort and caution, foster stillness and action, be prophetic and facilitate prayer. By divulging his compositional process and philosophy behind three choral works — 'Salvator Mundi: Great Love' (2011), 'O vos omnes' (2011), and his setting of the 'Stabat Mater' (2009) — Mealor explains that his music is in constant dialogue with that surrogate-priestly calling. Through these examples, he shows how fruitful the interchange between music and theology can be.

I. Developing a Sense of Vocation

Poet Gerard Manley Hopkins suggests that God's revelation may emerge gradually, 'stealing as Spring', or with the sudden force of an 'anvil-ding'.[4] Listening to Mealor share his personal history, one sees how his personal vocation emerged with the character of both. When his motet 'Ubi caritas' was performed in the Royal Wedding ceremony of His Royal Highness Prince William and Catherine Middleton in 2011, the composer achieved worldwide fame in classical music circles.[5] The first step towards his emerging vocation, however, is a humble and curious story.

By his own admission, Mealor was a 'hyperactive' child. Laughing, he remarks, 'we didn't have medication — or even political correctness — then'. His maternal grandfather, a psychiatrist, suggested music might pacify his untiring grandson: 'I was basically strapped down to a chair and music was played', Mealor recalls. 'As it turned out, it was brilliant for me. It was a great revelation that I could be lost in sound'. The symphonist's canvas was the world — and great ideas, rendered even to the smallest musical brushstroke, captivated the young boy's imagination. The music 'didn't calm me necessarily but it took my focus away from the mundane to something else'. Before he turned ten, Mealor composed his first symphony. Speaking about it now, he admits it was probably not the best work he has produced. Yet, it enabled him to step into 'this great drama and sound'. Mealor found the mystery of music marvellous: 'It is direct, but not direct. It is a language and it is not a language. It is an art and not an art. It is a science and it is not a science. It's a great contradiction, like prayer.' The comparison between music and prayer is not incidental — although it took the sudden 'anvil-ding' of a near-death experience to forge the indelible link between Mealor's music and his personal faith.

The watershed moment happened in the Din Lligwy river, in Anglesey, Wales. Then nine years old, Mealor was playing with his elder brother on the riverbank. His brother told him to remain behind while he went upriver, but Mealor decided to go after him. He fell into the water, unable to swim. As he began to drown, sinking in

---

4   Gerard Manley Hopkins, 'The Wreck of the Deutschland', in *Bartleby* < https://www.bartleby.com/122/4.html> [accessed 2 April 2019]

5   See Paul Mealor, *Biography* (Paulmealor.com, 2016), http://www.paulmealor.com/biography/

and out of consciousness, Mealor remembers not panic so much as a profound sense of comfort. The memory is vivid, but words fail him as he tries to convey how it felt: 'I have spent my whole life trying to intellectualize it, and it has taken me further away from it than when I was child and had no intellect at all', he confesses. The closest description he can muster is the feeling of being 'cradled in beautiful warmth'. For years since he was rescued, Mealor has been transfixed by what was, for him, a divine encounter: 'That's why I sought out music, and that's why I try to write the particular kinds of harmonies I write,' he says. 'It is trying to reach a kind of surrogate warmth of that [moment] — even though, of course, you can't'. Still, his tenacious search for its source led him to composition — and eventually to realize that music could be a kind of surrogate priesthood for the world.

After his chance rescue by an elderly passerby, Mealor's persistent questions about the spiritual nature of his experience led his parents to make an appointment with the Dean of St Asaph's Cathedral, the local Anglican presence: 'I don't know what they thought', he admits, 'but obviously, they thought they would take me to the only person they knew who might have some answers'. As they were waiting to see the Dean, the choir began rehearsing Orlando Gibbons' 'See, see the Word is Incarnate', a musical recapitulation of the life of Christ. The vastness of the cathedral, the cassocks and gowns donned by the choristers, and the sacred music created a wonderful theatre of sound: 'It was a very spiritual thing,' Mealor recalls, 'it was the first moment that the music I had been listening to as a hyperactive kid and this spiritual experience I had [in the water] suddenly came together'. Encountering a glimmer of that warmth again in the sacred choral music that day was more significant for Mealor than what the Dean later articulated in words. Looking back, he believes, 'it was then that I realized this was what was I was after'.

Not long afterwards, Mealor auditioned for and was accepted as a chorister at St Asaph's Cathedral. Beginning as a treble, he moved through alto, tenor, and bass roles and, subsequently, became a lay clerk. While the experience proved influential for his own compositions, Mealor is clear that 'it was not just the discipline of learning and practice' that made his time there formational: 'I was learning all this craft and learning to interact with people'. He was also becoming more rooted in Christian faith and practice. He reflects, 'There is a certain heartbeat to liturgy, which I love. I did not pursue theological studies at that point, but I was at mass every day because I was singing it. I remember the Dean used to say, "He who sings, prays twice."' 'Of course', he checks himself, 'it was all boys together…so it wasn't all practice and piety; it was a great amount of fun too'. Still, the liturgy — rooted in sacred music — provided a vital window for him into theology and prayer. Mealor even found himself considering the Anglican priesthood. At this point, however, his grandmother facilitated a critical introduction that inadvertently transposed his sense of calling from the traditional, clerical priesthood to the surrogate priesthood of composition.

Mealor recalls his grandmother — a survivor of Auschwitz — as direct and tenacious. Living in the same neighbourhood as the acclaimed twentieth-century Welsh composer, William Mathias, she took matters into her own hands: 'She just knocked on the door of William Mathias, who lived down the road, and said, "You've just retired and my grandson needs composition lessons."' The great composer agreed to take on the little student, then aged nine. 'There was no set agenda,' Mealor remembers: 'I'd show compositions that I had started, and then he would set me some Bach chorale exercises that I would have to harmonize. We would go through how that works, perhaps do some orchestration […]. Gradually, it got more and more complicated, but original composition was always going on as well'. By the time Mealor attended the University of York's music composition programme, he had learned the craft of composition from a master craftsman, including harmony, counterpoint, and orchestration. His vocation was also crystalizing: 'I certainly felt like I was being asked to something', but it was no longer clear that this vocation was to be a traditional, Anglican priest. Rather, he felt that 'what I was able to do was fulfil that calling' through communicating 'the sacred through sound'.

For Mealor, composing fulfills his surrogate-priestly calling. Through his music, he can reveal something of who God is, communicate the great stories of the Christian tradition, facilitate prayer, and create rare spaces for wrestling with faith and doubt, triumph and tribulation, love and fear, joy and grief. Mealor observes, 'The most profound prayers are often those that are meditative. They are not really saying anything in words; it's more a kind of "open thought"'. Music may thereby articulate the inarticulate cry so often at the root of real prayer: 'Music works like a language does in many ways, but does not express anything as hard-edged as a language does'. In the New Zealand premiere of his symphony *Passiontide*, Mealor remembers becoming aware of a woman weeping in the audience: 'She came up to me afterwards and she had had a profoundly religious experience. I talked to her for a long time'. Music fostered an encounter with the divine that was unexpected and revealing; and it also helped her seek a conversation.

Mealor believes that creating — and holding open — that hospitable space may be spiritually fruitful in a different way to that experienced through religious reflection in words, for example, through a sermon. If Luther is right that 'music is the art of the prophets,' Mealor maintains that music is an art that can speak of God today to a predominantly secular audience, where a spoken sermon might provoke alienation or indifference: 'It does a different thing than what words can do,' he says. To show us what he means, Mealor points to three of his sacred choral works: 'Salvator Mundi: Greater Love,' 'O vos omnes', and his setting of the 'Stabat Mater'.

II. Love's Endeavour, Love's Expense

The choral piece 'Salvator Mundi: Greater Love' is an extended, musical meditation on what theologian V. H. Vanstone so beautifully describes as 'Love's endeavour, Love's expense'.[6] His Royal Highness the Prince of Wales commissioned it for the retirement of his former Private Secretary, Dr. Manon Williams, LVO. Using Williams' history of service as inspiration, Mealor grapples with the fact that love is not without cost: the paradigm of Christ's life and death suggest that self-sacrifice may well be 'the ultimate quality of love'.

To open up this idea to his audience, Mealor recollects, 'I decided to set up a bitonality, which in my mind represents suffering'. The choir sings Jesus' words recorded in the Gospel of John: 'Greater love hath no man than this, that he lay down his life for his friends' (John 15.12). Arranged as a sustained, hushed processional in G Major, this English setting sits uneasily with the simultaneous Latin setting of the 'Salvator Mundi' prayer in G Minor.

Fig. 2.1 The bi-tonal relationship between the English setting of John 15.12 and the Latin setting of 'Salvator Mundi' evokes a sense of suffering.

In a 'Celtic-adapted' style of plainchant, four soloists (SATB) sing in lament:

> Salvator Mundi, salva nos:
> Qui per crucem et sanguinem redemisti nos,
> Auxiliare nobis, te deprecamur, Deus noster.
>
> [Saviour of the world, save us, who through thy cross and blood didst redeem us, help us, we beseech thee, our God].

Mealor cites the Finnish composer Jean Sibelius as once saying that 'the symphony is the smallest idea taken to its biggest conclusion.' Drawing inspiration from this compositional philosophy, Mealor uses micro-level structures to increase the macro-level strain. The opening motif is a fractal for the whole piece — a seed of an idea that

---

6   William Hubert Vanstone, *Love's Endeavour, Love's Expense: The Response of Being to the Love of God* (London: Dartman, Longman, and Todd, 2007).

grows, develops, and repeats throughout the remaining musical narrative. Notably, it is a musical crucifix: a technique with roots that reach back to the Baroque period.[7]

Fig. 2.2 The opening motif of 'Salvator Mundi: Greater Love' is cross-shaped.

Mealor arranges the choir in a clustered major third over a perfect fifth. He comments, 'On paper it resembles a cross'. Colouring the word 'love' in this way intimates love's expense — represented so vividly and paradigmatically in the Cross.

Fig. 2.3 The 'cross-shaped' arrangement juxtaposes suffering with love.

Together, these macro and microstructures propel 'the piece towards an enormous climax. At that point, the soloists and choir rest together in the key of G Major'. As with the resolution of the cross, this musical resolution does not represent the end of the narrative, but the beginning of a new stage in which what has begun is brought to its final and consummate conclusion.

This final section, set in the language of Williams' native land of Wales, draws from Celtic music's wellspring. Reminiscent of Scottish Bothy singing, 'the music evaporates

---

7   See also Jasmin Cameron, *The Crucifixion in Music: An Analytical Survey of Settings of the Crucifixus between 1680 and 1800* (Lanham, MD: Scarecrow Press, 2006), p. 212.

into shimmering lines'. It suggests nebulous swirls of rising incense, flickering flames, or even 'singing in tongues' — the latter of which is associated in the Bible with being receptive to and filled with the Holy Spirit.[8]

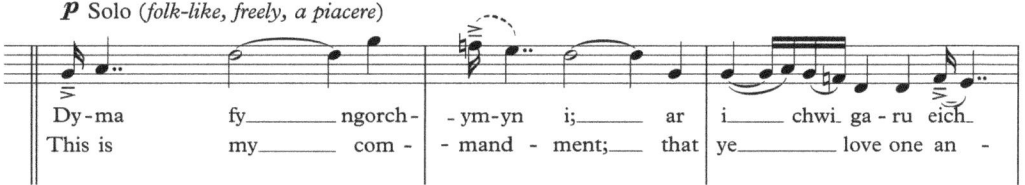

Fig. 2.4 The Celtic-inspired arrangement suggests a 'singing in tongues'.

Mealor believes, 'When your life is so filled by the Spirit, you do act differently'. Through the Spirit's indwelling, a person learns to know and walk in God's ways — including being strengthened to love others in the way of God's love. For this final section, Mealor set the text of John 15.13: 'Dyma fy ngorchymyn I; ar I chwi garu eich gilydd, fel y cerais I chwi' [This is my commandment, that you love one another, as I have loved you]. Referring to a reality and a mission, it is deeply relational. Mealor recalls, 'I wanted to present a vision of these mystical and powerful words of Jesus Christ'. Through 'Salvator Mundi: Greater Love', he offers audiences the opportunity to experience to some degree the suffering love of Christ for the sake of the world. Not all listeners will make that specific connection — or the further connection, i.e. that Jesus suffered for *their* sake — but that is not the composer's primary goal. Rather, Mealor holds open a space hospitable for deeper contemplation — where '[listeners] can just sit and *be* and let this music get into their hearts and souls without feeling that they should not be there'. With its likeness and unlikeness to language, art, and science, organized sound serves a formidable 'mode of knowing'; its characteristic indirectness may even facilitate greater openness to theological reflection.

As music appeals not only to the head but also to the 'emotions, inclinations, and affections', it can be an effective means of being united with Christ in his suffering. Luther, as noted above, believed that these three human characteristics 'impel men to evil or good'. With this in mind, then, the missional content of Jn 15.13 is provocative. Jesus commands that his disciples embody the reality of his love in their broader relationships. He intends that their experience of his love may impel them to greater love for one another. By wedding a form evocative of the Spirit with Jesus's words of command in this final section, Mealor accomplishes something unexpected. Together, word and form help listeners connect obedience to the command of 'greater love' with union with Christ through the Spirit.

Structurally, Mealor also connects Williams' legacy of service to the reality of self-sacrificial love: the divine love that she recognizes as ultimately supporting and giving her service character. Even if her image is not perfect, it is this Love that her love images.

---

8   For biblical verses on speaking in tongues, cf. Mark 16.17; Acts 2.4; 19.6, 1 Cor 12.8-11; 14.2, 27-28.

If one person's self-sacrificial service can serve as a 'fractal' for the character of divine love, so too can music. 'Meaning is more profound than what can be accomplished in words', Mealor reaffirms. By engaging tacit and experiential ways of knowing, organized sound fosters insightful theological and personal connections that might not be made (or might not be as easily made) in other more discursive modes of knowing. A composer may therefore help reframe how his audience attends to the world in fresh and even countercultural ways. For Mealor, music's potential for reorienting head and heart to the love of God, for weaving together personal and cosmic narratives, is one key way in which it may act as a kind of 'surrogate priesthood' for the world.

III. Praying for Peace in Troubled Times

Music also provides a means through which listeners may attend to realities in life that so often leave them struggling for words. C. S. Lewis writes, 'Pain insists upon being attended to. God whispers in our pleasures, speaks in our consciences, but shouts in our pains'.[9] Confronting pain and sorrow may therefore mean confronting God: in heartbreak, in anger and lament, in desperation, or in hope. To explore the sense of encountering God in the midst of suffering, Mealor turned to a Latin responsory based upon Lamentations [Lam] 1.12, entitled 'O vos omnes'.

In the Hebrew Bible, the Book of Lamentations bewails God's desertion of Jerusalem and its consequent fall to the Babylonians in 586 B.C. 'The book paints a picture of the Holy City, Jerusalem, in sorrow and desolation', the composer explains. Jerusalem is personified: 'She weeps bitterly in the night, with tears on her cheeks; among all her lovers she has no one to comfort her' (Lam 1.2).[10] To those that pass by, she calls: 'Look and see if there is any sorrow like my sorrow, which was brought upon me, which the Lord inflicted on the day of his fierce anger' (Lam 1.12). Even though 'O vos omnes' is based upon this text, Mealor says that his setting tries to 'concentrate on hope and the power of suffering to illuminate and make sense of our relationship with God'. 'Only by understanding the true nature of pain', he says, 'can we be fully set free from it'. Hope glimmers not in turning *away* from suffering, but in turning *towards* it. In 'O vos omnes', a personified Jerusalem thus bids:

> O all you that walk by on the road, pay attention and see,
> If there be any sorrow like my sorrow.
> Pay attention, all people, and look at my sorrow,
> If there by any sorrow like my sorrow.

In Mealor's setting, a solitary, tubular bell calls audiences to 'solemn meditation on this ancient text and prayer for peace in troubled times' — much as a bell might call monastic communities to the Daily Offices of Prayer. As the bell continues to toll in the piece, it marks the passage of time whilst perhaps also reiterating the summons. By employing

---

9   C. S. Lewis, *The Problem of Pain* (San Francisco: HarperSanFrancisco, 2001), p. 91.
10 Biblical references throughout are to the New Revised Standardised Version (NRSV).

the 'cross chord' as well as cruciform micro-arrangements similar to those found in 'Salvator Mundi: Greater Love', Mealor sustains a solemn, contemplative mood. The text is set in English and Latin, with a final verse from Psalm 133 in Hebrew: 'hinneh mah towb mah na'iym yashab ach gam yachad' [Behold how good, and how pleasant it is, for brothers to dwell together in unity].[11] Here, Mealor seems to suggest that the suffering world needs us not to turn away from, but rather to pay careful attention to, each other.

Mealor remarks, 'As we pay attention and see, the music climaxes into a triumphant F sharp major key (bar 28)'. For Schubert, the key of F sharp major represents 'triumph over difficulty, [a] free sigh of relief uttered when hurdles are surmounted; [an] echo of a soul which has fiercely struggled and finally conquered'.[12] This encouraging moment is not a final victory though, but rather a breath of success before approaching the next hurdle. When the work resolves in bar 49, it 'resolves on the dominant (C sharp)'. It is a highly significant, but perhaps surprising, choice for the concluding chord. Mealor explains, however, that C sharp 'has a tritone relationship to the opening, G' — a discordant interval traditionally known as the Devil's interval (or *'diabolus in musica'*).[13] For him, this concluding chord intimates that the work of Christ is not yet finished: 'The life of Christ is needed to complete the "word"'.

Mealor thus gestures towards another paradox at the heart of Christian faith — that Christ has conquered on the cross, yet Christians await his coming again for the final consummation of all things when '[God] will wipe every tear from their eyes, Death will be no more; mourning and crying and pain will be no more, for the first things have passed away.'[14] In the intervening time, the suffering of the world needs to be lamented, lifted up, and offered back to the God who created and loves it. From bar 24 onwards, therefore, Mealor has 'the soloists echo and imitate the chiming bell', imagining humanity responding to the call to pray for — and share — one another's joys and tribulations. This harks back to Mealor's message, expressed in Psalm 133, that pain is better alleviated through togetherness than withdrawal; its consistency throughout the piece is perhaps an indication that this experience should not be subdued. So, through 'O vos omnes', Mealor shows us how the surrogate priesthood of music can 'calm the agitations of the soul', opening space for listeners to lament suffering, to feel sorrow, and to turn to God in prayer for the salvation of the world.

IV. Personal Devotion

When asked to identify which piece has been the most personally significant, Mealor points to his choral setting of the thirteenth-century Latin poem 'Stabat Mater

---

11 Transliterations are taken from James Strong, *Strong's Exhaustive Concordance of the Bible: Updated and Expanded Edition* (Peabody, MA: Hendrickson Publishers, 2007).
12 Cited in James Webster, *Haydn's 'Farewell' Symphony and the Idea of Classical Style: Through Composition and Cyclic Introduction in His Instrumental Music* (Cambridge: Cambridge University Press, 1991), p. 117.
13 For more on the *'diabolus in musica'*, see Paul Griffiths, *The Penguin Companion to Classical Music* (London: Penguin Group, 2005), p. 223.
14 Revelation 21.4.

Dolorosa' [The mournful mother was standing]. Attributed to Jacopone da Todi, the poem depicts Mary's suffering as she witnesses the crucifixion of her beloved son.[15] According to the composer, 'The Stabat Mater is this cry out into the darkness by the Virgin Mary in seeing her son dying on the cross'. By sharing in her profound sorrow, listeners can participate in something of 'the spiritual and emotional bond that unites Mary — and all Christians — to the death of her Son'. Theologically, Mealor believes that the sequence 'teaches us that the crown of eternal life in Heaven can be reached when we each choose to share with Our Lord in His suffering and death on the cross at Calvary'. The mournful mother, then, shows us how to grieve.

After his paternal grandmother was diagnosed with terminal cancer, Mealor found unexpected comfort in Catholic liturgical readings: 'For the first time in my life, I was experiencing what real death is — death of someone I actually really cared about,' he recalls. With Western culture so heavily invested in minimizing the realities of death and dying, processing grief can be a difficult and lonely experience. Many people do not know how to respond, and so their instinct is to *turn away* from suffering or death as quickly as possible. In the 'Stabat Mater', however, Mealor found someone else who understood the desolation that the death of a beloved one brings. Mary did not turn away from Christ's (or her own) suffering; she stood at the foot of the cross and turned *towards* suffering. In the fullness of time, as John writes, 'he will wipe every tear from their eyes' and 'death will be no more; mourning and crying and pain will be no more, for the first things [will] have passed away' (Rev 21.4).

Through the eyes of his mother, Jesus' death becomes more poignant. By contemplating Mary's example, Mealor was able to process the grief of his grandmother's death. 'Being able to finish that amongst all [that grief] is probably the most difficult thing I have done so far.' Composing gave some release — and context — for his grief. Music brought the words to life, transforming the medieval hymn to a personal, living prayer:

> O thou Mother! Fount of love!
> Touch my spirit from above,
> Make my heart with thine accord:
>
> Make me feel as thou has felt;
> Make my soul to glow and melt
> With the love of Christ my Lord.
>
> Let me share with thee His pain,
> Who for all my sins was slain,
> Who for me in torments died.[16]

When he set out to render the text musically, Mealor made several structural decisions to signify the cost of suffering love. The key signatures were a critical macro-structural — and

---

15   Robert D. Hawkens, 'Stabat Mater Dolorosa', *The Encyclopaedia of Christianity*, ed. by Erwin Fahlbusch and others, 5 vols. (Grand Rapids, MI: W. B. Eerdmans, 2008), Vol. 5, p. 185.
16   See Margaret Miles, *Maiden and Mother: Prayers, Devotions, and Songs to Honour the Blessed Virgin Mary* (London: Burns & Oates, 2001), pp. 72–73.

numerological — decision. B♭ major, in which the central elegy is set, provides the harmonic axis of the entire piece. Dissecting this axis is E♭ major in the first and fourth movements, and F minor in the third movement. Connected through the interval of a fifth, these 'key' relationships may be rendered in the shape of a cross:

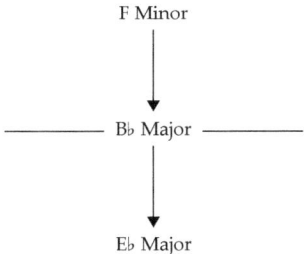

Fig. 2.5 The key signatures of the 'Stabat Mater' in cruciform configuration.

Furthermore, 'each key signature itself relates to the symbol of the cross some other way'. For instance, E♭ major (three flats) and B♭ major (two flats) suggest the five wounds of Christ in the first and second movement. In the third movement, Mealor represents the four points on the cross with F minor (four flats). In the journey from darkness to light, the fourth movement returns to E♭ major set in triumphant mode. With its three flats signifying the triune God, Mealor intimates the promised comfort of a day when pain and suffering will no more triumph. He represents these macro-structural decisions in Figure 2.6.

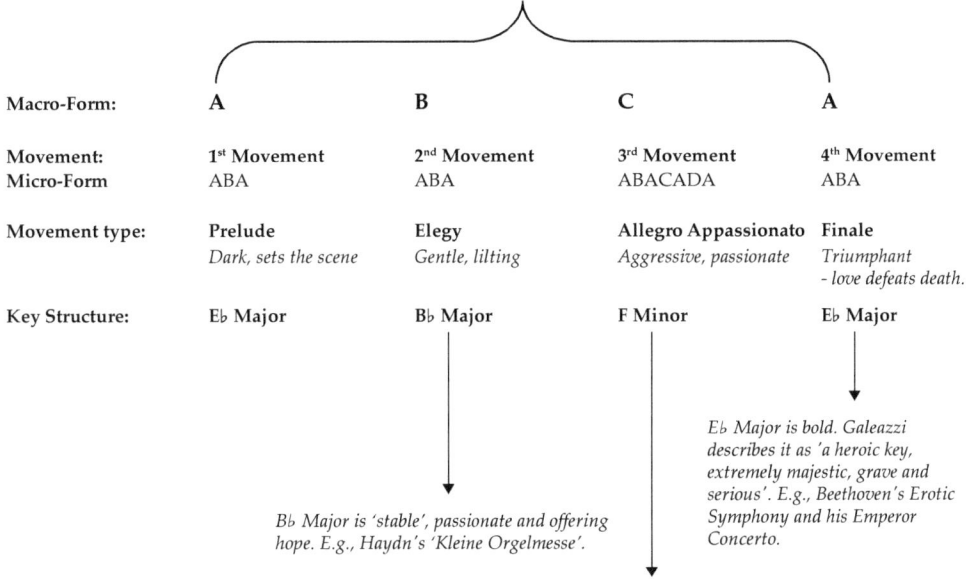

Fig. 2.6 Mealor's macro-structural outline of his 'Stabat Mater'.

As Mealor relates, 'the pre-compositional key-relationship design and structure are not the only "cross"-related semiotics in the piece'. Rather, 'throughout the entire work, the melodic and harmonic material are closely related to three "cross"-like motifs', such as these examples found in the first movement:

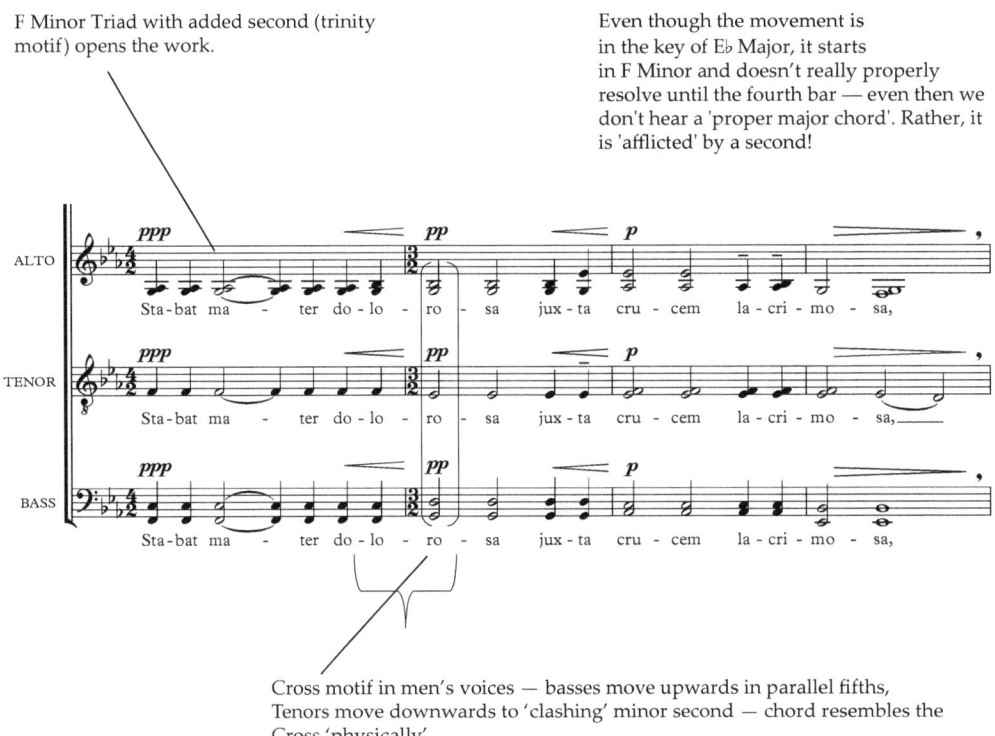

Fig. 2.7 Mealor's illustration of cruciform motifs present in the first movement of his 'Stabat Mater'.

Altogether, the arch-shaped design of the work, made possible through mirroring, stratification, and transposition, gives the work a sense of movement. It is as if Mealor is comforting his audience (and perhaps, himself). Death, as horrible as it is, does not have the final word.

Wrestling with mortality through the 'Stabat Mater' was a deeply personal process for the composer. Yet, he continues to find its broader appeal fascinating. He says, 'It is the piece that connects most immediately when people hear it'. His correspondence contains stories of people on their deathbeds who, with their relatives, have found honesty and comfort in listening to his music in their final hours. 'It was created in that moment [of grief]. Perhaps people can hear that in it', he suggests. For Mealor, it is one more way in which he can minister to Christians and non-Christians alike in a way that complements — and even opens up space for — participation in a more traditional community of faith.

If music is 'the art of the prophets', as Luther wrote, perhaps it is unsurprising that standing up as a composer and a Christian is no easy feat in the twenty-first century. Prophets have always stood in uneasy tension with their surrounding culture: reminding people of the cost of divine and human love, confronting them with the realities they would rather ignore, and calling for people to find the comfort of reconciliation with their loving God. For those who ask 'Where are today's prophets?', perhaps they might look to those whose dual sense of vocation — the universal call to love God and neighbour, and the specific call to be an artist — enables them not only to engage critically with their surrounding culture, but also to minister to it. While the artistic ministry might be less direct, it is arguably more accessible to those people who are outside (and sometimes inside) traditional, ecclesiastical communities. Less discursive, it may nonetheless involve the whole person by affecting the emotions, creating tacit connections, undermining cultural narratives, and moving the will. Less didactic, it is nonetheless a formidable mode of knowing. As we have seen in the three examples of Mealor's choral works discussed above, the interchange between music and theology can be fruitful for both the composer and his or her audience. As Mealor comments, 'theology and music are one. Theology not only inspires the creation, the structure, and the shape of music, but they are inseparable'.

List of Illustrations

2.1	The bi-tonal relationship between the English setting of John 15.12 and the Latin setting of 'Salvator Mundi' evokes a sense of suffering.	21
2.2	The opening motif of 'Salvator Mundi: Greater Love' is cross-shaped.	22
2.3	The 'cross-shaped' arrangement juxtaposes suffering with love.	22
2.4	The Celtic-inspired arrangement suggests a 'singing in tongues'.	23
2.5	The key signatures of the 'Stabat Mater' in cruciform configuration.	27
2.6	Mealor's macro-structural outline of his 'Stabat Mater'.	27
2.7	Mealor's illustration of cruciform motifs present in the first movement of his 'Stabat Mater'.	28

3. Mary as a Model for Creative People: Establishing Theologian-Composer Partnerships with James MacMillan

George Corbett

James MacMillan's understanding of the history of classical music, and of sacred music in particular, presents a challenge to a contemporary cultural climate frequently characterized as secular:

> Music is the most spiritual of the arts. More than the other arts, I think, music seems to get into the crevices of the human-divine experience. Music has the power to look into the abyss as well as to the transcendent heights. It can spark the most severe and conflicting extremes of feeling and it is in these dark and dingy places where the soul is probably closest to its source where it has its relationship with God, that music can spark life that has long lain dormant.[1]

MacMillan's conviction about the intrinsic relationship between music and spirituality emerged, nonetheless, in reaction to a prevalent attitude 'in university environments' of his generation: that music 'was complete in itself' and that 'anything else was extraneous and irrelevant'.[2] MacMillan subsequently considered such a retreat or 'divorce' from 'resonances and connections with life outside music' as sterile, a cerebral playing around with notes on the page in 'train spotterist fashion', a music which delighted in its own inaccessibility and unpopularity.[3] Only when — against this university music culture — he allowed the 'spiritual dimension to emerge' did

---

1 James MacMillan, 'God, Theology and Music', *New Blackfriars*, 81.947 (January 2000), 16–26 (p. 17). This article is reprinted in *Composing Music for Worship*, ed. by Stephen Darlington and Alan Kreider (Norwich: Canterbury Press, 2003), pp. 35–50.
2 *Ibid.*
3 *Ibid.* MacMillan again emphasizes the 'pre-musical or extra-musical starting point or impetus, its genesis, its inspiration' in James MacMillan and Richard McGregor, 'James MacMillan: A Conversation and Commentary', *Musical Times*, 151.1912 (Autumn 2010), 69–100 (p. 74): 'music is

MacMillan find his true voice as a composer.[4] He came to relish the 'extra-musical or pre-musical' impetus, and to compare the transformation of these ideas into music as 'to use a Catholic theological term, a transubstantiation of one to the other.'[5]

In this chapter, I first consider MacMillan's theology of music in relation to the book's theme of 'annunciations'. I suggest that, for MacMillan, the Annunciation may serve as a theological paradigm for the composition, performance, and reception of music. In being mentored by MacMillan, the composers on the TheoArtistry scheme were invited to reflect on his understanding of artistic inspiration. However, we neither required any faith commitments on the part of the composers (in order to apply), nor prescribed a particular approach, in the confidence that engagement with scripture of whatever kind (reverent, reactive, playful, etc.) would be generative of powerful new music and striking theological expressions or perspectives. In the chapter's second part, I outline how we approached the practical and theological issues that arose in setting up theologian-composer partnerships.

I. Composition as 'Annunciation': A Perspective on MacMillan's Theology of Music

Exploring the theme of 'annunciations', we focused on scriptural episodes in which God communicates directly with men or women. But, for MacMillan, the Annunciation also has resonances with the life of the Christian and with the vocation of the Christian artist. Describing his own compositional process, he draws on scriptural accounts of the interplay between divine and human creativity in the Old and New Testaments. He reflects on the word 'inspiration', as 'from the Latin *inspiratio*, mean[ing], "in-breathing", an arousal or infusion of an impulse of illumination that impels a person to speak, act or write under the influence of some creative power.'[6] MacMillan considers the Old Testament model of creativity par excellence to be Adam. In Genesis, 'God presents his limitless love for humanity in the gift of Creation and yet,

---

plugged in to something more than the notes on the page or the concept of moving those notes about the page in as successful a way as possible.'

4   MacMillan, 'God', p. 18. It is interesting to note that the composer Roxanna Panufnik (b. 1968), a decade on, had a similar reaction to the teaching of musical composition in the academy: 'I left music college swearing never to write another note again, because I wasn't getting good marks. It was during the mid-1980s when esoteric and cerebral avant-garde music was still considered the right kind of music to be writing. […] I felt very false and that I wasn't being true to myself in writing that kind of music, so I didn't.' See Roxanna Panufnik, 'Beyond a Mass for Westminster', in *Composing Music*, pp. 76–85 (p. 84).

5   MacMillan and McGregor, 'James MacMillan: A Conversation and Commentary', p. 75.

6   MacMillan, 'God', pp. 21–22. MacMillan notes that 'the engagement between theology and culture, between religion and the arts is now such a faded memory for most people that a whole generation has grown up without an understanding of the true meaning and implication in the word "inspiration". And when a creative person comes across the definition for the first time, it is a discovery made with undisguised delight — a recognition of a primal truth that has lain hidden for a long time'. See also MacMillan, 'Sandford Lecture', cited in Arnold, *Sacred Music*, p. 151: 'I believe it is God's divine spark which kindles the musical imagination now, as it has always done, and reminds us, in an increasingly de-humanized world, of what it means to be human'.

at the same time invites Adam, the archetype, to make his own sense of this new world. [...] Humanity's inner creativity is being inspired to express itself in the face of God's immeasurable love.'[7] The creation of Eve from Adam's rib is an image for how composers 'have always taken fragments of material, consciously or unconsciously, from elsewhere and breathed new life into them, creating new forms, new avenues and structures of expression'.[8]

It is nonetheless Mary, the second Eve, who provides MacMillan with the true model for the Christian composer:

> It is not just Mary's fecundity that is inspiring to a creative person. A more powerful and more pertinent metaphor for the religious artist is the balance between, on the one hand, Mary's independent free will and, on the other, her openness to the power of the Holy Spirit. There is something in the instinct of an artist or a composer, or any creative person, or any Christian for that matter, which is inexorably drawn to the idea of Mary's 'vesselship' — the notion of making oneself as a channel for the divine will.[9]

MacMillan has highlighted that 'the Christian believer is paradigmatically female: receptive to the seed of God's word. Receptive of the potency of God, the believer is waiting to be filled, longing to bear the fruit which will result from his or her union with God, to bring Christ to birth in our own life stories'.[10] This is a standard theological reading of the Annunciation, of course. Commenting on the words of St Paul ('My children, for whom I am again in labour until Christ be formed in you'; Galatians 4.19), Aquinas comments that 'just as the blessed virgin conceived Christ corporeally, so every holy soul conceives him spiritually'.[11] However, MacMillan draws out from this paradigm the very conditions of his own compositional process:

> Mary opens the door to the very heart of God, and in the silence of my own contemplation, in that necessary stillness where all composers know that music mysteriously begins, the following words from our sacred liturgy have lodged themselves in the womb of my soul, trapped in a scarlet room, gestating gently with a tiny pulse:
>
> Hail Mary, full of grace,
>
> The Lord is with thee
>
> Blessed art thou among women
>
> And blessed is the fruit of thy womb, Jesus.[12]

---

7 MacMillan, 'God', p. 22. See also MacMillan, 'Parthenogenesis', in Begbie (ed.), *Sounding the Depths*, pp. 33–38 (p. 34): 'All art is a kind of mirror image or a response to divine creation, to the first gesture of creation by the Creator. In many ways, artists have a tiny glimpse into the pathos with which God, at the dawn of creation, looked upon the work of his hand'.
8 MacMillan, 'God', p. 22. As MacMillan highlights, his own work *Adam's Rib* (1994–1995) is 'simply an acknowledgment of this eternally regenerative process of music as it develops through the ages'.
9 *Ibid.*, p. 23.
10 *Ibid.*, p. 24.
11 See Thomas Aquinas, *Summa Theologica*, IIIa, q. 30, a. 1, arg. 3, trans. by the English Dominican Province, 5 vols. (Notre Dame, IN: Ave Maria Press, 1981), Vol. 4, p. 2173.
12 MacMillan, 'God', p. 26.

MacMillan's compositional understanding is, then, incarnational: 'Mary, who was receptive to God; Mary who was filled by God; Mary who bore God's son. Mary is a paradigm of our receptivity [...] a model for all creative people [...] and an example for all Christian believers'.[13]

Springing from his faith, MacMillan's music is always, therefore, a witness to this faith. And that faith by virtue of the Incarnation is bodily as well as spiritual: 'I've always been drawn to a theology of music which emphasises [...] a sense of the physical, the corporeal, rather than a sense of the spirit being in some way divorced or set apart from the corporeal'.[14] Through the Incarnation, as through music itself, MacMillan believes that one can come to intimacy with God: 'there's an analogy between music and the mind of God: that in music there is, we see or even feel something of the thinking of God.'[15] But this is a journey to God *through* and not *away from* the body.[16] On reflecting on the first workshop performance of the six new compositions in the TheoArtistry scheme, MacMillan returned again to this incarnation metaphor:

> It is a huge thing for a composer to hear their work come alive in the hands and voices of interpreters. Up until the first rehearsal the composition remains in the inner imagination of the composer. But it comes to life, incarnationally, when conductor and singers (in this case) start to transform it into live musical flesh. The open rehearsal of these new works [...] was the moment when composer and theologian began to realise where their joint discussions had led.[17]

As the Annunciation provides a model for his composition of music (and for artistic 'conception' itself), so Christ incarnate is, for MacMillan, the pattern for musical performance — the transformation of the 'joint discussions' and 'inner imagination of the composer' into 'live musical flesh'. As music may represent the Incarnate living word through whom Christians come to know God, so musical creation is always fulfilled through the sensual, bodily communication of performance.

---

13 *Ibid.*, pp. 23–24.
14 MacMillan and McGregor, 'James MacMillan: A Conversation and Commentary', pp. 82–83: 'That's certainly a very Catholic way of understanding the theology of the body, the theology of spirituality which is about the here and now, as well as a sense of the Other. It's about the interaction — for us it has to be about — the interaction of the here and now, the mundane, the everyday, the joys and tragedies of ordinary everyday people, and some concept of the Beyond or something that we stretch towards, something that we're not completely fully aware of. And that tension brings about the great hope and potential for human beings to rise to the heights of what humanity is capable of'.
15 *Ibid.*, p. 99.
16 In this way, MacMillan distances his own theology of music and compositional language from those of his contemporary, John Tavener. See *Ibid.*, p. 98: 'I [MacMillan] don't share his [Tavener's] disparagement of the Western canon and indeed modernism, and I think we're even different kinds of Christian thinkers as well. And the way he talks in, I think, rather pessimistic terms about the body, although he, as a product of the 60s, is clearly someone who has taken full cognisance of hedonistic tendencies, probably more so than I have. But he talks about the body as quite distinct from the spirit and that always strikes me as rather odd, and a negation of full human potential. It seems an uneasy relationship in which to have the corporeal and the spiritual, and one could easily be dropped in relation to the other, and that worries me'.
17 MacMillan, 'A New Generation of Christian Artists', p. 21.

The Annunciation may also be, at the performance stage, a model for the reception of music and for how God may encounter a person through music: 'Being openly receptive to the transforming power of music is analogous to the patient receptivity to the divine that is necessary for religious contemplation.'[18] Indeed, MacMillan sees music as not only 'a striking analogy for God's relationship with us' but as a 'phenomenon connected to the work of God':

> Music opens doors to a deepening and broadening of understanding. It invites connections between organised sound and lived experience or suspected possibilities. In the connection is found the revelation, a realisation of something not grasped before. Such 'seeing' offers revelations about human living and divine relationships that can affect changes in our choices, our activities and our convictions.[19]

MacMillan therefore suggests a model for his 'ideal listener' who 'has to be not just open minded or open eared [...] but a hungry listener, a curious listener'.[20]

Maeve Louise Heaney underlines the Annunciation as a paradigm for the receptivity of the listener in remarkably similar terms: 'to be open and receptive to Christ's continued presence among us now through art and music is a doorway to a transformed and transforming experience of life and faith; a transforming presence theology needs to both receive from and speak to.'[21] Drawing on Bernard Lonergan's emphasis on an embodied experience of God, Heaney presents music as 'a gift of God to humanity' that frees a person from the 'pragmatic' to the 'contemplative', and opens a space or, in John Henry Newman's terms, a 'disposition' for the experience of God.[22] The encounter with the aesthetic is, in George Steiner's terms, 'the most "ingressive" transformative summons available to human experience' and, in the Annunciation, he sees the 'short hand image [...] of a "terrible beauty" or gravity breaking into the small house of our cautionary being'.[23] For Heaney, then, music 'enters "the small house" of our embodied self in a much more powerful way than any other form of art. It changes us. To not accept its potential at the service of a faith that is always experienced as Another entering one's life, be it in the invitation of a gentle breeze, be it as an interruption or intrusion, would be shortsighted.'[24] The model of Mary at the Annunciation is an invitation not just for the composer,

---

18   MacMillan, 'God', p. 25. MacMillan speaks or writes eloquently about the transformative power of music on many other occasions. See, for example, MacMillan, 'Parthenogenesis', pp. 35–36: 'Whether they are religious or not, people can and do speak in religious terms about the life-enhancing, life-changing, life-giving transformative power of music. This quasi-sacramental aspect of the form proves that music has a power and depth to touch something in our deepest secret selves, for music cannot be contained in its abstract parameters. It bleeds out into other aspects of our existences and experiences'.
19   MacMillan, 'God', p. 25.
20   MacMillan and McGregor, 'James MacMillan: A Conversation and Commentary', p. 87.
21   Maeve Louise Heaney, 'Towards a Theological Epistemology of Music', in her *Music as Theology: What Music Says About the Word* (Eugene, OR: Wipf and Stock Publishers, 2012), pp. 135–82 (p. 163).
22   Ibid., p. 165.
23   Ibid., pp. 167–68.
24   Ibid., p. 168.

then, but for the listener who, in receptive response to music, may be open to the communication of the divine.

II. The TheoArtistry Composers' Scheme: Forming Theologian-Composer Partnerships

Alongside setting scriptural, liturgical and secular texts to music, MacMillan has actively sought collaborations with other artists and theologians.[25] As he commented on the TheoArtistry scheme, 'collaborations between musicians and others can be wonderful things and can push the composer beyond their comfort zone to see the impact of their music outside of purely abstract considerations'.[26] Foremost amongst MacMillan's collaborators is the poet Michael Symmons Roberts. MacMillan first set Symmons Roberts' collection of poems as *Raising Sparks* (1997), considering his poetry as 'a search for the sacred that needs to ruminate in your mind' — a search which his music could 'enable and enhance.'[27] However, after over a decade of collaborations, he sought a more dialogic creative process: 'I really wanted to work with him from scratch on a piece so that we could both have some input into the other's work'.[28] This has led to a series of collaborative ventures, including *Quickening* (1998), *Parthenogenesis* (2000), *The Birds of Rhiannon* (2001), *Chosen* (2003), *The Sacrifice*: *Three Interludes* (2005–2006), *Sun Dogs* (2006), and *Clemency* (2009–2010).[29] Although their roles as poet-librettist and composer are delineated, MacMillan and Symmons Roberts see themselves as part of the other's creative process.[30] Underpinning the collaboration, moreover, is a shared

---

[25] See MacMillan, 'Parthenogenesis', pp. 34–35: 'Many of my works begin with an extra-musical starting-point. The pre-musical inspiration is an important factor on the specific nature and character of the music itself. It is important that this connectiveness between the pre-musical and the musical is always palpable and audible in the final creation'.

[26] MacMillan, 'A New Generation of Christian Artists', p. 21.

[27] Rhiannon Harries, 'How We Met: James MacMillan and Michael Symmons Roberts', http://www.independent.co.uk/extras/sunday-review/regulars/how-we-met-james-macmillan-michael-symmons-roberts-5340496.html. As MacMillan notes, *Raising Sparks* 'sprung forth initially from Michael's reading of the eighteenth-century Hasidic mystic and theologian Menahum Nahum' (MacMillan, 'Parthenogenesis', p. 33).

[28] Harries, 'How We Met'.

[29] Where *Quickening* (1998) celebrates the 'mysterious fragilities and ambiguous sanctities of human life', *Parthenogenesis* (2000) confronts head on the moral and theological issues of embryo research and genetic experimentation and manipulation: 'areas that are uncomfortable, messy and disturbing [...] theologians need to engage in these areas and be involved in debates pertaining to the nature of human life which are currently raging in our culture' (MacMillan, 'Parthenogenesis', pp. 33, 36). See also, for a brief discussion of some of these collaborations including Parthenogenesis, Michael Fuller, 'Liturgy, Scripture and Resonance in the Operas of James MacMillan', *New Blackfriars*, 96.1064 (July 2015), 381–90 (esp. pp. 286–90).

[30] MacMillan credits Symmons Roberts, indeed, with helping him to articulate his own theology of music. See MacMillan, 'God, Theology and Music', p. 20: 'Michael Symmons Roberts, whose poetry I have set a lot, has used the term "the deep mathematics of creation" about music. This is a term that chimes with me because music does seem to be a kind of calculus, a means of calculating something of our very nature. And because we are made in the image of God, music can be seen as a calculus of the very face of God'.

passion for the theological and human issues at stake: 'We spend a lot of time talking around our subjects, trying to get to the root of it before we work.'[31] As someone who highly values, and has considerable experience of, collaboration, MacMillan was an ideal mentor for the TheoArtistry Composers' Scheme.

For the project, *Theology Through the Arts* (*TTA*), Jeremy Begbie invited MacMillan and Symmons Roberts to collaborate, in addition, with Rowan Williams. Symmons Roberts reflects on this creative process in his poem 'Study for the World's Body', which concludes:

> '[…] an intimacy
> takes two people by surprise.
> It may be, in the world's eyes
>
> they should not be here,
> but without their risk the house is bare'[32]

Collaboration involves risk, but such risk — such openness to the other — is potentially generative. This is 'the open-endedness and risk involved in making any worthwhile art, and any worthwhile theology'.[33] Begbie's project yielded a provisional model for the TheoArtistry Composers' Scheme.[34] Four insights proved especially important for constructing these six theologian-composer partnerships: first, practical guidelines; secondly, the recognition of the revelatory power of such collaborations; thirdly, the emphasis on the value of *praxis*; and, fourthly, the issue of artistic integrity.

Begbie set up *TTA* in 1997 in Cambridge but, from 2000–2008, the academic work of *TTA* was undertaken at the Institute for Theology, Imagination and the Arts (ITIA) in St Andrews. TTA's stated aim was 'to discover and to demonstrate the ways in which the arts can contribute towards the renewal of Christian theology in the contemporary

---

31 Harries, 'How We Met'. In a revealing BBC radio interview, MacMillan comments: 'When I set poetry […] I live with the poem for a long time, a necessarily long time, so that I can fully understand it, and the music can wrap itself around the words in a way that brings about the deeper meaning which is not immediately apparent in first encounter'. See Susan Hitch, 'Poetry and the Divine. In Conversation with James MacMillan', Proms Literary Festival, BBC Radio 3, 24 August 2010, http://bobnational.net/record/390312

32 Michael Symmons Roberts, 'Study for the World's Body', in Begbie (ed.), *Sounding the Depths*, pp. 39–40 (p. 40).

33 Symmons Roberts, 'Author's Note', in Begbie (ed.), *Sounding the Depths*, p. 39.

34 The theologians and composers on our scheme were asked to engage with Begbie's research as well as with the reflections of James MacMillan, Michael Symmons Roberts and Rowan Williams on the fruit of their collaboration, *Parthenogenesis* (see Begbie, *Sounding the Depths*, pp. 1–13 and pp. 17–53). *Parthenogenesis* focused on an intriguing story, or urban myth, of 'a young woman in Hanover in 1944', who was injured by an Allied bombing raid, and gave birth nine months later to 'a child whose genetic profile was identical to hers. She insisted that she had not had intercourse before conceiving' (*Ibid.*, pp. 21–22). In addition to a methodological model, *Parthenogenesis* (etymologically, 'virgin-creation'), with its theme of a peculiar 'dark-Annunciation', provided, of course, a prompt for our own theme of 'Annunciations'. Although our collaborations explored 'positive' Annunciations — God communicating directly with humankind and, at the Incarnation, becoming man (and of the lived and artistic experiences associated with this) — one cannot but be acutely aware in contemporary Western culture of the 'negative mirror image of the Annunciation' (MacMillan, 'Parthenogenesis', p. 37) in the destruction and manipulation of human life at its earliest and most vulnerable stage.

world'.³⁵ Begbie brought together theologians and artists working in different media (poets, composers, sculptors, playwrights), and other interested parties (historians, local clergy, commissioners) to collaborate on new works of Christian art. Each of the four 'pod groups' was different, and the meetings arranged were flexible (some 'pod groups' met more frequently, others less so; some always together, others in smaller and bigger groupings). The freedom of the 'pod group' had many advantages, not least that the artistic work could develop organically through meetings: MacMillan describes fastening on to a 'common concept that provided the basis for much discussion and thought, bearing artistic fruit in due course'.³⁶

For the TheoArtistry Composers' Scheme, we experimented with a more compact and formal structure for the artistic collaborations, with a time frame of just six months.³⁷ The key collaboration was between one theologian and one composer; nonetheless, this 'theologian-composer partnership' was nourished by the mentoring of MacMillan, the wider research community of ITIA, the school of Divinity, and the University of St Andrews Music Centre. We established a strict framework for these partnerships: in the first two months, the six theologians researched six Old Testament 'annunciations', and the six composers were able to select one of the passages which resonated with them. At the first TheoArtistry workshop, the theologians then shared and discussed their research, and the composers also received guidance and mentorship from the faculty in theology and music. For the next three months, the theologians and composers collaborated through three scheduled one-to-one meetings (via Skype) and continued email correspondence, as the compositions started to take shape. In the final month, first drafts of the new compositions were given to St Salvator's Chapel Choir to rehearse before a second one-day workshop with MacMillan in which the six new choral pieces were performed.

We encouraged the theologians and composers involved to be receptive to the revelatory capacity of the arts 'to "open up" and disclose in unique ways [...] to contribute to *theology*'.³⁸ Begbie presents the arts as 'vehicles of *discovery*', as 'the materials, not simply the channels, of learning', citing Rowan Williams's insight, which it is worth reproducing once again:³⁹

---

35 Begbie, *Sounding the Depths*, p. 3. In 2009, Jeremy Begbie was appointed as the Thomas A. Langford Research Professor of Theology at Duke Divinity School, where he directs similarly dynamic projects at the interface of theology and the arts. See 'Duke Initiatives in Theology and the Arts' (DITA), https://sites.duke.edu/dita/

36 Begbie, *Sounding the Depths*, p. 33.

37 For a discussion of the scheme from the perspective of a participating theologian, see Margaret McKerron, 'TheoArtistry: Practical Perspectives on "Theologically Informed Art"', *International Journal for the Study of the Christian Church*, 1.5 (2018), 354–68 (pp. 355–57).

38 *Ibid.*, p. 355. See also Rowan Williams, 'Making it Strange: Theology in Other(s') Words', in Begbie (ed.), *Sounding the Depths*, pp. 19–32 (p. 29): 'Artistic work is always discovery, not illustration. Or, to put it slightly differently, but to connect it with the whole thesis of this essay, artistic work both engages with the real otherness of the environment and itself becomes "other" to the original planning mind as it moves towards its final form. It is not an empty cliché to repeat that the artist genuinely doesn't know until the work is coming to its expression just what is going to be'.

39 Begbie, *Sounding the Depths*, pp. 1, 5.

> [...] art, whether Christian or not, can't properly begin with a message and then seek for a vehicle. Its roots lie, rather, in the single story of metaphor or configuration of sound or shape which *requires* attention and development from the artist. In the process of that development, we find meanings we had not suspected; but if we try to begin with the meanings, they will shrink to the scale of what we already understand; whereas creative activity opens up what we do not understand and perhaps will not fully understand even when the actual work of creation is done.[40]

This was important in re-approaching the scriptures through the imaginative possibilities of the arts: always being open to how new meanings and perspectives might emerge. As MacMillan put it: 'At the Symposium, we presented the composers with this underlying research. We then encouraged them to engage deeply with their theologian collaborator, to be open to surprises, to what such collaboration might bring to the creative process'.[41]

Begbie's emphasis on *praxis* was also influential: 'art is first and foremost not a theory or an "aesthetics", but something done.'[42] By asking those involved to 'recount the process of collaboration' and 'what the group members believed could be learned from their experiences about the future of theology', Begbie valourises the doing and making of art as revelatory for the enterprise of theology itself.[43] He writes:

> the very activity of meeting together — praying, listening, responding, agreeing, disagreeing, exploring blind alleys, arguing at rehearsals, and so on — was not only intrinsic to the final result ('the play behind the play', as Ben Quash put it), but also the means through which a vast amount of the most important theology was actually done.[44]

Although research in biblical studies, the commentary traditions, reception history, liturgy and artistic representation was an important first stage, the participants similarly experienced the collaborative process as generative of ideas and theological insights.

Begbie addresses directly the issue of artistic integrity, recognising that his phrase 'theology through the arts' is in itself problematic.[45] At a theoretical level, Begbie seeks a *via media* between what he perceives as the 'double hazard' of 'theological instrumentalisation' (where 'music is treated as a vehicle; a mere tool at the behest

---

40 *Ibid.*, pp. 1–2, and see also, Williams, 'Making it Strange', p. 28. More controversially, Williams goes on to draw an analogy with the process of the composition of the Gospels themselves as 'not a story repeated, not a story invented to make a point, as the more mechanically minded critics might argue, but a set of narratives constantly being retold, and altered in the retelling because of what the very process of telling opens up, shows or makes possible' (*Ibid.*).
41 MacMillan, 'A New Generation of Christian Artists', p. 21.
42 Begbie, *Sounding the Depths*, p. 4.
43 *Ibid.*, p. 4.
44 *Ibid.*, p. 5.
45 *Ibid.*, pp. 10–11: 'In using the phrase "theology through the arts", I have often met with anxiety from both theologians and artists. [...] To speak of the arts serving theology — I have been told — inevitably means they will be dragooned into some kind of slavery, condemned to being mere carriers of predetermined theological "messages". Even worse, artistic freedom will likely be choked by some inflexible ecclesiastical orthodoxy. Either way, the arts don't get the "room" they need'.

of theology') and 'theological aestheticism' (where an overriding concern with the 'autonomy of music' leads people to give music 'a semi-independent role in relation to theology', and to attribute to it a 'veridical access to the divine').[46] Begbie's concern with 'theological aestheticism' is that music may be set against the 'norms derived from Scripture and its testimony to God's self-revelation', such that art becomes 'an ultimate measure of theological truth'.[47] One could argue, of course, that music does have the capacity to disclose the divine while maintaining, from a Christian viewpoint, that this cannot contradict the revealed doctrines of faith. But Begbie opposes this approach, explicitly rejecting 'a norm immanent to musical activity' as well as any 'foundational metaphysics or ontology elaborated prior to, or apart from, the specific dealings of the Christian God with the world'.[48]

Begbie's *via media* is, then, questionable: that Christian theology must have 'a distinct *orientation* as it engages with practices such as music — to the gospel, the dramatic movement of God by which he reconciles us to himself by the Spirit through the Son, witnessed to and mediated normatively by Scripture'.[49] This avoids 'theological aestheticism', but the claim that this will not 'suppress but *enable* a faithful honouring of music's integrities' because the Christian God 'is dedicated to the flourishing of creation in its own order (the order out of which music is made)' is, while theoretically plausible, problematic from a practical point of view, unless one works exclusively with Christian artists.[50] This seems to have been the case with the four 'pod groups' involved in *TTA*: Begbie suggests that it was 'just *because* of a joint orientation to the triune God of Jesus Christ, who is committed to the flourishing of the world in all its manifold particularity and diversity, that they were able to honour the integrity of the arts with which they were dealing, and the integrity of the artists in each group'.[51]

For the TheoArtistry collaborations, however, we did not request that either the theologians or the composers had any faith commitments; at the same time, we maintained that, whatever the individual beliefs of the participants, the compositions could potentially contribute constructively to theology. Gavin Hopps, the director of ITIA, presented new ways to envisage the relationship between theology and music.

---

46 Jeremy S. Begbie and Steven R. Guthrie, 'Introduction', in *Resonant Witness: Conversations between Music and Theology*, ed. by Jeremy S. Begbie and Steven R. Guthrie (Grand Rapids, MI: Eerdmans, 2011), pp. 1–24 (pp. 11–12). Although the introduction is co-written with Guthrie, the discussion of instrumentalisation, aestheticism, and orientation seems to expand directly on the passages cited in Begbie, *Sounding the Depths*. See also Jeremy Begbie, *Theology, Music and Time* (Cambridge: Cambridge University Press, 2000); and *Music, Modernity and God: Essays in Listening* (Oxford: Oxford University Press, 2013).

47 Begbie and Guthrie, *Resonant Witness*, p. 12; and Begbie, *Sounding the Depths*, p. 10. Begbie's concern, in this respect, is not specifically with regard to music but with any of the arts, insofar as an independent 'theology' might be derived from them. See *Ibid.*, p. 10: 'History is replete with examples of the arts over-determining theology: among the subtler forms, the keenness in much contemporary writing to identify the immense psychological power of music, film, painting or whatever as "spiritual" or "religious", and then cultivate some strand of "theology" accordingly'.

48 Begbie and Guthrie, *Resonant Witness*, p. 13.

49 *Ibid.*, p. 12.

50 *Ibid.*, p. 13.

51 Begbie, *Sounding the Depths*, p. 11.

He pursued approaches which move beyond Begbie's apparent insistence on pre-emptive Christological criteria, on particular musical forms, and on a privileging of cognitive over affective experiences of music.⁵² The work of David Brown, emeritus professor of ITIA, similarly seeks to validate less exclusive approaches to the presence of God in music, which are particularly valuable when working with theologians and composers in a more secular environment.⁵³ As Frank Burch Brown comments, 'it has become more imperative than ever for theology to expand its scope to consider culture, arts, and specifically music not as somehow illustrative, or as helpful analogies "outside" theology's intrinsic modes of thought, but, rather, as means of reshaping (and in turn being shaped by) that very thought — if, indeed, "thought" is the best word for what is called for'.⁵⁴ The theologians and composers on the TheoArtistry scheme were thus introduced to a rich, and developing dialogue about the contested relationship between theology and music, a dialogue which has been at the heart of ITIA research culture since the institute's inception.⁵⁵

In the theologian-composer collaborations, the relationship between theology and music was, in one sense, somewhat straightforward insofar as the composers (whether Christian or not) were responding to passages from the Old Testament. Perhaps especially because of this, it was important to stress that a 'correspondence', 'applicationist', or 'instrumental' method was but one way of approaching the task at hand. We were keen, then, that the theologians and composers had the license to explore these scriptural episodes with or without regard to particular doctrinal standpoints.⁵⁶

---

52 See Gavin Hopps, 'Popular Music and the Opening up of Religious Experience', in *The Extravagance of Music: An Art Open to God*, ed. by David Brown and Gavin Hopps (New York: Springer, 2018), pp. 161–296; and Chapter 17, in this volume.

53 David Brown has consistently advocated in his work a 'generous' understanding of God's self-revelation in the world through human history and culture. See, most recently, David Brown, *Divine Generosity and Human Creativity: Theology through Symbol, Art and Architecture*, ed. by Christopher R. Brewer and Robert MacSwain (London: Routledge, 2017). See also *God and Enchantment of Place: Reclaiming Human Experience* (Oxford: Oxford University Press, 2004); *God and Grace of Body: Sacrament in Ordinary* (Oxford: Oxford University Press, 2007); and *God and Mystery in Words: Experience through Metaphor and Drama* (Oxford: Oxford University Press, 2008). In this context, see also Begbie's response to David Brown's approach to theology and music, including his 'misgivings', in Jeremy Begbie, 'Openness and Specificity: A Conversation with David Brown on Theology and Classical Music', in *Theology, Aesthetics and Culture: Responses to the Work of David Brown*, ed. by Robert MacSwain and Taylor Worley (Oxford: Oxford University Press, 2012), pp. 145–56.

54 Frank Burch Brown, 'Preface', in Brown and Hopps (eds.), *The Extravagance of Music*. See also Burch Brown, *Religious Aesthetics: A Theological Study of Making and Meaning* (Princeton, NJ: Princeton University Press, 1989), pp. v–xvii (p. ix).

55 This dialogue, of course, contributes to an international scholarly discussion on the relationship between theology and music. For a descriptive summary of some of these scholarly viewpoints see, for example, Heaney, 'Theological Aesthetics in Contemporary Theology', in her *Theology as Music*, pp. 183–253.

56 In this respect, again, we were encouraging theologians and artists to exercise the freedom of their theological and artistic imaginations, without constraining them by excessive concern with scriptural or doctrinal 'orthodoxy' or 'correctness'. In his 'Afterword' to Begbie's *Theology Through the Arts* project, Nicholas Wolterstorff registers his own anxiety about envisaging artistic media as 'media of disclosure': there is, he affirms, always 'the need for *critical discernment*': a 'theological (or other) interpretation wrought in some artistic medium may prove *unacceptable* in one way or another; rather than being a means of disclosure, it may be a means of distortion if we allow

In each of the six collaborations, the scriptural passage spoke in a particular way to the theologians and composers; at the same time, the theologians and composers' own cultural beliefs, individual personalities and intellectual interests offered an enriched understanding of the biblical episode in question.

A Thomist paradigm for engaging with non-Christian truths may offer an additional way to articulate how theology may interact with music without infringing music's autonomy or intrinsic capacity to reveal God, while, at the same time, showing how music can be transformed and transfigured by the encounter with theology. Gavin D'Costa draws a parallel between twenty-first-century attitudes to Christian engagement with other religions and the three attitudes characteristic of early Christian engagements with philosophy: first, a rejection of engagement altogether; secondly, a critical encounter and accommodation; thirdly, an uncritical adoption of philosophy such that it determines Christianity rather than being transformed by it.[57] D'Costa favours the second as the most appropriate way for theology to engage with other disciplines, and sees in Aquinas' theology a key model. What happens, then, in this encounter with theology? Aquinas uses the scriptural image of water and wine: rather than the philosophy (water) diluting theology (wine), philosophical doctrines (water) become, are transformed into, wine. Crucially, as Martin Ganeri highlights, 'the water of [philosophical] thought still remains the material out of which the theology is made and without it we could not have the resultant theology in the form we have it'.[58] In other words, this wine is new to the cellar of divine wisdom, not replicating what was already there. Although the analogy with theology and music should be treated tentatively, there is a sense in which music (the water) can be transformed by its encounter with Christianity and come not to *serve* theology, but to *be* theology, or, more exactly, theoartistry, insofar as it may reveal God and His revelation in a new way through artistry.

---

ourselves to be led by it' (Nicholas Wolterstorff, 'Afterword', in Begbie (ed.), *Sounding the Depths*, pp. 221–32 (pp. 228–29)). This is a valid concern, which Wolterstorff shares, of course, with Begbie; however, an alertness to these dangers need not lead one to restrict the role of theological art to simply communicating a predetermined revelation (as *propaganda fidei*). We maintained, by contrast, that this is just one (albeit highly important) role of theological art, others being precisely to provoke and challenge (as by distortion, play, or irreverence). As Burch Brown insists, theology 'must exist in complementary and dialectical reaction not only with praxis but also with those richly aesthetic arts that can bring these relations imaginatively to life'. See Frank Burch Brown, *Religious Aesthetics: A Theological Study of Making and Meaning* (Princeton: Princeton University Press, 1989), p. 88. There are also important ecclesiological, and inter-denominational issues at stake here. McKerron interrogates the importance — in considering whether art is, in fact, theologically generative (rather than degenerative) — of the artwork's particular context and audience: 'What is "generative" is not necessarily fitting for worship purposes — at least, not without careful attention to ecclesiological, liturgical and even moral considerations' (McKerron, 'TheoArtistry: Practical Perspectives', pp. 362–65 (p. 363)).

57 Martin Ganeri situates his Thomist model for comparative theology in relation to the summary of approaches provided by Gavin D'Costa. See Martin Ganeri, 'Tradition with a New Identity: Thomist Engagement with Non-Christian Thought as a Model for the New Comparative Theology in Europe', *Religions* 3 (2012), pp. 1054–74 (p. 1058). See also Gavin D'Costa, *Theology in the Public Square: Church, Academy and Nation* (Oxford: Blackwell Publishing, 2005).

58 *Ibid.*, p. 1066.

The TheoArtistry partnerships, mentored by MacMillan, encouraged all concerned to reflect on the nature of scriptural exegesis and artistic creation. MacMillan proposes Mary as a model for the creative person, and the Annunciation may help us to understand theologically the performance and reception, as well as the composition, of music. Many composers, however, do not have faith commitments and, in establishing collaborations with artists, we did not want to prescribe an 'orientation' to a particular Christian doctrine or ecclesial denomination. Rather, we sought to highlight the scriptures as rich sources of creativity for artists, whatever their individual beliefs, and to support them in bringing their gifts to reading, seeing, and hearing those scriptures anew. As I think the six new pieces show, music can also go beyond the limits of language, contributing profoundly to the experience and knowledge of God. Hopefully, these new works, and the flexible and open model for collaboration that we adopted, will inspire more theologians to seek out and engage artists, as well as more artists to return to this perennial spring of creativity.

4. When Gods Talk to Men: Reading Mary with the Annunciations of the Hebrew Bible and the Ancient Near East

Madhavi Nevader

'The Annunciation' of Jesus' birth to Mary by the Angel Gabriel is the beginning of an illustrious story indeed. It comes to us from the third Evangelist, Luke, and, paired with its precursor narrative which tells the story of John the Baptist's birth, sets the stage for the entire gospel to come:

> [26] In the sixth month the angel Gabriel was sent by God to a town in Galilee called Nazareth, [27] to a virgin engaged to a man whose name was Joseph, of the house of David. The virgin's name was Mary. [28] And he came to her and said, 'Greetings, favoured one! The Lord is with you.' [29] But she was much perplexed by his words and pondered what sort of greeting this might be. [30] The angel said to her, 'Do not be afraid, Mary, for you have found favour with God. [31] And now, you will conceive in your womb and bear a son, and you will name him Jesus. [32] He will be great, and will be called the Son of the Most High, and the Lord God will give to him the throne of his ancestor David. [33] He will reign over the house of Jacob forever, and of his kingdom there will be no end.' [34] Mary said to the angel, 'How can this be, since I am a virgin?' [35] The angel said to her, 'The Holy Spirit will come upon you, and the power of the Most High will overshadow you; therefore the child to be born will be holy; he will be called Son of God. [36] And now, your relative Elizabeth in her old age has also conceived a son; and this is the sixth month for her who was said to be barren. [37] For nothing will be impossible with God.' [38] Then Mary said, 'Here am I, the servant of the Lord; let it be with me according to your word.' Then the angel departed from her.[1]

The whole episode is temporally oriented to Elizabeth's pregnancy (Luke [Lk] 1.26), but quickly moves on to the messenger, the Angel Gabriel, and to the recipient of the

---

1   Luke 1.26-38, NRSV. All biblical quotations are derived from the NRSV unless otherwise noted.

message, Mary, a virgin (Greek: *parthénos*) engaged to Joseph, a man of the house of David. The body of the exchange is the discourse between Gabriel and Mary: the former offering words of reassurance, the latter responding with perplexity. Because she has found favour with God (Lk 1.30), Gabriel informs Mary that she will give birth to a son named Jesus (Lk 1.31), who will grow in stature such that he will be given the throne of David (Lk 1.32) and will reign over Israel/Jacob in perpetuity (Lk 1.33). Though Mary initially responds with incredulity, Gabriel points to Elizabeth's mature pregnancy as a sign of divine potency (Lk 1.36), assuring Mary that 'nothing is impossible with God'. In response, she relents, commits to being a servant of God (Lk 1.38), and Gabriel duly departs.

Luke's annunciation is the foundation story of all foundation stories. To a young woman is revealed the destiny not simply of herself or even her extraordinary child (variously called 'great', 'Son of the Most High', 'holy', 'Son of God'), but that of the people to whom she belongs, the house of Jacob, who will see an ancient promise come to fruition. The particulars are grand to be sure — so much so that a new testament rests on its shoulders. But my hope here is to explore another story — in which the announcement that Mariam[2] will give birth to Jeshua[3] (the *mashiah* [Messiah] and son of God) is in fact the last episode in an inherited story just as illustrious. My wish, in effect, is to explore how the 'Annunciation' functions within its own, original context as Jewish literature. After all, before Luke's story could become the springboard for Christianity — the *start* of Jesus' story — it was written to demonstrate that Jesus was the culmination of the Jewish story. Thus, before we look to how Christianity has used the Annunciation in the arts, my hope is to explore how it fits into the tradition from which it arose, and how it itself engages with a complex constellation of texts. Indeed, the Annunciation can perhaps act as an object lesson for the force, merit and value of artistic and theological play.

To this end I shall consider the relation between the Annunciation in Luke's gospel and the biblical 'annunciation type-scene', to which, I suggest, Mary's Annunciation does not altogether conform. Instead, I argue that Luke's narrative structure more closely follows the sequence and progression of theophany scenes in the Hebrew Bible, suggesting that Luke has narrated his annunciation to be the theophany of theophanies. Next I shall examine the second annunciation of Jesus' birth in the Gospel of Matthew. Conveyed to Joseph in a dream, Matthew's annunciation also follows a well-established literary pattern in the Hebrew Bible and the wider ancient Near East. A variation on a 'prophetic dream-vision', Matthew's annunciation functions to demonstrate that the events surrounding the birth of Jesus unfold so as to fulfil the promise of Jewish scripture. Finally, I turn to the 'why' of the Annunciation, arguing that Matthew and Luke are engaged not only in a theological discussion, but a literary one as well.

---

2   'Mariam' is the Greek rendering of the name Miriam/Mary.
3   'Jeshua' is the Greek rendering of the name Joshua/Jesus.

1. Mary and the Annunciation Type-Scene

The contours of Mary's story are by no means unique. Each element of the exchange between Gabriel and Mary is intimately related to a group of texts in the Hebrew Bible, which when taken together form what many now refer to as the 'annunciation type-scene'; the function of which is to recount how a woman gives birth to a child (inevitably a son) because of the direct pronouncement and/or promise of God. Scholars disagree on the precise conventions of the type-scene — the arguments range across the spectrum from the overly simple[4] to the overly complex[5]—but most are happy to acknowledge five component parts to the type-scene: 1) plight of a woman; 2) prayer or appeal made to God; 3) annunciation scene proper; 4) birth report; 5) concluding statement.[6]

With this set of conventions in mind, one can identify seven annunciation type-scenes in the Hebrew Bible, used to initiate the narrative lives of Hagar (Genesis [Gen] 16), Sarah (Gen 18), Rebekah (Gen 25), Rachel (Gen 29-30), Manoah's wife (Judges [Judg] 13), Hannah (1 Samuel [Sam] 1), and Elisha's Shunammite Woman (2 Kings [Kgs] 4).

1) The plight experienced by all but one woman is barrenness (Sarah, Gen 18. 11; Rebekah, Gen 25.21; Rachel, Gen 29.31; Manoah's wife/Samson's mother, Judg 13.2; Hannah, 1 Sam 1.2; the Shunammite Woman, 2 Kgs 4.15). Here Hagar is the outlier — her plight is Sarah's wrath (Gen 16.8).

2) The prayer or appeal to God underpins Rebekah's type-scene (even if it is Isaac who prays in Gen 25.21), Rachel's lamentation of her continued infertility (Gen 29), as well as the narrative structure of Hannah's temple scene (1 Sam 2.13). Prayer, loosely conceived, provides some kind of pretext in the dealings between Abraham and Sarah in Gen 18. And yet again, Hagar appears to be the outlier.

3) There is a report concerning all seven of the women that they will either conceive and/or bear a son. A divine figure (be it God or an angel) pronounces the coming male child to Hagar and Manoah's wife. The respective narratives of Rebekah, Rachel and Hannah all report that their wombs have been opened. More straightforwardly, Sarah and the Shunammite Woman simply fall pregnant.

---

4 Robert Alter, 'How Convention Helps Us Read: The Case of the Bible's Annunciation Type-Scene,' *Prooftexts*, 3 (1983), pp. 115–30; Esther Fuchs, *Sexual Politics in the Biblical Narrative: Reading the Hebrew Bible as a Woman*, JSOTSupp 310 (London: Sheffield Academic Press, 2000).

5 James G. Williams, 'The Beautiful and the Barren: Conventions in Biblical Type-Scenes,' *JSOT*, 17 (1980), 107–19; Raymond E. Brown, *The Birth of the Messiah: A Commentary on the Infancy Narratives in the Gospels of Matthew and Luke*, AB Reference Library, 2nd edn. (New York: Doubleday, 1993).

6 Timothy D. Finlay, *The Birth Report Genre in the Hebrew Bible*, FATII 12 (Tübingen: Mohr Siebeck, 2005).

4) All seven scenes contain a birth report, even if at times truncated and interwoven with the pronouncement of the child's name: Hagar and Ishmael, Sarah and Isaac, Rebekah, Esau and Jacob; Rachel and Joseph; Manoah's wife and Samson; Hannah and Samuel. The outlier here is the Shunammite Woman, though all minor characters in the story appear anonymous, suggesting that the type-scene plays second fiddle to Elisha the prophet.

5) All good stories must come to an end, as all seven of our type-scenes do.

Working with this set of conventions for an annunciation type-scene, one can also include the precursor story to Mary's: Elizabeth's narrative that begins the gospel, which follows each convention perfectly. Elizabeth is barren (Lk 1.13, 25) despite the prayers of Zechariah (Lk 1.13). Gabriel announces that she will bear a son, John the Baptist (Lk 1.13), which in due course she does (Lk 1.57); the story ends with a report of how he grows and thrives to adulthood (Lk 1.80). Elizabeth's annunciation type-scene is, therefore, the most pristine in the biblical corpus. Though Elizabeth's husband, Zechariah, acts as a model of what *not* to do as recipient of an annunciation (Lk 1.8-23), the larger narrative typifies the conventions of the scene to perfection.

What does not typify the conventions of the type-scene, however, is Mary's own version of it. She is neither barren, nor in plight. She does not pray to God in the initial iteration of the type-scene. There is no birth report. And while all good stories must come to an end, the concluding statement, 'Then the angel departed from her' (Lk 1.38), hardly relates to the nature or instantiation of the annunciation.[7]

The scholarly escape routes from the problem are diverse, though all in some way tweak the convention to keep Mary's Annunciation as part of the type-scene. Robert Alter, for example, suggests that it is the nature of type-scenes to 'surprise' the reader, subverting expectations by means of purposefully breaking the established convention.[8] Athalya Brenner nuances the convention itself, arguing that deviation is allowed if and when it is concerned with pre-conception difficulties.[9] And James G. Williams argues that the discord between Mary and her putative type-scene is evidence of innovation, 'which manifests the concerns of a newly formed religious tradition that is still partially linked to its parent tradition'.[10]

All three of these avenues of argument are troublesome, because each forces Mary into a type-scene into which she clearly does not fit. I do not take issue with the existence of a type-scene that might tie together all of the biblical matriarchs (as we will see later, on some level, I think this *is* what the text is attempting to do), nor with the reconfiguration of conventions so as to allow for variation. Profound transformation can

---

7   Ending the type-scene as some do in Lk 1.56 and thus including the Magnificat and the report that Mary returned home does not rehabilitate the convention.
8   Alter, 'How Convention Helps Us Read', pp. 127–29.
9   Athalya Brenner, 'Female Social Behaviour: Two Descriptive Patterns within the "Birth of the Hebrew" Paradigm,' *Vetus Testamentum*, 36 (1986), pp. 257–73.
10 Williams, 'Beautiful and the Barren,' p. 113.

occur as a result of adaption — as evidenced by most of the biblical canon. Instead, the issue lies with the title — the Annunciation — that we employ, inasmuch as it leads the type-scene to be defined by an episode that runs contrary to the scene's conventions. Because the announcement of Jesus's birth to Mary is considered to be *the* ultimate and greatest annunciation, the type-scene is determined by the subject of the announcement (birth of a child) rather than its narrative conventions, which overwhelmingly point to the barrenness of the woman. In fact, there appears no benefit in referring to the child-miraculously-born-to-barren-woman type-scene in the Hebrew Bible as a 'type-scene' to *the* Annunciation (i.e. Mary's annunciation in the New Testament); to do so is to collapse two different narratives onto one another for the sake of raising the New Testament iteration, that is, the Christian iteration, over the Old Testament, that is over the Jewish iteration.

If, however, we excise Mary from the barren-woman type-scene, we must also excise Hagar. But it is precisely in the similarities shared by these two women, long noticed by Islam,[11] that the importance of Mary's type-scene begins to emerge: both are young women; both are promised a son whose destiny is fixed; both are commanded to give the child a predetermined name. Both women converse directly with, and see, a divine being, moving our type-scene away from barren mother to that of theophany, where, perhaps, the Annunciation is most at home.

2. Mary's Annunciation and the 'Theophany' Type-Scene.

George Savran has explored the various conventions that make up the theophany type-scene in the Bible.[12] Also opting for five conventions, Savran lays out the theophany type-scene as follows: 1) scene setting wherein the protagonist is separated (intentionally or unintentionally) so as to experience the theophany; 2) the appearance and speech of Yahweh (YHWH) (or his representative); 3) human response to the presence of the divine; 4) expression of doubt or anxiety; 5) externalization, wherein the protagonist re-enters the external realm and is reintegrated into society.

Mary's story gains new life when we read her as the protagonist of a theophany before the recipient of a divine promise. Gabriel is sent by God to Mary, and she encounters the angelic figure whilst alone (convention 1). He speaks to her and relays an announcement built upon Mary's status as a favoured one (Lk 1.28; convention 2). Mary, initially perplexed by the angel's greeting, is told not to be afraid (Lk 1.20; convention 3). Indeed, after the first pronouncement concerning her as yet unborn son, Mary asks the question upon which the entire theophany turns, 'how can this be, since I am a virgin?' (Lk 1.34). Somehow satisfied with Gabriel's response (that she will be overshadowed by the power of the Holy Spirit), Mary accepts her future,

---

11 For a larger discussion, see Robert C. Gregg, *Shared Stories, Rival Tellings: Early Encounters of Jews, Christians, and Muslims* (New York: Oxford University Press, 2015), pp. 543–91.
12 George W. Savran, 'Theophany as Type Scene,' *Prooftexts*, 23 (2003), pp. 119–49.

self-identifying as 'the servant of the Lord' (Lk 1.38) and handing over agency to Gabriel (convention 4). Finally, Mary is externalized first with the departure of the angel and then with the next step she takes, which is to leave Nazareth in search of Elizabeth (Lk 1.39; convention 5). Whereas Mary was an awkward outlier for the conventions of the 'annunciation type-scene', she is fully accounted for when we evaluate her according to the conventions of a theophany type-scene.

Suggesting we read Mary as a theophany heroine is not to jump out of bed with one type-scene and back into bed with another for the sake of theological warmth. It is to offer a wider textual canvas with which Luke's Mary is in conversation, hopefully bringing her out from under the weight of the promise given to her and into a context in which she acts with other protagonists of the theophany tradition(s). The promise that she will conceive and bear a son unquestionably tethers Mary to the great women of Jewish scripture — Hagar, Sarah, Samson's mother, Hannah, and the mother-to-be of Isaiah [Isa] 7.14. But Mary's *story* tethers her to the great heroes of that very same scripture (Abraham, Jacob, Moses, Samuel, Gideon) and to YHWH's prophets (Isaiah, Jeremiah and Ezekiel), all of whom are recipients of a divine annunciation. With a simple statement, conveyed by the single Greek word *idou*, Mary's response to Gabriel, 'here I am', evokes the Hebrew *hinneni*, and with it the response of Jacob (Gen 31; 46), the response of Moses (Exodus [Exod] 3), and the response of Samuel (1 Sam 3) to a divine call. Through this one word, Akedah itself (Gen 22) — the story of the sacrifice of Isaac, without which Jesus would mean very little — is called into the constellation of Mary's theophany.

The greatest dividend of reading Mary's story as a theophany is the transformation she undergoes. Theophany type-scenes are most often used to recount first-time encounters with the divine (e.g. Isa 6), functioning not just as the preface to a major change in the life of the protagonist, but as the narrative transformation of that protagonist from one stage to another, one person to another (e.g. Abraham; Jacob; Moses). And so, the importance of the Annunciation is not what, or even that, God pronounces something to Mary, it is that she meets Gabriel as God's messenger and takes up the unthinkable (even unfathomable) commission that he has for her, transfiguring from a young woman to the mother of God.

3. Joseph's Annunciation and the Prophetic Dream Vision

I have purposefully ignored Mary's second annunciation scene, as found in Matthew [Mt] 1.18-25, because it is not an annunciation to Mary at all, but a divine dream given to Joseph. It shares certain similarities with the Luke passage, but is logically distinct:

> ¹⁸Now the birth of Jesus the Messiah took place in this way. When his mother Mary had been engaged to Joseph, but before they lived together, she was found to be with child from the Holy Spirit. ¹⁹Her husband Joseph, being a righteous man and unwilling to expose her to public disgrace, planned to dismiss her quietly. ²⁰But just when he had resolved to do this, an angel of the Lord appeared to him in a dream and said, 'Joseph, son of David, do not be afraid to take Mary as your wife, for the child conceived in her is from the Holy Spirit. ²¹She will bear a son, and you are to name him Jesus, for he will save his people from their sins.' ²²All this took place to fulfil what had been spoken by the Lord through the prophet: ²³'Look, the virgin shall conceive and bear a son, and they shall name him Emmanuel,' which means, 'God is with us.' ²⁴When Joseph awoke from sleep, he did as the angel of the Lord commanded him; he took her as his wife, ²⁵but had no marital relations with her until she had borne a son; and he named him Jesus.

The Matthean 'annunciation' has a number of similarities with its Lukan counterpart: there is a Mary, a child conceived from the Holy Spirit, a prediction of the son and his function, and an angelic figure with whom Joseph converses as a proxy for God. Here is where the similarities end. While there is a 'Mary', this story of the 'birth of Jesus' hovers around and is concerned solely with the actions and reactions of Joseph. Like Rebekah's barren-wife variation, which is told initially in relation to Isaac (Gen 25), Mary's inexplicable pregnancy is resolved between the divine representative and Mary's betrothed, against whom presumably the offence has been committed. Moreover, though the pericope ends with the statement that Joseph named the child 'Jesus', at no point does Joseph speak. No one in this version, bar the divine messenger, utters a word. One supposes, then, that it is a true 'annunciation'.

The story stands out in two further, and much more significant ways. Firstly, the knowledge that Joseph receives is conveyed in the format of a dream. Two of the Bible's early protagonists experience life-changing dreams: Jacob (Gen 28) and Abimelech (Gen 20). When implicitly associated with prophetic revelation (e.g. Joseph, Daniel), divine revelation through dreams appears to be the textual and revelatory canvas for royalty (e.g. Solomon in 1 Kgs 3; Pharaoh in Egypt).[13] Moreover, it is in this scene, and this scene alone, that we find larger, ancient Near Eastern conversation partners.[14] Both the Legend of King Kirta and the Aqhat Legend, known to us from the Levantine Ras Shamra archive, begin with a royal protagonist whose dynasty is either under threat or entirely compromised.[15] Each king induces a dream through ritual and receives

---

13 Koowon Kim, *Incubation as a Type-Scene in the Aqhatu, Kirta, and Hannah Stories: A Form-Critical and Narratological Study of KTU 1.14 I-1.15 III, 1.17 I–II, and 1 Samuel 1:1-2:11*, VTSupp 145 (Leiden: Brill, 2011).

14 On the discussion more broadly, see Scott A. Ashmon, *Birth Annunciations in the Hebrew Bible and Ancient Near East: A Literary Analysis of the Forms and Functions of the Heavenly Foretelling of the Destiny of a Special Child* (Lewiston, NY: Edwin Mellen Press, 2012).

15 For the texts, see the various entries in *Context of Scripture. Volume 1: Canonical Compositions from the Biblical World*, ed. by W. W. Hallo and K. Lawson Younger, 3 vols. (Leiden and New York: E. J. Brill, 1996).

divine assurance from the head of the pantheon (the God El) regarding the birth of a child. Of King Kirta, we read:

> As he wept, he fell asleep,
> > As he shed tears, he slumbered.
> Sleep overcame him and he lay down,
> > Slumber and he curled up.
> In a dream Ilu descended,
> > In a vision, the father of mankind.
> He came near, asking Kirta:
> > Who is Kirta that he should weep?
> > Should shed tears, the goodly lad of Ilu?
> …
> What need have I of silver and of yellow gold?
> …
> [Permit] me to acquire sons,
> > [Permit] me to multiply [children].
> …
> Rather, you must give what my house lacks:
> > Give me maid Hurraya,
> > The best girl of your firstborn offspring;
> …
> That she might bear a scion for Kirta, a lad for the servant of Ilu.
>
> Kirta looked about and it had been a dream,
> > The servant of Ilu, and it had been a vision.[16]

The second aspect that distinguishes Matthew's annunciation is more obvious: why does Joseph find himself with a soon-to-be wife impregnated by the Holy Spirit? All this took place, claims the evangelist, 'to fulfil what had been spoken by the Lord through the prophets' (Mt 1.22). For Matthew, there is no question of agency on the part of either Joseph or Mary. God may speak and pronounce, but even divine speech in the present is tethered to an earlier promise once given to Ahaz through Isaiah, concerning Hezekiah (Isa 7.14). History unfolds, and God communicates so as to enable promises of the past to be fulfilled.

4. Theophanies and Cognitive Dissonance: The Problem of Mary

But what does all of this mean? What is the purpose of an annunciation? In short, why have Matthew and Luke gone to the trouble? Unfortunately, we do not have anything even approximating a foolproof answer.[17] The enterprise of identifying type-scenes,

---

16   Dennis Pardee, 'Kirta Epic,' in *Context of Scripture*, Vol. 1, pp. 333–43.
17   Ashmon is the most comprehensive in his list of "functions" served by annunciation narratives from the ancient Near Eastern and the Hebrew Bible (*Birth Annunciations*, pp. 277–321; pp. 328–30). By

and assessing biblical narratives according to their conventions, was intended to avoid questions of genre, historical priority, and causation. Yet such evasions are frustrating, skirting as they do the ever important question, 'why?'. Allow me then to offer two possible answers to the 'why' of the Annunciation: one historical, the other literary.

Let me turn first to the historical. In the textual world of the ancient Near East, Gods talk to men when there is a problem, most usually concerning the men themselves. Divine speech is used time and again to smooth over and alleviate cognitive dissonance. Positively, the outcome for the men to whom Gods speak is a change in their person: a new name and thus identity in the case of Jacob (from Jacob to Israel [cf. Gen 32]), and a new vocation or calling in the case of Moses (from run-away shepherd to the leader of God's people [cf. Exod 3]). For Mary, then, as a result of God's speech to her, she is called to take on the task of all tasks, the vocation of vocations — to be, as we noted earlier, *the* mother of God.

Negatively, however, we might query what the cognitive dissonance is that Luke and Matthew endeavour to assuage in the first place? One option that immediately comes to mind is the problem of Jesus' origins. In accounting for Jesus, the gospels do not sing from the same hymn sheet. Mark, for one, is not compelled to muse on the birth of Jesus (nor, for that matter, is Paul). By contrast, John masterfully weaves Jesus into the very fabric of creation: 'In the beginning was the Word, and the Word was with God, and the Word was God' (John 1.1). But whatever soteriological function Jesus has for either Mark or John, it is not one based on his human lineage or the nature of his birth.

Matthew and Luke, on the other hand, orient Jesus into the history of Israel, each providing a genealogy for Jesus which ties his salvific function to lineage. For Luke, the genealogy begins with Jesus (Lk 3.23) and works itself backwards, weaving through King David (albeit through an obscure son[18]), the royal tribe of Judah, Abraham and Adam, and ending with God: 'son of Adam, son of God' (Lk 3.38). Matthew's approach travels in the other direction, beginning with Abraham and weaving through King David and his most prominent sons. For Matthew, Jesus is the latest and last king of Judah; the genealogy demonstrates precisely what it claims of itself in Mt 1.1, that Jesus is 'the Anointed One, the son of David, the son of Abraham'. Perhaps the annunciation scenes are meant to act as further justification — lending both heroic and scriptural weight to the contested royalty of a man of no known origin, ignominiously put to death by Rome for political insurrection.

    Ashmon's count, the former grouping of texts serves twenty different functions, the latter twenty-two, the two corpora sharing approximately seven elements (e.g. Legitimate Destiny[ies]; Show God's Character; Elevate Mother's Status; *et. al.*). I am very much in favour of allowing annunciation texts to serve a diverse set of different, even unique purposes, but we must be careful not to freight the biblical version with more theological importance than other ancient Near Eastern texts. The promise that a son will be born to a young woman in Isa 7.14 is no less political than the announcement of a coming, salvific king in the Egyptian *Prophecies of Neferti*, for example.

18 Nathan as David's son as distinct from his admonishing court prophet is attested only in 1 Chron 3.5; cf. 14.4.

However, Matthew's genealogy gives further pause for thought, not because of the genealogical route by which he traces Jesus' lineage, but because of the five women he mentions in that lineage: Tamar, a woman who pretends to be a prostitute; Rahab, a prostitute; Ruth, a widow who arguably prostitutes herself; the wife of Uriah, a woman taken and impregnated in adultery; and Mary. Matthew's genealogy therefore draws our attention to Mary herself. Is it possible that she is the problem the annunciation must tackle?

If so, how does each of the annunciation scenes address the problem of Mary's putatively illegitimate pregnancy? Matthew is the most straightforward and the least subtle of the two. Mary is pregnant because scripture said she must be so: 'All this took place to fulfil what had been spoken by the Lord through the prophet' (Mt 1.22). One might also suggest that Matthew's Mary is made a virgin for the same reason, to fulfil every aspect that might point to Jesus as *christos* even at the expense of the integrity of his mother. Mary's agency is eclipsed by the demands of fulfilment of prophecy and scriptural allusion. By contrast, Luke appears to take on the question of Mary's integrity through Mary's own actions. By accepting the call to divine servanthood through a proclamation of existence — *hinneni/idou*/I am here — Mary becomes a member of a rich constellation of servants to God. For Luke, then, Mary's scriptural pedigree renders void any doubt over her virtue.

Now, the second of the two explanations for the 'why' of the Annunciation — the literary. Whatever we decide about a possible historical 'why' for the Annunciation texts, their rich textuality is undeniable. Each engages with scripture in complex ways that — at least in this initial iteration — do not seem to 'replace' the scriptural antecedent, but endeavour to demonstrate that Mary stands in relation to an expansive hinterland of texts. The historical problem of Mary in Matthew was *created* by the demands of scripture. In Luke, by contrast, the historical problem of Mary was *resolved* by the fluidity of scripture. Addressed from a different perspective, each Annunciation text is in complex conversation with the multiple stories of the Hebrew Bible. As Yair Zakovtich reminds us:

> The Bible's profusion of interpretative strategies testifies to its being a branching network of relationships that connect distant texts, binding them to one another. Writings from different historical periods and a variety of literary genres call out and interpret one another, with the interpreted texts being reflected back — somewhat altered — from a multitude of mirrors. Indeed, it is not an exaggeration when I propose that no literary unit in the Bible stands alone, isolated and independent, with no other text drawing from its reservoir and casting it in a new light.[19]

---

19 Yair Zakovitch, 'Inner-Biblical Interpretation,' in *Reading Genesis: Ten Methods*, ed. by Ronald Hendel (Cambridge: Cambridge University Press, 2011), pp. 92–118 (p. 95).

What goes for the Hebrew Bible continues into its next iteration, the New Testament.[20] The profusion of interpretative strategies testifies to the Bible being a branching network of relationships that connect texts, binding them to one another. So, let me encourage you to read Mary at the end of the story, concluding that God talks to women and that the art of reworking a biblical text can act as a model for us all.

---

20 See, for example, Richard B. Hays, *Echoes of Scripture in the Letters of Paul* (New Haven: Yale University Press, 1993); Gregory K. Beal, *Handbook on the New Testament Use of the Old Testament: Exegesis and Interpretation* (Grand Rapids, MI: Baker Academic, 2012).

5. Old Testament Typology: The Gospel Canticles in the Liturgy and Life of the Church

William P. Hyland

The Infancy Narratives (the first two chapters of the Gospels of Matthew and Luke) are marked by powerful moments of divine annunciations and epiphanies, as well as by human and angelic response in song. These accounts of the birth and childhood of Jesus have served as profound inspiration for Christian theology and art throughout history, and the truths they embody are central to the Christian imagination. The thirteenth-century Franciscan theologian, Bonaventure, treats in an exemplary way the evangelists' detailed discussions of the birth of John the Baptist, as well as of the events surrounding and following the nativity and epiphany of Jesus. Far from seeing the Infancy Narratives as a prelude to the main events of the Gospel, Bonaventure sees in them an indispensable summation of the main themes of the Christian faith and the fulfilment of the promises of the Old Testament.

This chapter focuses on Bonaventure's discussion of the three Gospel canticles recited in the Divine Office: the *Benedictus*, *Magnificat* and *Nunc Dimittis*. His treatment of these songs makes it clear how the Infancy events found in the Gospel are the culmination of the history of Israel, and are thus suitable focal points for the liturgy. Drawing upon a venerable tradition of exegesis from the patristic and earlier medieval period, Bonaventure explicates the meaning of these three canticles from Luke's gospel in the daily liturgical prayer of the Church. In doing so, Bonaventure relies upon the idea of typology: the figurative reading of the Old Testament in light of its fulfilment in the Christian dispensation. These exegetical and liturgical contexts at the heart of the Christian tradition may open up many opportunities for rich and original forms of artistic expression.

1. St Bonaventure, and Typology in the Bible and Christian tradition

Typology is a method of biblical interpretation whereby an element found in the Old Testament is seen to prefigure one found in the New Testament. The initial one is called 'the type' and the fulfilment is designated 'the antitype'. Either type or antitype may be a person, thing, or event, and somehow relates to the person and mission of Christ and the salvation of believers. The use of biblical typology was fundamental to much Christian exegesis before the rise of modern critical biblical scholarship, and persists in various forms to our own day. With deep roots in Hellenistic Greek and Hebrew literary and religious cultures, it also became central to Christian biblical interpretation. Beyond being a tool for Christian exegetes, typology has become central to the Christian imagination over the centuries, shaping liturgical, artistic and literary expression.

When examining the history of Christian biblical exegesis, typology specifically refers to the interpretation of the Old Testament based on the fundamental theological unity of the two Testaments — with God as the ultimate inspiration — whereby something in the Old foreshadows or prefigures something in the New. This view of the theological unity of scripture is expressed in *Catechism of the Catholic Church*:

> The Church, as early as apostolic times, and then constantly in her Tradition, has illuminated the unity of the divine plan in the two Testaments through typology, which discerns in God's works of the Old Covenant prefiguration of what he accomplished in the fullness of time in the person of his incarnate Son. Christians therefore read the Old Testament in the light of Christ crucified and risen. Such typological reading discloses the inexhaustible content of the Old Testament; but it must not make us forget that the Old Testament retains its own intrinsic value as Revelation reaffirmed by our Lord himself. Besides, the New Testament has to be read in light of the Old. Early Christian catechesis made constant use of the Old Testament. As an old saying put it, the New Testament lies hidden in the Old and the Old Testament is unveiled in the New.[1]

Christian exegetes felt empowered to take this approach because they found it utilized within the New Testament itself. Firstly, authors of various New Testament books use the Old Testament as a source of prophecy pointing forward to Jesus.[2] Christ himself used a reference to Jonah as a prefiguring of himself (Matthew [Mt] 12.40). St Paul, too, portrays the desert wanderings of the ancient Israelites as a type of the Christian life (1 Corinthians 10.1–6), and the story of Hagar and Sarah is seen as typologically representing the contrast between slavery to the Law in the Old Covenant with the freedom of the Christian New Testament (Galatians [Gal] 4.21-31). Likewise, the

---

1 *Catechism of the Catholic Church*, Canons 128-29 (Rome: Urbi et Orbi Communications, 1994), p. 36.
2 Restricting ourselves just to the Infancy Narrative of Matthew's Gospel, examples include: Matthew 1. 23; and 2. 6, 14-15, 17-18, 23.

Epistle to the Hebrews portrays many aspects of the Old Testament, such as the priest, Melchizedek (Heb 7.15-19), as typologically looking forward to Christ. Inspired by these New Testament examples, early Christian exegetes discovered many typological connections in Hebrew scripture, such as how the manna in the desert may prefigure the Eucharist, or animal sacrifice may prefigure the death of Christ on the Cross. To give an example from the Infancy Narratives, Mary's song *Magnificat* was seen to echo clearly the Prayer of Hannah in 1 Samuel [Sam], where Hannah would be a type of Mary.

Furthermore, over time these typological readings were tied to an idea of the different "senses" of scripture. These came to be seen in terms of four senses, usually adhering to the following pattern: 1) Literal sense, or 'the meaning conveyed by the words of scripture and discovered by exegesis'[3]; 2) Allegorical sense, or how the Old Testament person or thing stands for or prefigures a New Testament counterpart; 3) Tropological or Moral sense, how the text teaches virtue; 4) Anagogical sense, how the text teaches something about salvation. Throughout the patristic and medieval centuries, the relationship of these 'senses', and how the three 'figurative' senses related to the literal or historical, resulted in a great deal of variety and creativity among a wide range of authors.[4]

Seen from this rich and complex viewpoint, the Old Testament antecedents of the Gospel Narratives would have resonated with their Christian audiences, echoing, calling to mind, and providing a deeper meaning to the Infancy Narratives and, indeed, to the whole of the Gospels. This view of the fundamental unity of the two testaments was imaginatively put to use in the earliest traditions of the Church. Most basically, the Church enshrined typology in the liturgy, from the great sequences of Easter, to the readings for every single Sunday, where usually an Old Testament passage was read, which either would foreshadow or be fulfilled in some readings from the Gospels. This liturgical practice also accentuates the moral meanings of the scriptures: that is, how they are meant to be applied in the lives of Christian believers today. The liturgical expression of typology could also lend itself to the full resources of music and art, opening out and articulating these multivalent theological connections.

This way of reading the scriptures arguably reaches its apogee in the scriptural commentary of Bonaventure. This Franciscan master envisaged scriptural exegesis as preaching the Word of God and aiding other teachers to do likewise. As he expresses it in his prologue to the *Commentary on Luke*, 'Now to expound and teach the Gospel of God is to preach the divine word. And therefore, the teacher must be inflamed by

---

3   *Catechism of the Catholic Church*, Canon 116.
4   Seminal studies of the medieval senses of scripture include Henri de Lubac, *Medieval Exegesis: Volume I: The Four Senses of Scripture*, trans. by Marc Sebanc (Grand Rapids, MI: Eerdmans Publishing Co., 1998) originally published in 1959; and Beryl Smalley, *The Study of the Bible in the Middle Ages* (Oxford: Blackwell, 1952). For an excellent discussion of recent scholarship in this area, see Christopher Ocker and Kevin Madigan, 'After Beryl Smalley: Thirty Years of Medieval Exegesis, 1984–2013', *Journal of the Bible and its Reception*, 2 (2015), 87–130.

fraternal love'.⁵ Bonaventure's method reflects this ideal. As Robert Karris expresses it, 'Briefly put, Bonaventure's hermeneutical method is to interpret Scripture by Scripture'.⁶ This view of scripture, interestingly, has often been described in artistic terms. The Quarrachi editors of Bonaventure's works see his commentary as 'a mosaic constructed from innumerable and varied stones'; it uses other scriptural texts, in other words, to expound on the text of scripture he is considering in any given moment, to bring out its full meaning.⁷ Moreover, in his *Collations on the Six Days of Creation*, Bonaventure compares scripture to a stringed instrument, a zither, that is a cithara or psaltery: 'All of Scripture is like a single zither. And the lesser string does not produce the harmony by itself, but in union with the others. Likewise, one passage of Scripture depends upon another. Indeed, a thousand passages are related to a single passage.'⁸

This theory of scriptural interpretation, so beautifully articulated through artistic metaphors, is set forth succinctly in the prologue of his *Breviloquium*, a short compendium of theology meant for the training of fellow Franciscans. Bonaventure identifies theology with sacred scripture: its origin is God; it surpasses knowledge, but is geared toward our capacity; and its end or fruit consists of eternal happiness. Faith in Christ is a fundamental prerequisite for understanding scripture, for grasping its full meaning and how it unfolds before our mind.

Using imaginative metaphors, Bonaventure then describes the breadth, length, height and depth of scripture. He compares the breadth of scripture to a river that is enriched by a diversity of books and genres as it flows from its source. The length of scripture is seen in how it covers all periods from creation until the Day of Judgment. Moving from his river metaphor, Bonaventure describes the whole course of salvation history as being like a beautifully composed poem: an integral view of the poem is necessary to fully appreciate its individual words and stanzas. The height of scripture testifies to how Jesus is the mediator of all grace and knowledge of heavenly things, and the means by which they descend for our own apprehension. The depth of scripture is experienced in its four-fold senses, all of which correspond to its content, audience, source and final end. Each passage of sacred scripture, then, provides the reader with a number of meanings from a single text. For Bonaventure, it is fitting that the teaching of Christ should be humble in word but profound in meaning.⁹

---

5   Bonaventure, *Commentary on the Gospel of Luke*, trans. and ed. by Robert J. Karris (St Bonaventure, NY: Franciscan Institute Publications, 2001–2004), p. 4. For the context of this statement vis-à-vis Stephen Langton, Peter Comestor and Peter Cantor, as well as the early Franciscans, see Jacques Guy Bougerol, 'Bonaventure as Exegete', in *A Companion to Bonaventure*, ed. by Jay M. Hammond and others (Leiden and Boston: Brill, 2014), pp. 168–74.

6   Robert J. Karris, 'St Bonaventure as Biblical Interpreter: His Methods, Wit, and Wisdom', *Franciscan Studies*, 60 (2002), 159–208 (p. 163).

7   *Ibid.*

8   Quotation and translation found in Karris, 'Introduction', *Commentary on the Gospel of Luke*, pp. xxi–xxii. The original is found in Bonaventure, *Doctoris Seraphici S. Bonaventurae Opera Omnia*, 10 vols. (Quarrachi: Collegium S. Bonaventurae, 1882–1902), Vol. 5 (1891), p. 421.

9   This paragraph is a summary of the Prologue to *Breviloquium*. St Bonaventure, *Breviloquium*, trans. with notes by Dominic V. Monti (St Bonaventure, NY: Franciscan Institute Publications, 2005), pp. 1–22.

The most effective way to bring out these spiritual meanings once the basic, literal understanding has been established is, in Bonaventure's view, by quoting other, more direct scriptural passages.[10] The role of the exegete is to guide the uninitiated Christian soul through the intimidating and seemingly impenetrable forest of the scriptures to an understanding of true theology found in its text. This requires, first and foremost, a hermeneutical lens of humility, desire and charity. The purpose of such exegesis is, then, to illuminate the mind and ignite the heart of the reader or listener.[11] The key, however, in an exegetical process far from straightforward or self-evident, is for the exegete to possess a profound knowledge of *all* scripture in order to bring appropriate scriptural texts forward in the analysis of a particular biblical episode. Let us now turn to analyse how Bonaventure implements these hermeneutical principles in his exegesis of the canticles in the Lukan Infancy Narratives, keeping in mind the central importance of typology to his method.

2. The Three Canticles

The Divine Office of the Roman Rite from early centuries included three canticles (usually referred to by their first words in Latin) from the Gospel of Luke as integral parts of the liturgy. The Canticle of Mary, known as *Magnificat* (Luke [Lk] 1.46-55), is sung by the Virgin Mary when she is greeted by her cousin Elizabeth. This song forms an integral and climactic moment as part of Vespers every evening.

> 'And Mary said: "My soul doth magnify the Lord. And my spirit hath rejoiced in God my Saviour.
>
> Because he hath regarded the humility of his handmaid; for behold from henceforth all generations shall call me blessed. Because he that is mighty hath done great things for me, And holy is his name.
>
> And his mercy is from generations unto generations, to them that fear him. He hath shewed might in his arm: he hath scattered the proud in the conceit of their hearts. He hath put down the mighty from their seat, and hath exalted the humble; He hath filled the hungry with good things; and the rich he hath sent empty away. He hath received Israel his servant, being mindful of his mercy: As he spoke to our fathers, to Abraham and to his seed forever."'[12]

The song of Thanksgiving (Lk 1.68-79), uttered by Zechariah at the birth of his son John the Baptist, known as the *Benedictus*, is full of gratitude and hope for the fulfilment of

---

10 See Bougerol, 'Bonaventure as Exegete', pp. 175–79; Christopher Cullen, *Bonaventure* (Oxford: Oxford University Press, 2006), pp. 113–17.

11 This insight about Bonaventure was first voiced by the fifteenth century Parisian master Jean Gerson. See Marianne Schlosser, 'Bonaventure: Life and Works', in *A Companion to Bonaventure*, pp. 7–59 (p. 57).

12 Lk 1:46-55. The translation known as the Douay-Rheims Version of the Bible, first published in 1582 (New Testament) and 1609 (Old Testament) is quoted here and in the next two canticles, as it is a literal translation of the Latin Vulgate Bible used by Bonaventure. *The Holy Bible, Translated from the Latin Vulgate* (New York: P. J. Kenedy & Sons, 1914).

Messianic promise, and the child who is to be the forerunner of the Messiah. It is sung as part of the early morning hour of Lauds, and like the *Magnificat* is accompanied by appropriate seasonal and festal antiphons.

> "Blessed be the Lord God of Israel; because he hath visited and wrought the redemption of his people: And hath raised up an horn of salvation to us, in the house of David his servant: As he spoke by the mouths of his holy prophets, Who are from the beginning: Salvation from our enemies, and from the hand of all that hate us: To perform mercy to our fathers, and to remember his holy testament, The oath which he swore to Abraham our father, that he would grant to us, That being delivered from the hand of our enemies, we may serve him without fear, In holiness and justice before him, all our days. And thou, child, shalt be called the prophet of the Highest: for thou shalt go before the Lord to prepare his ways: To give knowledge of salvation to his people, unto the remission of their sins: Through the bowels of the mercy of our God, In which the Orient from on high hath visited us: To enlighten them that sit in darkness, and in the shadow of death: to direct our feet into the way of peace."[13]

Finally, the *Nunc Dimittis*, sung by Simeon (Lk 2.29-32) upon his encounter with the infant Jesus at his presentation in the Temple, is sung every night at Compline, the final liturgical service of the day.

> "Now thou dost dismiss thy servant, O Lord, according to thy word in peace: Because my eyes have seen thy salvation which thou hast prepared before the face of all peoples: A light to the revelation of the Gentiles, and the glory of thy people Israel."[14]

The placement of these three canticles in the liturgy of the Church was seen as having profound significance by Bonaventure, as is evidenced by the following statement in his Lukan commentary:

> And because this canticle [*Nunc Dimittis*] contains in itself the fullness of the praise of Christ, and the consolation of a dying old man, it is, therefore, sung in the evening at Compline. Wherefore, these three canticles of Mary, Zechariah and Simeon are ordered so that one begins where the other leaves off: the first at Vespers, the second in the morning, and third in the evening. Also it is signified in this that every station in life must praise God for the incarnation: virgins, married people, and widows; those in contemplative life, prelates, those in active life; lay and clerics and religious, who must be consecrated to God.[15]

Let us now turn more closely to what Bonaventure has to say about each canticle and about what the episodes surrounding them can reveal about the nature of revelation. It is also important to include the *Ave Maria*, which, although not liturgical, was becoming, in Bonaventure's time, a cornerstone of private devotion. Bonaventure draws his sources primarily from Jerome (in particular, for his references to Hebrew words); from Ambrose and Bede (especially for their comments in the *Glossa Ordinaria*);

---

13   Lk 1.68-79 (Douay-Rheims Version).
14   Lk 2.29-32 (Douay-Rheims Version).
15   Bonaventure, *Commentary on the Gospel of Luke*, p. 193.

and from the Marian sermons of Bernard of Clairvaux. As in all his works, however, Bonaventure takes things selectively from his predecessors, creatively fashioning his thoughts with his own voice and style in fidelity to received tradition.

The *Ave Maria*, or the Angelic Salutation, as drawn from Lk 1.28 and Lk 1.42, was becoming an important private prayer in his day, and was developing into the practice of the Rosary.

> Hail Mary, full of grace,
>
> The Lord is with thee!
>
> Blessed art thou among women,
>
> And blessed is the fruit of thy womb, Jesus.[16]

Bonaventure's discussion of these verses gives him the opportunity to portray the Virgin Mary, at the moment of the Annunciation and thus Incarnation, as the fulfilment of all great Old Testament women, with explicit mention of Esther, Jael, Abigail, Ruth and Judith.[17] Focusing on the Incarnation as fundamentally a realization of promise, Bonaventure provides a lens through which to read the story of all Old Testament women as major players in salvation history, in the promise, its fulfilment, and now redemption itself.

This continues with his treatment of the *Magnificat*. This song is the climax of Vespers and, on Saturday evening, the beginning of the liturgical celebration of the resurrection. In discussing the *Magnificat*, Bonaventure makes clear that it is related to various Old Testament canticles, including the Song of Hannah (1 Sam 2.1-10), which it intentionally echoes: 'Her canticle shows that the fulfilment of all promised blessings has come about, and therefore brings about the fulfilment of all praise and canticles and even of the scriptures.'[18] Unlike many modern biblical scholars, Bonaventure does not make the leap to say that Luke has essentially put these words in the mouth of Mary in order to make the theological point. Rather, he believes the Virgin, inspired by the Holy Spirit, is quite capable of echoing the songs and plaintive aspirations of her Hebrew mothers on her own. Bonaventure asserts that the *Magnificat* bridges the gap to the New Testament, as these previous promises are now fulfilled.

A similar significance is given to the *Benedictus*, the song of Zechariah. This is placed by the Church in the morning service of Lauds to signify, as its final lines make clear, the dawn on the day of resurrection. The only response, Bonaventure asserts, should be praise and thanksgiving. For him, this canticle is all about divine Mercy, which is at the heart of the Infancy Narratives. In this canticle, he asserts that three important facets of divine Mercy are established: the mystery of the Incarnation; the

---

16   The now familiar final sentence of this prayer, 'Holy Mary, Mother of God, pray for us sinners, now and at the hour of our death', did not become common or universal until the sixteenth century.
17   Bonaventure, *Commentary on the Gospel of Luke*, pp. 63–66.
18   Bonaventure, *Commentary on the Gospel of Luke*, p. 102.

price of redemption; the triumph of the resurrection. 'In these', he states, 'is the remedy of our salvation'.[19] The song of Zechariah, moreover, speaks of the beginning of our reparation, giving knowledge of salvation, and of the promise to enlighten those who live in darkness. This, he says, is a perfect expression of the theme of Consolation for Israel and ultimately for everyone.

The culmination of the Infancy Narratives for Bonaventure is the Presentation of Christ in the Temple, an episode where both Christ and his Mother, through his presentation and her ritual purification, submit themselves to the law. This, he asserts, is a profound act of humility, for such purification is needed, in fact, by neither of them. The infant Christ is presented to the elderly Simeon who, embodying Old Testament wisdom, is enabled to experience the promised, but long-awaited Consolation of Israel. His ecstatic song is prayed every night by the Church at Compline, which Bonaventure feels is appropriate as it encapsulates the whole gospel story and its central theological meaning:

> Thus in this canticle Christ is praised as peace, salvation, light and glory. He is peace, because he is the mediator. He is salvation, because he is the redeemer. He is light, because he is the teacher. He is glory, because he is the rewarder. And in these four consist the perfect commendation and magnification of Christ, indeed the most brief capsulation of the entire evangelical story: incarnation in peace; preaching in light; redemption in salvation; resurrection in glory.[20]

For Bonaventure, Simeon can only be explained in light of Old Testament scriptures because he is the antitype of the 'just' man, responding for all the just who had come before him. Simeon, then, is himself a figure of scriptural fulfilment, traversing the trestle between the Old and New. Indeed, Bonaventure tells us how the Holy Spirit continued to speak to Simeon through the scripture, making more annunciations — especially on the theme of looking for the Consolation of Israel: 'Thus the Holy Spirit in a most powerful way said to him what is read in Habakkuk 2.3: *"if he tarries a little, look for him, for he will surely come and will not delay"*'.[21] Bonaventure argues that the Spirit was present with Simeon through grace and love — characteristics of the New dispensation — and thus the full meaning of this Lukan text can be best understood by quotations from the New Testament, such as Romans 5.5: *"and hope does not disappoint us, because God's love has been poured into our hearts through the Holy Spirit which has been given to us."* This interweaving of Old and New Testament passages illuminates the actions of Simeon. Simeon also received, in response to his long years of prayer, a special response of Revelation from the Holy Spirit. As Bonaventure says:

> Finally, Simeon was told by the Spirit of truth, and prompted to comprehension infused with Joy, that he himself would meet the Lord with the suddenness promised in Malachi 3.1: *Behold I send my angel and he shall prepare the way before my face. And presently the Lord,*

---

19 *Ibid.*, p. 119.
20 *Ibid.*, p. 193.
21 *Ibid.*, p. 187.

whom you seek, and the angel of the testament, whom you desire, shall come to his temple. Behold he is coming, proclaims the Lord of hosts.[22]

The use of Malachi by Bonaventure is not incidental or arbitrary, as it was also the Old Testament reading (Malachi 3.1-4) for Mass for the Feast of the Purification of the Blessed Virgin Mary. Thus, Bonaventure links his own interpretation of the method of the Spirit's inspiration of Simeon to the ancient typological teaching of the Church. Indeed, he seems to be giving future preachers (and artists) the exegetical tools to explain the liturgical mystery in light of the proper readings for the feast.

As Wisdom literature leads Simeon to the brink of encounter with the Lord, so the language of the Song of Songs is used to describe the moment when prophecy, wisdom, and justice through grace bring Simeon to union with Christ. Simeon, Bonaventure explains, 'exposes himself completely to Christ'. Thus, Simeon fulfils what Song of Songs 8.6 says about having a seal on his heart and also his arm. Bonaventure goes beyond the text to exclaim how Christ is to be comprehended and held with both arms, congruous with the verse Song of Songs 3.4 about not letting go. This demonstrates how, like Simeon, the Christian must serve God with both hands and all of his or her strength, to spiritually work and battle like in Nehemiah 4.17.

Bonaventure then turns to another key figure in this episode, the prophetess and aged widow, Anna. Here, there is even more theological richness to be found in the canticle of Simeon. Bonaventure explains why Anna is a suitable witness to these great events, but, initially, he makes an important digression to assert that witnesses were needed from every stage of life and both genders, as Christ was coming to restore *everything* and *everyone*:

> After the testimony of an old man there now follows the testimony from a woman. For it is fitting that there be testimony to the advent of Christ from every sort of person, so that those who do not believe the Gospel might be without excuse. Whence there was angelic and human testimony to Christ, and also of the simple and of the perfect of both sexes to show that both sexes looked for redemption just as both had fallen. Therefore to show that there was no crack in the firm foundation of the testimony, there was sevenfold testimony to the birth of Christ.[23]

Bonaventure then sets forth the sevenfold testimony: 1) heavenly testimony from the star (Mt 2.2); 2) a source above heaven, the angels (Lk 2.13); 3) a source from under heaven, simple men like the shepherds (Lk 2.20); 4) wise men like the Magi (Mt 2.1); 5) elderly men, like Simeon (Lk 2.27); 6) elderly women like Anna; 7) infants who gave their lives (citing the 28 December Holy Innocents oration from the liturgy; and Mt 2.16; also Ps 8.3): 'And every nature, every sex, every age produced testimony to the

---

22 *Ibid.*, p. 188.
23 *Ibid.*, p. 199. Here one is reminded of canon 130 of the *Catechism of the Catholic Church*: 'Typology indicates the dynamic movement toward the fulfilment of the divine plan when God "will be everything to everyone"'.

birth of Christ, because he had to restore all things.'[24] Bonaventure sums this point up dramatically by citing Lk 19.40 about how all things, even the stones and material world, will cry out in response to God's appearance among us, even if some keep silent. As Simeon is the antitype or fulfilment of all the just men of the Old Testament, so Mary and the Prophetess Anna could be seen as functioning in the same way for all of the Old Testament women, whether in their prophecies, laments, songs of praise, or periods of thoughtful silence.

3. Art, Liturgy and the Typological Imagination

The centrality of typology to patristic and medieval exegesis of scripture manifested itself in an incredible variety of artistic expression of all kinds, such as statues, stained glass, painting, manuscript illumination, poetry, musical composition and performance, and preaching. Many examples could be adduced to demonstrate the interplay of typological exegesis and the arts within a liturgical and performative context. The well-known eleventh-century Bernward Doors of Hildesheim Cathedral are a fitting illustration. These immense bronze doors depict, on the one side, scenes from the book of Genesis; paralleled on the other are episodes from the life of Christ, which the scenes from Genesis are meant to prefigure. This extraordinary masterpiece of Ottonian art reflects a long trajectory of artistic portrayals of typology and, in the medieval period, it was used in tandem with preaching and liturgical celebrations.[25] Cathedrals such as Chartres and Canterbury contained series of stained glass depictions of Old and New Testament typological parallels, often meant to accompany and articulate the meaning of a parable such as the Good Samaritan.[26] The reciprocity and interplay between artists, exegetes and liturgists in these particular contexts inspired ongoing creativity throughout the medieval period. As William Flynn has shown, evidence suggests that in the eleventh-century monasteries and cathedrals, the makers and composers of liturgical music and texts were marked by 'a reflection and meditation upon memorized scripture provided by the liturgy itself, and deepened by the study of commentary […] [their] training — poetic, musical, liturgical and exegetical — fed into the study of scripture and these seemingly diverse activities were often experienced as a unified pedagogy that had its origin and culmination in the liturgy'.[27]

Thus, typology has long provided rich artistic opportunities for the juxtaposition of Old and New Testament texts in dialogue with one another. Furthermore, these heartfelt and ecstatic utterances, themselves in response to divine messengers or

---

24 Bonaventure, *Commentary on the Gospel of Luke*, p. 200.
25 For an excellent description and analysis, see Aloys Butzkamm, *Ein Tor zum Paradies. Kunst und Theologie auf der Bronzetür des Hildesheimer Doms* (Paderborn: Bonifatius, 2004).
26 See e.g. Christopher G. Hughes, 'Art and Exegesis', in *A Companion to Medieval Art*, ed. by Conrad Rudolph (Oxford: Blackwell, 2006), pp. 173–92.
27 William T. Flynn, *Medieval Music as Medieval Exegesis* (London: The Scarecrow Press, 1999), p. xix.

divine inspiration, are moments of great dramatic potential. They are intimate, conversational, but also glorious and awe-filled. And what makes them even more so is that the audience understands that these powerful New Testament moments of divine annunciation and human response are anchored and prefigured deeply in the salvation history of the people of Israel. Pope Paul VI, quoting the second century theologian Irenaeus, expressed this tradition about the *Magnificat*:

> It is in Mary's canticle that there was heard once more the rejoicing of Abraham who foresaw the Messiah (cf. Jn. 8:56) and there rang out in prophetic anticipation the voice of the Church: 'In her exultation Mary prophetically declared in the name of the Church: "My soul proclaims the glory of the Lord…"'. And in fact Mary's hymn has spread far and wide and has become the prayer of the whole Church in all ages.[28]

Thus in this most mysterious way, the Gospel canticles in the liturgy are simultaneously moments of apprehension transformed into relief, promise and fulfillment, always looking toward the future in hope for an eternity of joy. This patristic and medieval tradition of typology can challenge and inspire contemporary artists to perceive in the scriptural narratives manifold openings for creative parallels, juxtapositions, and meaningful, multi-layered connections. A reappraisal of the reciprocal enrichment of theologians and artists in past expressions of the typological imagination may lead, in turn, to a re-invigoration of contemporary Christian art.

---

28 Pope Paul VI, 'Apostolic Exhortation of His Holiness Paul VI: *Marialis Cultus*' (Vatican.va, 1974), para. 18, http://w2.vatican.va/content/paul-vi/en/apost_exhortations/documents/hf_p-vi_exh_19740202_marialis-cultus.html.

6. Composing for a Non-Professional Chapel Choir: Challenges and Opportunities

Tom Wilkinson

Writing sacred music for a non-professional chapel choir presents the composer with many challenges. One important theme of this discussion is that, in the most successful choral writing, challenges are treated as opportunities. Clichéd though it may appear, I hope to demonstrate that it is true. The most common circumstance is that the solution to a technical problem will present an opportunity for a mode of expression that would not otherwise have occurred. The first half of the chapter explores this principle, initially with reference to Benjamin Britten's 'Rejoice in the Lamb'. The majority of the musical examples, however, are taken from the CD, *Annunciations: Sacred Choral Music for the 21st Century*, and include several ingenious passages by the six TheoArtistry composers. The second half of the chapter focuses on harmony in some detail, citing James MacMillan's '*Ave Maria*'. Arguably, the challenges and opportunities afforded by harmony are especially significant for composers today.

While I take a broadly analytical approach, it will become evident that my perspective is that of a performer; specifically, that of a choral conductor with several years' experience of observing singers' responses to a wide range of sacred music. A discussion of what constitutes 'difficulty' from the performer's perspective leads to a breaking-down of this concept into two distinct parameters: practical difficulty and intelligibility of expression. A given passage of music might be practically challenging in some way, while its expressive purpose — emphatic textual declamation, say — might be obvious. In my experience, choral singers will readily engage with moderate technical challenges, provided that they can discern an underlying expressive purpose in the music. Such formulation comes close to being paradigmatic of a rewarding rehearsal process. Nonetheless, composers should not be afraid to produce music that is easy to learn: such repertoire is invaluable, not least because a choir's morale and confidence can be uplifted by the experience of rapidly learning and performing a new piece.

On the theme of expression, my experience is that singers admire pieces for what I would term 'expressive coherence': the ability to communicate emotive purpose. Britten's 'A Hymn to the Virgin' has enduring popularity with singers due to the unique sense of prayerful intensity it creates. This property of the work might alternatively be described as its 'expressive essence'.[1] Indeed, several terms and phrases in common musical parlance today seem related to this concept, such as 'sound-world' and 'the core of the piece'. From this perspective, today's composers are in a difficult position: the rich inheritance of sacred music is bound to seem intimidating. Moreover, the climate of purported artistic freedom is as much a curse as a blessing: with no universally accepted norms of musical language either to adopt or from which to deviate, achieving expressive coherence is a significant compositional challenge. One underlying theme of this chapter is the various possible responses to this problem.

It is useful to approach this theme systematically, by identifying some key parameters of choral music:

- voice-leading (the 'horizontal' aspect of music);
- harmony (for the purposes of this chapter, I take this to mean the 'vertical' aspect of music);
- individual rhythm;
- ensemble rhythm;
- metre;
- texture;
- text.

From a choral singer's perspective, rewarding pieces are often characterized by varied levels of difficulty across the parameters listed above. In other words, singers enjoy a challenge, but find it difficult to cope with being challenged from many angles simultaneously. Given the importance that Britten attached to writing music for amateurs, it is perhaps unsurprising that his music provides such an apposite starting-point from this perspective. His 'Rejoice in the Lamb' begins ominously, with a single held organ note (middle C); the choir subsequently enters on that same note

---

1   The notion that a musical work has a unique 'expressive essence' is, arguably, part and parcel of the modern 'work' concept, by which a piece of music is conceived essentially as a work of art. Lydia Goehr has argued — controversially — that this concept came of age c. 1800; it is worth remembering that much of the corpus of Western sacred music originated prior to this, thus providing a window onto earlier implied musical ideologies. See Lydia Goehr, *The Imaginary Museum of Musical Works* (Oxford: Oxford University Press, 1994).

(Fig. 6.1). The resultant lack of harmony (there is only one note) is rather unsettling for the listener, since it gives no clue as to the sound-world that might develop. From a practical perspective, though, one could hardly imagine a more approachable opening. In terms of the parameters listed above, there is nothing challenging.

Probably, the ever-practical Britten aims to give the choir a gentle start to a relatively long and challenging piece. The simplicity of the material leaves the singers free to focus on rewarding aspects of choral performance such as ensemble (i.e. 'togetherness'), vocal production, and blend. Britten's genius is to provide music that is intrinsically mysterious — as a result of the lack of harmony — and that enables the performers to enhance this property, by imbuing its delivery with expressive intensity.

Fig. 6.1 Benjamin Britten, 'Rejoice in the Lamb' (1943), bars 1–3. © Boosey & Hawkes.

In the second section, 'Let Nimrod, the mighty hunter', the vocal parts are characterized by metrical irregularity and fast-moving text (Fig. 6.2), making the music more challenging for the singers. Probably in recognition of this, Britten ensures that the music is straightforward in other ways: the 'horizontal' motion is diatonic and largely step-wise, and there is a unison texture. Thus, the singers' mental energies can be focused on the rhythmical and textual complexities.

Fig. 6.2 Benjamin Britten, 'Rejoice in the Lamb' (1943), bars 19–25. © Boosey & Hawkes.

The tables turn for the third section, 'Hallelujah from the heart of God' (Fig. 6.3). Here, the relatively complex four-part texture is enabled, as it were, by the motivic economy: each voice-part sings music based on a simple scalic/triadic figure, creating an imitative effect. The simple diatonic chords heard in the right hand of the organ part provide a stable backdrop for the singers.

Fig. 6.3 Benjamin Britten, 'Rejoice in the Lamb' (1943), bars 60–63. © Boosey & Hawkes.

Britten's practical approach is also evident in the more challenging sections of the work ('For I am in twelve Hardships' and 'For the Shawm rhimes are lawn fawn and the like'), which are underpinned by pedal points (bass drones) on the organ, providing harmonic stability. In sum, from a singer's perspective, 'Rejoice in the Lamb' is characterized by achievable challenges.

While the human voice is a remarkably flexible instrument, there is certainly such a thing as idiomatic vocal writing; Figures 6.2 and 6.3 contain useful examples. The voice likes to move in small intervals; usually within an octave, and with a predominance of seconds and thirds. Passages containing successive leaps of more than an octave, or indeed remaining on the same pitch for an extended period, are physically challenging (and the former is also mentally challenging). This is not to say that such writing must be avoided at all costs, but rather that it should be treated with caution. The composer of vocal music has one significant advantage over the composer of instrumental music: they can easily test what they have written by singing it themselves. Of course,

74 *Annunciations*

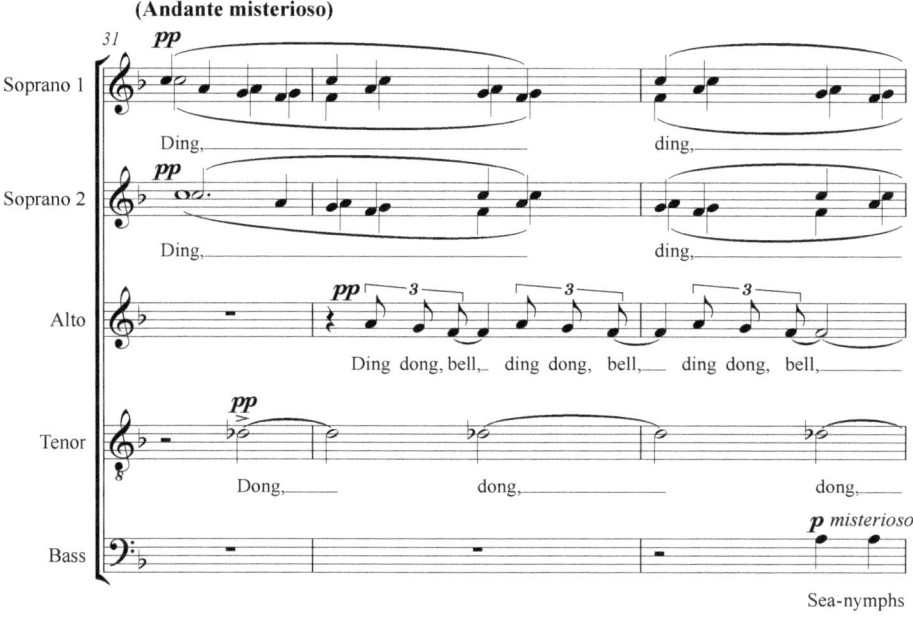

Fig. 6.4 Ralph Vaughan Williams, 'Three Shakespeare Songs', I. 'Full fathom five' (1951), bars 31–35.
© Oxford University Press.

a trained singer will have greater technical ability than a non-singer; nevertheless, self-testing is a broadly reliable route to idiomatic writing.

Another important consideration for the composer of vocal and choral music is pitching. While many instrumentalists locate pitches mechanically — by pressing the appropriate key on the piano, for example — the singer must always conceive the correct note mentally, in relation to what has gone before. (This does not apply to the tiny percentage of singers who possess 'perfect pitch'; these fortunate people can find any note 'out of thin air'). Therefore, the composer must consider harmonic context. Naturally, the more complex or dissonant the harmony, the greater the challenge that pitching presents. Britten seems to avoid anything more than mild dissonance in the choral writing of 'Rejoice in the Lamb'. Therefore, in order to consider how more pronounced dissonance might be approached accessibly, I shall turn to an example by Ralph Vaughan Williams': 'Full fathom five', from 'Three Shakespeare Songs'. The passage in Figure 6.4 begins on a unison C, in the soprano parts; the dissonance then increases steadily, achieving a particularly beautiful cluster chord on the third beat of bar 33. Had the composer begun the section with this chord, even professional singers would find the necessary pitching to be extremely challenging, or impossible. Aware of this issue, Vaughan Williams provides each voice-part with a clear reference-point: the tenors can pitch their D-flat from the sopranos' C, while the altos and basses can take their entry note directly from the soprano parts. Crucially, the melodic (i.e. 'horizontal') intervals within any given part are generally diatonic and straightforward. The soprano and alto parts are constructed as repeating units of four and three notes respectively; these simple cells are layered (i.e. presented out-of-phase with each other), thereby creating a complex texture. As a result, while the pitching required to sing any one vocal line is relatively simple, the resultant harmonies are complex. Vaughan Williams thus makes an artistic virtue out of a practical necessity: the shimmering, oscillating effect evokes the mystical eeriness of Ariel's song as experienced by Ferdinand (*The Tempest*, I, ii).

Adopting the same compositional principle as Vaughan Williams, TheoArtistry composer Anselm McDonnell achieves a quite different effect in his commissioned work, 'Hinneni' (Fig. 6.5). Bars 22–27 present God's question to Adam 'Have you eaten from the tree, of knowledge, of good and evil?' The anchor note E in the bass-line has both a practical and an expressive function: it provides a stable reference point for the other singers, while its immovability seems to communicate God's authority. The repeated motif heard initially in the first tenor part at bar 22 is layered, creating dissonance — and, as a result, tension — perhaps reflecting man's anticipation of God's impending judgement. Bars 28–29 employ the principle of conjunct melodic intervals: though each voice-part is straightforward to sing, the resultant harmony is very discordant. The climactic dissonant chord in bar 30 communicates God's anger with startling immediacy.

Listen to Anselm McDonnell, 'Hinneni', bars 22-30, in *Annunciations: Sacred Music for the 21st Century*, St Salvator's Chapel Choir and Sean Heath, cond. by Tom Wilkinson (Sanctiandree, SAND0006, 2018), © 2017 University of St Andrews. Track 07. Duration: 3.37 (1.10-1.35).

https://hdl.handle.net/20.500.12434/dd5c37bc

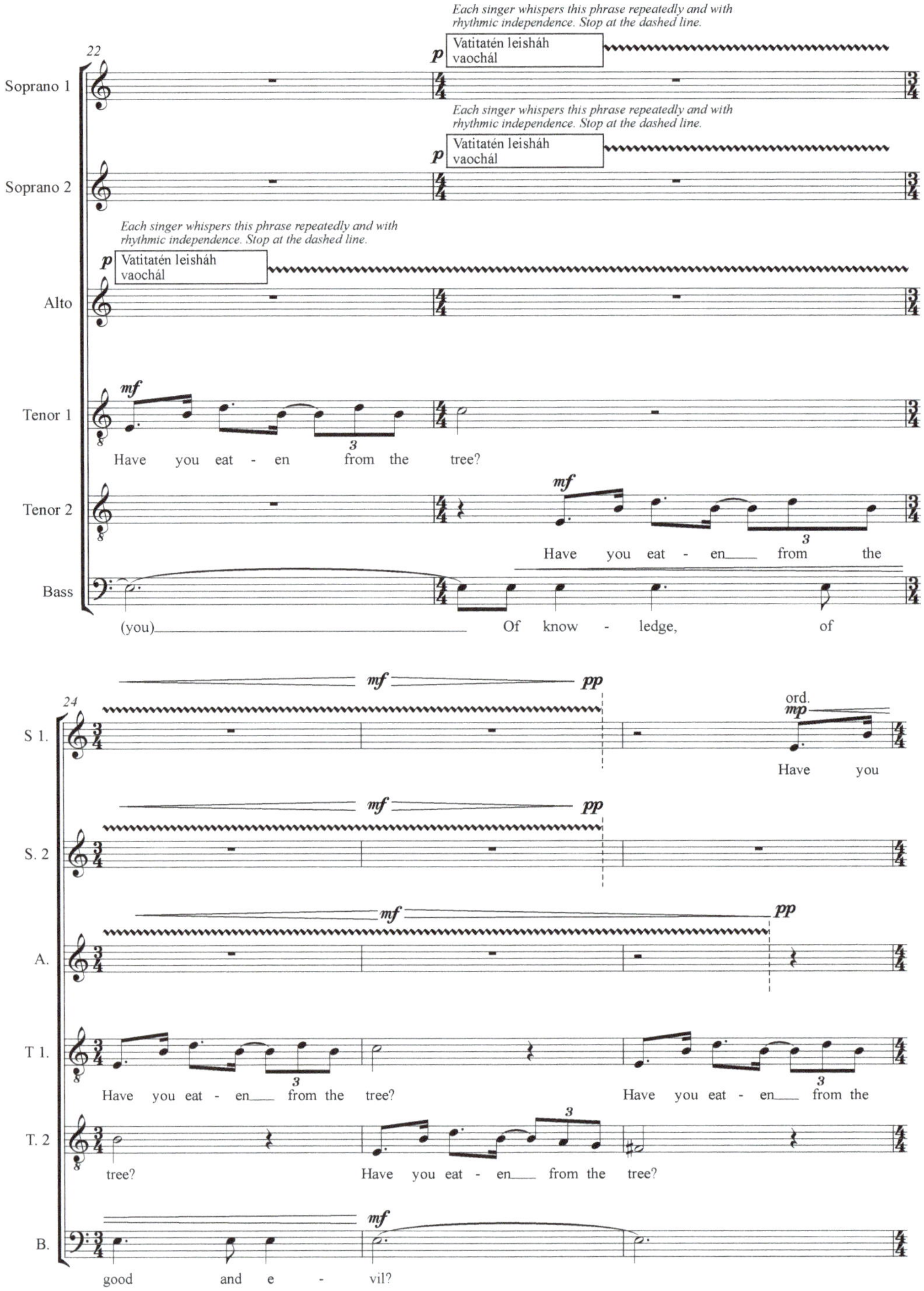

Fig. 6.5 Anselm McDonnell, 'Hinneni' (2016), bars 22–30.

Having begun by addressing the relative difficulties of the different parameters of choral music — in terms of practicality of performance — the discussion has broadened to include aspects of expressivity. That this has proved unavoidable is surely symptomatic of the sophistication of the music being analysed: the examples by Vaughan Williams and McDonnell present a synthesis of practicality and expressivity. I shall continue to discuss the manipulation of musical parameters in terms of expression as well as practicality. Contrast and juxtaposition are seen to be effective devices, especially concerning dramatic textual communication.

Lisa Robertson's 'The Silent Word Sounds' provides a striking example of dramatic textural contrast (Fig. 6.6). Its opening two bars depict God calling to Eliyahu (Elijah). The texture is complex: though essentially in only two parts, both of these are subjected to heterophony (the simultaneous variation of a single melodic line).[2] The following passage — God's command — is presented in emphatic unison. This is an effective use of a classic compositional technique: textural complexity abruptly gives way to textural simplicity, thus drawing the listener's attention to an especially significant line of text.

---

2 In a TheoArtistry composers' workshop, Sir James MacMillan remarked that the effect reminds him of Gaelic psalm singing (a tradition to which he himself alludes in, for example, 'A New Song'). MacMillan describes this tradition thus: 'a precentor leads the singing and the voices follow in an almost canonic fashion heterophonically masking and ghosting the line'. See Shirley Ratcliffe, 'MacMillan', *Choir and Organ*, 8 (1999), 39–42 (p. 40). Quoted in Stephen A. Kingsbury, 'The Influence of Scottish Nationalism on James MacMillan's "A New Song"', *The Choral Journal*, 47 (August 2006), 30–37 (p. 36).

Lisa Robertson, 'The Silent Word Sounds', bars 1-5, in *Annunciations: Sacred Music for the 21st Century*, St Salvator's Chapel Choir and Sean Heath, cond. by Tom Wilkinson (Sanctiandree, SAND0006, 2018), © 2017 University of St Andrews. Track 11. Duration: 3.41 (0-0.20).

https://hdl.handle.net/20.500.12434/c771e04a

Fig. 6.6 Lisa Robertson, 'The Silent Word Sounds '(2016), bars 1–5.

MacMillan's Christmas motet, 'And lo, the Angel of the Lord Came upon Them', which depicts the angels' annunciation to the shepherds, employs this technique in an even more rhetorical fashion. At the point of annunciation, the narrative voice switches from polyphony to quasi-unison (Fig. 6.7). This vivid portrayal seems to emphasize that the angels' entrance was entirely unexpected. However, the use of this technique is not limited to such overt gestures. In the meditative Advent motet, 'A New Song', it helps to articulate a cyclical structure (ABABA), in a rather understated manner.

James MacMillan, 'And lo, the angel of the Lord came upon them', bars 26-31, in *Annunciations: Sacred Music for the 21st Century*, St Salvator's Chapel Choir and Sean Heath, cond. by Tom Wilkinson (Sanctiandree, SAND0006, 2018), © 2017 University of St Andrews. Track 13. Duration: 4.42 (2.00-2.24).

https://hdl.handle.net/20.500.12434/94a29191

Fig. 6.7 James MacMillan, 'And lo, the Angel of the Lord Came upon Them' (2009), bars 26–31. Choir 3 parts are omitted. © Boosey & Hawkes.

This technique is also a key feature of Kenneth Leighton's 'Second Service' ('*Magnificat*' and '*Nunc dimittis*'), which tends to contrast passages of rhythmic (and often melodic) unison with imitative writing (Fig. 6.8). Furthermore, textures are not only alternated, but also super-imposed: in Figure 6.8, the *staccato*, dissonant, rhythmically unpredictable organ writing contrasts sharply with the longer, *legato* choral phrases. This creates a complex, yet intelligible, texture.

Other examples include passages from 'A Hymn to the Virgin' (Britten) (Fig. 6.9) and, again, MacMillan's 'And lo, the Angel of the Lord Came upon Them' (Fig. 6.10). In both cases, the syllabic writing serves to bring the text into sharp focus against a more expressive, melismatic, backdrop. The joyful text of the MacMillan — 'Glory to God in the highest, and on earth peace, goodwill towards all men' — is dazzlingly portrayed by this juxtaposition of decorative polyphony and emphatic homophony, in a passage equally thrilling for performer and listener.

 Kenneth Leighton, 'Magnificat' from 'The Second Service', bars 20-32, in *Annunciations: Sacred Music for the 21st Century*, St Salvator's Chapel Choir and Sean Heath, cond. by Tom Wilkinson (Sanctiandree, SAND0006, 2018), © 2017 University of St Andrews. Track 04. Duration: 7.12 (1.31-1.51).
https://hdl.handle.net/20.500.12434/0f9f5f56

Fig. 6.8 Kenneth Leighton, 'The Second Service' (1972), 'Magnificat', bars 20–32. © Oxford University Press.

Benjamin Britten, 'Hymn to the Virgin', verse 3, in *Annunciations: Sacred Music for the 21st Century*, St Salvator's Chapel Choir and Sean Heath, cond. by Tom Wilkinson (Sanctiandree, SAND0006, 2018), © 2017 University of St Andrews. Track 14. Duration: 3.27 (2.12-2.33).
https://hdl.handle.net/20.500.12434/230df508

Fig. 6.9 Benjamin Britten, 'A Hymn to the Virgin' (1930, rev. 1934), verse 3. © Boosey & Hawkes.

James MacMillan, 'And lo, the angel of the Lord came upon them', bars 43-44, in *Annunciations: Sacred Music for the 21st Century*, St Salvator's Chapel Choir and Sean Heath, cond. by Tom Wilkinson (Sanctiandree, SAND0006, 2018), © 2017 University of St Andrews. Track 13. Duration: 4.42 (3.17-3.30).
https://hdl.handle.net/20.500.12434/efa6e2a0

Fig. 6.10 James MacMillan, 'And lo, the Angel of the Lord Came upon Them' (2009), bars 43–44. © Boosey & Hawkes.

A fundamentally different approach to creating textural complexity is explored by Seán Doherty in 'God calls Samuel'. The effect of complex imitation is achieved by syllabic repetition *within* individual voice parts (Fig. 6.11). This technique has to be used with care: the risk is that the vocal lines lose their individual integrity, and consequently become counter-intuitive for the singers. Doherty successfully avoids this danger through the use of static harmony and pitch. This is a clear example of complexity in one musical parameter being compensated by simplicity in another.

 Seán Doherty, 'God Calls Samuel', bars 22-24, , in *Annunciations: Sacred Music for the 21st Century*, St Salvator's Chapel Choir and Sean Heath, cond. by Tom Wilkinson (Sanctiandree, SAND0006, 2018), © 2017 University of St Andrews. Track 10. Duration: 4.11 (1.30-1.43).
https://hdl.handle.net/20.500.12434/8c6be779

Fig. 6.11 Seán Doherty, 'God Calls Samuel' (2016), bars 22–24.

In 'God calls Samuel', then, Doherty's writing is technically challenging yet 'intelligible' for the performers, since its expressive purpose is clear: the music communicates the power of God's voice as it echoes around the temple, and Samuel's intense fear in hearing it. As discussed in the introduction, choral singers tend to enjoy rehearsing and performing music in which they can discern a clear expressive purpose, whether this is overt and dramatic (as in 'God calls Samuel'), meditative (as in the music of John Tavener, for example), or otherwise.

Having discussed the interplay between various musical parameters in both practical and expressive terms, it is worth considering what is perhaps a more contentious issue: harmony. I have already cited harmonic language as one of the most important issues faced by composers today. Notwithstanding the alleged 'breakdown of tonality' of the early-twentieth century,[3] it could be argued that most listeners familiar with Western music still perceive common-practice tonality as their musical mother tongue. Since the mid-twentieth century, the normative status of atonality has, arguably, lessened. Assessing the state of choral music in the late-twentieth and early-twenty-first centuries, Nick Strimple writes the following:

> After the explosion of new ideas in the early decades of the twentieth century, and the resistance to them exemplified by traditionalists and later by minimalists, the last third of the century gradually relaxed into an era where virtually nothing new was brought to the compositional table. Rather, choral composers experimented with various combinations of twentieth-century devices, eventually abandoning atonality and dodecaphony in favor of an essentially — but not exclusively — diatonic language (often derived from folk music or chant) which could be manipulated to function in association with any known compositional technique. Arvo Pärt (b.1935), James MacMillan, Tan Dun, and a few others were able to turn this situation to their advantage and create choral works of genuine originality. Some, such as Morten Lauridsen, chose to ignore trends altogether and developed exceptionally distinctive and inviting styles.[4]

It is worth noting the distinction between tonality and what Strimple describes as 'an essentially — but not exclusively — diatonic language'. 'Tonality' implies a system of functional harmony that, fundamentally, is governed by the need for a dominant chord to resolve to a tonic chord. Strimple's phrase implies no such temporal energy: music can be diatonic without being tonally functional. However, for most amateur singers of classical music — in the UK, at least — diatonicism carries with it the baggage of tonality. Consequently, amateur singers respond positively to diatonic music that obeys the conventions of tonality to some extent. Certainly, my experience is that choirs enjoy getting to grips with a harmonic language that acknowledges dissonances as in need of resolution (however 'consonance' and 'dissonance' might be defined). This acknowledgement can even take the form of non-resolution. From this perspective, one challenge for the composer of choral music today is that of finding a

---

3   See Carl Dahlhaus '3.iv: Early 20th Century', in Richard Cohn, Brian Hyer, Carl Dahlhaus, Julian Anderson and Charles Wilson, 'Harmony', *New Grove Online*, http://doi.org/10.1093/gmo/9781561592630.article.50818. See also Christopher Butler, 'Innovation and the avant-garde, 1900–20', in *The Cambridge History of Twentieth-Century Music*, ed. by Nicholas Cook and Anthony Pople (Cambridge: Cambridge University Press, 2004), pp. 69–80 (esp. pp. 77–79); and Jim Samson, *Music in Transition: A Study of Tonal Expansion and Atonality, 1900–1920* (New York and Oxford: Oxford University Press, 1977).

4   Nick Strimple, 'Choral Music in the Twentieth and Early Twenty-first Centuries', in *The Cambridge Companion to Choral Music*, ed. by André de Quadros (Cambridge: Cambridge University Press, 2012), pp. 43–60 (p. 60).

consistent harmonic language. When achieved, it can make a powerful contribution to the aforementioned sense of 'expressive coherence'.

MacMillan's choral music is neither tonal nor exclusively diatonic: as Strimple recognizes, it is imbued with modality, betraying the influence of Celtic music and, arguably, Gregorian chant.[5] However, voice-leading patterns and harmonic progressions familiar from tonal music are employed frequently — sometimes at moments of structural demarcation — creating memorable effects. His '*Ave Maria*'

James MacMillan, 'Ave Maria', bars 51-58, in *Annunciations: Sacred Music for the 21st Century*, St Salvator's Chapel Choir and Sean Heath, cond. by Tom Wilkinson (Sanctiandree, SAND0006, 2018), © 2017 University of St Andrews. Track 1. Duration: 4.30 (1.48-2.15).
https://hdl.handle.net/20.500.12434/70c2774c

---

5   See, for example, Richard McGregor, '"A Metaphor for the Deeper Wintriness": Exploring James MacMillan's Musical Identity', *Tempo*, 65 (July 2011), 22–39.

Fig. 6.12 James MacMillan, 'Ave Maria' (2010), bars 51–58. © Boosey & Hawkes.

Bars 52–56 (Fig. 6.12) are, it seems to me, the core of the work: five bars of intimate yet emotionally-charged music, containing only one word, 'Jesus'. Bar 55 is something of a climax: canonic writing between soprano and tenor voices abruptly gives way to a unison rising sixth, which seems to embody a sense of longing. Modally, the passage could be considered as in E Dorian or E Aeolian (notwithstanding the 'tonal' raised leading note, D sharp, in bar 56). Listening to the work from beginning to end, one has the sense that everything is focused on this atmospheric passage. How is this effect achieved?

Examining the work as a whole, one discovers a three-part harmonic structure: G 'major' (beginning) — E 'minor' (bar 43) — G 'major' (bar 85). Listeners familiar with tonal music will discern the major/minor contrast between these sections. Tonally speaking, this structure is markedly traditional: E minor, as the 'relative minor' of G major, is the standard secondary key. Another tonal feature is the use of pedal points (bass drones), found primarily in the organ part: G (bars 1–6), B (bars 23–35), E (bars 43–48), and finally G again (bars 85–89 and 110–17). An obvious next step, analytically speaking, would be to consider the B pedal point as having a dominant role in the overall tonal scheme. On this view, its role would be to prepare for the section in E 'minor' beginning at bar 43. The listening experience, however, reveals that the B pedal point is heard as a tonic; moreover, the music has a modal flavour at this point, owing to the unconcealed non-functionality of the surrounding harmonies, and especially the non-sharpened leading notes.

However, the pedal point does move subsequently to an E, in bar 36, retrospectively hinting at a dominant role for the B. Richard McGregor discusses a similar case in MacMillan's percussion concerto, *Veni Veni Emmanuel*, in which a C# drone eventually becomes the fifth degree of an F# triad.[6] McGregor argues further that '[t]here are places in MacMillan's music where individual pitches assume a hierarchical importance, not simply in the sense of defining some tonality but expressing an aspect of a work's developing narrative'.[7] It seems that the note B falls into this category in '*Ave Maria*': in addition to its prominent role as a pedal point, a recurrent dotted motif — first heard in the alto line in bar 26 — emphasizes the note B in a more overt manner by 'circling around it' (Fig. 6.13). By the time that the E pedal point of bars 43–48 is reached, then, the note B has been imbued with an ambiguous significance.

 James MacMillan, 'Ave Maria', bars 25-28, in *Annunciations: Sacred Music for the 21st Century*, St Salvator's Chapel Choir and Sean Heath, cond. by Tom Wilkinson (Sanctiandree, SAND0006, 2018), © 2017 University of St Andrews. Track 1. Duration: 4.30 (0.50-0.59).

https://hdl.handle.net/20.500.12434/e639d3cd

Fig. 6.13 James MacMillan, '*Ave Maria*' (2010), bars 25–28. © Boosey and Hawkes.

Bars 51–52 present, for the first time, an unambiguous perfect cadence in the key of E minor (Fig. 6.12). The quiet dynamic belies the significance of this gesture from a tonal perspective: finally, the note B has been accorded a definitive role — that of the dominant of E. Since the listener has been primed to hear the note B as significant yet tonally undefined, this cadence draws the listener in by laying this indistinctness to rest. An additional possibility is that the listener experiences the cadence as a kind of

---

6   Richard McGregor, 'A Metaphor for the Deeper Wintriness', p. 30.
7   *Ibid.*

telescoped memory of the earlier B and E pedal points. The harmony of '*Ave Maria*' is largely non-functional: it is not driven by dominant/tonic polarity. Yet MacMillan is unafraid to employ the perfect cadence — an overtly tonal technique — in order to highlight a particularly significant moment of structural demarcation. This subliminally exploits the listener's memory, and familiarity with tonality, in order to create narrative cohesion. Overall, the work seems to embody principles of musical structure that are eloquently captured by Roger Scruton:

> We should see [musical form] not as the unfolding or 'composing-out' of some underlying 'deep structure', but in the way that we see the composition of a painting — as forms and figures in a unified surface, each answering to, completing, or complementing the others. The pleasure that we take in musical forms depends … upon their abstract quality — on their emancipation from the figurative aims which tie painting to the world of objects. Music shows us movement without the thing that moves; it can therefore present us with a reality that we know otherwise only through the workings of consciousness — movements outside physical space, which do not merely coincide but which coalesce as a unity. And these movements find in music a completion which ordinary consciousness denies.[8]

The compositional techniques found in '*Ave Maria*', discussed above, achieve the 'completion' and 'unity' which Scruton considers. The same could be said of Tavener's 'Annunciation', though the compositional means are quite different from MacMillan's. Characteristically, this work does not aggressively subvert the listener's experience of linear time, as can sometimes seem to be the case in the Minimalism of Terry Riley and Steve Reich. Rather, the music of the so-called 'Holy Minimalists' (Tavener, Arvo Pärt, etc.) seems to offer a space in which the listener is invited to meditate. This is achieved partly through repetition of a ritualistic kind. Whereas musical interrelation is exploited by MacMillan to create a sense of heightened focus in a specific passage, Tavener seems to invite the listener to move 'beyond' linear time altogether.

In markedly different ways, then, MacMillan and Tavener exploit music's capacity to evoke reflection on a verbal text, and on itself. The composers on the TheoArtistry scheme also exploit this potential. Stuart Beatch, for example, provides a reflective ending to his work 'The Annunciation of Solomon'. The text, 'Go forth, O ye daughters of Zion, and behold King Solomon in the day of the gladness of his heart', seemingly a forthright command, is presented simply in syllabic and homophonic music (Fig. 6.14). This provides effective contrast with the preceding impassioned music, and, more importantly, invites the listener to reflect on the musical work as a whole.

 Stuart Beatch, 'The Annunciation of Solomon', bars 57-59, in *Annunciations: Sacred Music for the 21st Century*, St Salvator's Chapel Choir and Sean Heath, cond. by Tom Wilkinson (Sanctiandree, SAND0006, 2018), © 2017 University of St Andrews. Track 12. Duration: 4.11 (3.25-4.06).
https://hdl.handle.net/20.500.12434/2f7de31a

---

8   Roger Scruton, *The Aesthetics of Music* (Oxford: Oxford University Press, 1997), pp. 340–41.

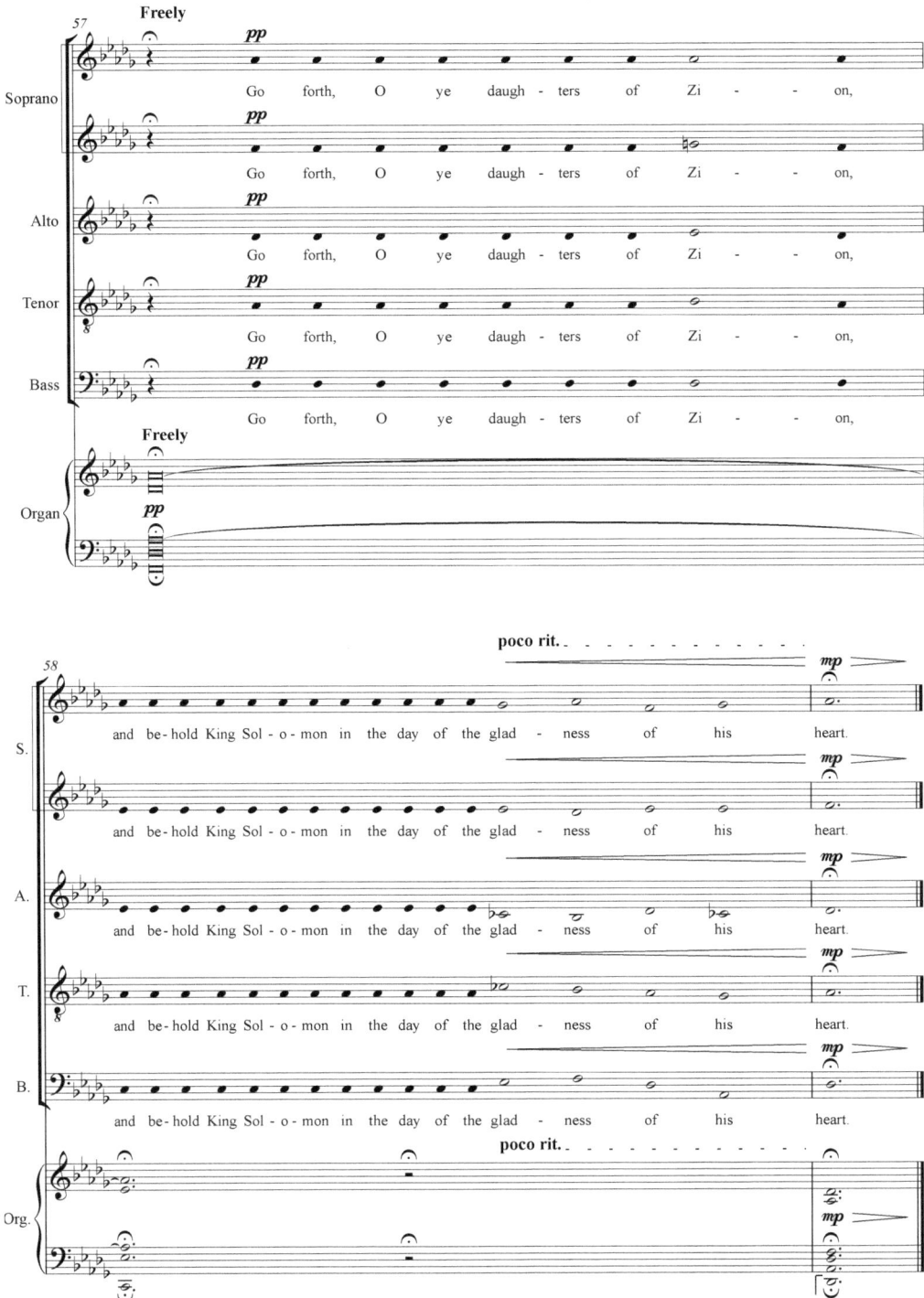

Fig. 6.14 Stuart Beatch, 'The Annunciation of Solomon' (2016), bars 57-end.

My primary purpose in exploring these aspects of sacred choral music has been to examine what makes a work rewarding to rehearse and perform. As many of the musical examples above demonstrate, rewarding music is often challenging in one area while being straightforward in others. Command of texture has emerged as a crucial aspect of the composer's art: it can shape the narrative of a work in myriad ways, the most apparent being its ability to draw the listener's attention to a significant passage of text. This technique is but one example of expressive intelligibility — a concept that has emerged as significant not only for listeners, but also for performers. With regard to harmony, composers of sacred choral music today operate in a post-tonal — and, arguably, post-atonal — world. MacMillan's *Ave Maria* has been analysed from this historically-defined perspective: tonal and non-tonal techniques coalesce in a unique sound-world, which reveals its secrets only gradually to performers and listeners. In particular, it exploits music's capacity for internal-reference, to great expressive effect.

Composers today possess a rich inheritance of sacred music. This chapter has explored ways in which this legacy is materially-reflected in twentieth- and twenty-first-century sacred choral music, including in the six TheoArtistry commissions. The discussion has edged towards a conception of the contemporary composer's situation as, potentially, postmodern. The techniques and conventions developed over centuries continue to be adopted and adapted today, yet this occurs in an environment that is acutely aware of its own historical contingency. As W. H. Auden identified in 1948, our situation is one in which we are 'no longer supported by tradition without being aware of it'.[9] Thus, the 'meaning' of any musical gesture cannot be 'purely expressive' or 'purely functional'. Rather, every compositional decision seems to carry with it an uncertainty as to whether its validity should or could be defined in relation to the vast legacy of sacred music. I would argue that our inheritance of sacred music remains relevant to us today in ways that we cannot fully rationalize or understand. Perhaps part of its attraction — to composers, performers and listeners alike — may lie precisely therein.

List of Illustrations

6.1	Benjamin Britten, 'Rejoice in the Lamb' (1943), bars 1–3. © Boosey & Hawkes.	71
6.2	Benjamin Britten, 'Rejoice in the Lamb' (1943), bars 19–25. © Boosey & Hawkes.	72
6.3	Benjamin Britten, 'Rejoice in the Lamb '(1943), bars 60–63. © Boosey & Hawkes.	73
6.4	Ralph Vaughan Williams, 'Three Shakespeare Songs', I. 'Full fathom five' (1951), bars 31–35. © Oxford University Press.	74
6.5	Anselm McDonnell, 'Hinneni '(2016), bars 22–30.	77
6.6	Lisa Robertson, 'The Silent Word Sounds '(2016), bars 1–5.	78

---

9   W. H. Auden, 'Yeats as an Example', *Kenyon Review*, 10 (1948), 187–95 (pp. 191–92).

6.7	James MacMillan, 'And lo, the Angel of the Lord Came upon Them' (2009), bars 26–31. © Boosey & Hawkes.	79
6.8	Kenneth Leighton, 'The Second Service' (1972), 'Magnificat', bars 20–32. © Oxford University Press.	81
6.9	Benjamin Britten, 'A Hymn to the Virgin' (1930, rev. 1934), verse 3. © Boosey & Hawkes.	82
6.10	James MacMillan, 'And lo, the Angel of the Lord Came upon Them' (2009), bars 43–44. © Boosey & Hawkes.	83
6.11	Séan Doherty, 'God Calls Samuel' (2016), bars 22–24.	84
6.12	James MacMillan, 'Ave Maria' (2010), bars 51–58. © Boosey & Hawkes.	87
6.13	James MacMillan, 'Ave Maria' (2010), bars 25–28. © Boosey and Hawkes.	88
6.14	Stuart Beatch, 'The Annunciation of Solomon' (2016), bars 57-end.	90

List of Recordings

Anselm McDonnell, 'Hinneni', bars 22-30, in *Annunciations: Sacred Music for the 21st Century*, St Salvator's Chapel Choir and Sean Heath, cond. by Tom Wilkinson (Sanctiandree, SAND0006, 2018), © 2017 University of St Andrews. Track 07. Duration: 3.37 (1.10-1.35). — 76

Lisa Robertson, 'The Silent Word Sounds', bars 1-5, in *Annunciations: Sacred Music for the 21st Century*, St Salvator's Chapel Choir and Sean Heath, cond. by Tom Wilkinson (Sanctiandree, SAND0006, 2018), © 2017 University of St Andrews. Track 11. Duration: 3.41 (0-0.20). — 78

James MacMillan, 'And lo, the angel of the Lord came upon them', bars 26-31, in *Annunciations: Sacred Music for the 21st Century*, St Salvator's Chapel Choir and Sean Heath, cond. by Tom Wilkinson (Sanctiandree, SAND0006, 2018), © 2017 University of St Andrews. Track 13. Duration: 4.42 (2.00-2.24). — 79

Kenneth Leighton, 'Magnificat' from 'The Second Service', bars 20-32, in *Annunciations: Sacred Music for the 21st Century*, St Salvator's Chapel Choir and Sean Heath, cond. by Tom Wilkinson (Sanctiandree, SAND0006, 2018), © 2017 University of St Andrews. Track 04. Duration: 7.12 (1.31-1.51). — 80

Benjamin Britten, 'Hymn to the Virgin', verse 3, in *Annunciations: Sacred Music for the 21st Century*, St Salvator's Chapel Choir and Sean Heath, cond. by Tom Wilkinson (Sanctiandree, SAND0006, 2018), © 2017 University of St Andrews. Track 14. Duration: 3.27 (2.12-2.33). — 82

James MacMillan, 'And lo, the angel of the Lord came upon them', bars 43-44, in *Annunciations: Sacred Music for the 21st Century*, St Salvator's Chapel Choir and Sean Heath, cond. by Tom Wilkinson (Sanctiandree, SAND0006, 2018), © 2017 University of St Andrews. Track 13. Duration: 4.42 (3.17-3.30). — 82

Seán Doherty, 'God Calls Samuel', bars 22-24, in *Annunciations: Sacred Music for the 21st Century*, St Salvator's Chapel Choir and Sean Heath, cond. by Tom Wilkinson (Sanctiandree, SAND0006, 2018), © 2017 University of St Andrews. Track 10. Duration: 4.11 (1.30-1.43).   84

James MacMillan, 'Ave Maria', bars 51-58, in *Annunciations: Sacred Music for the 21st Century*, St Salvator's Chapel Choir and Sean Heath, cond. by Tom Wilkinson (Sanctiandree, SAND0006, 2018), © 2017 University of St Andrews. Track 1. Duration: 4.30 (1.48-2.15).   86

James MacMillan, 'Ave Maria', bars 25-28, in *Annunciations: Sacred Music for the 21st Century*, St Salvator's Chapel Choir and Sean Heath, cond. by Tom Wilkinson (Sanctiandree, SAND0006, 2018), © 2017 University of St Andrews. Track 1. Duration: 4.30 (0.50-0.59).   88

Stuart Beatch, 'The Annunciation of Solomon', bars 57-59, in *Annunciations: Sacred Music for the 21st Century*, St Salvator's Chapel Choir and Sean Heath, cond. by Tom Wilkinson (Sanctiandree, SAND0006, 2018), © 2017 University of St Andrews. Track 12. Duration: 4.11 (3.25-4.06).   89

PART II:
'ANNUNCIATIONS' IN THE HEBREW BIBLE

7.1. 'Where are you?': The Temptation of Adam and Eve (Genesis 3)

Margaret McKerron

Commenting on Adam and Eve's temptation (Genesis [Gen] 3), biblical scholar George Knight bids his readers consider, 'Have any 24 verses in all literature had quite such an impact on human thought *everywhere* as has this chapter?'[1] From art and advertising to justice and gender relations, few narratives have arguably influenced Western culture so pervasively. Even in a secular age, the narrative's three movements are relatively well-known: Adam and Eve live in the Garden of Eden (Gen 2.7-25), they are tempted by the serpent and the forbidden fruit (Gen 3.1-13), and God expels them from Eden as punishment (Gen 3.14-24). Despite how familiar the story is — or perhaps *because* of how familiar it is — two 'conventional' interpretations govern much of the theological and cultural imagination. Whereas the first interpretation fixates on the temptation-judgment dialectic, the second interpretation views Adam and Eve's action as commendable self-determination. This chapter maps these two conventional interpretations of Gen 3 before considering how artistic, imaginative, and exegetical responses to a text reveal new avenues of understanding — even challenging received cultural wisdom about a text. Finally, I explore a response that germinated into 'Hinneni', a choral work by Belfast composer Anselm McDonnell that reflects on God's agency and provision in the Gen 3 narrative.

---

1 George Knight, *Theology in Pictures: A Commentary on Genesis Chapters One to Eleven* (Edinburgh: Handsel, 1981), p. 35.

I. Genesis 3 in the Theological and Cultural Imagination

Michelangelo's Sistine Chapel fresco, *Adam and Eve Tempted and Expelled from Paradise* (c. 1509–1510), illustrates the two dramatic moments that have typically preoccupied artists' imagination of the Gen 3 narrative: the couple's temptation and their expulsion. In this fresco, Eve grasps an apple offered to her by a human-looking serpent in Adam's company. In the next scene, the grief-stricken couple are then expelled from Eden at sword-point. Albrecht Dürer similarly suspends the narrative where husband and wife are balancing precariously on the precipice of transgression in *Adam and Eve* (1504). With four animals in the background representing the humours in harmonious equilibrium, the couple's foregrounded moment of temptation ripens with disordering potential.[2] Jan Brueghel the Elder reverses the composition in his *Adam and Eve in the Garden of Eden* (1615), but achieves a similar dramatic escalation. With flora and fauna commanding the immediate context and the couple just perceptible in the distance, Brueghel suggests that Adam and Eve's small act of sinfulness will have cosmic ramifications. Masaccio, on the other hand, uses his fresco in the Brancacci Chapel, Florence (1424–1425) to arrest the husband and wife in the midst of their anguish: perceiving the price of their actions, an angel expels the couple from Eden as they weep with despair. Depicting the same episode, Gustave Doré's *Adam and Eve Driven out of Eden* (1865) evokes the couple's profound isolation.

Although such artistic concentration upon Adam and Eve's temptation and expulsion invites us to contemplate their grave transgression, it also privileges what Denis Danielson calls the 'maximizing position' of the doctrine of the Fall of Man: an interpretation that 'exalts Adam's original perfection and righteousness in Eden [and also] maximizes the physical and spiritual consequences of Adam's sin.'[3] St Paul writes, 'sin came into the world through one man, and death came through sin, and so death spread to all because all have sinned' (Romans [Rom] 5.122); 'by the one man's disobedience the many were made sinners' (Rom 5.18a).[4] From the maximizing perspective, the couple's 'original sin' rends a deep chasm between pre-Fall paradise and post-Fall corruption.

In self-conscious contradistinction to these theological preoccupations, modern cultural narratives reframe Adam and Eve's temptation in terms of self-determination, and their Edenic expulsion in terms of liberation. Theatrically, George Bernard Shaw's *Back to Methuselah* (1921) adopts Adam and Eve's story as the setting for a plot depicting 'a benevolent "force" directing evolution towards a future perfection', while

---

2   Bruce Cole and Adelheid Gehalt, with an introduction by Michael Wood, *Art of the Western World: From Ancient Greece to Post-Modernism* (London: Simon & Schuster Paperbacks, 1989), p. 130.
3   Denis Danielson, 'Fall', in *A Dictionary of Biblical Tradition in English Literature*, ed. by David Lyle Jeffrey (Grand Rapids, MI: Eerdmans, 1992), pp. 271–73 (p. 272).
4   Unless otherwise noted, all biblical quotations are taken from the *New Revised Standard Version* (NRSV) of the Holy Bible.

7.1. 'Where are you?'

Fig. 7.1.1 (Left to Right) Details of: (2.4-24) Jan Brueghal the Elder, *The Garden of Eden with the Fall of Man* (c. 1613); (3.1-13) Lucas Cranach the Elder, *Adam and Eve* (1526); (3.14-24) Michelangelo, *The Fall and Expulsion from the Garden of Eden* (1509–1510). Many people can describe the basic contours of Adam and Eve's disobedience. First, Adam and Eve live a paradisiac life in Eden. Then, the serpent tempts Eve to eat of the only fruit forbidden in the garden. Finally, when she shares it with her husband, God expels them from Eden. While this model captures three plot 'landscapes,' it obscures God's role by focusing on creaturely (not divine) actions and their consequences.

Archibald MacLeish's *Songs for Eve* (1954) portrays the couple's sin as emancipatory.[5] By reconceptualising Adam and Eve's disobedience as a daring act of progress, these narratives imply that Eden is a counterfeit of genuine paradise. If a person only has the courage and fortitude to reach out and take it, a paradise of one's own design is within grasp here and now.

A similar approach undergirds the modern marketing industry's appropriations of the Gen 3 narrative. Katie B. Edwards, author of *Admen and Eve*, shows that messages focused on individuals' exercise of personal freedom or self-determination subvert consumers' apprehension of self-indulgence — even when that act means a temporary lapse from more collective or relational ideals.[6] The temptress archetype, in particular, encourages grasping one's own bliss — whether to emulate her or to possess her. Highly sexualised images of 'Eve the temptress' are not a new phenomenon. She is provocative in Michelangelo's Sistine Chapel (Fig. 7.1.1), alluring in Lucas Cranach the Elder's *Adam and Eve* (1538), and even dominant in Tintoretto's *Adam and Eve* (1550). Yet, unlike Renaissance depictions of the temptress archetype, modern marketing campaigns conflate sin with paradise. Paradise is found in sin: the tacit message is that a simple act of consumerism is all that bars individuals from their own, self-constructed paradise. Consequently, interpretations of Gen 3 tend to be polarised: there are those people who understand Adam and Eve's act of disobedience as regressive, and those who understand it as progressive. The question, then, is whether other modes of engaging with the narrative can be used constructively to move beyond this interpretive dichotomy.

If two scenes — temptation and expulsion — form a diptych visual representation of Gen 3, then what does subsequent scholarly discourse reveal? Biblical and theological commentators have largely been engrossed by questions regarding the nature of sin and divine judgement. R. R. Reno, in his theological commentary *Genesis*, skips from considering the couple's awareness of sin after their temptation (Gen 3.7) to their judgement (Gen 3.14).[7] Iain Provan, in *Discovering Genesis*, divides his analysis between doctrinal interpretations of sin and theological interpretations of sin's consequences.[8] John Day, although arguing against importing 'the full-blown Augustinian concept of original sin' into the narrative, nevertheless asserts that 'it is difficult to see why the Garden of Eden story should not be understood as one of sin and judgment comparable to others which follow in Genesis 4-11'.[9] These commentaries shed valuable light upon on-going cultural and theological dialogues about the nature of sin and God's

---

5 These two examples are discussed by Iain Provan in his *Discovering Genesis: Content, Interpretation, Reception* (Grand Rapids, MI: Eerdmans, 2015), p. 85.
6 Katie B. Edwards, *Admen and Eve: The Bible in Contemporary Advertising* (Sheffield: Sheffield Phoenix Press, 2012), p. 11. See also Chapter 3, 'Bad Girls Sell Well', in *ibid.*, pp. 64–126.
7 R. R. Reno, *Genesis*, Brazos Theological Commentary on the Bible (Grand Rapids, MI: BrazosPress, 2010).
8 Provan, *Discovering Genesis*, pp. 82–83.
9 John Day, *From Creation to Babel: Studies in Genesis 1-11* (London: Bloomsbury T&T Clark, 2013), p. 45.

judgement. Yet, in highlighting these discussions, other vital parts of the narrative are overshadowed.

Bruce Waltke is one of the few biblical commentators to note the chiasm unifying Gen 2.4-3.24 into one coherent narrative unit (or pericope) — a significant, structural observation, which challenges the view that the human act of sin and the divine act of judgement represent *the* imaginative dialectic through which the story of Adam and Eve's temptation should be interpreted.[10] In the Hebrew scriptures, chiasms focus attention on a central assertion or idea. Often, they are patterned by a sequence of subjects or concepts (A, B, C), followed by a focal or pivot assertion to which the author wishes to draw attention (X), and then the opening subjects or concepts repeated in reverse order (C', B', A').[11] In the Gen 2.4-3.24 pericope, the ABC structure consists of the creation of man (Gen 2.4-17), creation of woman (Gen 2.18-25), and serpent conversing with the woman (3.1-5). The C'B'A' structure is the judgment of the serpent (Gen 3.14-15), the woman (Gen 3.16), and the man (Gen 3.17-19). The focal point, then, is not only Adam and Eve's sinful act but also God's striking response in the moments that follow: moments in which, through a series of queries, he invites Adam and Eve to reveal themselves and reestablish their relationship (Gen 3.6-13).[12]

Waltke, however, only partially develops the implications of this insight. Uncovering this chiastic structure, he claims, 'exposes the crucial moment as Adam and Eve's choice to eat the forbidden fruit'.[13] This moment is significant: even the textual pronunciation bears witness to its gravity. In English, we read that Eve 'took of its fruit and ate; and she also gave some to her husband, who was with her, and he ate' (Gen 3.6b). In Hebrew, only eight words are needed to convey the same message; however, as Victor Hamilton observes, 'the first four words [...] contain six instances of doubled consonants,'[14] thus demanding 'merciless concentration on each word'.[15] Understandably, then, commentators dwell upon this significant moment of human sin. Still, Waltke neglects to follow his reasoning to its full conclusion: if the chiastic structure dictates that the moment of Adam and Eve's sin is important (Gen 3.6), then it also dictates that the developments involved in its uncovering (Gen 3.7-14) must be crucial too.

---

10   Bruce K. Waltke with Cathi J. Fredricks, *Genesis: A Commentary* (Grand Rapids, MI: Zondervan, 2001), p. 81. Waltke credits David. A. Dorsey for this insight. See David A. Dorsey, *The Literary Structure of the Old Testament: A Commentary on Genesis — Malachi* (Grand Rapids, MI: Baker, 1999), p. 50.
11   *Ibid.*, p. 36. See also, R. L. Pratt Jr., *He Gave us Stories* (Brentwood, TN: Wolgemuth & Hyatt, 1990), pp. 179–230.
12   *Ibid.*, p. 81.
13   *Ibid.*
14   Victor Hamilton, *The Book of Genesis: Chapters 1–17*, New International Commentary on the Old Testament (Grand Rapids, MI: Eerdmans, 1990), p. 190.
15   J. T. Walsh, 'Genesis 2:4b-3:23: A Synchronic Approach', *Journal of Biblical Literature*, 96 (1977), 161–77 (p. 166), cited in Hamilton, *The Book of Genesis*, p. 190.

English: She took of its fruit and ate; and she also gave some to her husband. (Gen 3.6)

In Hebrew, a mere eight words capture the moment of sin.

Hebrew: Vatiqáh mipiró vatachál vatitén le-isháh imáh va-ochál. (M. Navader)

Hamilton notes, however, that 'the first four words… contain six instances of doubled consonants.' He writes that 'such extremely difficult pronunciation… forces a merciless concentration on each word'.

(Hamilton, *NICOT*, 190)

Chiastic structures are narrative techniques following a structure similar to A-B-C-X-C′-B′-A′. While unifying a narrative, they also draw attention to a central point.

This model suggests that the central climax is the act of disobedience and its discovery by God.
(Bruce Waltke, *Genesis*, 80)

Fig. 7.1.2 Details of: (2.4-17) Michelangelo, *Sistine Chapel Ceiling: 4th Bay* (1508–1512); (2.18-25) Carlo Francesco Nuvolone, *Creation of Eve* (c. 1662); (3.1-5) Unknown artist, *Drawing, Adam and Eve, The Temptation, Early 19th century* (19th c.); (3.6-13) Gerard Hoet, *Figures de la Bible illustration* (1728); (3.14-15) Lucas Cranach the Elder, *Adam and Eve* (1526); (3.16) John Roddam Spencer Stanhope, *The Expulsion from Eden* (1900); (3.17-19) Domenichino, *The Rebuke of Adam and Eve* (1626).

Compared to temptation, sin, and judgement, the moments *after* God uncovers Adam and Eve's sin, and *before* he presents his judgement, are underrepresented in artistic, cultural, and scholarly engagement.[16] According to the narrative, sometime after the couple eats the forbidden fruit, the evening breeze stirs marking the hour customary for taking a stroll.[17] God walks through the garden but no one is in sight (Gen 3.8). Adam and Eve, suddenly conscious of their nakedness, conceal themselves, first sewing clothes out of leaves to hide from one another (Gen 3.7) and then camouflaging themselves among the trees of the forest to hide from God (Gen 3.8). As Hamilton remarks, the 'silliness, stupidity, and futility of the couple's attempt to hide' from an omniscient God is on full display.[18] However, so too is the gracious character of God's response.

Rather than coming in 'guns blazing' or posing a question laden with interpretive baggage (e.g., that Adam and Eve are, indeed, hiding), God calls out, 'Where are you?' It might have been expected for Adam to respond 'Hinneni' — the response Abraham (Gen 22.1), Moses (Exodus [Exod] 3.4), and Samuel (1 Samuel 3.4; 6-8) give to God's calling. Roughly translated 'Here I am', 'hinneni' connotes presenting one's whole self to God for service or commission. Adam, though, does not answer God's 'Where are you?' with 'Hinneni'. Instead, Adam pre-emptively answers the question God did not ask (i.e., why are you hiding?): 'I heard the sound of you in the garden, and I was afraid, because I was naked; and I hid myself' (Gen 3.10).

In the verses that follow, God continues to encourage Adam and Eve to reveal themselves, and to interpret their sinfulness within this relational context: 'Who told you that you were naked? Have you eaten from the tree of which I commanded you not to eat?' (Gen 3.11). First, Adam turns away from the opening God offers. Placing the blame at the feet of his wife and of God, he hides his own responsibility: 'The woman whom you gave to be with me, she gave me fruit from the tree, and I ate' (Gen 3.12). Next, God asks Eve, 'What is this you have done?' She also passes on the responsibility to another, saying 'The serpent tricked me, and I ate' (Gen 3.13b). Through these questions, God offers three spurned openings for the couple to turn to him, confess, and repent. When he judges, therefore, he does so as one who is 'merciful and gracious, slow to anger and abounding in steadfast love and faithfulness' (Exod 34.6b) — as one committed to genuine relationship with human beings and the whole of creation.

In some respects, attending to these neglected moments magnifies Adam and Eve's sin. It suggests that the original act of eating the forbidden fruit may be a

---

16 For artistic exceptions, see also the mosaic of Gen 2-3 in the Cathedral of the Assumption, Monreale, Sicily (12th c.); and William Blake's *The Angel of the Divine Presence Clothing Adam and Eve with Coats of Skins* (1803). For exceptions in biblical scholarship, cf. Knight, *Theology in Pictures*, pp. 41–43; and Donald E. Gowan, *From Eden to Babel: A Commentary on the Book of Genesis 1-11*, International Theological Commentary (Grand Rapids, MI: Eerdmans, 1988), pp. 55–57.
17 Hamilton, *The Book of Genesis*, p. 192.
18 *Ibid.*, p. 193.

prelude to the greater betrayal of refusing God's invitation to turn back to Him. What envenoms a child's disobedience is their concerted effort to cover it up. Whilst acknowledging the greater magnitude of Adam and Eve's sin is significant and insightful, therefore, it is nevertheless but part of the emerging story: God's agency and God's continued grace are the other (often neglected) part of the story. When one engages the wider pericope (Gen 2.4-3.24) with an imaginative hermeneutic, God's agency and continued commitment to a responsive relationship with the whole of creation comes into clearer focus.

II. Fruits of an Imaginative Hermeneutic Response

When certain 'conventional' interpretations of a text such as Gen 3 dominate the theological and cultural imagination, approaching the text with an imaginative hermeneutic often reveals overlooked (or forgotten) avenues of interpretation. Drawing from practices of *lectio divina*, Ignatian contemplation, and a theatre workshop entitled 'Word by Heart', reveal three significant structural elements uncommon in biblical and theological scholarship: a repeated 'call-and-response' pattern that stresses divine agency, three rebuffed overtures that focus the narrative on divine grace, and the reassurance signified in Adam and Eve's re-clothing. Together, these three elements reframe Adam and Eve's encounter with God and signify God's continued presence and provision for creation even after the fall and judgement.

Lectio divina is the oldest of the three practices. It refers to a practice of deep reading that involves 'chewing' upon a passage of scripture: reading it or hearing it read aloud, repeating it to oneself, listening meditatively for certain words or images that strike the heart and mind, and contemplating them in prayer.[19] As a contemplative response to scriptural text, *lectio divina* invites readers to become more receptive to the manifold meanings existing in a passage of scripture. Drawing from this practice, I listened to the larger pericope (Gen 2.4-3.24) repeatedly over several days. A distinctive pattern in the narration emerged: God recognises a need in creation ('call') and God supplies an appropriate response ('response'). For instance, the narrator notes that the growing of crops calls for 'rain upon the earth' and someone to 'till the ground' (Gen 2.5). God responds by causing a stream to 'rise up' (Gen 2.6) and creates man to live 'in the garden of Eden to till and keep it' (Gen 2.15). Next, God observes 'it is not good for man to be alone', so God creates animals (Gen 2.19) and forms woman (Gen 2.20-22). The recurring call-and-response pattern reinforces the image of an active, responsive God. Therefore, when we hear creaturely agency abruptly displacing divine agency (Gen 3.1-6), it is arresting. Not only does the serpent dictate the imperative (the tree is *'to be desired* to make one

---

19 Christine Valters Paintner and Lucy Wynkoop, *Lectio Divina*: *Contemplative Awakening and Awareness* (New York: Paulist Press, 2008), pp. 2–3.

7.1. 'Where are you?'

Fig. 7.1.3 (Left to right) Details of: (2.5-17) Étienne Colaud, *The Creation of the Animals and the Birds* (Minature, Book of Hours, Rome, Early Morning) (c. 1525); (2.18-25) Raphael Coxie, *The Creation of Eve* (c. 1601–1610); (3.1-7) Károly Patkó, *Adam and Eve* (c. 1920); (3.8-13) Johann Elias Ridinger, *Adam and Eve Cover Their Nakedness as God Makes His Wrath Felt in the Garden of Eden* (c. 1750); (3.14-19) Master Bertram, *Fall of Man* (1375–1383); (3.20-21) William de Brailes, *God Clothing Adam and Eve*, from a Book of Bible Pictures, illumination on vellum (c. 1250); (3.22-24) William Wailes of Newcastle, *St Mary de Castro Nave Window 4* (1866). The 'Call-and-Response' model focuses on the theme of 'Who provides?' In Gen 2, God is the provider. God recognises the needs of creation — whether it is a spring, or a gardener, or a partner — and takes it upon himself to address these needs. The serpent questions God's trustworthiness as provider, suggesting that the human beings should look to their own best interests. Once Adam and Eve decide to 'be like God' though, a cascade of new problems emerge. They become aware of their vulnerability and fashion makeshift clothes from fig leaves. They become afraid of God's punishment, first hiding behind bushes and then blaming each other. Remarkably, before the couple are expelled from Eden — and after his judgement — God again confirms his role as their provider, by endowing them with more substantial clothing. In the end, the narrative shows God addressing Adam and Eve's needs in ways that go beyond what they are able to do for themselves.

wise', Gen 3.6a), but the serpent also implies that Eve will only get what she needs if she provides it for herself (Gen 3.5).[20] Despite God's evident care and consistent commitment to the flourishing of creation, Adam and Eve choose creaturely agency over divine agency. Appreciating God's divine care magnifies the couple's subsequent desolation, but it also underscores the grace in God's choice to seek the young couple out afterwards. It is a grace that can be appreciated further using two related imaginative, hermeneutic practices.

Jesuit founder, Ignatius of Loyola, suggests readers of scripture attempt to walk prayerfully 'in the shoes' of different characters in the biblical narrative to open up new questions and horizons of meaning within a given biblical narrative.[21] It is illuminating to try to imagine the story from the divine perspective. After Adam and Eve's sinful act, God calls, 'Where are you?' Does he demand to know where the couple is, as if haranguing two people who have failed to materialise at an appointed time? Does his tone command them to reveal themselves, as a parent might in calling a child whose disobedience has been discovered? When God calls 'Where are you?' is his query coloured with concern or regret? Might it be said with sadness, as one whose foresight appreciates the full cost of their actions? Ignatian contemplation does not lead us to any hard or fast conclusions, but its empathetic approach does open more interpretive possibilities to be investigated and evaluated.

Similarly interested in imaginative and empathetic responses to the text, Broadway actor Bruce Kuhn teaches workshops entitled 'Word by Heart', which retell biblical stories as if the participants were present — guided by a facilitator versed in historical-cultural and biblical background for accuracy.[22] Reading the Gen 3 narrative line-by-line, pausing to imagine the experience from the characters' perspective, two often-overlooked events within the narrative surface are considered: Adam and Eve's clothing of themselves and God's re-clothing of Adam and Eve. First, having grasped their naked vulnerability, the narrator relates that the couple 'sewed fig leaves together and made loincloths for themselves' (Gen 3.7b). It is possible to appreciate the discomfort Adam and Eve would have felt: hyper-vigilant lest leaves rip unexpectedly, unprotected against a cool evening breeze, and irritated with insects and stems. Acknowledging God's substantial provision of clothing later in the narrative, the difference in experience is palpable. We can envision how Adam and Eve were comforted and reassured as they were tenderly dressed and protected by

---

20 Bruce Waltke with Charles Yu, *An Old Testament Theology: An Exegetical, Canonical, and Thematic Approach* (Grand Rapids, MI: Zondervan, 2007), p. 262.

21 For more information on practices of imaginative prayer, see, for example, the chapter entitled 'Pray with Your Imagination', in David L. Fleming, *What is Ignatian Spirituality?* (Chicago, IL: Loyola Press, 2008), pp. 55–60.

22 I am grateful to Kirstin Jeffrey Johnson for an introduction to Bruce Kuhn's methodology during the 2016 *Linlathen Lectures* ('InActing Word: Theology & Theatre') held in Carleton Place, ON, Canada. See Linlathen, *Past Conferences and Retreats* (Linlathen.com, 2016), https://www.linlathen.com/past-conferences; and Bruce Kuhn, *Word by Heart: Truth by Story* (Wordbyheart.org, 2015), http://www.wordbyheart.org/

God's own hand — notably, after they had received his judgement. In this action, God's role in the call-and-response motif is re-established: while divine judgement is not lessened, re-clothing Adam and Eve with the garments they will need for life outside Eden is an intimate act that reaffirms God's care and commitment to creation even in the midst of their sinfulness.

Together, these three imaginative, hermeneutic responses to the text challenge conventional interpretations of Gen 3 that tend to distil the 'moral of the story' into a rumination on human agency: either God is feared (sovereign judge) or forgotten (oppressor). Instead, an imaginative hermeneutic reveals the central place of God's agency and mercy in the narrative, as well as the deep tragedy and profound cost of sin. God is intimately and actively involved in recognising and providing for creation — both before and after human sinfulness and divine judgement. Indeed, as Belfast composer Anselm McDonnell portrays in his choral arrangement 'Hinneni', it is God Himself — on behalf of creation — who freely and finally provides the only sufficient answer to sin. Only the divine, self-emptying agency of Jesus Christ in the incarnation, passion, and resurrection makes possible God's redemptive purposes.

III. Fruits of an Artistic Collaboration

Collaborating with someone whose background, commitments, and interests are unknown to you is a daunting proposition — especially when the narrative with which you are engaging has attracted so much theological, artistic, and cultural attention historically. How do you grapple with the cultural imagination of a person you have never met? And how do you balance presenting background information with creating space for the other's own imaginative engagement? While wrestling with these concerns in preparation for the first *TheoArtistry* workshop, I decided that *how* I presented the information I uncovered in my research would be as important as *what* I uncovered.

In the end, my approach was simple. Mapping out the theological and emotional topography of the larger pericope for McDonnell, I observed the more challenging theological terrain (e.g., doctrine of original sin) and how others have navigated such areas historically (e.g., maximizing and minimizing positions). As well as well-worn paths of cultural and artistic interpretation, I documented the less-explored expanses within the narrative: particularly, the interval between Adam and Eve's first sin (Gen 3.6) and their judgement (Gen 3.14), in which God's three overtures to Adam and Eve are rebuffed. At the first TheoArtistry workshop, I invited McDonnell — with 'map' in hand — to encounter the text imaginatively, using much the same exercises that I had myself used to open up new horizons of meaning within the text.

> Christ Jesus, who, though he was in the form of God, did not regard equality with God as something to be exploited, but emptied himself, taking the form of a slave being born in human likeness. And being found in human form, he humbled himself and became

obedient to the point of death — even death on a cross. Therefore God also highly exalted him, and gave him the name that is above every name.[23]

Unlike Adam and Eve who sought to become 'like God', Jesus *was* in the form of God. Whereas they disobeyed and filled themselves with forbidden fruit, Christ emptied himself, becoming obedient to the point of death. When Adam and Eve sought to exalt themselves, God humbled them; when Christ humbled himself, God exalted him. These parallels and contrasts between Adam and Christ provide ample inspiration.

In 'Hinneni', McDonnell weaves together the threads of divine grace that bind Eden to Golgotha. Whereas two scenes — temptation and expulsion — tend to dominate the imaginative fabric of Gen 3, McDonnell roots his choral composition in the moments of divine grace *after* Adam and Eve eat the forbidden fruit and *before* God pronounces their judgement. With Hebrew pronouncing the sin in the hushed background, the libretto recounts God's encounter with Adam and Eve through his queries: 'Where are you? […] / Who told you you were naked, / Have you eaten from the tree, / Of knowledge of good and evil?' As the questions continue, the choir's initial unison becomes fragmented, mirroring the division that sin precipitates. Using vocal unison, volume, and staccato rhythm, the tension mounts to God's climactic demand: 'What is this you've done…my son?' In the stillness between the staccatos, listeners sense the profound weight of Adam's disobedience — a weight made heavier when Adam's sonship is reflected ('my son').

Perhaps in homage to the reversal motifs recurring in our research — i.e., the structural reversal in the chiasm and the typological reversal of Adam and Christ — the climactic moment is followed by a role reversal in the libretto: encountering Jesus on the cross, Adam and Eve are confronted with the true cost of their sinfulness. Struck by the self-sacrifice of Christ's incarnation and passion, the couple marvels:

> For whom are you naked?
> Hanging cursed from the tree,
> Of death, of wrath, and sorrow?
> What is this you have done…
> …for me?

Thus, the 'Tree of Knowledge of Good and Evil' becomes the tree of the cross, while the grasping disobedience of the first Adam is interwoven with the self-sacrificial obedience of Christ, the second Adam. The refrain, 'Hinneni', provides the warp and weft of Anselm's choral tapestry: the consistent thread holding together the whole composition and the frame against which the parallels and divergences of Adam, Eve, and Christ are drawn out. With God's unanswered questionings echoing in the background, the choir's first cries of 'Hinneni' are dissonant and pathos-filled — an uncomfortable reminder of the response Adam and Eve failed to give God when

---

23 Philippians 2.7-9a.

he sought them in the garden. As the piece turns and the couple encounters Christ, however, 'Hinneni' takes on reassuring overtones: this is a God who declares 'Here I am' to his creation, even in the midst of sin and judgement, and on the cross. By interweaving the couple's story with the gift of the Son, McDonnell's piece suggests that God himself answers 'Hinneni' to human sinfulness — showing the lengths to which Love will go to pursue the restoration and reconciliation of the world to Himself and to one another.

List of Illustrations

7.1.1   Details of: (2.4-24) Jan Brueghal the Elder, *The Garden of Eden with the Fall of Man* (c. 1613), oil on copper, Wikimedia, https://commons.wikimedia.org/wiki/File:Jan_Brueghel_the_Elder_-_The_Garden_of_Eden_with_the_Fall_of_Man.jpg, public domain; (3.1-13) Lucas Cranach the Elder, *Adam and Eve* (1526), oil on maple wood, Courtauld Institute of Art, London, United Kingdom, Wikimedia, https://commons.wikimedia.org/wiki/File:Lucas_Cranach_d.%C3%84._-_Adam_und_Eva_(Courtauld_Institute_of_Art).jpg, public domain; (3.14-24) Michelangelo, *The Fall and Expulsion from the Garden of Eden* (1509–1510), fresco, Sistine Chapel, Vatican, Wikimedia, https://commons.wikimedia.org/wiki/File:Michelangelo,_Fall_and_Expulsion_from_Garden_of_Eden_00.jpg, public domain.   99

7.1.2   Details of: (2.4-17) Michelangelo, *Sistine Chapel Ceiling: 4th Bay* (1508–1512), fresco, Sistine Chapel, Vatican, Wikimedia, https://commons.wikimedia.org/wiki/File:Michelangelo_-_Sistine_Chapel_ceiling_-6th_bay.jpg, public domain; (2.18-25) Carlo Francesco Nuvolone, *Creation of Eve* (c. 1662), oil on canvas, Dulwich Picture Gallery, London, United Kingdom, Wikimedia, https://commons.wikimedia.org/wiki/File:Nuvolone,_Carlo_Francesco_-_Creation_of_Eve_-_Google_Art_Project.jpg, public domain; (3.1-5) Unknown artist, *Drawing, Adam and Eve, The Temptation*, Early 19th century (19th c.), pen and ink, brush and watercolor, black chalk on paper, Cooper Hewitt, Smithsonian Design Museum, Manhatten, USA, Wikimedia, https://commons.wikimedia.org/wiki/File:Drawing,_Adam_and_Eve,_The_Temptation,_early_19th_century_(CH_18121969).jpg, public domain, museum purchase through various donors; (3.6-13) Gerard Hoet, *Figures de la Bible illustration* (1728), engraving, Bizzell Bible Collection, University of Oklahoma Libraries, USA, Wikimedia, https://commons.wikimedia.org/wiki/Category:Figures_de_la_Bible#/media/File:Figures_004_God_called_to_Adam_and_said,_Where_are_you.jpg, public domain; (3.14-15) Lucas Cranach the Elder, *Adam and Eve* (1526), oil on maple wood, Courtauld Institute of Art, London, United Kingdom, Wikimedia, https://commons.wikimedia.org/wiki/File:Lucas_Cranach_d.%C3%84._-_Adam_und_Eva_(Courtauld_Institute_of_Art).jpg, public domain; (3.16) John Roddam Spencer Stanhope, *The Expulsion from Eden* (1900), tempera on canvas, Walker Art Gallery, Liverpool, United Kingdom, Wikimedia,   102 https://commons.wikimedia.org/wiki/File:John_Roddam_Spencer_Stanhope_-_The_Expulsion_from_Eden,_1900.jpg, public domain; (3.17-19) Domenichino, *The Rebuke of Adam and Eve* (1626), oil on canvas, National Gallery of Art, Washington, D.C., USA, Wikimedia, https://commons.wikimedia.org/wiki/File:The_Rebuke_of_Adam_and_Eve.jpg, public domain, Patrons' Permanent Fund.

7.1.3 Details of: (2.5-17) Étienne Colaud, *The Creation of the Animals and the Birds* (Minature, Book of Hours, Rome, Early Morning) (c. 1525), illumination on parchment, Bibliothèque nationale de France, Paris, France, Wikimedia, https://commons.wikimedia.org/wiki/File:Livre_d%27heures_%C3%A0_l%27usage_de_Rome_-_Bodleian_Lib_Douce135_f17v_(cr%C3%A9ation).jpg, public domain; (2.18-25) Raphael Coxie, *The Creation of Eve* (c. 1601–1610), oil on panel, Galerij Bernaerts, Antwerp, Belgium, Wikimedia, https://commons.wikimedia.org/wiki/File:Raphael_Coxie_(attr.)_-_The_creation_of_Eve.jpg, public domain; (3.1-7) Károly Patkó, *Adam and Eve* (c. 1920), oil on canvas, private collection, Wikimedia, https://commons.wikimedia.org/wiki/File:Patk%C3%B3_Adam_and_Eve_1920.jpg, public domain; (3.8-13) Johann Elias Ridinger, *Adam and Eve Cover Their Nakedness as God Makes His Wrath Felt in the Garden of Eden* (c. 1750), etching, Wellcome Collection, United Kingdom, Wikimedia, https://commons.wikimedia.org/wiki/File:Adam_and_Eve_cover_their_nakedness_as_God_makes_his_wrath_fe_Wellcome_V0034432.jpg, CCA 4.0. This file comes from Wellcome Images, a website operated by Wellcome Trust, a global charitable foundation based in the United Kingdom; (3.14-19) Master Bertram, *Fall of Man* (1375–1383), tempora on wood, Kuntshalle Hamburg, Hamburg, Germany, Wikimedia, https://commons.wikimedia.org/wiki/File:Meister_Bertram_von_Minden_009.jpg, public domain; (3.20-21) William de Brailes, *God Clothing Adam and Eve*, from a Book of Bible Pictures, illumination on vellum (c. 1250), Collezione Naya-Bohm, Venice, Italy, public domain; (3.22-24) William Wailes of Newcastle, *St Mary de Castro Nave Window 4* (1866), stained glass window, Leicester, United Kingdom, Wikimedia, https://commons.wikimedia.org/wiki/File:St_Mary_de_Castro_nave_W_window_5.jpg, CCA-SA 2.0.

105

7.2. Composer's Reflections

Anselm McDonnell

The British composer, Harrison Birtwistle, compared his compositional process to an outdoor stroll: there is a general destination, but the walker may linger along the path — caught by the sight of a gnarled tree here, an intriguing tunnel there, or the dappled sunlight reaching through a net of leaves.[1] My own artistic endeavours often mirror this approach. Once a destination is set, the journey itself may unfold in a myriad of ways. Musically, I have an aversion to lingering, so perhaps a more apt comparison is a walk that bristles with energy and exploration: a chord or motivic fragment may seize my imagination briefly until it is cast by the wayside as my curiosity wanes and I find something else to tinker with.

Taking such a walk with someone else — as in interdisciplinary collaboration — risks the possibility that one disciplinary approach may hinder or obstruct the other, or one inflexible vision may dominate the direction and progress. Any concerns that I had as a composer about being given a task that was overly prescriptive were quickly put to rest after my first meeting with Margaret McKerron. McKerron presented themes and information regarding our Gen 3 passage to see what provoked inspiration. I had a pre-conceived notion that, once the theological groundwork had been done, I would take that information and use it as an extra-musical starting point; however, in practice the interaction between the activities of theological and musical thought became inseparably intertwined. To hijack Birtwistle's analogy, rather than theology sending music out for a walk while it remained in the armchair with its feet up, both set out to explore together (although it is inevitable that at some point theology will reprimand music for having left the map at home).

---

1   In conversation with Ryan Wigglesworth, Birtwistle alludes to artist Paul Klee's practise of 'taking a line for a walk'. While specifically related to Birtwistle's use of monody, he also uses this language to describe compositional exploration. Interview with Birtwistle, 12/07/11, NMC Recordings, https://www.nmcrec.co.uk/recording/nights-black-bird

This collaborative attitude was vital not only for the conception of the initial ideas, but also for the project's development as the piece began to take shape. On several occasions, the work took unanticipated twists and turns, highlighting nuances to our themes we had not noticed. This experience caused me to reflect with more self-awareness on the nature of art as 'a vehicle of discovery'.[2] Frequently, this revelatory aspect takes the form of self-discovery. As W. B. Yeats observes, 'Out of the quarrel with others we make rhetoric; out of the quarrel with ourselves we make poetry'.[3] Collaboration, therefore, is not an invitation to produce rhetoric, but to enter the inner world of quarrelling that takes place within the artist. This invitation contributes to making collaboration more daunting, for it requires a self-exposure of truths and intentions in our art that we often avoid verbalising. To add theology creates a potent mix, for the self-discovery of sinful man in the light of God's holy character is an uncomfortable experience.

The text of Gen 3 picks up on these very themes with Adam and Eve's discovery of their own nakedness, both physically and spiritually, before God. They attempt to hide themselves, first by physical concealment and then by blame-shifting. Initially, after my discussions with McKerron at the TheoArtistry Symposium (November 2016), I had been taken with the idea of Adam and Eve avoiding blame, and implicitly rebuking God. I began sketching out a piece that would contain active polyphonic textures between combating male and female voices. After a frustrating week, I jettisoned both the musical material and the theological theme; I asked McKerron if we could start afresh. Calming my concerns about what seemed to me a wasted week, McKerron suggested that we approach the passage by focusing on a more general concern that both of us had noted at the symposium. McKerron's research showed the chiastic structure of the Hebrew prose running from Gen 2.4 to the end of Gen 3. The chiasm draws the reader's attention not to Adam and Eve's sin or punishment, but rather to the surprising grace God shows to his disobedient creation — a grace that crystallizes in his merciful and gentle invitation to them to approach him and confess.

I was struck by this theme of grace, especially when McKerron pointed out that commentaries (and works of art inspired by Gen 3) tend to neglect this aspect, instead focusing on temptation and judgement. Musical structure that derives its architecture from literary models is, moreover, a compositional interest of mine. I had already experimented, for example, with using parallelism in the Psalms as source material. There, the returning in parallelism was used to elicit the sense of eternal truth contained within a finite structure (in defiance of the notion that both music and poetry are bound to a temporal plane). With the importance of these themes highlighted, McKerron and I produced a text based on the questions God asks in the garden and framed them in a chiastic structure.

---

2   Jeremy Begbie, *Sounding the Depths*: *Theology Through the Arts,* ed. by Jeremy Begbie (London: SCM Press, 2002), p. 1.

3   Cited in Steve Turner, *Imagine*: *A Vision for Christians in the Arts* (Downers Grove, IL: Intervarsity Press, 2001), p. 55.

The resulting text has a strong typological element to it, using the object of the tree as a locus. The inclusion of typology seemed fitting as it is, arguably, a clear instance where artistic and theological concerns aligned. The idea of motivic seeds and organic growth found in the musical concept of Jean Sibelius' profound logic, or the developing variation of Arnold Schoenberg, is very reminiscent of the hermeneutical categories of type, anti-type and recurrence throughout the biblical narrative. McKerron did some research finding typological links that could be drawn out between the 'Tree of Knowledge of Good and Evil', the tree of the cross, and the tree of life in Rev 22. After some deliberation, we decided to focus solely on the link between the trees of Eden and Golgotha. This had more dramatic potential and would be clearer than adding in too many references to the mix.

One area which we had not yet addressed was the theme of annunciation. Elements integral to other annunciations are missing from the Gen 3 text, such as God's repeated calling of a particular person or the response 'Hinneni', which means 'Here I am' in Hebrew (e.g. 'Moses, Moses' and 'Here I am', Exod 3.4). It was, however, possible to work a more explicit allusion to annunciation language into the text: Adam, Eve and God are named repeatedly, and the response 'Hinneni' plays a key role in the narrative.

I had begun composing at this stage, starting off with the central elements of the piece and working outwards so the chiastic structure would be an integral part of the composition. I reflected on the questions that God asks Adam and Eve, realizing that there was an opportunity for role reversal: the questions could be repeated, but their direction changed. Such an approach would fit well with the chiastic structure and typological associations I wanted to impress. In the first half of the piece, God asks Adam and Eve, 'Where are you? Who told you, you were naked?' and, 'Have you eaten from the tree? What is this you have done?' Musically, these questions are represented by falling musical motifs, as the divine descends to the earthly. Then, the roles are reversed with the revelation of 'the second Adam' on the cross. Adam and Eve now ask God with rising musical lines, 'For whom are you naked? What is this you have done? Where are you?'. God's annunciation to man is placed parallel to man's search for the only one who can grant forgiveness. The repeated 'Hinnenis' provide an emotional barometer of the narrative: the listener is taken from Adam and Eve's initial reluctance to emerge from hiding to the final, comforting 'Hinneni' as God answers the searching sinners. He is not aloof or far off, but on the cross: paying for their sins and welcoming them with grace and forgiveness.

Using 'Hinneni' as an identifying marker in my piece, I wanted to integrate a further cohesion with the Hebrew prose of Gen 3. McKerron found one biblical commentator who emphasized that the verse narrating Adam and Eve's disobedience is challenging to pronounce in Hebrew (Gen 3.6). Madhavi Nevader, who was consulted on Hebrew textual issues, pointed out that the description of Adam and Eve's sin is staccato and phonologically percussive, characterized by the repetitive 'va' consonant. I decided to exploit the aural effect of the Hebrew syllables by creating three susurrating backgrounds to various sections of the text. At a basic level, these sounds could be taken to represent the hushed rustling of leaves and wind in the garden that form the soundscape for the encounter between man and God, or Adam and Eve's desire to conceal and cover up. However, this technique serves a deeper, dual purpose. The first was to re-introduce the blaming concept that I had initially abandoned. The first Hebrew phrase, vocalized by the men, is an accusatory denunciation of Eve's role in the sin: 'she took of its fruit and ate.' The second phrase, whispered by the sopranos and altos, is a responding condemnation of Adam: 'and she also gave some to her husband who was with her, and he ate.' Mankind's imprecations, however, fall silent in the face of Christ's sacrifice: the third phrase ('then the eyes of both were opened') is uttered not as a realization of sin but as a recognition of the grace that has paid the price.[4]

The second purpose of these backdrops is the subtler intention of layering, based upon the chiaroscuro oil-painting technique of Renaissance painters such as Caravaggio. Strong tonal contrasts of light and dark are used to create dramatic and three-dimensional effects. Here, the canvas is painted entirely dark and then light is gradually worked up in layers to create a focal point. The heart of the concept is that the eye is always drawn to a light that has overcome darkness. The unpitched, hissing accusations of rebellion are overcome by the powerful redemption and justification achieved by grace. This technique is known to theology. In Ephesians, when Paul describes the state of the Christian, he begins with a dark description of their previous ignorance of Christ ('and you were dead in the trespasses and sins in which you once walked') and progresses to the contrasting light ('But God, being rich in mercy, because of the great love with which he loved us, even when we were dead in our trespasses, made us alive together with Christ – by grace you have been saved').[5] In my choral work 'Hinneni', grace is all the brighter because it takes place over and against a backdrop of murmured and hidden sin.

Composing this piece was an enjoyable learning curve, both as my first experience of this kind of collaboration and as a project with explicit intention to explore theology and the arts. Although already an area of interest for me, the interactions and ideas of the staff of ITIA (the Institute for Theology, Imagination and the Arts), James MacMillan and especially my theological guide, McKerron, have greatly increased my appreciation and understanding of what it means to produce art as a Christian. I am very grateful to have been introduced to so many artists and theologians in whom I have found a similar concern for the place of contemporary Christian art. Perhaps the annunciation to Isaiah provides a fitting summary for the Christian of any discipline: 'Whom shall I send? And who will go for us?' 'Hinneni, send me.'

 Listen to Anselm McDonnell, 'Hinneni', in *Annunciations: Sacred Music for the 21st Century*, St Salvator's Chapel Choir and Sean Heath, cond. by Tom Wilkinson (Sanctiandree, SAND0006, 2018), © 2017 University of St Andrews. Duration: 3.37. Track 07. Duration: 3.37.
https://doi.org/10.11647/OBP.0172.31

---

4   All biblical quotations in this chapter are taken from the ESV translation, unless otherwise noted.
5   Ephesians 2.1-5.

'Hinneni'

Anselm McDonnell

Preface

Composed by Anselm McDonnell Nov-Dec 2016 for the St. Salvator's Chapel Choir as part of the Theoartistry composers' scheme.

Text produced in collaboration with Margaret McKerron, based on Genesis 3. Hebrew transliteration by Dr. Madhavi Navader.

Instrumentation:

SATB choir with divisions

Duration: '3:00' c.

Text:

Vatiqáh mipiró vatochál.	**Pronounced:** (Va-tee-ka mi-peer-row va-toe-chal) 'ch' as in loch 'mi' as in miss

Where are you?
Where are you Adam?
Where are you Eve?

Hinneni	**Pronounced:** (Hi-nay-nee) 'hi' as in him

Vatitatén leisháh vaochál.	**Pronounced:** (Va-tee-ta-tayn lay-eesh-ah va-oh-chal) 'ch' as in loch

Who told you you were naked?
Have you eaten from the tree,
Of knowledge, of good and evil?
What is this you have done,
My son?

Hinneni

For whom are you naked?
What is this you have done?
My lord, my God, my Saviour?
Hanging cursed from the tree,
Of wrath, of death?
For me?

Vatipaqáchna ene shnehém.	**Pronounced:** (Va-tee-pa-ka-chna ay-nay shne-chem) 'ch' as in loch

Where are you?
Where are you, my Saviour?
My lord, my God, my Saviour?

Hinneni

Hinneni
הִנֵּנִי

For St. Salvator's Chapel Choir

Anselm McDonnell/Margaret McKerron

Anselm McDonnell

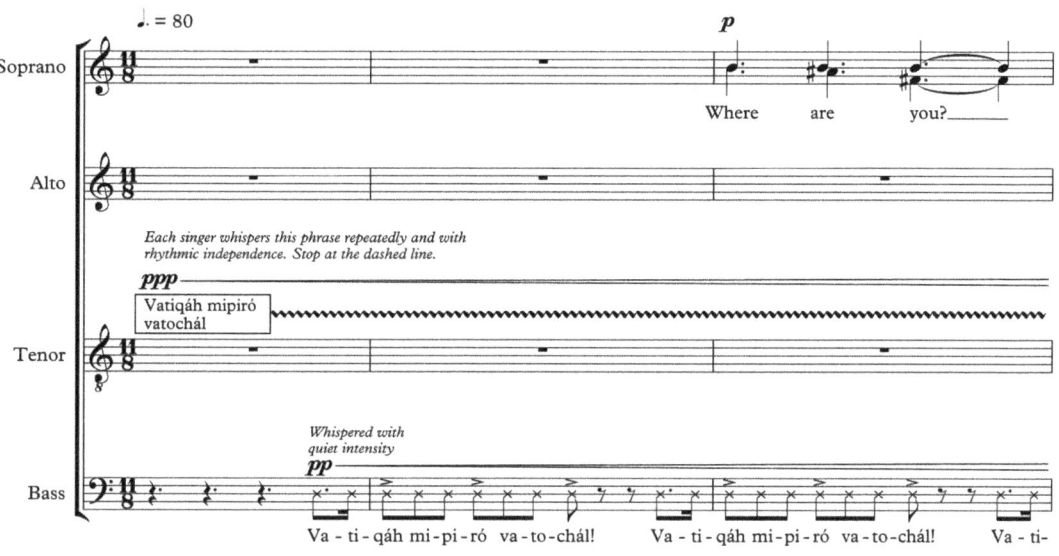

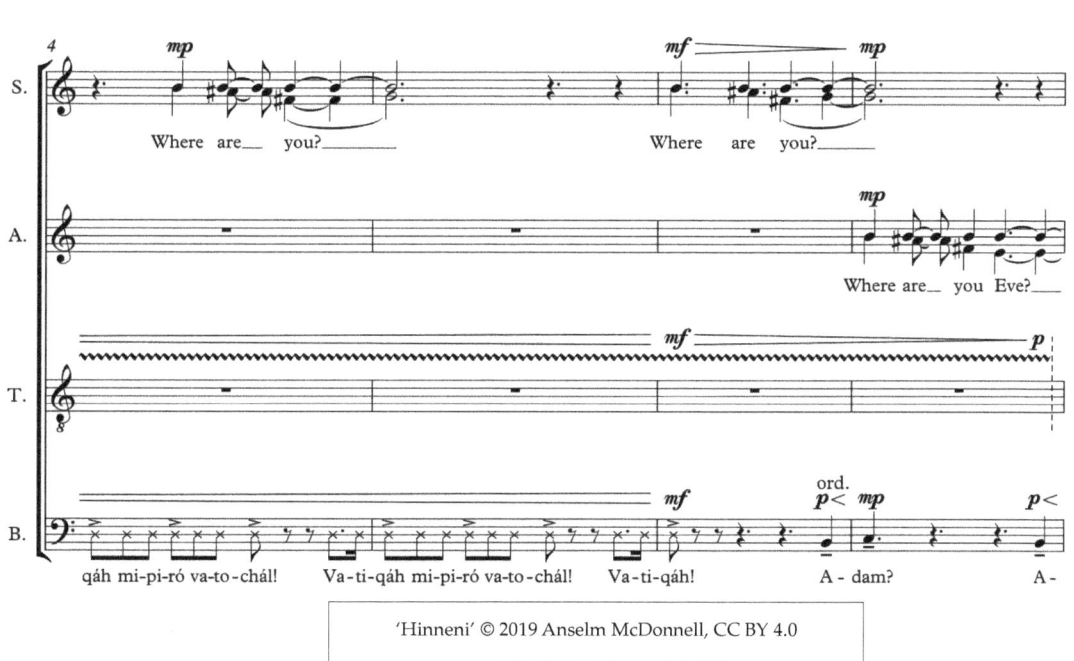

'Hinneni' © 2019 Anselm McDonnell, CC BY 4.0
https://doi.org/10.11647/OBP.0172.09

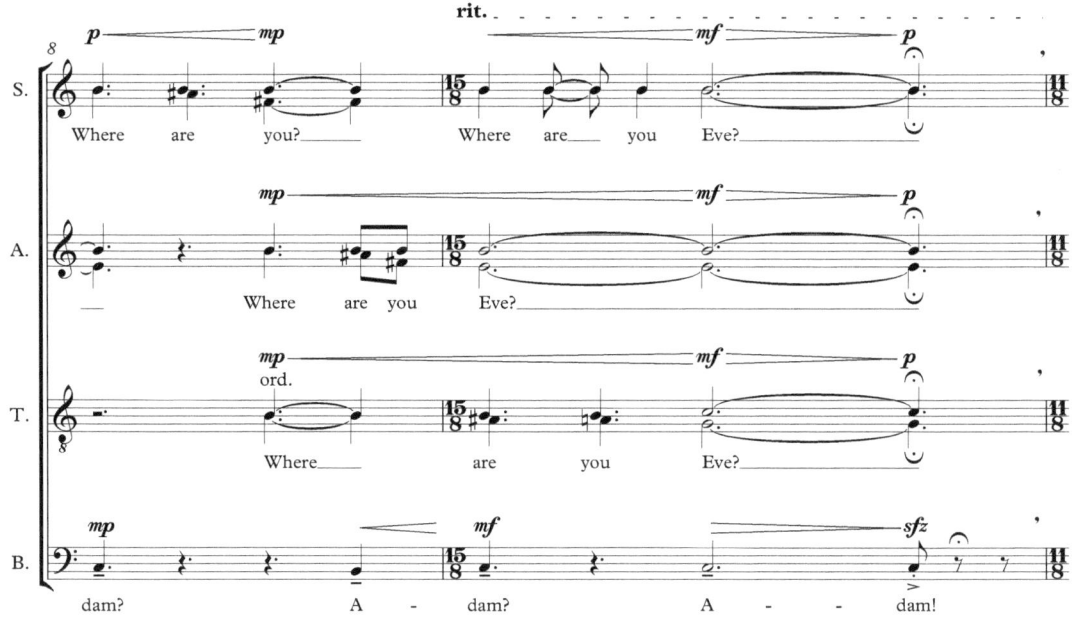
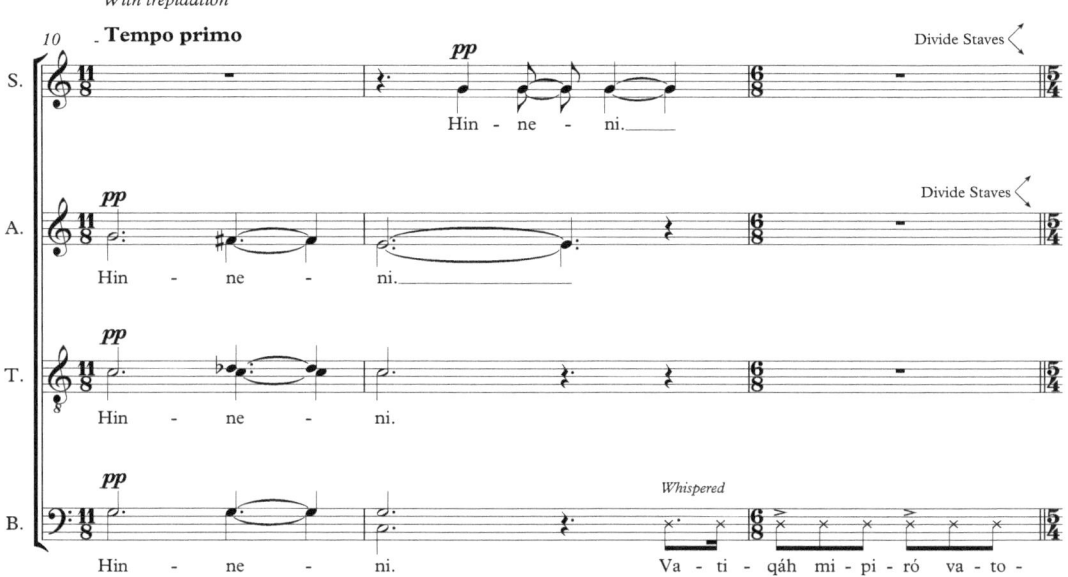

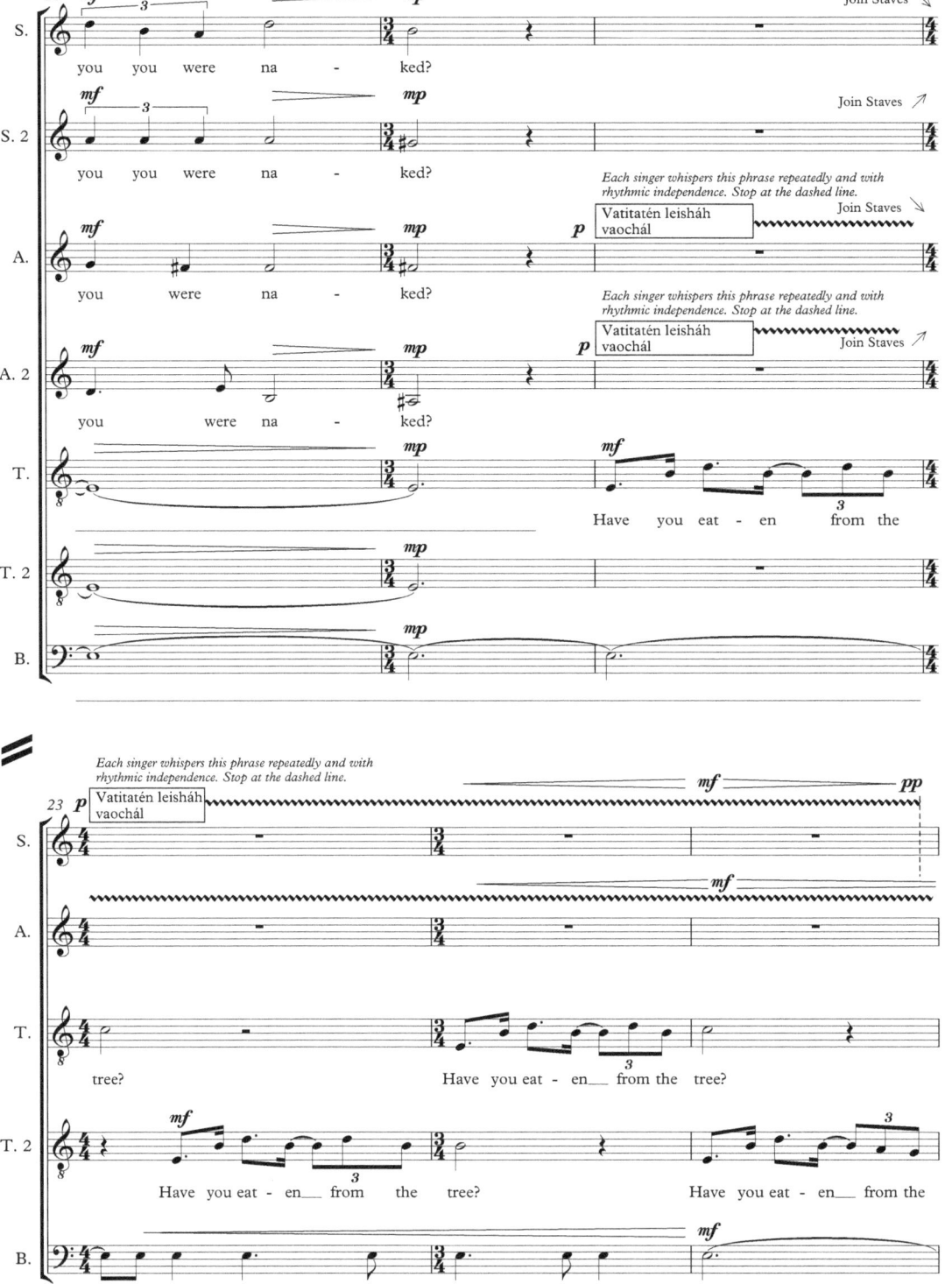

With anguish
31
S.
A.
T.
B.
Hin - - ne - - - - - ni!
mp
Divide Staves

33
S.
A.
T.
T. 2
B.
B. 2
mp
mf
For whom are you
For whom are you na - ked? Are you na - ked?
For whom are you na- ked? For whom are you na - ked?
For whom_ are you na- ked? For whom are you_ na - ked?
For whom_ are you na- ked? For whom are you na - ked?
Join Staves
3

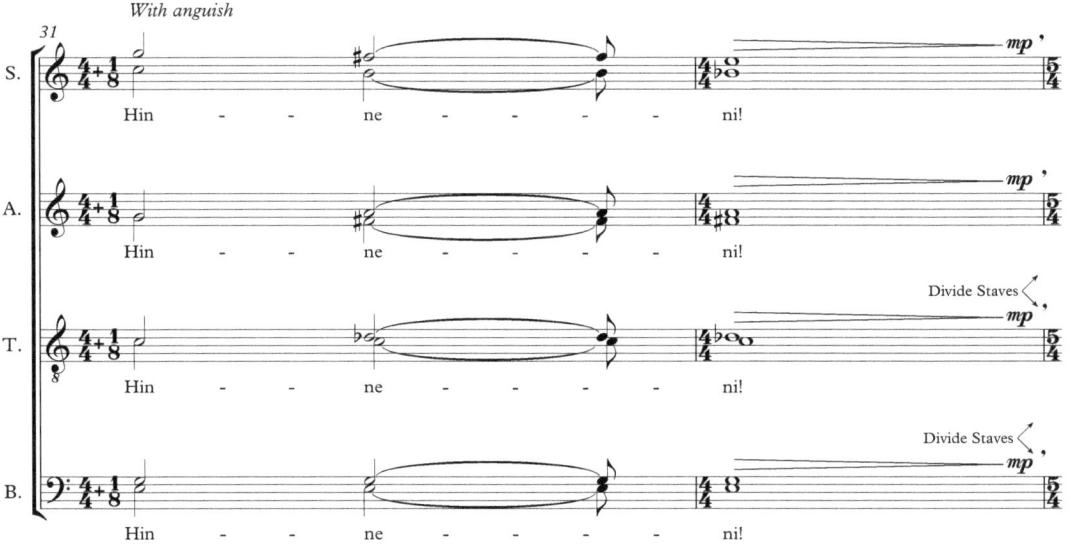

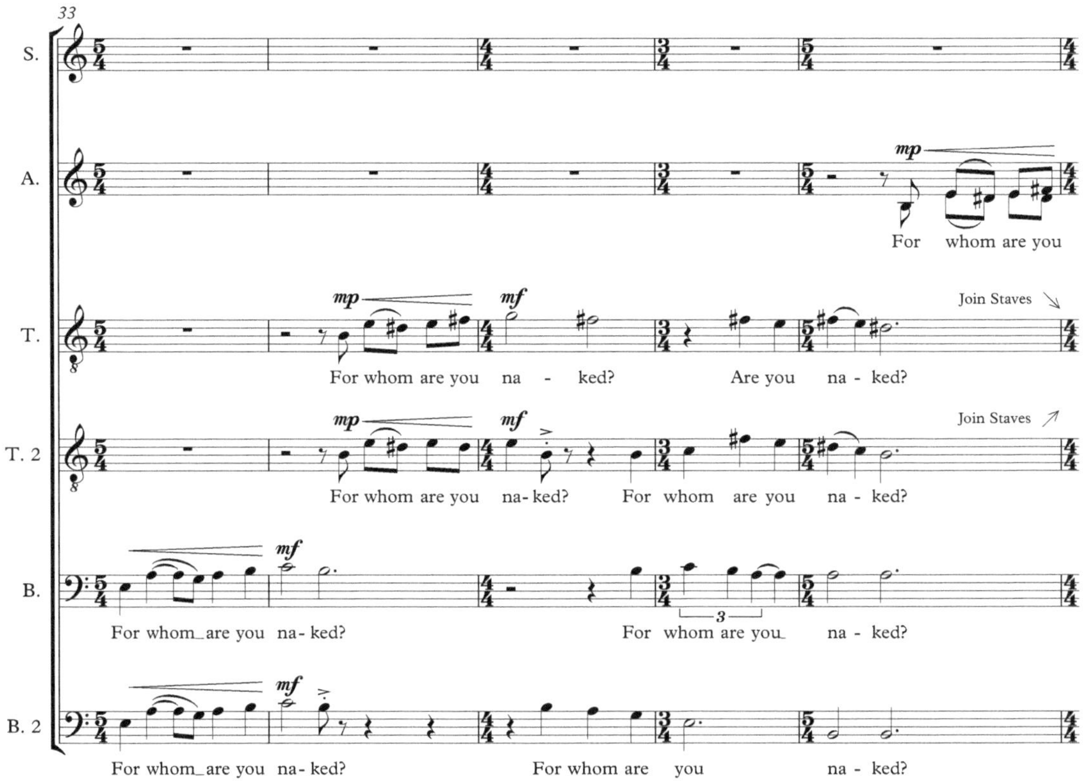

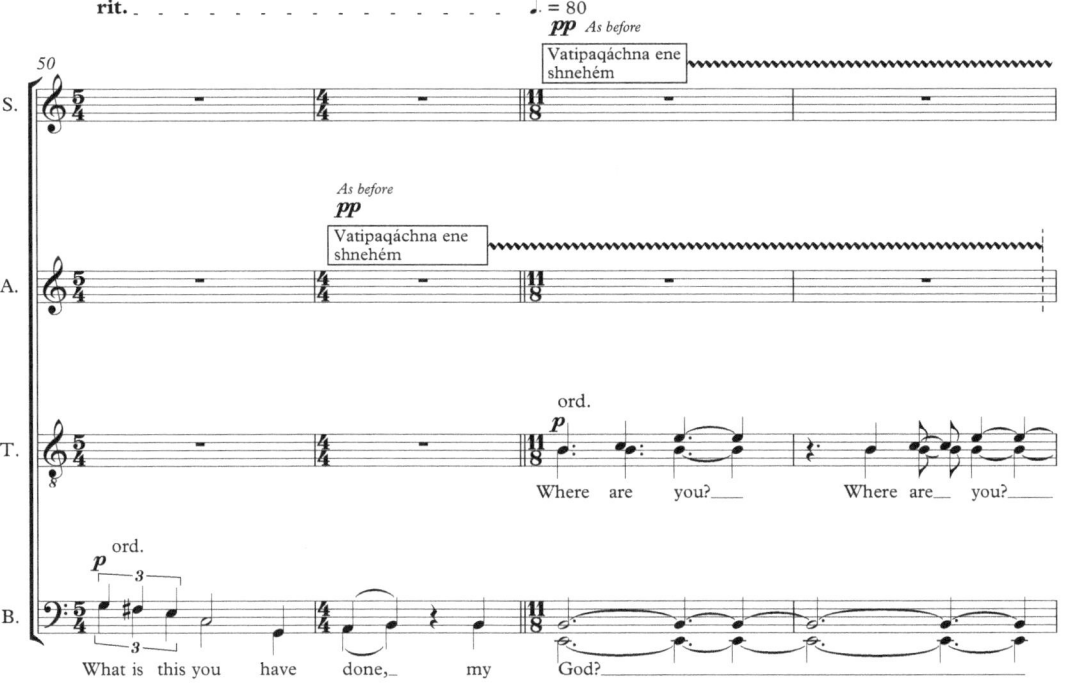

8.1. Jacob Wrestling (Genesis 32.22-32)

Marian Kelsey

Genesis [Gen] 32.22-32 is a richly ambiguous text that recounts a nocturnal wrestling match between the patriarch, Jacob, and a mysterious opponent. It has provided resources for many artists, poets and hymn-writers down the centuries, and continues to do so today. In the first section of this chapter, I introduce the wider biblical context and internal ambiguity of the text, with particular attention to the implications of Jacob's renaming and the enigma of his opponent's identity. Secondly, I explore appropriations of this famous biblical episode in liturgy, literature, and visual art. Finally, I reflect on the collaboration itself, and on how Dominic de Grande found a way to respond, in an intensely personal way, to the creative potential of this biblical episode.

I. Jacob's Re-Naming by a Mysterious Opponent.

The passage that describes Jacob's wrestling match is laconic, but succeeds in prompting a host of questions. Who is Jacob's opponent? Did Jacob leave in triumph, or barely escape with his life? What is the significance of the blessing Jacob wins and the new name he is given? Such questions have led to the passage being interpreted in many different ways in theological, liturgical and artistic explorations. It is a process that may continue with each new reader of the text:

> The same night he got up and took his two wives, his two maids, and his eleven children, and crossed the ford of the Jabbok. He took them and sent them across the stream, and likewise everything that he had. Jacob was left alone; and a man wrestled with him until daybreak. When the man saw that he did not prevail against Jacob, he struck him on the hip socket; and Jacob's hip was put out of joint as he wrestled with him. Then he said, 'Let me go, for the day is breaking.' But Jacob said, 'I will not let you go, unless you bless

me.' So he said to him, 'What is your name?' And he said, 'Jacob.' Then the man said, 'You shall no longer be called Jacob, but Israel, for you have striven with God and with humans, and have prevailed.' Then Jacob asked him, 'Please tell me your name.' But he said, 'Why is it that you ask my name?' And there he blessed him. So Jacob called the place Peniel, saying, 'For I have seen God face to face, and yet my life is preserved.' The sun rose upon him as he passed Penuel, limping because of his hip. Therefore to this day the Israelites do not eat the thigh muscle that is on the hip socket, because he struck Jacob on the hip socket at the thigh muscle.[1]

In the wider context of the passage, Jacob is returning home after years of exile. He had fled long before in fear of his brother, Esau, whom he had tricked out of their father's blessing. Momentarily separated from his family, Jacob is attacked at night by an unknown person. This occurred at the Jabbok, the stream which marked the border of the promised land. Both landscape and plot put Jacob's status as patriarch of God's chosen people under threat.

The dangerous situation in which the patriarch found himself seemed at first to resolve triumphantly. Jacob prevailed over his opponent and received from him both a blessing and a new name. Naming and renaming are significant acts in the Bible: when God renames a person, it implies God's favour.[2] Jacob's grandfather Abram was similarly renamed when God made a covenant with him (Gen 17.5). Moreover, the narrative contains the first biblical occurrence of the name 'Israel'. Jacob is thereby confirmed as the father of the people whose story is to follow. Thus, the biblical narrative reaches a climactic moment in which the father of the nation Israel entered the future land of Israel with the favour of God on his side.

Nonetheless, the initial sense of danger was not entirely banished; in fact, with the coming of morning, it arguably grew. Jacob's unnamed opponent refused to identify himself when Jacob asked, but Jacob reached his own conclusion and declared that he had seen God face to face. Throughout the Bible, seeing God 'face to face' implies great intimacy in the encounter, but also a high degree of risk. As God said to Moses: 'You cannot see my face, for no one shall see me and live' (Exodus 33.20).[3] Had Jacob not released his opponent before the dawn, when the veil of darkness would have been removed, the risk might have been too great for him. Despite Jacob's apparent victory in the struggle, he was left to declare in wonder that his life had been preserved.

---

1   Genesis 32.22-32. All biblical quotations in this chapter are taken from the NRSV translation, unless otherwise noted.
2   Gerhard von Rad, *Genesis: A Commentary*, rev. edn. (London: SCM, 1972), p. 83. By contrast, George Ramsey suggests that names, determined by events or the nature of the one named, are an act of discernment on the part of the one naming. For this he cites, among other texts, Hagar's naming of the Angel of the Lord/God in Gen 16.13 (George W. Ramsey, 'Is Name-Giving an Act of Domination in Genesis 2:23 and Elsewhere?', *The Catholic Biblical Quarterly*, 50 (1988), 24–35).
3   See also Isa 6.5 for the idea that no-one can see God and live (Rad, p. 323; Gordon J. Wenham, *Genesis 16-50*, Word Biblical Commentary (Waco, TX: Word Books, 1994), II, p. 297). Alternatively, in Ezek 20.35, the particular description of encountering God 'face to face' is associated with the threat of unfavourable judgment. For the intimacy of encounters 'face to face', see Exod 33.11, p. 336; also Deut 5.4 and 34.10.

The first impression of God's favour within the story, furthermore, is not without reservation. Both Jacob's new name and the implication of land and descendants appear to be provisional at this stage. Neither the narrator nor the other characters use Jacob's new name in the chapters immediately following. Jacob's children were still known as the sons and daughter of Jacob (Gen 34.3; 34.7). The narrator continues to address him only as Jacob (Gen 33.1; 35.1). Moreover, the assurance of land and descendants was at best obliquely indicated in the opponent's renaming and blessing of Jacob. Explicit assurance does not appear until a second encounter some chapters later, in which God appeared to Jacob at Bethel (Gen 35). Here, the (re-)giving of Jacob's new name was accompanied by an overt promise of the kind traditionally given to the patriarchs: 'I am God Almighty: be fruitful and multiply; a nation and a company of nations shall come from you, and kings shall spring from you. The land that I gave to Abraham and Isaac I will give to you, and I will give the land to your offspring after you' (Gen 35.11-12). The uncertain status of Jacob when leaving the Jabbok, and the sense of his life having been spared despite his prevailing, both provide a contrast to the notes of triumph and reassurance inherent in Jacob's new name.

As it is usually translated, Jacob claims to have seen 'God'. Similarly, the opponent's statement is usually rendered 'you have striven with God'. In each case 'God' is being used to translate the Hebrew *'ĕlōhîm*. This Hebrew word, however, can refer to divine beings more generally, including angels or members of a heavenly council, as seen in Job 1.6: 'One day the heavenly beings (*'ĕlōhîm*) came to present themselves before the LORD.'[4] It is possible that the same sense of 'heavenly being' or 'angel' is meant in Gen 32. From the wording alone it cannot be affirmed definitively, then, that Jacob's opponent is God. The narrator is reticent concerning the identity of Jacob's opponent and only refers to the opponent as a 'man' (Hebrew *'îš*). This is significant; elsewhere in biblical narrative, in every episode of God appearing to one of the patriarchs to assure them of God's favour, God explicitly identifies himself.[5] To Abraham, God said 'I am the LORD who brought you from Ur of the Chaldeans' (Gen 15.7) and 'I am God Almighty' (Gen 17.1). To Isaac, God said 'I am the God of your father Abraham' (Gen 26.24). Even to Jacob, in other passages when it was clearly God who appeared, God said 'I am the LORD, the God of

---

4   Examples of the word referring to other god(s) and their images can be found in Deut 4.7; Judg 16.23-24; 1 Kgs 18.24-25. Examples of the word referring to a divine being other than God are in Ezek 28.2, 6; Gen 6.2-4 (in which the sense is probably 'members of the class *'ĕlōhîm*' rather than 'sons [i.e. children] of God') and Job 1.6, 2.1, 38.7. While all these meanings imply an angel-like character, there is one use in Deut 32.17 in which the word is in parallel to 'demons'. A final meaning of the word is in 1 Sam 28.13 in which it appears to mean shade(s) of the dead. See *The Dictionary of Classical Hebrew*, ed. by David J. A. Clines (Sheffield: Sheffield Academic Press, 1993), I, pp. 277–86.

5   Gen 12.1-3; 15; 17.1-19; 26.24; 28.13-15; 35.9-13 and 46.2-4. Each of these involved an encounter with God, a self-identification formula, and an explicit promise of progeny. Gen 12.1-3, the first promise to Abraham, is the exception to this pattern as it has no self-identification formula. However, as it is the first in the series of those promises which take the form 'I am the God who brought you…', 'I am the God of your father…', it is unsurprising that in the initial encounter with this God there was no incident to which God could refer in order to identify himself. The promises without such descriptive qualification use instead the self-identification 'El-Shaddai'.

Fig. 8.1.1 (Left) Details of: Jean-Baptiste Larrivé, *Lutte de Jacob et de l'Ange* (c. 1920); (Right) Léon-Joseph-Florentin Bonnat, *Jacob Wrestling the Angel* (1876). Although some English translations render the term for Jacob's opponent ('ĕlōhîm) as 'God', the term can also refer to a divine being such as an angel. The narrator simply refers to his opponent as a man (îš). Whereas Larrivé is suggestive regarding the opponent's identity in his sculpture *Lutte de Jacob et de l'Ange* (left), Bonnat heightens the human physicality of the patriarch's opponent in *Jacob Wrestling with the Angels* (right). While his wings belie the opponent's heavenly origins, note his muscular definition and flexion as he wrestles with Adam.

Abraham your father and the God of Isaac' (Gen 28.3) and 'I am God, the God of your father' (Gen 46.3). By contrast, in Gen 32 Jacob's opponent avoids such self-identification even when asked directly by Jacob ('Why is it that you ask my name?').

The mystery figure's refusal to give a name does bear similarities to an angelic appearance elsewhere in the Bible.[6] In Judges 13 the 'Angel of the Lord' appeared to announce the birth of Samson. When Samson's father-to-be asked the angel his name, the angel refused to give it, using the same words as Jacob's opponent (in Hebrew): *lāmmâ ze tišʾal lišmî*. The Angel of the Lord is a puzzling figure who appears occasionally in the Bible. Often, he is not clearly distinguished from God, to the point that it is unclear whether the Angel is merely a messenger or the manifestation of the divine on earth. The Angel of the Lord can speak with divine authority in the first person, but also refers to God in the third person.[7] The danger that is attached to seeing God face to face also attaches to seeing the Angel.[8] The Angel can be referred to as both *malʾāk* (angel) and *ʾĕlōhîm* (God or divine being).[9] The identity of God and the Angel of the Lord therefore appears to be blurred in several places in biblical literature.[10] This is characteristic of Jacob's larger story, occurring in Gen 31.11-13 and Gen 48.15-16. In each of these, Jacob referred to the same figure as 'angel' and 'god/God'.[11] The uncertainty regarding the identity of Jacob's opponent in Gen 32, then, fits with this pattern.

Whatever uncertainty there is concerning the opponent's *identity*, the subsequent narrative demonstrates that *the favour* of God was indeed with Jacob. When the encounter with his estranged brother does occur, it resolves amicably. Jacob fled in fear having stolen a blessing, but returns in peace with a blessing he has won.[12]

---

6   Dmitri M. Slivniak, 'Our God(s) is One: Biblical and the Indeterminacy of Meaning', *Scandinavian Journal of the Old Testament*, 19.1 (2005), 3–23 (p. 10), https://doi.org/10.1080/09018320510032411

7   See Gen 16.7-14 and Gen 22.1-19. Similar blurring of identity is suggested in Gen 31.10-13, which uses 'angel of *God*' (rather than 'Angel of the Lord') in a similar context.

8   See Judg 6.22 concerning Gideon's encounter with the Angel of the Lord. There is some ambiguity in the narrative, as first the Angel of the Lord appeared to Gideon (Judg 6.12), and later what seems to be the same figure is referred to as Yahweh (Judg 6.14 and 6.16). However, when Gideon realised that he has encountered a divine being he cried out for help because he had seen 'the Angel of the Lord face to face' (Judg 6.22). This suggests that the danger attached to seeing a divine figure applies both to God in person and to the Angel of the Lord.

9   Gen 48.15-16.

10 In addition to the passages already referenced, there is also Exod 3.1-6, Judg 6.19-23 and Judg 13.3-22, and implicitly in Exod 23.20-24 and Josh 13-15 (see discussion in Camilla Hélena von Heijne, *The Messenger of the Lord in Early Jewish Interpretations of Genesis*, Beihefte Zur Zeitschrift Für Die Alttestamentliche Wissenschaft, Bd. 412 (Berlin: Walter De Gruyter, 2010), pp. 49–113).

11 There is also ambiguity elsewhere in the Bible concerning the divine figures whom Jacob encounters. Hosea 12:5 reads: 'He [Jacob] strove with the angel and prevailed/he wept and sought his favour/ he met him at Bethel/and there he spoke with him.' The phrase 'he met him at Bethel' can only refer to Jacob and the angel from earlier in the verse. This might imply that Jacob's experiences at Bethel, which in the Genesis accounts are indisputably encounters with God, are understood by the author of Hosea to be encounters with an angel. This fluidity of identity even within the various biblical accounts is reminiscent of the passage in Gen 31.11-13 in which the '*angel* of God' appears to Jacob and declares 'I am the *God* of Bethel'. Discussion of this issue can be found in von Heijne, *The Messenger of the Lord*, 108–10.

12 This has led Hamori to suggest that the blessing stolen under a false name in Gen 27.1-45 was thus ratified by the blessing given under Jacob's true name in Gen 32.23-33 (Esther Hamori, *'When Gods*

Similarly, although the promise of land and descendants is implicit at best in Gen 32, later chapters confirm it. In Gen 35, God appears to Jacob at Bethel for a second time in the patriarch's life, reaffirming Jacob's new name with an explicit promise of land and descendants. Directly afterwards, Rachel gives birth to Benjamin, Jacob's twelfth and last son. Subsequently, the focus of the biblical narrative shifts from Jacob the patriarch to his twelve sons, the fathers of the twelve tribes of Israel.

II. Appropriations of Jacob's Wrestling in Art and Worship

Jacob's encounter with his divine opponent has been the inspiration for many personal and collective reinterpretations of the struggle. In the Revised Common Lectionary, it is set alongside Psalm 17.1-7, 15, in which the psalmist asserts that, were God to visit him by night and test him, no wickedness would be found in him. The psalmist goes on: 'As for me, I shall behold your face in righteousness; when I awake I shall be satisfied, beholding your likeness' (Psalm 17.15) The juxtaposition of these two passages suggests an interpretation of Gen 32 in which the encounter was intended as a spiritual trial: in granting Jacob a new name and a blessing, God acknowledged that he has passed the test. The liturgical appropriation implies that, like Jacob, those who are righteous will come through their own trials, adversities and temptations, and when they stand before God will be enriched rather than endangered by the encounter. The Lectionary also places Gen 32 alongside the parable of the unjust judge (Luke 18.1-8). In this passage, an analogy is established between a widow's pleas for justice from an unjust judge and someone praying to God for justice. The use of an unjust judge in the place of God in the analogy is quite as startling as the thought of God attacking his chosen patriarch. Yet just as Jacob prevailed over his opponent, so the widow prevailed against the judge. In both of the texts, it is the characters' persistence — Jacob refusing to release the opponent, and the widow refusing to drop her case — which is eventually rewarded. In the liturgy, then, the congregation is encouraged to take Jacob, as well as the widow, as a model of persistence in both prayer and their lives of faith. In an eighteenth-century hymn by John Newton, for example, the congregation sing: 'Lord, I cannot let Thee go, / Till a blessing Thou bestow: / Do not turn away Thy face, / Mine's an urgent, pressing case.'[13]

Were Men': *The Embodied God in Biblical and Near Eastern Literature*, Beihefte Zur Zeitschrift Für Die Alttestamentliche Wissenschaft, Bd. 384 (Berlin: Walter De Gruyter, 2008), pp. 101–02). However, it is important to point out that Jacob was certainly not devoid of God's favour until the Jabbok incident. This is demonstrated by God's protection of Jacob while he was in Laban's house (Gen 31.3, 11-13). Rather, it seems that Isaac's promise was ratified by Jacob's first encounter with God at Bethel. Thus, the early conflict between Jacob and Esau reached its climax when Jacob took Esau's blessing while in a disguised identity, and then the blessing was confirmed by God at Bethel. Similarly, the rivalry between Jacob and Laban and the danger of returning to his brother reached a climax when Jacob demanded a blessing from a disguised opponent (an *'ĕlōhîm* in the form of *'îš*). Then, the hinted-at promise was again confirmed by God in a second encounter at Bethel.

13 *The Methodist Hymnal* (New York and Cincinnati, OH: The Methodist Book Concern, 1905), pp. 410–11.

Fig. 8.1.2 (Left to Right) Details of: (Ps 17.1-7, 15) Unknown artist, *Agony in the Garden* (15th c.); (Lk 18.1-8) John Everett Millais, *The Unjust Judge and the Importunate Widow* (1865). 1921. In the Revised Common Lectionary, the narrative of Jacob wrestling with the divine figure (Gen 32.22-32) is set alongside a prayer for deliverance (Ps 17.1-7, 15) and the parable of the unjust judge (Lk 18.1-8). After the Psalmist invites God to 'try my heart' and 'visit me by night' (Ps 17.3), he writes 'as for me, I shall behold your face in righteousness; when I awake I shall be satisfied, beholding your likeness' (v. 15). In the parable, the widow's persistent petitioning leads to the unjust judge finally deciding 'I will grant her justice' (Lk 18.5). Resonances in these pairings suggest Jacob's encounter is a spiritual trial, where God acknowledges his persistence with a new name and blessing. For Christians, Jacob's struggle has become a model for wrestling with God in faithfulness and prayer.

In several literary explorations of the text as well, Jacob is presented as a model for readers. Jones Very's 'Jacob Wrestling with the Angel' applies Jacob's experience to the religious lives of contemporary readers.[14] After retelling the story, the poem goes on:

…

Deem not that to those ancient times belong
The wonders told in history, and in song;
Men may with angels now, as then, prevail;
Too oft, alas! they in the contest fail.
Their blessed help is not from man withdrawn,
Contend thou with the angel till the dawn;
A blessing he to earth for thee doth bring,
Then back to heaven again his flight will wing.

Jacob's struggle with God is also appropriated as a metaphor for broader descriptions of human struggles with spiritual and emotional crises, as depicted in Rainer Maria Rilke's 'Der Schauende' [The Beholder] and Gerard Manley Hopkins' 'Carrion Comfort'.[15] Hopkins' poem captures the sense of danger in the biblical text, and places the narrator of the poem side by side with Jacob in wrestling their demons and their gods:

Not, I'll not, carrion comfort, Despair, not feast on thee;
Not untwist — slack they may be — these last strands of man
In me ór, most weary, cry *I can no more*. I can;
Can something, hope, wish day come, not choose not to be.
But ah, but O thou terrible, why wouldst thou rude on me
Thy wring-world right foot rock? lay a lionlimb against me? scan
With darksome devouring eyes my bruisèd bones? and fan,
O in turns of tempest, me heaped there; me frantic to avoid thee and flee?

Why? That my chaff might fly; my grain lie, sheer and clear.
Nay in all that toil, that coil, since (seems) I kissed the rod,
Hand rather, my heart lo! lapped strength, stole joy, would laugh, chéer.
Cheer whom though? the hero whose heaven-handling flung me, fóot tród
Me? or me that fought him? O which one? is it each one? That night, that year
Of now done darkness I wretch lay wrestling with (my God!) my God.

---

14 Jones Very, 'Jacob Wrestling with the Angel', cited in *Chapters into Verse: Poetry in English Inspired by the Bible*, ed. by Robert Atwan and Laurance Wieder, 2 vols. (Oxford: Oxford University Press, 1993), I, p. 96.

15 For Rilke's poem, see Rainer Maria Rilke, *Das Buch der Bilder*, 2nd edn (Berlin: Axel Junker Verlag, 1906), pp. 151–54. For Hopkins' poem, see Gerard Manley Hopkins, *The Poems of Gerard Manley Hopkins*, ed. by William Henry Gardner and N. H. MacKenzie (Oxford: Oxford University Press, 1967), p. 99.

Hopkins' poem exploits the dramatic dénouement of the biblical narrative. With the coming of morning, the poet, like Jacob, draws the startling conclusion that he has been struggling with God.

Similarly, Emily Dickinson's poem 'A Little East of Jordan' ends with the revelation (at least in Jacob's mind) that his opponent was God.[16] However, Dickinson imitates the biblical narrator's reticence in otherwise referring to the opponent as an angel. In sharp contrast to Hopkins' poem, however, the tone of 'A little East of Jordan' is light and playful. The Angel wishes to leave for breakfast, and Jacob is left bewildered rather than in fear. The whole encounter is cast as a poet's retelling of a story, rather than as intense personal reliving of the experience (Hopkins), or as the moralizing self-application urged by Very:

> A little East of Jordan,
> Evangelists record,
> A Gymnast and an Angel
> Did wrestle long and hard —
>
> Till morning touching mountain —
> And Jacob, waxing strong,
> The Angel begged permission
> To Breakfast — to return!
>
> Not so, said cunning Jacob!
> 'I will not let thee go
> Except thou bless me' — Stranger!
> The which acceded to —
>
> Light swung the silver fleeces
> 'Peniel' Hills beyond,
> And the bewildered Gymnast
> Found he had worsted God!

Although the struggle between Jacob and his opponent is depicted frequently in visual art, the tendency towards personal application evident in liturgical and poetic explorations is almost entirely absent. Nonetheless, the variety of ways in which artists have appropriated the biblical account is clear. Some of the modern, abstract portrayals are full of jarring lines and colours; these seem intended to reflect the confusion and ambiguity of the biblical account. More often, however, the artist has explored the passage by choosing between the various possible understandings of the text.

---

16 Atwan and Wieder, *Chapters into Verse*, pp. 95–96.

136 *Annunciations*

Fig. 8.1.3 Left: Details of: Alexander Louis Leloir, *Jacob Wrestling with the Angel* (1865); Right: Rembrandt, *Jacob Wrestling with the Angel* (c. 1659). Jacob's encounter with the angel is diversely portrayed in art. A few painters and sculptors portray a very physical, forceful fight. Leloir's *Jacob Wrestling with the Angel* (1865) falls in this category (left). This struggle reflects the initial sense that Jacob's encounter is fraught with danger. During the struggle, it is far from clear that it will end in blessing. In other artistic portrayals, such as Renoir's 1695 painting *Jacob Wrestling with the Angel* (c. 1659), the angel is shown with a serene expression as if the struggle is not taxing.

Visual art, perhaps unavoidably, resolves the ambiguity concerning the identity of the opponent, most often depicted straightforwardly as an angel. Given the practical and theological difficulties of representing God, this is unsurprising and does not necessarily constitute an interpretive decision either way. There is more variety in the portrayal of the wrestling itself. A few painters and sculptors portray a physical, forceful fight, such as Alexander Louis Leloir in *Jacob Wrestling with the Angel* and Jean Larrivé in *Lutte de Jacob et de l'Ange*. This reflects the initial sense of danger in the biblical narrative, when, during the struggle, it is far from clear that it will end in blessing, and the patriarch seems truly under threat. In other artistic portrayals, including Rembrandt's *Jacob Wrestling with the Angel*, the angel is shown with a serene expression, as if the struggle is not taxing. In other cases, the visual representation seems to reflect discomfort at the thought of a divine or angelic person being overpowered by a man, for example in Gustave Doré's *Jacob Wrestling with the Angel*, in which the angel calmly holds at arm's length a seemingly straining Jacob. The biblical narrative itself insists, nonetheless, that the opponent had no difficulty in giving Jacob a serious injury as a memento of their fight, despite having pleaded for release. The serenity of the angel in these portrayals might therefore reflect the precariousness of the situation, as yet unrealized by Jacob. It is noticeable that in numerous artistic representations of the scene the 'struggle' looks more like an embrace. These representations include the previously mentioned Rembrandt, Johann Friedrich Glocker's *Kampf Jakobs mit dem Engel*, and depictions of the scene in the Haggadah shel Pesaḥ or the 'Sister Haggadah' in the British Library, and the mosaics of the Palatine Chapel in Palermo. In such depictions, the multiple layers of the biblical account have arguably found their fullest visual expression. The physical struggle remains, with all the danger that it connotes. However, the audience is also presented with the aftermath beyond the events of Gen 32. The embrace between angel and Jacob, between divine favour and human strength, communicates Jacob's intimacy with God and the divine protection he experienced through the course of his life.

III. The TheoArtistry Collaboration

When de Grande and I first spoke about the passage, he was interested in the Hebrew text. The Hebrew contains various puns and wordplays that rarely come across in translation, and we discussed the possibility of using some Hebrew in the choral piece. Unfortunately, it was quite difficult for de Grande to write a score using a language unfamiliar to him. After wrestling with the problem for some weeks, de Grande instead decided to set the choral piece in the context of a grandmother telling the story of Jacob to her grandchild at bedtime. He integrated a solo human whistle into the piece, as one of his memories of his own grandmother is of her whistling. Such personal application of the biblical text was pleasing as it fits with how artists and musicians have interpreted it down the centuries. The slightly unearthly quality of a whistle also provides an atmospheric backdrop to the account of a mysterious nocturnal encounter.

De Grande used Dickinson's poem as the basis of the words of the choral piece. The story starts gradually and continues to the crucial moment at which the 'Angel', as Dickinson introduces him, blesses Jacob. At this point, in a sudden burst of voices, de Grande switches to the biblical text and the opponent's demand that Jacob release him as dawn is breaking. The outburst from the whole choir at once cuts sharply through the gentle prose of Dickinson, evoking the sense of danger that exists in the biblical text, yet is not prominent in Dickinson's poem. It marks the turning point in the story from Jacob's apparent overpowering of his opponent to the realization of the true nature of the situation. It is as if the opponent himself has stepped out of the piece and spoken directly to the listeners. Afterwards, de Grande returns to the words of Dickinson and her gentler tone. The movement back to the poem seems to reflect the aftermath of the encounter in the Bible, where only Jacob is aware of the nocturnal events and their significance. For Jacob, however, the encounter shapes his life. The piece ends by softly musing on Jacob's realization that the opponent he has fought is none other than God.

Gen 32 provides deep resources for theological and artistic exploration. It is the first appearance in biblical narrative of the name 'Israel'. It comes at the moment when the ancestors of that nation are entering the land promised to them. The story thereby contains the first steps in the span of Judeo-Christian history which follows. At the same time, the multi-layered uncertainties of the passage — danger or blessing, wrestling or embrace, God or angel — resist assimilation into any smooth recounting of the tale. Hence, the passage has been appropriated in many different ways in liturgy, literature and art. It has especially lent itself to personal re-application. When faced with a confusing and uncertain situation, Jacob stubbornly persisted in the pursuit of a blessing. Like Jacob, those in search of God's blessing often struggle with ambiguous or elusive experiences. They, too, may find resolve through clinging on, even when that to which they cling is trying its best to escape. De Grande's choral piece continues in the tradition of personal applications of the story, while also bringing out much of the richness of a text that resists simplistic interpretation. Hopefully, there will be many more explorations to come.

List of Illustrations

8.1.1 Details of: Jean-Baptiste Larrivé, *Lutte de Jacob et de l'Ange* (c. 1920), stucco and plaster, Museum of Fine Arts of Lyon, Lyon, Wikimedia, https://commons.wikimedia.org/wiki/File:Jean_Larriv%C3%A9_-_Lutte_de_Jacob_et_de_l%27Ange_-_stuc_et_pl%C3%A2tre_(1920)_01.jpg, CCA-SA 4.0, photo by Scailyna; Léon-Joseph-Florentin Bonnat, *Jacob Wrestling the Angel* (1876), pencil and black chalk on paper, Dahesh Museum of Art, New York, USA, Wikimedia, https://commons.wikimedia.org/wiki/File:Jacob_Wrestling_with_the_Angel_by_Leon_Bonnat.jpg, public domain. — 130

8.1.2 Details of: (Ps 17.1-7, 15) Unknown artist, *Agony in the Garden* (15th c.), fresco, Saint Michael Church, Veringenstadt, Germany, Wikimedia, https://commons.wikimedia.org/wiki/File:Veringendorf_St._Michael_Gethsemane-Szene_Detail.jpg, CCA-SA 3.0 Unported, photo by Roman Eisele; (Gen 32.22-32) Giulio Benso, *Jacob Wrestling with the Angel* (1601–1608), pen and brown ink with brush and brown wash over traces of black chalk, Metropolitan Museum of Art, New York, USA, Wikimedia, https://commons.wikimedia.org/wiki/File:Jacob_Wrestling_with_the_Angel_MET_DP807858.jpg, CC0 1.0, gift of Harry G. Friedman, 1964; (Lk 18.1-8) John Everett Millais, *The Unjust Judge and the Importunate Widow* (The Parables of Our Lord and Saviour Jesus Christ) (1865), wood engraving with proof on India paper, Metropolitan Museum of Art, New York, USA, Wikimedia, https://commons.wikimedia.org/wiki/File:The_Unjust_Judge_and_the_Importunate_Widow_(The_Parables_of_Our_Lord_and_Saviour_Jesus_Christ)_MET_DP835791.jpg, CC0 1.0, Rogers Fund. — 133

8.1.3 Details of: Alexander Louis Leloir, *Jacob Wrestling with the Angel* (1865), oil on canvas, Musee des Beaux-Arts, Clermont-Ferrand, France, Wikimedia, https://commons.wikimedia.org/wiki/File:Leloir_-_Jacob_Wrestling_with_the_Angel.jpg, public domain; Rembrandt, *Jacob Wrestling with the Angel* (c. 1659), oil on canvas, Gemäldegalerie, Staatliche Museen zu Berlin, Berlin, Wikimedia, https://commons.wikimedia.org/wiki/File:Rembrandt_-_Jacob_Wrestling_with_the_Angel_-_Google_Art_Project.jpg, public domain. — 136

8.2. Composer's Reflections

Dominic de Grande

I have collaborated on projects with choreographers, actors, lyricists and poets, other composers, and musicians of all ages and backgrounds. Yet, I have never collaborated with a theologian. As a teetering agnostic, there was something special about this collaboration from the start. In particular one question arose: what part (if any) would my own sense of religiosity, or lack thereof, have to play in this project?

As a young child, neither of my parents were musicians but they did have a love of music. Both grounded me in a musical tradition that emphasized the importance of lyrical content, which included the works of Leonard Cohen, Paul Simon, Bob Dylan: three men of Jewish heritage who have all made countless allusions to the New and Old Testaments. I remember my mother waking me in the middle of the night to listen to the repeated phrase *'with God on their side'*, which dovetailed every verse: these were amongst my first lessons in lyrical criticism and consciousness. In my mid-teens, I found a recording of choral classics belonging to my mother, which included Wolfgang Amadeus Mozart, Johann Sebastian Bach, Gabriel Fauré, and Charles Gounod, amongst others. For the first time, I discovered music that could match the splendour, the beauty, the dignity and the embrace, which, up until that point, I had found in the lyrical allusions of singer-song-writers such as those mentioned above. Throughout my compositional career, I have sought to include the lyrics and the music that changed my life.

My background in lyrics and narrative allusions inspired my involvement in the TheoArtistry project. It presented an opportunity to form a partnership with someone who could influence and nourish the lyrical content in my compositions. In a way, the TheoArtistry collaboration started before the first meeting at St Andrews. Concern for what was expected of me, how religion was to figure in the project, and the powerful reputation of St Andrews were all considerations leading up to the first official meeting. This meeting was crammed with seminars, meetings, lectures and conversations. It was exhausting, intriguing and inspiring, and the power of this initial event perhaps overawed my first attempts to find my compositional feet.

On the first day, my theologian-partner, Marian Kelsey, provided me with a document entitled 'Jacob Wrestling: Genesis 32.22-32', which contained information about the biblical context, cultural background, and a section dedicated to 'Possibilities for Musical Exploration'. It also included examples of how the story had inspired poets, artists and musicians throughout history. Initially, the goal was to find a suitable text — whether from the material provided or by composing new words. The original Hebrew material immediately sparked my interest so Kelsey suggested YouTube links for the purposes of aiding pronunciation; she also provided me with a word-by-word breakdown of the literal and poetic translation. In my mind's ear, I could hear complex sounds, antiphony and polyphony alike, multiple time signatures and syncopated rhythms. The enjoyment of finding a musical counterpart, manifested in the freshness of this unfamiliar language, was palpable.

However, allocating sufficient space to each idea proved frustrating. What was wrong? There seemed to be two things inhibiting the flow of composition. First, the specified duration of the piece (three minutes). Typically, my pieces last under ten minutes. Secondly, I felt committed to the high standard demanded by the first meeting. How was I going to achieve this in three minutes? I realized that whilst my initial ideas might have worked on another occasion, they simply were not the sounds suggested to me by the text in this context, and I began to pare away what I considered unnecessary.

During our final Skype interview, I voiced my concerns about the piece and my need for a new approach. I explored Kelsey's motivations for the project: taking theology out of an academic context and into a musical one. She also highlighted a salient attribute about Jacob's struggle: namely, the ambiguity of the protagonists' identity and how that had inspired wonderful interactions and responses in art and literature. I found this very encouraging, and I took the least convoluted poem that Marian had included in her original document ('A little East of Jordan' by Emily Dickinson) and interpolated a small fragment from the original biblical text in English ('Let me go, for the day is breaking'), which summed up the energy of the story in a clear and honest way.

I struggled with many starts and stops (the irony of wrestling with a narrative about wrestling was not lost on me). I began to treat the words more gently and let them guide the music, I tried to help the narrative '*speak*' itself. I began to realise that I needed to develop a deeper and more personal relationship with the text, something that I could feel invested in. The turning point for me came when I thought about my grandmother who was religious and the way she was full of music and stories. She would improvise bedtime stories and I would often have to wake her for conclusions that seldom came. I realized that it was not only the words working with the music but feeling comfortable with the numinous context that bound them together. It turns out that my own sense of religiosity was found through the memory of my grandmother.

The harmonic underpinning of this piece consists of three chords: (1) A minor 7/11. (2) G major 7/9 and D major 7. The first three stanzas of the poem spell out the notes of each of these chords by descending or ascending melodically through them. I used this musical idea to create a homogenous and comfortable texture, allowing the narrative to remain prominent. The departure from this harmonic language occurs with the interpolated words 'Let me go for the day is breaking.' The first three syllables make use of the three chords mentioned above, but the remaining six syllables introduce six new chords. This section is particularly important, and, just as the words are interpolated, so the harmonies and dynamic range hopefully provide the listener with a sense of otherness. The final stanza makes melodic use of the initial three chords as if to consolidate and recapitulate their fundamental character.

The music is not intended to represent the meaning of the text. For example, there is little word painting. The music is there to help frame the meaning of the poem in a way that a declamation of it cannot, whilst still allowing the words narrative supremacy. My interests were concerned with the absorption of the narrative. With this in mind, it was important to use simple cyclical juxtapositions of repeating chords and melodies with sprinklings of dissonance. I hope that listeners will take the time to think about the title, as it encapsulates the soul of my piece. If the listener can imagine or remember the joy of being young and somewhere between sleep and wakefulness in a summer sunset that stains the edges of the curtains with a halo of light whilst your grandmother tells you stories, then he or she will have a sense of my intentions.

The piece is bookended by a vocalization harmonized by human whistling. The beginning and end had to be simple to allow the listener a moment of meditation once the piece had finished. Throughout, the whistling can be heard at moments to depart and compliment the mechanics of the sung melody. At other times they are in unison. Perhaps as representation, this compositional aspect came closest to my experiences of introspection on the TheoArtistry program — inflections of the numinous reveal themselves to be sometimes consonant and sometimes indivisible with, or invisible to, my perceptions of my life. For this reason, I wanted the melody lines of the voice and the whistle to soar with and into one another almost above the composition itself.

 Dominic de Grande, 'Whilst falling asleep, Savta told me of Jacob', in *Annunciations: Sacred Music for the 21st Century*, St Salvator's Chapel Choir and Sean Heath, cond. by Tom Wilkinson (Sanctiandree, SAND0006, 2018), © 2017 University of St Andrews. Track 08. Duration: 4.10.
https://doi.org/10.11647/OBP.0172.32

'Whilst falling asleep, Savta told me of Jacob'

Dominic de Grande

9.1. Setting Fire to Music: Theological and Aesthetic Approaches (Exodus 3)

Rebekah Dyer

When the Institute for Theology, Imagination and the Arts (ITIA) circulated a call for theologians to participate in a new collaborative initiative with composers, I could not resist the prospect of a 'TheoArtistic' approach to the burning bush of Exodus [Exod] 3. The self-revelation of God through fire represents a particular area of interest in my research, which explores the multifaceted interpretations of fire in biblical and contemporary experience. The dramatic first encounter between God and Moses never stopped flickering away in the back of my mind during the period of my doctoral research.[1] The TheoArtistry Theologian-Composer Partnerships invited me to consider the passage anew: to open up my own imagination to fresh insights and interpretative possibilities of Exod 3. Firstly, this chapter outlines the context of Moses' encounter with God in the burning bush, before offering some reflections on the challenges of representing the burning bush in music, and the method that emerged as a result. I discuss how drawing upon experiential 'ways of knowing' helped forge a more integrative approach, shaping the collaboration as a whole and opening up new creative and theological possibilities.[2] I then examine how composer Kerensa Briggs — my TheoArtistry partner — characterizes God and Moses in her choral piece to create and explore theological meaning. Finally, this chapter concludes with suggestions as to how experiential approaches to the text might be cultivated in future artistic responses to Exod 3.

---

1   Rebekah M. Dyer, 'Multivalence, Liminality, and the Theological Imagination: Contextualising the Image of Fire for Contemporary Christian Practice' (unpublished doctoral thesis, University of St Andrews, 2018), http://hdl.handle.net/10023/16452.
2   Terminology derived from Hui Niu Wilcox, 'Embodied Ways of Knowing, Pedagogies, and Social Justice: Inclusive Science and Beyond', *NWSA Journal*, 21 (2009), 104–20.

I. Finding God in the Flames

Both narratively and theologically, the burning bush constitutes much more than a single miraculous incident in the wilderness. It is but one of many wonders told in the book of Exodus, which is an account of human conflict, treachery, divine judgement, salvation, and survival. At this point in the biblical narrative, the Hebrew people are enduring forced labour in Egypt. The days of their forefathers, whose lives were shaped by God, seem to be long past. Nothing short of divine intervention will bring them relief from this oppression; yet God seems ignorant of their suffering. The descendants of Abraham, Isaac, and Jacob appear to have been forgotten by the deity, while their Egyptian slave-masters mark even infants for death. Into the bleakness of Hebrew captivity, Moses is born. Saved from death by the courage of two Hebrew midwives, and a second time by the ingenuity of his mother, the infant Moses is found and adopted by the Pharaoh's daughter. He is raised in the safety and luxury of the royal household. Yet, confronted by the oppression of his kinsfolk as an adult, Moses perpetrates the murder of an Egyptian slave-master. Fearing for his life, Moses flees to Midian. He settles among a foreign tribe, marries Zipporah, and earns his keep by tending to his father-in-law's flock.

When Moses stumbles upon an inexplicable fire in the wilderness, he courts death yet again. To be so near a deity is to risk being struck down by divine power; but, like the burning bush, Moses is not consumed. Instead, God speaks from the flames. Moses is called by name and charged with leading the Hebrews out of captivity. What follows is a conversation — or a negotiation — in which Moses hesitantly accepts his role in the redemption of his people. He is a fugitive, an exile, a criminal. How will his testimony of a strange deity in the desert possibly convince the king of Egypt? And how can he speak on behalf of the Hebrews when he once lived as an Egyptian royal, complicit in their oppression? Yet God bestows authority upon Moses as a divinely-appointed envoy to the Pharaoh. Moses asks for the name of the one who sends him. 'I am that I am,' God responds. Then, for the first time in the biblical narrative, God discloses the divine name, Yahweh (YHWH). This is a cosmic moment of intimacy at the edge of the wilderness. The personal and geographical isolation of Moses from other human beings only heightens the immediacy of his encounter with the divine. In the burning bush, God seems so overwhelmingly *present* — and yet the form of his presence is inexplicable and paradoxical. God, later called 'consuming fire' (Hebrews 12.29), here appears in fire which does not consume. For Moses, the long-absent deity of his ancestors is almost within reach, yet unapproachably holy.

Briggs was particularly interested in capturing the emotional complexity of Exod 3. As with many biblical texts, Exod 3 is laden with theological and interpersonal tensions. Questions about Moses' conflicted identity, the nature of God, the suffering of the Hebrews, and the potentially consuming power of divine presence each offered compelling avenues for musical exploration. We explored these tensions first through a narrative approach to the text, situating the passage within the broader biblical account of the life of Moses and the history of Israel. This gave us a starting point for tracing thematic and artistic possibilities, which we then considered in dialogue with aspects of the imagery, typology, and reception history. Ongoing conversations gave us the opportunity to articulate the themes and ideas we saw emerging at each stage of the composition. As the work came together, it became clear that even the most practical of musical decisions could have unanticipated theological implications. The decision to include a portrayal of the burning bush presented a particular compositional challenge, one that required the integration of musical, experiential, and theological approaches. Likewise, the characterization of God and Moses required making particular theological, as well as musical, choices. In this way, Briggs' composition does not present its source text passively, but actively interprets and explores theological meaning.

Fig. 9.1.1 Rebekah Dyer, *Exodus — 1 — Beach Fire* (2017). A beach bonfire kindled in celebration of the TheoArtistry Composers' Scheme in St Andrews.

II. Re-Imagining the Burning Bush for Music

There is no single starting point for a creative response to a biblical passage — except, perhaps, the text itself. A creative response need not precisely correspond to the narrative; Briggs and I proceeded with the understanding that any representation of Exod 3 should not be at the cost of imaginative discourse. At the same time, there were certain elements of the passage which Briggs wished to portray: namely, the dialogue between God and Moses, and the flames of the burning bush. We both felt that the burning bush contained a great depth of creative and theological potential and should be included, if possible, within the final composition. However, communicating the presence of fire through choral music would not be a straightforward task.

The portrayal of fire was, in some ways, the linchpin of our collaborative interest. It was a creative and theological experiment which compelled us to examine how we understood fire with regard to our respective fields. It was only in preparing for the Composers' Scheme that I realized I had formerly conceived of the burning bush as a primarily visual image. Grappling with the question of how fire might be portrayed in music, I became acutely aware of my reliance on the visual imagination as the basis for my analysis of Exod 3. This quickly proved insufficient for conceptualizing fire within a non-visual medium. Another approach was required — alternative 'ways of knowing' based on more than what existed in my mind's eye.

A solution arose from an experience of an entirely different art form: fire spinning. Fire spinning is a performance art that involves manipulating a burning staff (or other apparatus) to create whirling movements with the flame. It has associations with the circus arts, along with other fire-based performance skills such as fire breathing and fire juggling. In these arts, fire is drawn close to the body, engendering a responsive relationship between the performer and the flames. The motion of the flame is determined by bodily movements that are governed, in turn, by the momentum of the burning staff. It is an intimate and intensely physical experience of fire.

Fire spinning, like dance, is guided by the sensations of the body. The performer maintains near-continuous movement to prevent the flames blooming to a treacherous scale. The fire behaves as though it has a life of its own, and can burn in unpredictable ways. The ever-changing volume and direction of the flames results in a shifting centre of gravity which must be accommodated by the body. The performer must decide whether to embrace the fire's effect on their movement or to try to work against it. With each motion, the flames roil through the air. The performer is enfolded by heat. Usually, there is little smoke, but the smell from the burning paraffin can be overwhelming. The entire body is involved in the experiential knowledge of fire.

The mind's eye may conjure an image of light and heat but reduce — or forget entirely — the sensory impact of the smell, movement, and sound of a flickering flame. Privileging the non-visual aspects of fire worked as a corrective to the limitations in

Fig. 9.1.2 Rebekah Dyer, *Exodus — 2 — Fire Spinning* (2013). In fire performance art, there is a reciprocal relationship between fire and the body.

my initial approach. I took my experience of fire spinning as a prompt for thinking more holistically about the nature and behaviour of fire. By incorporating physical 'ways of knowing' into our partnership, Briggs and I were able to utilize an additional resource by which to address the creative and theological conceptualization of the burning bush.

In seeking to portray fire in music, our collaborative methodology evolved like this:

1. Within the partnership, we agreed on a mutual goal: to represent the burning bush in the final composition.
2. An apparent limitation was identified. How could fire be represented in musical performance without visual cues?
3. Experiential forms of knowledge were integrated into the thought process and applied to theological aspects of the research (i.e. narrative and textual analysis; artistic and theological implications of the imagery, etc.).
4. These experiential perspectives were articulated to the composer through academic writing and discussion.
5. The composer allowed these perspectives to inform the process of composition.
6. In concert, the audience encounters a portrayal of the burning bush through sensory and aesthetic experience.

Participation in the arts gives rise to ways of thinking and feeling which integrate the physical, intellectual, and spiritual dimensions of the self.[3] In terms of the *Exodus III* composition, experiential knowledge helped overcome barriers in the way certain ideas were being conceptualized intellectually. Specifically, a physical understanding of fire generated fresh ideas for a musical portrayal based on experience of fire performance art. This improvised methodology perhaps falls into A. Abby Knoblauch's definition of 'embodied rhetoric,' in that it involved 'a purposeful decision to include embodied knowledge […] as forms of meaning making' during the project.[4] Presented through academic forms of writing and analysis, embodied knowledge became integrated into more traditionally 'scholarly' approaches to the text. Moreover, embodied ways of knowing revealed a route to theological understanding:

> […] fire is an intensely multi-sensory experience. Not only do we see, hear, feel it; it provokes an emotional response. Just as fire is ungraspable, so is God; so, too, is music. The three are compatible, even complementary, concepts. Exploring their complementarity is an act of theology — whether that exploration is conducted in writing, music, or both.[5]

Using experiential knowledge of fire as a starting point, Briggs and I discussed how the music could evoke an impression of the burning bush in the audience's imagination. In particular, the sounds and rhythms of fire took precedence as characteristics that might be captured by the music. We took time to consider the correspondence between sound and movement. Volume could be suggestive of scale: fire blazing through the air booms, while a stable fire crackles and single flames whisper. During *Exodus III*, the burning bush is represented through steady, repetitive sequences given to the organ part. The piece opens with the organ, and so the portrayal of fire provides the entry point into this divine-human interaction — appropriately enough, since the burning bush constitutes the meeting point of the dialogue partners. The rise and fall of musical notes signal the rise and fall of flames. Variations in volume and rhythm suggest fluctuations in intensity as the burning bush continues to burn throughout the theophany.

Within Briggs' composition, no direct mention is ever made of the burning bush. Yet fire generates its own sense of presence, as anyone who has enjoyed the welcoming flicker of a hearth may attest. It draws attention, not only as a source of potential danger but as a point of fascination, aesthetic pleasure, or reverie. Likewise, in *Exodus III*, the organ is given time to establish itself in the mind of the audience, which must take note of this unique voice. As the music progresses, the organ plays for several bars between the choir vocals, carving out space in the midst of the conversation. Like fire, the organ generates its own, distinctive presence within the piece.

Just as the organ is more than an accompaniment in the music, so the burning bush is more than a background feature of Exod 3. It is integral to this divine self-disclosure:

---

[3] Jeremy Begbie, 'Introduction', in *Sounding the Depths: Theology Through the Arts*, ed. by Jeremy Begbie (London: SCM Press, 2002), pp. 1–13 (p. 7).

[4] A. Abby Knoblauch, 'Bodies of Knowledge', *Composition Studies*, 40.2 (2012), 50–65 (p. 52).

[5] Excerpt from research by the author, presented within the Composers' Scheme partnership (unpublished, 2016).

not only as the means by which God speaks, but also as a manifestation of God's presence on earth. It is both context and content; backdrop and mouthpiece. As an image for divine presence, fire offers a tangible example of something powerful, elusive, and other-than-human. It changes everything it touches and moves with a will of its own. Fire never stands still as it burns, yet always remains fire. Like God, its nature remains constant.

The consistency of divine presence is captured through the portrayal of the burning bush in 'Exodus III'. Through the organ music, the burning bush is present throughout the piece. Though the vocals may fall silent, waiting or listening, the organ's reminder of divine presence is continuous. At times, the organ's complexity falls away to privilege the vocals, notably the soprano and baritone solos — but its music is never silenced by the conversation.

Fig. 9.1.3 Rebekah Dyer, *Exodus — 3 — The Bush That Burns* (2017). The composition draws inspiration from the sound and movement of flames.

III. The Characterization of God and Moses, and Constructing New Theological Meanings

Setting the burning bush to music provided new ways to conceptualize old ideas, and revealed how different forms of perception can stimulate both the imagination and the intellect. Collaboration between theology and the arts is beneficial not only as a 'mutually enriching conversation,' as Jeremy Begbie reminds us, but also for reintegrating intellectual, spiritual, aesthetic, and bodily ways of knowing.[6] There is an alchemical interaction between scripture and art, between physicality and intellect, and between theology and the imagination.

God's act of self-disclosure in Exod 3 is difficult to capture in all its narrative and existential complexity. At the burning bush, God's eternal presence is revealed amidst a finite creation. Moses is initiated into the faith of his ancestors through nothing less than direct contact with divine reality. Divinely commissioned to lead his people out of slavery, it is not difficult to imagine that Moses is overcome with terror, wonder and self-doubt. Exploring Moses' emotional landscape may open up a route to aesthetic and theological engagement for both the artist and the audience, taking us beyond the scope of the text to contemplate the complexity of divine-human encounter. In Briggs' composition, there is no description or narration; only the words of God and Moses. Although historical and narrative context informs the piece, it is not overtly presented. As a result, there is a sense of dislocation from events which come before and after: a kind of narrative wilderness that reflects the liminality of the encounter. The themes of isolation and intimacy are evident here, as much for the audience as for Moses. Without the explicit narrative framing of the original text, the fragments of dialogue hang together like echoes of a distant conversation. It is as though the listener comes upon the conversation *in media res.* They must piece together its meaning line by line. They are required to pay attention, to discern (aesthetically, intellectually, spiritually) the significance of this encounter.

While Moses is called by name near the very beginning of the piece, the identity of the one who calls him is ambiguous. It is not until the first solo (beginning at bar 33) that we are offered a glimpse into God's eternal selfhood: 'I am that I am…' The phrase constitutes a double revelation, disclosing not only divine identity but the sound of the divine voice. The biblical text does not give an indication of what God's voice sounded like to Moses. However, God is conventionally portrayed in masculine terms and associated with masculine conceptions of power and sovereignty. In 'Exodus III', such expectations are subverted. When the soprano's voice rises to announce divine identity, the listener might be surprised by the feminine portrayal of divine presence. The strength of the soprano's solo conveys the authority of such presence as effectively as a baritone, yet the distinctiveness of this musical choice generates much

---

6 Begbie, 'Introduction', p. 9.

greater theological meaning. If God is usually portrayed as masculine, the femininity of the soprano allows the association of God with another gender, providing a way to express divine transcendence of human assignations.

By virtue of the soprano's pitch, the divine voice seems to soar from another plane. Moses' baritone solo achieves the converse effect, grounding Moses' voice in the earthly realm. Theologically, the distinction between the divine and human voices is significant, suggesting the transcendent otherness of God and the historically-bound nature of human existence. The multiplicity of voices that call to Moses draw attention to a transcendent reality which is greater than Moses' individual circumstance. In contrast, the Israelite voices (bar 77 onwards) are dense and overlapping — urgently seeking the end of oppression. Moses himself is heard clearly only at the epicentre of the piece when his solo is both the counterpart of, and counter-balance to, the ethereal voice of God.

Yet, intriguingly, divine and human identity are sometimes obfuscated through the precise setting of the text. This reflects some of the tensions regarding identity which Briggs and I identified in our initial conversations. In the original text, God calls Moses by name ('Moses, Moses') and Moses answers ('Here I am'). In the musical rendition of these words, there is no change in voice. Narrative elucidation regarding the speaker is absent. The elision of divine and human speech juxtaposes divine and human identity to the point that they lose distinction. When the altos and sopranos sing 'Moses, Moses, Here I am,' is it Moses who declares his presence, or God? Either attribution would be appropriate. While the original narrative is clear about the pattern of call and response — in which God calls, and Moses responds — the music offers an alternative suggestion. By calling to Moses through the fire of the burning bush, God also declares, in effect, *Here I am*. As the piece draws towards its conclusion, the growing urgency of the choir creates an air of expectancy. The members of the audience are invited to respond, with Moses, to the call of the choir: 'Go…'. The audience, thereby, may reflect on their aesthetic (and perhaps emotional) experience in thought and action, and ask what it might mean to respond to divine presence — the same divine presence which called Moses by name.

The Composers' Scheme was more than a collaboration of individuals; it was a collaboration of approaches, of ways of knowing. Within the music, theological and aesthetic ideas converge and are placed in conversation with one another in active mediation of the biblical text. As composer and theologian respectively, Briggs and I found that we needed to reach beyond our respective disciplines to navigate the creative and conceptual demands of the partnership. The process of composition led us to explore ways of incorporating physical, emotional, and spiritual perspectives into the project — with both artistic and theological implications.

Aesthetic expression and perception are rooted in the body. Music is perceived and processed through the senses, and it is on this physical basis that the sensations called forth by music can be conceptualized through the intellect.[7] Embodied knowledge

---

7   Bruce Torff and Howard Gardner, 'Conceptual and Experiential Cognition in Music', *The Journal of Aesthetic Education*, 33.4 (1999), 93–106 (pp. 93–94).

became the catalyst for our methodology, and may also be fruitful not only for future artistic work on Exod 3 but also on other, sensually rich biblical episodes. It is a strength of 'TheoArtistic' collaboration that it provides the opportunity to consider 'alternative narratives and discourses not privileged by current research.'[8] To this end, it is worth exploring what insights might be gained through locating the text within the embodied nature of human existence.

Exod 3 is not only a conversation between God and Moses; it is an encounter between divinity and humanity. While God's nature is eternal, human existence is finite and takes on countless expressions of self-disclosure and identity construction. There is no single way to be human. God calls not only Moses towards divine encounter but all of humanity: so what would it mean for Moses to be portrayed as a young man, rather than an ageing patriarch? As a refugee? As female? These questions concern the embodied nature of human life and identity. They encourage the creative artist to explore the relationship between bodily and spiritual experience — especially for individuals and communities whose bodies are vulnerable, exploited, or heavily politicized, and therefore not typically understood as the receivers of divine revelation.

Indeed, the association of oppressed bodies with *divine* identity is another important consideration for creative approaches to Exod 3. Portrayals of God that subvert traditional expectations give both artists and theologians the chance to explore a conception of divine personhood which far transcends the conventional picture of a singular (white) male authority. The soprano solo of *Exodus III* provides a straightforward example in which a feminine voice is associated with God's self-disclosure. Picturing God in yet more diverse ways may, in turn, suggest greater variety in the ways human beings are made in 'the image and likeness' of God (Genesis 1.26).

When Moses encounters the overwhelming power of divine presence, he cannot leave unchanged. The music of *Exodus III* embraces the uncertainty of such a moment, destabilizing the encounter by moving between elements of the conversation as expressed by different voices. The portrayal of flames in constant motion also signals the unfolding transformation, suggesting that the mysteries of divine and human selfhood burn almost within reach — yet remain ungraspable. The sensory and spiritual resonances of fire connect Moses' encounter with God to both physical sensation and emotional response. Further engagement with experiential ways of knowing could arise from considering changes in Moses' body language, voice, syntax, or physical appearance. In a more abstract portrayal, the fabric of the aesthetic work might itself bear the marks of transformation through alterations in form, tone, or colour palette. In such cases, aesthetic, emotional, and embodied forms of knowledge combine to convey a transformational spiritual

---

8 Ian Sutherland and Sophia Krzys Acord, 'Thinking with Art: From Situated Knowledge to Experiential Knowing', *Journal of Visual Art Practice*, 6 (2007), 125–40 (p. 135).

experience. At the burning bush, all humanity is invited to approach God's presence and contemplate the mysteries of divine personhood. It is the task of both artist and theologian to help facilitate and interpret this moment of encounter. Knowing that eternal mysteries are beyond human thought, we may attempt to render them with an aesthetic experience that resonates with spiritual and emotional ways of knowing over and above the limitations of human language and intellect.

List of Illustrations

9.1.1 Rebekah Dyer, *Exodus — 1 — Beach Fire* (2017), digital photograph, St Andrews, United Kingdom. © Rebekah Dyer, CC BY-ND 4.0. A beach bonfire kindled in celebration of the TheoArtistry Composers' Scheme in St Andrews.   163

9.1.2 Rebekah Dyer, *Exodus — 2 — Fire Spinning* (2013), digital photograph, St Andrews, United Kingdom. © Rebekah Dyer, CC BY-ND 4.0. In fire performance art, there is a reciprocal relationship between fire and the body.   165

9.1.3 Rebekah Dyer, *Exodus — 3 — The Bush That Burns* (2017), digital photograph, St Andrews, United Kingdom. © Rebekah Dyer, CC BY-ND 4.0. The composition draws inspiration from the sound and movement of flames.   167

9.2. Composer's Reflections

Kerensa Briggs

I first applied to the TheoArtistry project as a composer with a long-standing but waning connection to the Christian faith. Sacred music played a large part in my upbringing and the connection between music and spiritual (or emotional) directness is something that I continue to explore within all of my compositional work. TheoArtistry was a truly collaborative process from start to finish: an alchemy in which the theologian was influencing the experience of the composer and the composer was influencing theological experience. My theologian partner, Rebekah Dyer, was exploring 'Fire in the theological and social imagination' as her PhD thesis topic at the time of the collaboration, and was also an amateur Fire Art performer. From the early stages of the project, where the six composers were offered a selection of biblical extracts, I was immediately drawn to the evocative imagery found within Exod 3. The power and mystery of fire, as a force which can both give, sustain and take life, was something that I thought would be fascinating to explore musically. The text is full of expressive harmonic, textural and melodic possibilities. Moments of darkness and plight are juxtaposed with moments of hope and light. Using Dyer's extensive research, we decided to delve deeper into the context and connections surrounding our choice of text.

We discussed how these underlying connections might provide stimuli which could be translated into musical ideas or responses. Our biblical extract, for example, provides several contextual questions surrounding the notion of identity. The identity of the voice calling Moses from the bush is initially ambiguous. Contextually, there are also questions surrounding Moses' own identity and, indeed, that of God. One way of expressing these issues seemed possible through texture. The opening, 'Moses, Moses, here I am' is set between the upper voice parts (S/A I, II and III) and starts on a unison note. It then grows out of itself into a three-part, largely homophonic, texture which then proceeds back to a unison note. The three-part writing here often features a turn-like semiquaver motif in the S/A III part, reflecting the flickering flame movement found, initially, within the organ part. This idea also appears later in a T/B I, II and III split at the text 'Who am I?' The fact that the texture is divided into three parts during these phrases also refers to the nature of the Holy Trinity: Father, Son and Holy Ghost.

The solo sections of the piece feature a more direct narrative; the baritone solo, for example, reflects the questions of Moses. The people of Israel then ask 'What is His name?' in homophony across all voice parts. This is the first time that this texture appears within the piece. At the moment where the identity of the voice emanating from the bush is revealed, 'I Am' (or 'Yahweh'), there is a sense of annunciation, or divine revelation, as God responds to Moses' plight and exclaims, 'I Am that I Am. I Am hath sent me unto you'. The moment of annunciation — the moment where God is communicating directly — is the climax of the piece, and I sought to approach this in a subtle and special way. At this point, an ethereal solo emerges from a single triad. This follows on from the more harmonically challenging, bitonal section in which the people of Israel have asked 'What is His name?' The final section of the piece concludes with the soprano solo, 'I will lift you up, I will lift you up out of the affliction of Egypt', using textual repetition for emphasis. This is followed by the final response of the people, 'Now let us go', set in polyphony across all SATB parts.

Dyer and I discussed Moses' sense of mystery when he first encountered the bush, unconsumed through the flickering flames. Perhaps this had some metaphorical connection to the survival of the Hebrew slaves afflicted in Egypt. The flickering flame depicted in the text influenced the continually flickering quaver writing in the organ part. The juxtaposition of tonal harmony and melody against more challenging bitonal sections was used to express different sections found within the text. These moments of dissonance often feature suspensions against trills, which tend to resolve to consonance or conclusion. Similarly, the piece begins with a minor and somewhat ambiguous form of modal tonality but then ends diatonically in the major, bringing with it a sense of hope that is reflective of the discourse of the text: the people of Israel will be lifted up 'out of the affliction of Egypt'.

I find it quite difficult to describe the actual formation of musical ideas. The compositional process was influenced by an awareness of practicality for the performing forces and the subconscious influence of my own musical education, aesthetic taste and experiences. I wanted to create a piece that would be both enjoyable and thought-provoking for the performers and listeners. I also wanted to make the most of the acoustical possibilities of the space in which the composition would be performed and recorded. Throughout the process, I sent Dyer several musical ideas and examples, which we then discussed over Skype over a three-month period. For me, this collaborative approach was a new, unconventional way of working; it was productive and enjoyable. This process made me question the broader 'role' of the composer, particularly in terms of sacred music. Perhaps the composer is always subconsciously working as part of a team or cooperatively, considering that there is frequent input from other sources outside of the composer's own creativity and background.

Arguably, composing relies on the expression of the 'inner ear'. Many aspects of theology and music, then, are often inspired by a search for truth and spiritual directness (or emotional meaning), and also an openness to sharing this emotional or spiritual discourse with others. This is something that will differ for every individual, but there appears to be a communal theological and musical interaction united by threads of thought, connection and expression. This is particularly the case in sacred music performed within a holy space, whereby the visual and sensory aspects of the space, alongside the ceremony and ritual of a service, combine with the musical elements into something more.

It has been fascinating to work with Dyer's input and the influence of the TheoArtistry symposia. I believe that, for many of the partnerships, the process led to an enhanced incorporation of theological perspective, depth and aesthetic. The process deepened our levels of engagement with the text. Although much of the musical creation came from a subconscious place, it has been interesting to evaluate what artistic choices were made with relation to the depiction of the composition's textual, theological and contextual ideas. This has made me question the way I work and has also opened my eyes to the rich possibilities of collaboration. It was a moving experience hearing the fruits of our labour at the first performance, and to hear the work of the other partnerships involved in the project.

 Kerensa Briggs, 'Exodus III' (2017), in *Annunciations: Sacred Music for the 21st Century*, St Salvator's Chapel Choir and Sean Heath, cond. by Tom Wilkinson (Sanctiandree, SAND0006, 2018), © 2017 University of St Andrews. Track 09. Duration: 5.10.
https://doi.org/10.11647/OBP.0172.33

'Exodus III'

Kerensa Briggs

Exodus III

For members of the TheoArtistry Scheme,
St Salvator's Chapel Choir and Tom Wilkinson.

'Exodus III' © 2019 Kerensa Briggs, CC BY 4.0

https://doi.org/10.11647/OBP.0172.15

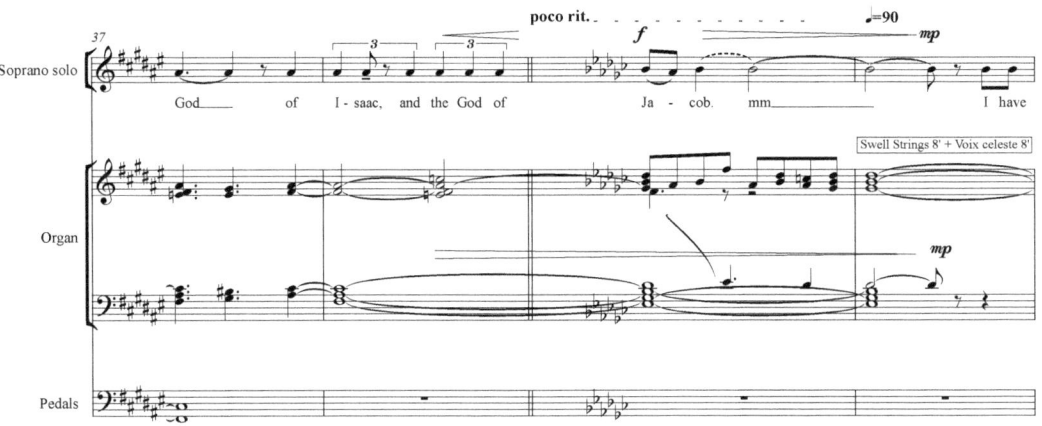

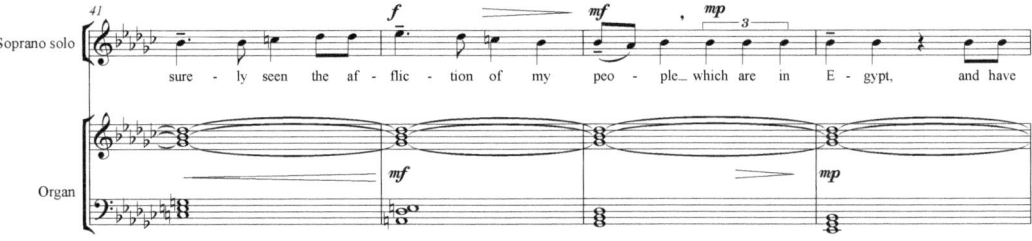

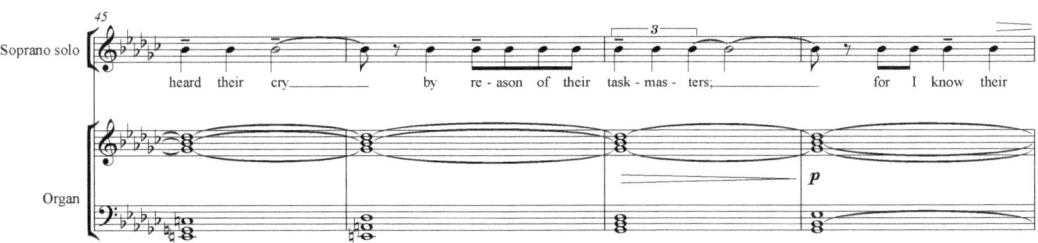

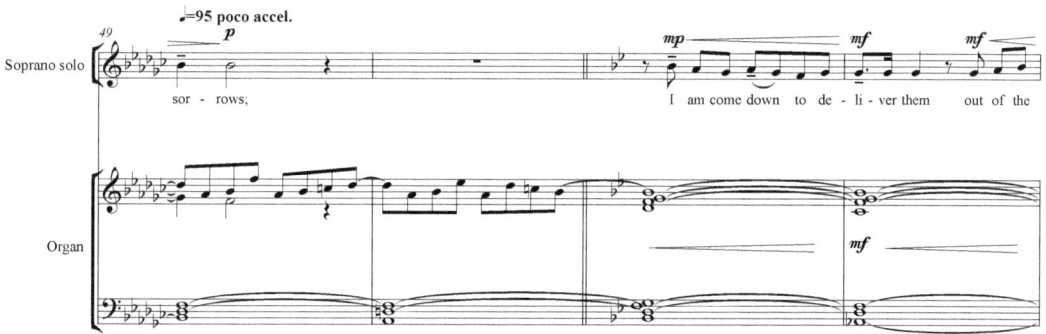
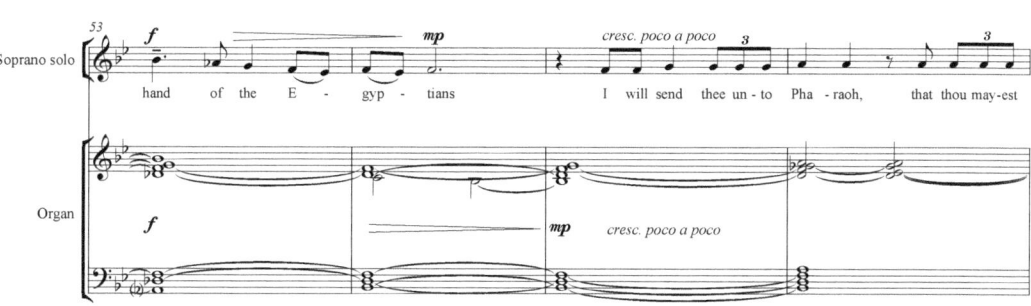
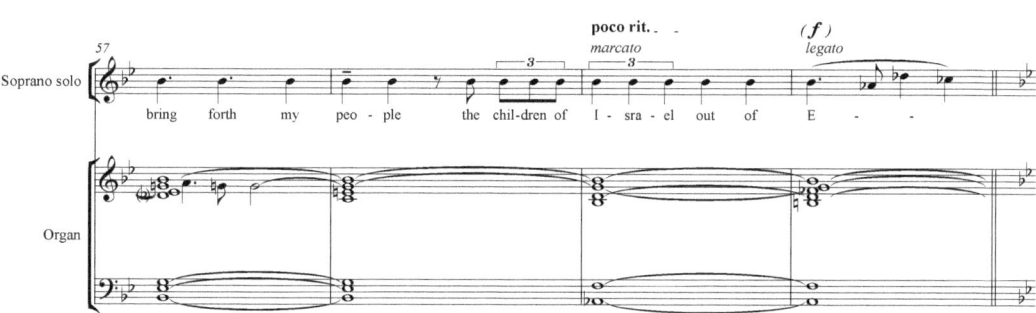

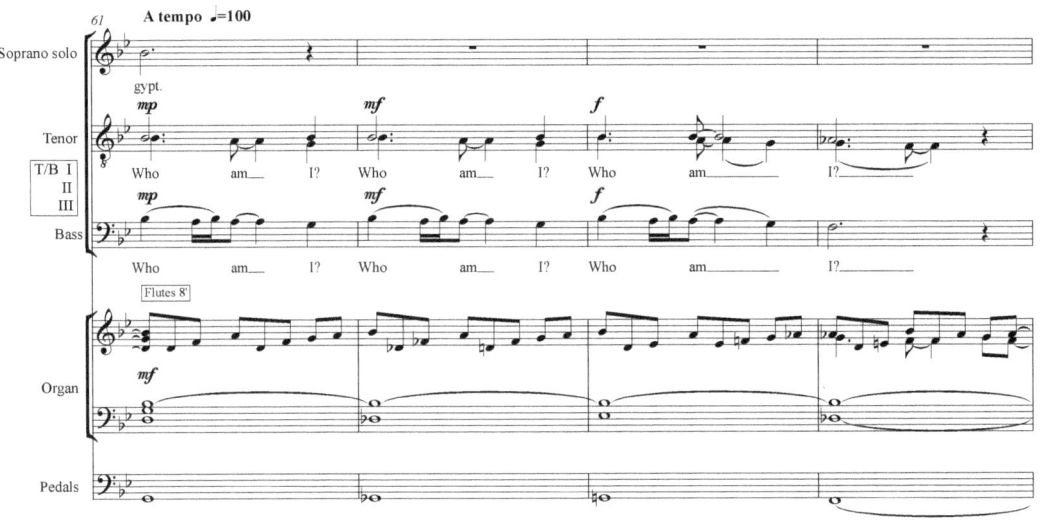

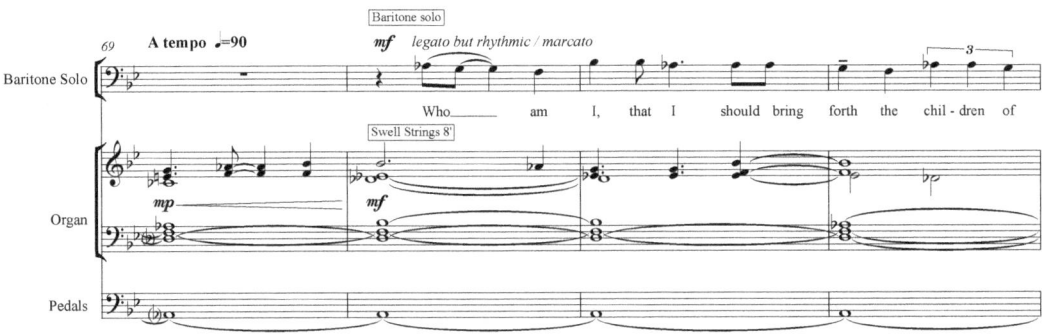

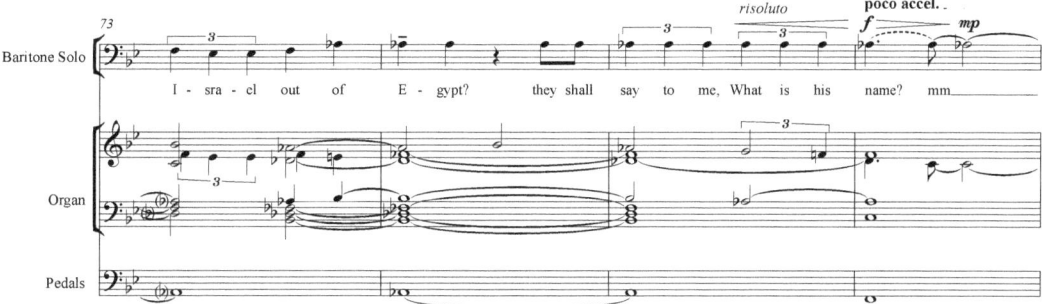

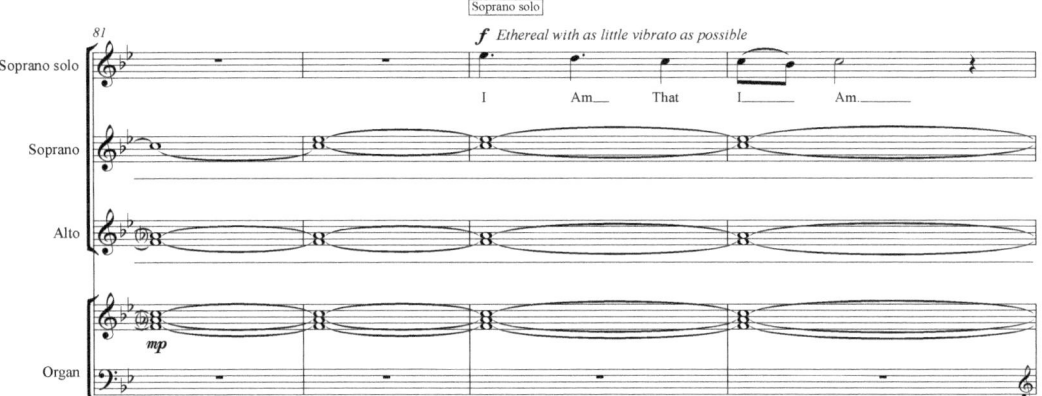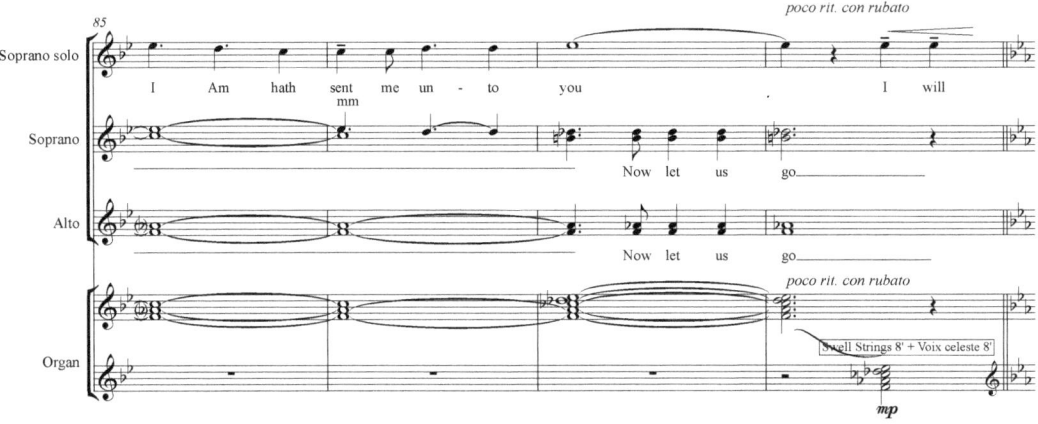

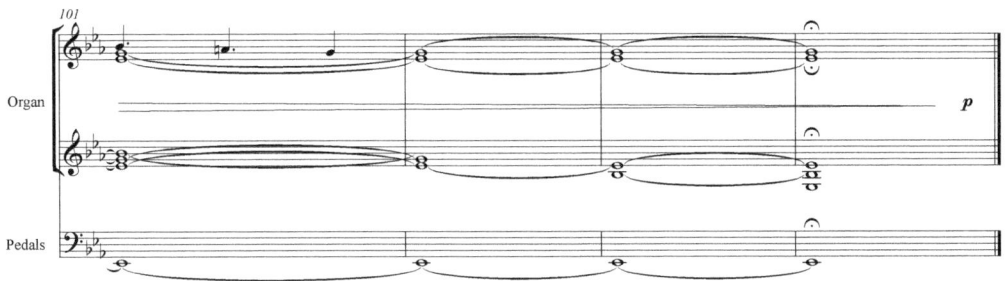

10.1. A Dark Dream: God's Calling of Samuel and the Ministry of Eli (1 Samuel 3)

Caleb Froehlich

God's calling of Samuel in the temple of Shiloh is a story typically associated with children, a story told in children's books, Sunday school lessons, and animated Bible films. A number of the story's features easily lend themselves to this audience. Most obviously, its main protagonist is a child, providing young listeners with a character to whom they can easily relate. Moreover, the central part of the story, God's three-fold call and Samuel's turning to Eli, exhibits the kind of repetition reminiscent of classic tales such as *Goldilocks and the Three Bears*, *The Gingerbread Man* and *Little Red Riding Hood* — a pedagogically useful feature for keeping a child's attention and relating particular themes.[1] Partly because of this dominant association, the story is widely viewed even by biblical scholars as simple, straightforward, and charming. Thus, for example, Walter Brueggemann accepts that God's calling is an 'idyllic childlike exchange' and paraphrases this part of the narrative to focus attention, instead, on wider socio-religious themes.[2] Other scholars see the threefold repetition as a purely rhetorical device for clarity of structure and dramatic emphasis.[3] Some regard it as an example of human frailty; at best, a misunderstanding; or, at worst, a display of

---

1 Irving Wood discusses the similarities between God's Calling of Samuel and folk-tales in Irving Wood, 'Folk-Tales in Old Testament Narrative', *Journal of Biblical Literature*, 28 (1909), 34–41.
2 Walter Brueggemann, *First and Second Samuel* (Louisville, KY: Westminster John Knox Press, 2012), p. 25. See also Robert Polzin, *Samuel and the Deuteronomist: A Literary Study of the Deuteronomic History Part Two: 1 Samuel* (Bloomington, IN: Indiana University Press, 1993), p. 44; P. Kyle McCarter, *I Samuel* (New Haven, CT: Doubleday Religious Publishing Group, 1995), p. 98; Robert P. Gordon, *I & II Samuel: A Commentary* (Grand Rapids, MI: Zondervan, 1999), pp. 88–91; Ralph W. Klein, *1 Samuel* (Nashville, TN: Thomas Nelson, 2008), p. 31.
3 Two scholars who interpret it this way are: Robert Karl Gnuse, *The Dream Theophany of Samuel: Its Structure in Relation to Ancient Near Eastern Dreams and Its Theological Significance* (Lanham, CT: University Press of America, 1984), p. 145; Jacob Licht, *Storytelling in the Bible* (Jerusalem: Magnes Press, 1986), p. 54.

obtuseness.[4] With only a few exceptions, scholars fail to deal with the full implications of God's calling in a more serious manner.[5]

In researching this scriptural passage for the composer, Seán Doherty, I did not attempt to remedy these scholarly omissions, but rather to establish a broader theological framework through which to explore the under-examined aspects of the narrative. It was gratifying to find that those elements of the story which most interested me also resonated with him and served as the basis for our discussions throughout the collaborative process. Since some of the elements are contained within a larger context of 1 Samuel [Sam] 3, I first relate the setting for God's call and its possible connection with many people's experience of God today; secondly, I examine what is revealed about the voice of God in the passage and the challenge this presented for the final composition; thirdly, I consider the psychological and emotional turmoil Samuel must have experienced; and, finally, I reflect on how these different elements were refined in Doherty's choral piece 'God Calls Samuel'.

The Setting for God's Call

The setting for God's calling of Samuel is what initially prompted me to select this passage for the TheoArtistry Composers' Scheme. It seemed to me that the narrative's opening statement is arresting, particularly in our contemporary context: 'The word of the Lord was rare in those days; there was no frequent vision (1 Sam 3.1).'[6] Is the word of God scarce because, to use Friedrich Nietzsche's famous adage, 'God is dead'? Is it because people have stopped going to church and have ceased to engage with religious concerns? If so, is God angry with us? Has God abandoned us because we have abandoned God? In popular Western culture, the silence of God has become a recurrent motif in film, theatre, literature and music, from acclaimed television series such as *The Leftovers* (2014) and *Preacher* (2016) to contemporary tracks such as As Cities Burn's 'Contact' (2007) or Vampire Weekend's 'Ya Hey' (2013) which, playing on the name *Yahweh*, directly addresses God and proclaims: 'you won't even say your name'.[7]

Such contemporary sentiments arguably reflect the scriptural setting for God's calling of Samuel. However, they are expressed less through a lack of hearing, as through a lack of vision. The account begins by highlighting the symbolic significance of sight. 'Vision' was precious in those days, it pronounces, leading directly to the statement that Eli, the high priest, 'could not see' because his eyes had 'begun to grow dim' from old age (1 Sam 3.1-2). In placing these parallel phrases, the narrative links

---

4 See, for example, Lyle M. Eslinger, *Kingship of God in Crisis: A Close Reading of 1 Samuel 1-12* (Sheffield: JSOT Press, 1985), p. 150; Polzin, *Samuel and the Deuteronomist*, p. 50.
5 For a scholarly perspective which does address Samuel in a substantial way, see Walter Moberly, 'To Hear the Master's Voice: Revelation and Spiritual Discernment in the Call of Samuel', *Scottish Journal of Theology*, 48 (1995), 443–68.
6 All biblical passages will be quoted from the English Standard Version (ESV).
7 Ariel Rechtshaid, Rostam Batmanglij, and Ezra Koenig, 'Vampire Weekend Lyrics — Ya Hey' (AZLyrics.com, 2018), http://www.azlyrics.com/lyrics/vampireweekend/yahey.html

Eli's physical deterioration with the religious decline of that period. The connection is made more explicit in the details of the preceding chapter (1 Sam 2.12-36). Here, the sons of Eli abuse their priestly duties before the Ark — God's visible token of His presence among the Israelites, housed in the temple at Shiloh. Years of stealing sacrifices from the deity and sleeping with female servants in the tabernacle are the causes for the termination of the family's election. With the priesthood in disrepute, there seems to be no suitable mediator for God's revelation.

Fig 10.1.1 Detail of William de Brailes, *Eli's Sons Commit Sacrilege* (1 Sam 2.13-17) (c. 1250). This page from the Walters manuscript (W.106) is comprised of two scenes from the second chapter of 1 Samuel. In the top image, the priest Eli's sons—Hophni and Phinehas— are depicted treating 'the offerings of the Lord with contempt' (1 Sam 2.17). They are shown taking meat for themselves from the Israelite's sacrifices before burning the fat as an offering to the Lord. The bottom image shows Elkanah and Hannah presenting the child Samuel to God at the temple. Unlike Eli's own sons, 'the boy Samuel continued to grow both in stature and in favor with the Lord and with the people' (v. 26).

1 Sam 3 represents this religious decadence with twilight hanging over the land of Israel. A nation without the mediating office of the priesthood is a nation falling into spiritual obscurity: the 'no frequent vision', reported at the beginning of the story, is not only reflected in Eli's poor eyesight but in the light slowly fading from the temple and its surroundings. All of Israel has settled down for the night and the high priest himself is 'lying down in his own place', away from his responsibilities at the temple. The nation is in a state of visionless sleep, oblivious to the voice of God. Even as the temple sinks into darkness, however, God has not completely forsaken Israel. A single lamp illuminates Samuel, sleeping dutifully beside the Ark. The juxtaposition of Samuel and Eli is arresting. While the high priest lies in the comfort of his own room, the boy lies near the very symbol of God's presence. This contrast identifies Samuel as the glimmer of light in an otherwise dismal situation. It is precisely in this moment of transition from day to night, a moment characterized by ambivalence and ambiguity, that the word of God strikes. The voice in the darkness does not address Eli or his progeny, the expected recipients of divine revelation, but the child. Its sound is so unexpected that Samuel repeatedly fails to recognize the source: God calls out to him three times and three times he turns to Eli.

There is much in common between the silence of Samuel's time and the silence which many believe characterizes our contemporary religious climate. The repeated call of God, however, throws this supposed silence into a different light. Samuel's failure to recognize the voice of God raises a number of questions which may pertain directly to current preconceptions: is God truly silent or are we simply not recognizing His voice? Similarly, what is the role of religious structures and particular figures within them in mediating the word of God? How would we know if God's silence has to do with our own inhibited hearing or some sort of divine anger? These all lead to the simple, yet profound, question: what does God's voice sound like?

The Voice of God

Doherty and I discussed how to portray the voice of God in the composition. Biblical stories typically provide little by way of description, leaving the sound of God's speech chiefly to the discretion of the artist.[8] In the animated film *Prince of Egypt* (1998), the directors had the entire cast simultaneously whisper God's lines, resulting in a reverberating chorus of voices. In *Exodus: Gods and Kings* (2014), Ridley Scott cast an eleven-year-old school boy to speak as God who, he said, 'exudes innocence and purity, and those two qualities are extremely powerful.'[9] Although 1 Sam 3 provides

---

8   When God's voice is described in Scripture, it is often associated with the sound of thunder. See, for example, Exod 19.19; 1 Sam 7.10; Job 37.2-5. 1 Kgs 19, however, qualifies this association with natural forces. Here, Elijah discovers that God is not present in the wind, earthquake or fire, but rather in 'a still small voice' (19.12).

9   Carrie Dedrick, 'Ridley Scott Casts 11-Year Old Boy to Speak as God in "Exodus: Gods and Kings"' (ChristianHeadlines.com, 2014), http://www.christianheadlines.com/blog/ridley-scott-casts-11-year-old-boy-to-speak-as-god-in-exodus-gods-and-kings.html

no explicit description, the voice of God is given two primary characteristics which the composer has to take into consideration.

The first is that the voice of God is not recognizable as such. It is easy to assume that when God speaks, the verbalization should exhibit qualities that suggest the transcendence or divinity of the speaker. We may be reminded of the common depiction of God's voice booming from heaven, loud and clear, as if James Earl Jones were speaking through a megaphone.[10] Or we might imagine a more phantasmal sound which emphasizes an otherworldliness, such as the cacophony of whispers in *Prince of Egypt*. The voice of God in 1 Sam 3, however, does not exhibit these kinds of qualities. There is no angelic chorus accompanying God's call, or sonorous voice emitting from a celestial echo chamber. Rather, the speech of God sounds ordinary; so much so that Samuel immediately assumes it is human.

The second characteristic follows directly from the first; the voice of God sounds very similar to the voice of Eli. As Walter Moberly points out, the correspondence is evident in the way Samuel responds to God's call:

> If one tries to imagine a situation in which a voice in the night were in any way unfamiliar, the initial response of Samuel to the voice would presumably be one of uncertainty or anxiety and might well be expressed by the question 'Who are you?' Or, when Samuel goes to Eli he could have said something along the lines of 'I heard a voice. Wasn't it you calling me?'[11]

Samuel's response to the call of God, however, does not take the form of a question. Instead, the boy responds with 'Here I am, for you called me', revealing his own belief that it was in fact Eli who summoned him in the night.[12] It is particularly telling that Samuel uses this familiar expression in all three instances (1 Sam 3.4-8).

These two characteristics presented Doherty with a duality: the voice of God as distinct from that of Eli and the voice of God being essentially the same as that of Eli. Regardless of how we tried to conceive God's voice — privileging one of these divergent aspects — questions emerged concerning the possible experience of the listening audience. Should the voice of God be distinct from the voice of Eli? If not, how does one convey the similarity while still allowing listeners to distinguish between the two? In our desire to enable the audience to experience something of this subtle dichotomy, we realized that it would be beneficial to use Samuel's own experience as the starting point.

---

10 This popular representation corresponds with those biblical passages where God's voice is associated with thunder. Loudness is probably used to indicate the transcendent power or importance of the speech or speaker.
11 Moberly, 'To Hear the Master's Voice', p. 459.
12 'Here I am' or *hinnēnî* can be said to equals, superiors and inferiors. It does not have any special theological meaning. See Douglas Stuart's comments in *Exodus*, New American Commentary (Nashville: B&H Publishing Group, 2006), II, p. 114.

The Experience of Samuel

If we imagine God's calling from the perspective of Samuel, the voice of God sounding like Eli's voice takes on a new significance. Biblical scholars generally agree that Eli not only served as Samuel's teacher, but also as his surrogate father.[13] From the time his mother gave him over for service at the temple — probably at the age of five — the majority of what Samuel heard and learned about God was through the high priest.[14] Considering the high priest's formative role, it may not be unreasonable to propose that Samuel's own idea of God might well have been informed also by his interactions with Eli. Recent studies in child psychology suggest, indeed, that children's ideas of God are mainly modelled on their teachers and parents.[15]

At this point, we might be tempted to adopt the Feuerbachian or Freudian supposition that God is merely a projection of Samuel's mind, an imaginary objectification of Eli, his surrogate father. The question, however, is whether this is true for Samuel. 1 Sam 3 seems to challenge precisely this supposition. It does not repudiate the tremendous formative role that Eli is likely to have exerted on the boy's idea of God. Yet, it shows that this might be the means through which to encounter a greater reality, taking up such ideas and transforming them. Indeed, the third time Samuel hears God's call and turns to Eli, his surrogate father points beyond himself. The high priest encourages the child to detach his understanding of God from his parental figure so that Samuel might relate to God on his own.

Eli provides Samuel with a response that not only identifies God as the caller, but also articulates the kind of respect, humility and willingness that seems appropriate

---

13 See, for example, George Savran, *Encountering the Divine: Theophany in Biblical Narrative* (London: T&T Clark, 2005), p. 141; Hillel I. Millgram, *The Invention of Monotheist Ethics: Exploring the First Book of Samuel* (Lanham: University Press of America, 2009), p. 145; Stephen B. Chapman, *1 Samuel as Christian Scripture: A Theological Commentary* (Grand Rapids, MI: Eerdmans, 2016), p. 84; Mark A. Leuchter and David T. Lamb, *The Historical Writings: Introducing Israel's Historical Literature* (Minneapolis, MN: Fortress Press, 2016), p. 199.2005

14 Samuel's mother, Hannah, gave her son over to the temple after 'she weaned him' (1 Sam 1.23-25). Scholars generally suppose that this means Samuel was between three and five years old. See the discussion, for example, in Dorothy Kelley Patterson and Rhonda Harrington Kelley, *Women's Evangelical Commentary: Old Testament* (Nashville: B&H Publishing Group, 2011), p. 428; Bruce K. Waltke, *The Book of Proverbs, Chapters 1–15* (Grand Rapids, MI: Eerdmans, 2004), p. 277. A few scholars, however, argue that weaning refers to the time the child is ready leave his mother's care, placing Samuel around twelve or thirteen. See comment in Charles Taze Russell, *Expanded Biblical Comments — Commentary of the Old and New Testament* (Chicago: Chicago Bible Students, 2014). The text states that Samuel 'was still young' when she handed him over (1.25). Hence, I place his age close to five years old.

15 In 2004, a study of 363 Dutch pre-schoolers, for example, found that the children's ideas of God mainly derived from interactions with their teachers and parents. The data showed that the stricter these interactions were, the more punitive God became in the minds of the children. See Simone A. de Roos, Jurjen Iedema and Siebren Miedema, 'Influence of Maternal Denomination, God Concepts, and Child-Rearing Practices on Young Children's God Concepts', *Journal for the Scientific Study of Religion*, 43 (2004), 519–35. Another study, conducted in 2006, discovered that teachers and parents remain the primary predictors of a child's conception of God well into young adulthood; however, from then on, the link between God and these attachment figures starts to weaken. See Jane R. Dickie, Lindsey V. Ajega, Joy R. Kobylak, and Kathryn M. Nixon, 'Mother, Father, and Self: Sources of Young Adults' God Concepts', *Journal for the Scientific Study of Religion*, 45 (2006), 57–71.

Fig 10.1.2 Detail of Unknown Artist, *Bible Primer: Old Testament by Adolf Holt* (1919). Following Samuel's dedication at the house of the Lord in Shiloh, Samuel goes to live with Eli where he learns how to minister before the Lord. For the young boy, therefore, Eli served not only as a teacher but also as something of a father figure. Samuel's experience becomes more harrowing when we consider the close relationship he had with Eli.

for one who is addressing God: 'Speak, LORD (*Yahweh*), for your servant hears' (1 Sam 3.9).[16] What is peculiar, however, is that when Samuel hears God call out to him the fourth time, he does not respond by using God's proper name, *Yahweh*, as Eli instructed. This omission seems to imply a certain reluctance or trepidation in the mind of Samuel as he steps into a new understanding (1 Sam 3.10).

Samuel's Bewilderment

As aforementioned, the dominant association of 1 Sam 3 with children has, in part, resulted in overly simplistic or reductionist interpretations of the story. One manifestation of this proclivity has been to characterize Samuel as a prime example of willing obedience. Yet, the story presents the boy as a more complex person. Samuel's responses to each call intimate a growing puzzlement. He initially pronounces 'Here I am!', *runs* to Eli, and repeats his declaration, stating 'Here I am' a second time. His eager willingness to respond to his teacher is obvious. After the second and third call, however, Samuel simply *goes* to Eli and only speaks once he has arrived. He does

---

16 Klein, p. 133. YWHW is usually replaced by LORD in bible translations. Here I have changed it back to YHWH so as to better convey that this is God's name rather than a title.

not appear less willing to respond, but his actions seem to show that he is perplexed, perhaps even discouraged, by what is occurring.

Visual representations of Samuel's response to God's calling typically coincide with the picture of Samuel as an eager respondent. Some works, however, depict a more nuanced expression that seems aligned with how one would expect a child to react under these bizarre circumstances. Newell Wyeth's painting, *Samuel Mistakes God* (1929), for example, portrays a tension-laden scene.[17] Samuel stands across from Eli with a disappointed look across his face. The slight tilt of his head and subtle frown give the impression that he is uncertain about what he has just experienced. Another painting entitled *The Infant Samuel* (circa 1853), by James Sant, shows a more dramatic response to God's calling. Here the boy suddenly rises out of bed and turns his head, intently searching for something in the darkness. Samuel's wide eyes exude alarm and bewilderment.

Samuel's Terror

Adaptations of 1 Sam 3 typically downplay the climax of the story. Some omit God's judgment against the house of Eli altogether, ending the retelling with Samuel's dutiful response to the fourth call of God. This neglect is not surprising, especially if the adaptation is for children. As Brueggemann candidly observes, 'the dream narrative is used to articulate a most disruptive, devastating assertion'.[18] When the judgment is included, however, it is usually told from Eli's viewpoint, with little or no regard to its immediate effects on Samuel. The message itself is weighty and abrasive. God tells Samuel that his surrogate family will be punished for their blasphemous behaviour, not just for a lifetime, but 'forever' — there is no hint of appeal or recourse. God's verdict is so severe that 'the two ears of everyone who hears it will tingle' (3.11-14). If we imaginatively place ourselves in the perspective of the child, it is easy to see how terrifying this message could be.

There are very few visual representations of Samuel listening to the judgment of God. A painting by Joshua Reynolds, however, seems to capture the kind of fear he likely endured during this intense nocturnal visitation. In *The Infant Samuel* (1776), we see the boy kneeling on the ground with his face turned up to heaven. There is a certain innocence to his posture with hands pressed tightly together. But Samuel's face clearly looks distressed. His furrowed brows and intense gaze suggest that he is alarmed by what he is hearing. Reynolds produced this scene in another painting *The Infant Samuel at Prayer* (1776), where his heavy use of shadow makes Samuel's distress even more apparent.

---

17 Wyeth painted this image for Bruce Barton, 'The Boy who Anointed Two Kings', *Good Housekeeping*, 88 (March 1929), 50–58.
18 Brueggemann, *First and Second Samuel*, p. 25.

Fig. 10.1.3 (Left) Joshua Reynolds, *The Infant Samuel* (1776), oil on canvas. (Right) Joshua Reynolds, *The Infant Samuel at Prayer* (1776). Joshua Reynolds' two paintings — both created circa 1776 — are suggestive of Samuel's earnestness and apprehension. In *The Infant Samuel* (left), the child's furrowed brows and intense gaze suggest he is alarmed with what he is hearing. In *The Infant Samuel at Prayer* (right), Reynolds intensifies this sense of consternation by using heavy shadowing in both the background and in depicting the features of Samuel's face.

The story hints at the trauma Samuel endured that night. It states that he 'lay until morning' and 'was afraid to tell the vision to Eli' (3.15). We can imagine the boy turning the devastating words over and over in his head. Samuel may have noticed that, while God specified a terrible judgment to be exacted on the house of Eli, the voice did not tell him to pass this message on to the high priest. Confusion and anxiety most likely compelled him to keep the events of that night to himself. Indeed, when Eli calls Samuel over to his quarters, the high priest has to encourage the child to relate God's message with a threat: 'May God do so to you and more also if you hide anything from me of all that He told you' (3.17).

The Collaboration

In our collaboration, Doherty was particularly taken by the experience of Samuel and decided to adopt a more child-centric interpretation of the narrative. He wanted the choral setting to express the events of the narrative through Samuel's eyes, rather than through the perspective of Eli or a third person narrator. The elements of the boy's nocturnal experience — the darkness, detachment, bewilderment, terror — struck the composer as being those of a true nightmare. This became the overarching theme and set the mood and texture for the final composition. Doherty wanted to invite the listening audience to enter into Samuel's dark dream, to sense something of the child's bewilderment and terror.

We talked about several possible textual sources for the choral setting that could have been fruitful thematic avenues. For example, we thought about using sources outside of the biblical narrative such as verses from a poem or even texts of our own making. The account of God's calling of Samuel also offered a number of ideas worth investigating musically. However, we could not explore them all due to the time restriction on the composition (three minutes). This brief duration challenged Doherty to be concise and economical in his textual choices, concentrating our ideas into a taut musical and narrative structure.

Appreciating these limitations, Doherty decided to build his text primarily from the names of the protagonists in 1 Samuel 3. The meanings of these names encapsulate the drama of the calling portion of this narrative. I pointed out to Doherty that names which contain 'el' typically speak of some relationship to God. The letters 'el' derive from God's name, *Elohim* (אֱלֹהִים) . Thus, the name Eli (אלי) signifies 'my God' whereas Samuel (שְׁמוּאֵל) means 'God hears' or 'the one who hears God'. In recognizing the meanings of these names, we understood the poignancy contained in the calling portion of the narrative. God calls out 'Samuel!' meaning 'the one who hears God'. The boy answers 'Here I am!' and runs to Eli, whose name significantly means 'my God'. God calls 'The one who hears God!' two more times, and two more times the boy turns to 'my God', rather than to the true God. Doherty kept these names in Hebrew for the setting so as to communicate directly the complexity of the protagonists' relationships with one another.

Collaborating with Doherty in the creation of 'God Calls Samuel' opened up a perspective on the narrative that neither of us had anticipated. We both came to the partnership with different expectations as to what would be expressed in the choral setting but, in the course of our discussions, we each shifted somewhat to arrive at a common concept. This enabled us to have a symbiotic relationship in which my theological insights served to inspire his musical creativity and his music brought an emotional richness to my theological understanding of the narrative. The final product of our collaboration, we hope, captures both the terror and the wonder of God's calling of young Samuel.

List of Illustrations

10.1.1 Detail of William de Brailes, *Eli's Sons Commit Sacilege* (1 Samuel 2.13-17) (c. 1250), ink and pigment on parchment, Walters Art Museum, Baltimore, USA, Wikimedia, https://commons.wikimedia.org/wiki/File:William_de_Brailes_-_Top_-_Eli%27s_Sons_Commit_Sacrilege_(1_Samuel_2_-13-17)_-_Walters_W10617V_-_Full_Page.jpg, public domain.   191

10.1. God's Calling of Samuel and the Ministry of Eli

10.1.2 Detail of Unknown Artist, *Bible Primer: Old Testament by Adolf Holt* (1919), illustration, Library of Congress, Washington, DC, USA, Wikimedia, https://commons.wikimedia.org/wiki/File:Bible_primer,_Old_Testament,_for_use_in_the_primary_department_of_Sunday_schools_(1919)_(14801957523).jpg, public domain.   195

10.1.3 Joshua Reynolds, *The Infant Samuel* (1776), oil on canvas, Fabre Museum, Montpellier, France, Wikimedia, https://commons.wikimedia.org/wiki/File:InfantSamuel.jpg, public domain. Joshua Reynolds, *The Infant Samuel at Prayer* (1776), oil on canvas, National Gallery, London, UK, Wikimedia, https://commons.wikimedia.org/wiki/File:The_Infant_Samuel_at_Prayer_-_Sir_Joshua_Reynolds.png, public domain.   197

10.2. Composer's Reflections

Seán Doherty

For the TheoArtistry project, I was paired with the theologian, Caleb Froehlich, and we collaborated in creating a choral setting of 1 Sam 3. In this passage, the boy Samuel hears his name being called three times during his nightly task of tending the lamp in the temple at Shiloh. Each time, Samuel thinks he is being summoned by his guardian, Eli, the high priest of the temple, and answers 'Here I am!'.[1] Eli tells Samuel that this is God's voice and to respond with the words, 'Speak, for your servant hears'. Whereupon, God speaks to Samuel and promises to destroy the house of Eli because his wicked sons had blasphemed and Eli had failed to restrain them. In the morning, Samuel, although hesitant to do so, recounts the prophecy to Eli. Froehlich had prepared a comprehensive, yet concise, information packet on the passage, which he presented to me at the symposium and which we talked through over several video calls. This packet included analyses of the historical and biblical context of the passage, the important theological themes and symbols, and other works of music and media which had used this passage as inspiration.

I. The Collaborative Process

At the symposium, I asked a group of theologians: what do you imagine Samuel's age to have been when he received this prophecy? Their answers ranged from four to eight years. This made the passage more personal to me as I reflected on my godson and nephew, Aodhán (the dedicatee of this piece), who was six years old at the time. I thought of what my own reaction would be to a child who was visibly distressed after waking up: to comfort them immediately. I imagine that this is a natural human reaction that traverses history and cultures.

This reflection inspired me to compose a setting from the viewpoint of Samuel. For Samuel, this call was not the saccharine story of the Sunday school lesson, nor a

---

[1] All biblical quotations are taken from the New International Version.

glorious annunciation that would forever change the course of history by instigating Samuel's role as Israel's priest, prophet, and judge. Instead, it was a terrifying ordeal which prophesied the destruction of the only family he had ever known. Eli evidently regarded Samuel as his son ('Samuel, my son'; 1 Sam 3.16) and Samuel was traumatized to the extent that he 'was afraid to tell Eli the vision' (1 Sam 3.15). Samuel's calling is unlike other prophetic call narratives because it does not involve confession nor an immediate charge to prophesy. It is significant, in this respect, that Eli had already received the divine word of his household's termination from an unnamed prophet in 1 Sam 2: 'The time is coming when I will cut short your strength and the strength of your priestly house, so that no one in it will reach old age, and you will see distress in my dwelling' (1 Sam 2.31-32). Accordingly, it seemed possible that Samuel had heard the rumours of the prophecy circulating about Eli's household as he went about his daily chores. The promise of the destruction of the house of Eli weighed heavily on his mind. Usually, preoccupations during waking hours are given vivid realization in dreams. For Samuel, the rumours of the prophecy had manifested as a nightmare.

Froehlich was meticulous in drawing my attention to the significance of the names in this passage. He informed me that Hebrew names are typically drawn from other words that give the names their meaning. Thus, names in the Hebrew scriptures often play a significant role in signaling a character's origin, personage, or purpose within the story. Names that contain 'el' usually mean that they are associated with God: the letters 'el' derive from Elohim, another name for God; Eli means 'My God'; Samuel means 'the one who hears God'. The three speaking characters in this passage, then, share the syllable 'el' in their names: El, Eli, and Samuel. When I analysed the passage to understand its basic dramatic structure, I therefore realized that the story could be told primarily through these names. The only other texts that I used were 'Hinneni' (*Here I am*) and 'Daber ki shomea abdecha' (*Speak, for your servant hears*), both in original Hebrew. The rest of the narrative could unfold in the music itself.

I determined that my setting would be a dramatic presentation of the biblical passage rather than a reflection on its theological meaning. Each group of performers is a distinguishable character, in the manner of an oratorio: the soprano soloist is the boy Samuel; the choir with organ is the voice of God; the choir without organ is the voice of Eli. In deciding on this characterization, I was influenced by the use of the organ as a metaphor for the word of God in seventeenth-century sources.[2] In addition to the use of the oratorio style and the metaphorical use of the organ, other Baroque elements, such as word-painting, are used throughout the piece, and will be discussed below.

Froehlich and I talked at length about the theological significance of God's three-fold call. I realized, additionally, that in the course of the passage there is not just one call, but three, and all names share the Hebrew root 'el': God calls Samuel, Samuel calls

---

2   Kerala J. Snyder, *The Organ as a Mirror of Its Time: North European Reflections, 1610–2000* (Oxford: Oxford University Press, 2002), p. 84.

Eli, and Eli calls Samuel. This realization was important to my compositional process, as this was the natural basis on which to structure the piece. I took considerable artistic license with the dramatic presentation of the biblical passage, notably by excluding Eli's remarks during the three-fold call ('I did not call; go back and lie down'). This was done for three reasons: to focus the reading on the viewpoint of Samuel, to make the dramatic structure of the three-fold call as clear as possible, and to eliminate all but the most essential elements of the narrative in order for the piece to remain within the stipulated duration in performance (three minutes).

There is a notable parallelism in this passage. At night, God calls Samuel, and Samuel thinks it is the voice of Eli. Samuel never attributed the voice to a stranger (he would have said, 'Who are you?'), but recognizes it as the voice of Eli every time, by running to him and saying 'Here I am!'. In the morning, however, Eli really does call Samuel, and in much the same way that God had done. The voices of God and Eli, I determined, should sound similar in my musical setting, in order to draw out the theme of the discernment of God, and in order to emphasize this parallelism. In my setting, the musical material of three-fold call is echoed by Eli but without the organ accompaniment, signifying that the voice of God has now departed, and it is Eli, alone, who speaks.

Table 10.2.1: Structure of Seán Doherty, 'God Calls Samuel'

Section	Text	Action	Verse of 1 Samuel 3
A bars 1-28	God: Samuel, Samuel. Samuel: Eli? Hinneni, Eli. God: Samuel, Samuel. Samuel: Eli? Hinneni, hinneni, Eli. God: Samuel, Samuel Samuel: Eli? Hinneni, hinneni, hinneni, Eli God: Samuel, Samuel Samuel: Daber ki shomea abdecha.	God Calls Samuel (*Eli? Here I am, Eli.*) (*Speak, for your servant hears*)	2-10
B bars 29-42	God: El! Eli! Samuel: Eli! Eli!	God gives the prophecy to Samuel	11-14
A' bars 43-55	Eli: Samuel? Samuel: Eli? Hinneni, Eli. Eli: Samuel.	Eli finds Samuel	15-16

II. The Compositional Process

Most of the ideas that Froehlich and I discussed at the TheoArtistry symposium, — all of which were viable — were jettisoned in the compositional process, in favour of thematic clarity, dramatic impact, and musical coherence. Practicalities must remain foremost for the composer, or the piece may lose its effectiveness in performance, or may not be performed at all. These practicalities included the prescribed duration of three minutes, which demanded a compression of the dramatic structure, the time constraints in rehearsal (which necessitated that the choir be able to perform the piece with limited preparation), and the balance between the organ, the choir, and the soloist (which needed to be distinguishable at all times for the sake of narrative clarity). In order to focus the dramatic structure, I limited my setting to 1 Samuel 3.2-16, from when God first calls Samuel, to when Eli finds Samuel in the morning.

2.1 Section A, Bars 1-28

At the TheoArtistry symposium, Froehlich and I discussed the symbolism of the first verse of this passage, and the possibility of exploring this idea creatively: 'In those days the word of the Lord was rare; there were not many visions' (1 Sam 3.1). Owing to the restricted duration of the piece and my desire to convey the passage from Samuel's viewpoint, this idea was distilled into a wordless fricative consonant (Sssshh), evoking the sound of wind across a barren land (bar 1). After the symbolic entry of the organ (the voice of God in my characterization), this wind sound emerges at the first phoneme of the word 'Samuel'. God's three-fold call, though theologically significant, risks being monotonous in performance owing to the lack of variation. I wanted a clear dramatic arc in the music, to reflect Samuel's increasingly distressed state of mind; to this end, I imposed an increase in musical tension with each of God's calls to Samuel. In the first of God's calls, the choir sing homophonically in stark open fifths (D and A); in the second call, the choir sing the words at different times and in a full triadic harmony (B minor); in the third call, the 'S' of Samuel is fragmented and repeated by the lower voices (Altos, Tenors, and Basses). Furthermore, there is an increase in dynamic level with each call (from *mezzo-piano* to *fortissimo*). The sibilance of the fragmented and repeated 'S' of Samuel has an effect which is increasingly ominous and disorientating. The increase of urgency in the choir is matched by the increasing urgency of Samuel's answers; this is accentuated by an increase in speed, pitch, and length, dynamic level, and in the number of repetitions of 'Hinneni'. (Table 10.2.1)

2.2 Section B, Bars 29-42

I wanted to convey the awesome sense of God's statement, 'See, I am about to do something in Israel that will make the ears of everyone who hears about it tingle'. To achieve this involved employing a number of extended vocal techniques. I ensured that the voice-leading (how the singer moves from one note to the next) is mostly by step, but with techniques that emphasize the sense of terror: *glissandi* (sweeping from one note to the next) are used in ascending and descending motion, which gives a sensation of extreme harmonic instability (e.g. bar 29); indeterminate pitches are used, and notated with a triangle note-head, which, depending on the direction of the triangle, indicates that the singer is to sing the highest or lowest possible (bar 35); and non-pitched notes are used in the emphatic last 'Eli!' before the final climax, where the singers are asked to roar (bar 38). The shift from standard to extended vocal techniques is difficult to perform, and so these shifts in technique are always underpinned by a strong harmonic foundation from the organ, which has clear notes in the lowest range (performed on the organ pedals) for the singers to use as a point of reference.

In relating the prophecy, God makes direct reference to himself six times and to Eli three times, as well as referring to himself in the third person ('his sons blasphemed God'), and to Israel (which also contains the Hebrew root word 'el'). It seemed justifiable, therefore, to restrict the text in the B section to 'El' and 'Eli', and let the music bear the narrative load. The chorus repeat 'El!' independently until the repetitions are as fast as possible, to give the effect of a mob baying for vengeance. The 'l' of 'Eli' is fragmented in the sopranos, and, through repetition, a *glissando* to a pitch high in their range (e″), and an *accelerando* (speeding up), becomes an ululation: a long, wavering, high-pitched vocal sound resembling a howl with a trilling quality. This vocal sound has manifold meanings depending on the geographical, historical, cultural, and ritual contextual factors of its performance, ranging from joy to grief.[3] I have chosen, however, to use it to denote fury and vengeance, as in Aeschylus' *Agamemnon*, when the ululation of Clytemnestra anticipates the impending slaughter of Agamemnon. In Greek tragedy, the ritual act of *ololugmas* or uluaalation is a choral activity, and the cue for performing this act is said to lead to *kata-stasis*, 'arranging' of *khoroi* 'choruses'.[4] Bars 39-42 serve as the *kata-stasis*, drawing together the independent rhythms of each voice, before the climax for the piece.

2.3 Climax, bars 43-50

The soprano solo in this section is written to imitate the cries of a child in the throes of a night terror. The cry is in a pitch register distinct from the rest of the choir: a diminished fifth or a perfect fourth above the sopranos ululation on e″. Every cry is a suspension (bar 43); this is when a note that is dissonant with the underlying harmony (the suspension) resolves downwards by step to a note consonant with the underlying harmony (the resolution). In species counterpoint, theorized in the Baroque era from the vocal

---

3   Joel C. Kuipers, 'Ululations from the Weyewa Highlands (Sumba): Simultaneity, Audience Response, and Models of Cooperation', *Ethnomusicology*, 43 (1999), 490–507 (pp. 490–93).
4   Gregory Nagy, *The Ancient Greek Hero in 24 Hours* (Cambridge, MA: Harvard University Press, 2013), pp. 479–80.

polyphony of the Renaissance, the suspension and the resolution are the same length. In these cries of 'Eli!', however, the suspension is elongated in comparison to the resolution. This frustrated and unsatisfying resolution heightens the distress of these cries.

This suspension is then contracted to form a pair of semiquavers (bar 45). Pairs of slurred descending notes with dissonant beginnings, such as these, were known as *Seufzer* — 'sigh' or 'groans' — and originated as a kind of word-painting or madrigalism in the Baroque era.[5] This sigh is made more realistic with a *glissando*, which, again, has the effect of minimizing the resolution and maximizing the harmonic instability and effect of disturbance (bar 46). These cries are made increasingly realistic by the reiteration of the vowel 'i', as Samuel chokes on his cries (bar 47). Samuel's final cry is cut off mid-word — where Eli is truncated to 'El', symbolizing that Samuel has been subsumed by the baying mob of his nightmare. The clamour of the chorus, too, is abruptly cut off, leaving a single note on the pedal, which decreases in volume until it is barely perceptible.

2.4 Section A', bars 51-55

The organ (the voice of God) has retreated, indicating that this is now Eli, rather than God, who is speaking. The chorus reprise the opening call of 'Samuel', which is now marked to be sung *semplice* (in a simple style); at the beginning of the piece it had been *lontano* (as from a distance). Too, the sound of the wind has now transformed into the sound of Eli hushing and comforting Samuel after his nightmare (bar 53). Where the soprano solo had outlined the melodic interval of a tritone in Samuel's first utterance (f''–b', bars 8-9) — once known as the *diabolus in musica* or 'the devil in music' — the soprano now sings a perfect fourth in its reprise at the end (f''–c'', bars 53-54): Samuel is glad to see that it was just a dream; his guardian is here, and he is comforted.

The creative partnership with Froehlich has been extremely valuable in the composition of 'God Calls Samuel', which would have been vastly different had I not enjoyed the benefit of his comprehensive contextualization. After our initial discussions, I completely changed my approach to setting this piece — owing solely to the collaboration — encouraging me to look at the passage in far greater detail, and more reflectively, than I had done beforehand. Froehlich was supportive of my personal reading of the biblical passage, which, in turn, gave me the confidence to pursue a more dramatic setting. I had never before collaborated with a theologian, and it proved a catalyst for inspiration.

 Seán Doherty, 'God Calls Samuel' (2017), in *Annunciations: Sacred Music for the 21st Century*, St Salvator's Chapel Choir and Sean Heath, cond. by Tom Wilkinson (Sanctiandree, SAND0006, 2018), © 2017 University of St Andrews. Track 10. Duration: 4.11.
https://doi.org/10.11647/OBP.0172.34

---

5   Richard Taruskin, *The Oxford History of Western Music*, 5 vols. (Oxford: Oxford University Press, 2010), II, p. 254.

'God Calls Samuel'

Seán Doherty

PROGRAMME NOTE

In 1 Samuel 3, the boy Samuel hears his name being called during his nightly task of tending the lamp in the temple at Shiloh. Samuel thinks he is being summoned by his guardian, Eli, the high priest of the temple, and answers 'Here I am!'. Eli tells Samuel that this is God's voice and to respond with the words, 'Speak, for your servant hears', whereupon God speaks to Samuel and promises to destroy the house of Eli because his wicked sons had blasphemed and Eli failed to restrain them. This setting takes the viewpoint of the boy Samuel, who is traumatised by this nightmarish prophecy to the extent that he is afraid to tell Eli about it in the morning.

TEXT

Text	Hebrew	Transliteration	Translation
Samuel	שְׁמוּאֵל	šə-mū-'êl	*God hears / the one who hears God*
Eli	אֵלִי	'ê-lî	*My God*
Hineni	הִנֵנִי	hine-nî!	*Here I am!*
Daber ki shomea abdecha	דַּבֵּר, כִּי שֹׁמֵעַ עַבְדֶּךָ	Dab-bêr, kî šhō-mê-a' ab-de-kā.	*Speak, for your servant hears*

PERFORMANCE NOTES

———————— *glissando*

Upwards triangle note head: as high as possible
Downwards triangle note head: as low as possible

Crossed note head: non-pitched note

For my Godson, Aodhán
God calls Samuel
written in collaboration with theologian Caleb Froehlich,
for TheoArtistry Scheme, Institute for Theology, Imagination, and the Arts, University of St Andrews.

1 Samuel 3

Seán Doherty

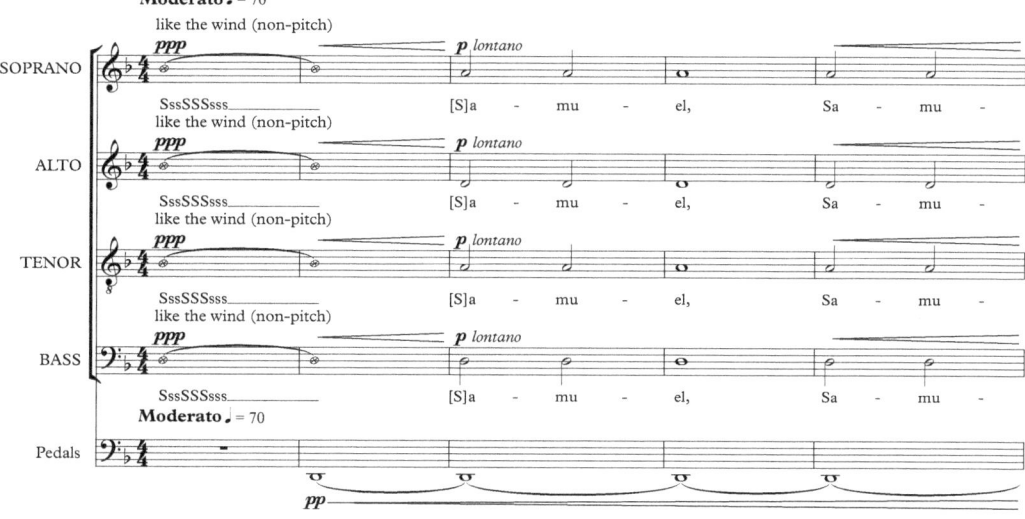

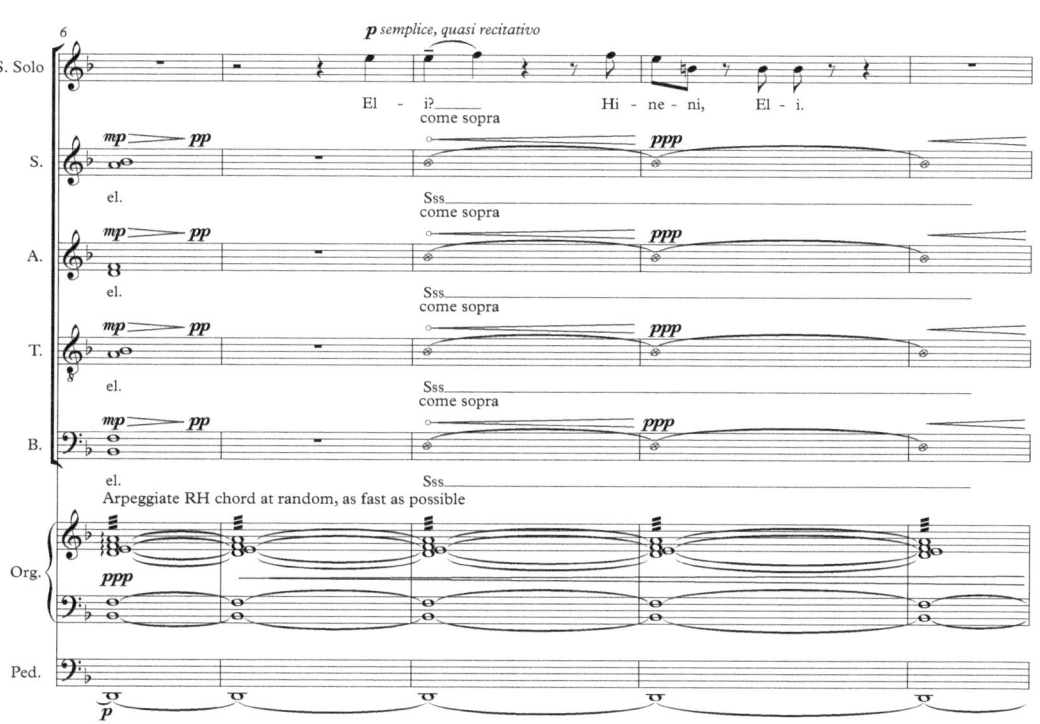

'God Calls Samuel' © 2019 Seán Doherty, CC BY 4.0

https://doi.org/10.11647/OBP.0172.18

11.1. Elijah's Silent Annunciation (1 Kings 19.8-15)

Mary Stevens

There are aspects of the biblical texts, comprising both theological themes and geographical references, which have resonances to scholars but which are not obvious to the present-day general reader. The biblical narrative depends heavily on these wider meanings, replete as it is with both concrete experience and the religious tradition of the original audiences. In preparing my collaboration with the composer, Lisa Robertson, a musician without theological training, I sought to present the essential religious and theological components of the text as well as to engage her imaginative involvement. To facilitate this, I presented both biblical and theological research, alongside a number of photographs of geographical scenes, seeking through the latter to bring her into contact with the location and external elements of the story. Although I was concerned that Robertson might feel overwhelmed with the amount of information given, this did not seem to have been the case. Instead, Robertson developed her own ideas in relation to those aspects of my research which resonated with her. Our subsequent theologian-composer conversations reflected her desire to understand the import of the text and its interpretation. As the process developed, Robertson articulated some of her inchoate plans, but I carefully tried to limit my role to aiding her own penetration of the text. This was truly a dialogue in which, as a theologian, I facilitated her understanding of the text while she, as a composer, responded both with her own questions and insights and, finally, with her fresh and original musical representation of the biblical episode. In this chapter, I try to give a sense of some of the theological research underpinning our collaboration, hopeful that it might enrich the appreciation of her piece of music and, also perhaps, that it might stimulate other artistic or theological interpretations of this seminal episode of the biblical narrative: Elijah's encounter with God in the 'still small voice'.

I. The Visual and Literary Dimensions of the Elijah Episode

The story from the Elijah Cycle is embedded in a specific geographical scene. Before introducing either textual or theological analysis, I sought, therefore, to highlight the visuality intrinsic to the scene: the vast and barren mountain range of Sinai where 1 Kings [Kgs] 19 is set. In the Bible, the mountain is itself a protagonist; it draws us beyond the quotidian to a place of transcendence — of encounter with God — and, at the same time, stirs a wealth of resonances from the Judeo-Christian tradition. This dual aspect of physical geography and religious tradition is the backdrop to several of the mighty phenomena that are narrated in the episode under consideration: thunder, lightning, mighty earthquake and gale. Imaginative immersion in this physical world should come prior to an unpicking of theological resonance. This is especially true for this biblical episode, which has at its heart a deliberate and major contrast between the natural phenomena shaping the setting of the 'annunciation' and the 'annunciation encounter' itself. To penetrate its meaning, one must be immersed in the images in order, paradoxically, to transcend them and receive the message held at its interstices.

Mount Horeb is situated in Sinai, though its exact geographical location is unknown. It bears a unique symbolism in the biblical repertoire, which gives it a precise symbolic and theological locus. Horeb is where Moses encounters the burning bush from within which Yahweh (YHWH) pronounced his Name, entrusting it to the people of Israel and summoning them out of Egypt (Exodus [Exod] 3). In continuity with this, and increasing the significance of Horeb, it is also the place of the Covenant (Exod 24; Deuteronomy 5.2). Additionally, the fire, thunder and earthquake of the present episode evoke the memory of the appearance of YHWH on a mountain in Sinai, immediately after the People of Israel had been led out of Egypt. On Horeb, too, there is an incident to which 1 Kgs 19 bears close resemblance: Moses was made to stand in a cleft of the rock while the glory of YHWH passed by.[1]

The main character in the story is the Prophet Elijah who lived in the ninth century BCE. To this day, Elijah is a powerful presence in Judaism, remembered at every Sabbath meal, Passover and ritual circumcision. He is known as the prophet who will usher in the coming of the Messiah to the people of Israel. The name, 'Elijah', affirms God's choice of the people of Israel and their choice of him as their God. It is

---

1 Cf. Exod 2; 24; Deut 5: 2. Mordechai Cogan, *I Kings: A New Translation with Introduction and Commentary* (New Haven, CT and London: Yale University Press, 2008), p. 456. For an exposition of the major biblical resonances in the text, see Marvin A. Sweeney, *I & II Kings: A Commentary* (Louisville, Ken.: Westminster John Knox Press, 2013), p. 231; Gina Hens-Piazza, *1-2 Kings* (Nashville, TN: Abingdon, 2006), pp. 184–95. Other particularly useful commentaries include Jerome T. Walsh and David W. Cotter, *1 Kings* (Collegeville, Minn.: Liturgical Press, 1996), pp. 264–78; Walter A. Brueggemann, *1 & 2 Kings* (Macon, GA: Smyth & Helwys Publ., 2000), pp. 233–43; Jerome T. Walsh and Christopher T. Begg, '1-2 Kings', in *The Jerome Biblical Commentary*, ed. Raymond Edward Brown, et al. (Dallas, TX: CDWord Library, 1989), p. 172.

11.1. Elijah's Silent Annunciation

(Above) Detail of Dorothea Reinecke, *Late Afternoon in South Sinai's Desert* (2016).

(Below) Detail of Berthold Werner, Sinai Peninsula, *View from Mount Sinai* (2010).

(Above) Detail of Berthold Werner, Sinai Peninsula, *Way to Mount Sinai* (2010).

Fig. 11.1.1 Elijah's encounter with God takes place on Mt. Horeb (the 'Mountain of God'). Although the exact location is disputed, the mountain is believed to be located in the vast and largely barren mountain range of Sinai.

a compound, formed from the general Hebrew word for God (*El*) and one syllable (*ja*) from the particular name of God revealed to Moses (YHWH). The two sounds combined create the name: 'El is YHWH'. The name YHWH is so sacred that to this day it will not be spoken by Jews and is always replaced with another name, which may be spoken without danger of blasphemy. The name Elijah therefore recalls and invokes the holiness of God and his self-revelation to Moses on Horeb.

In keeping with the project's theme of 'annunciation', I focused on the moment Elijah hears the sound of a 'still small voice' and leaves the cave to respond to God. To explore this intimate encounter with God, I introduced the mystical writings of St John of the Cross, the sixteenth-century Spanish Carmelite mystic who co-founded the Discalced branch of the order with St Teresa of Avila. The motto of the Carmelite Order is taken from the words of Elijah in this episode when he responds to God's question 'What are you doing here Elijah?' with the words 'With zeal have I been zealous for the Lord God of Hosts' (*zelo zelatus sum pro Domino Deo exercituum*). Members of the order emphasize attending to the 'still small voice' of God in contemplation. St John of the Cross directly refers to this episode, moreover, in *The Spiritual Canticle*, which I suggested as part of a paratext for the musical composition.[2] Before turning to this in more detail, however, I will present a brief textual analysis of the Elijahan story in order to identify its main elements.

The structure of this Elijah episode has been described variously as chiastic, binary, and composite.[3] The different structural identifications of the text emphasize the flexibility with which the components may be examined and the impossibility of imposing a rigid limitation on what is a dynamic and vibrant episode. All the possible structures with which it is accredited have a developmental movement to a centre and back: YHWH and Elijah are there at the beginning; the dialogue between them is repeated with slight yet significant variation; they move to a closer intimate encounter in the central silence and subsequent dialogue, before moving out in the re-commissioning. Various elements are repeated in different places: the cave appears at the beginning, the middle and the end; the same words are used in the dialogue between Elijah and YHWH in two places; to name the more obvious practical elements. With all this in mind I invited the composer to read the text of 1 Kgs 19.8-15 through the following binary structure:

---

2 Cf. Stanzas 14 and 15 in St John of the Cross, 'The Spiritual Canticle', in *The Collected Works of Saint John of the Cross, Volume II*, trans. by David Lewis (New York: Cosimo, 2007), II, pp. 160–67 (pp. 162–63).

3 Cf. Dan Epp-Tiessen, '1 Kings 19: The Renewal of Elijah', *Direction, A Mennonite Brethren Forum*, 35 (Spring 2006), 33–43; Ernst Würthwein, 'Elijah at Horeb: Reflections on 1 Kings 19:9-18', in *Proclamation and Presence: Old Testament Essays in Honour of Gwynne Henton Davies*, ed. by John I. Durham and Gwynne H. Davies (Macon, GA: Mercer University Press, 1970), pp. 152–66; Gwilym H. Jones, *1 and 2 Kings. Vol. 2* (London: Marshall Morgan & Scott, 1984).

11.1. Elijah's Silent Annunciation

    ⁸So he got up and ate and drank, and strengthened by that food he walked for forty days and forty nights until he reached Horeb, God's mountain.

A: ⁹There he went into a cave and spent the night there.

B: Then the word of Yahweh came to him saying, 'What are you doing here, Elijah?'

C: ¹⁰He replied, 'I am full of jealous zeal for Yahweh Sabaoth, because the Israelites have abandoned your covenant, have torn down your altars and put your prophets to the sword. I am the only one left, and now they want to kill me.'

D: ¹¹Then he was told, 'Go out and stand on the mountain before Yahweh.'

E: For at that moment Yahweh was going by.

    A mighty hurricane split the mountains and shattered the rocks before Yahweh. But Yahweh was not in the hurricane. And after the hurricane, an earthquake. But Yahweh was not in the earthquake. ¹²And after the earthquake, fire. But Yahweh was not in the fire. And after the fire, a light murmuring sound.

A1:   ¹³And when Elijah heard this, he covered his face with his cloak and went out and stood at the entrance of the cave.

B1:   Then a voice came to him, which said, 'What are you doing here, Elijah?'

C1:   ¹⁴He replied, 'I am full of jealous zeal for Yahweh, God Sabaoth, because the Israelites have abandoned your covenant, have torn down your altars and put your prophets to the sword. I am the only one left and now they want to kill me.'

D1:   ¹⁵'Go,' Yahweh said, 'go back by the same way to the desert of Damascus.'

What is the climax of the story? Is it E? Or perhaps A1 or B1? Or, conceivably, even D1? Each of these stages underlines something crucial: E is the 'still small voice' highlighting the difference of God from the pagan idols, and also his intimacy. A1 emphasizes the willing response of Elijah who has 'heard' God. Yet, did he hear God in the silence? Or was it that, hearing the silence, he was prepared for meeting God in a way even more unknown? B1 has God addressing anew the prophet and recommissioning him in a way which, given the name of Eli-jah, the Mt of Horeb, and the preceding phenomena, recalls the Mosaic drama and seems to suggest a new calling of Israel. With the episode's structure thus laid out, we may now turn to Elijah and Carmel.

Fig. 11.1.2 Details of: (18.9a) Unknown artist, *Fiery Ascent of the Prophet Elijah* (18th century); (18.9b) Unknown artist, *Holy Prophet Elijah with Selected Saints in the Fields* (1850); (18.10) Juan de Valdés Leal, *Ascension of Elijah* (c. 1655–1645); (18.11a) Adolf von Meckel (attrib.), *Landschaft in Sinai* (c. 1893); (18.11b–g) Herbert Sanchez, *Lighting* (2010); (18.13a) Unknown Artist, *Elijah the Prophet in the Desert* (15th century); (18.13b) Unknown Artist, *Fiery Ascension of the Holy Prophet Elijah* (c. 1800); (18.14) Photograph by Wikimedia User Léna of Marc Arcis, *Elijah, Prophet of the Carmelites*; (18.15) Washington Allston, *Elijah in the Desert* (1818). The structure of 1 Kings 19.9-15 is composed of repeated motifs, separated by a description of Elijah's dramatic experience of God. It invites readers to consider what is important about the passage: God's repeated invitation to Elijah to reveal why he has come to God's mountain (Mt. Horeb), Elijah's declaration of his zealousness for God or his willing response to God's commissions, or that intimate encounter of the 'still small voice' that is so unlike characteristic contact with pagan 'gods'.

II. The Elijah Episode and Carmelite Spirituality

The Carmelite Order was founded at the turn of the thirteenth century on Mt Carmel. The first hermits who settled there were crusaders who exchanged their military existence for a hermit religious life, living in prayer, contemplation and silence. According to their 'Rule of Life', this group of men gathered together 'around the spring of Elias on Mt Carmel'.[4] The Carmelites had no great founder but looked to scripture for their inspiration. They were known as 'The Brothers of the Virgin Mary of Mt Carmel'. Due to his association with Mt Carmel, Elijah became an important figure in their corporate identity, while Elijah's silent ineffable encounter with God became a key text for their contemplative spirituality. When the Carmelites subsequently moved to Europe, and it became politically expedient to have a single founding father, they adopted Elijah. Episodes from his life, which had been the subject of the brothers' reflections, remained central to the spiritual attitude of the Carmelite order in their contemplative searching for the 'still small voice' of God.

As a young Carmelite friar, St John of the Cross (b. 1542) met Teresa of Avila, his elder by twenty-seven years. She persuaded him to be involved in the reform of the Carmelite order. The two of them are known as the founders of the reformed, or discalced, Carmelite Order. This religious order is contemplative and largely silent. St John of the Cross is acknowledged as one of the greatest mystics in Christianity, and he is recognized as a doctor of the universal Church (meaning that the Church accepts his teaching as having outstanding worth for the whole people of God). The centre point and summit of his teaching concerns the most profound and intimate union of the human person with God and the way to that union.[5] He struggles to express through his poetry the knowledge learned through mystical experience.[6] He describes intense suffering on the way to union with God, which he understands entirely within the context of the salvific suffering of Christ. He writes of a journey of purification made at night, from which is derived the phrase 'the dark night of the soul'; one of John's poems begins: 'One dark night, my soul being now at rest, I went out…' He uses images such as 'silent music' and 'sounding solitude' in his attempt to articulate something of the experience of union with God.

---

[4] OCSD, 'Rule of St Alebert and the Constitutions of the Secular Order of the Teresian Carmel' (Ocd.pcn.net, 2003), http://www.ocd.pcn.net/ocds_Aen.htm

[5] For an introduction to mystical experience in John of the Cross, see Edward Howells, *John of the Cross and Teresa of Avila: Mystical Knowing and Selfhood* (New York: Crossroad, 2002), pp. 9–14. For a succinct analysis and basic description of the goal of human life as union with God in St John of the Cross, see Iain Matthew, *The Impact of God: Soundings from St. John of the Cross* (London: Hodder & Stoughton, 1995), p. 17; and Howells, pp. 125–28.

[6] Matthew, *The Impact of God*, pp. 10–12. Matthew describes the experience as 'white hot in poetry, cooled down and shared out in prose'.

Fig. 11.1.3 Juan Rodrìguez Juárez, *The Virgin of the Carmen with Saint Theresa and Saint John of the Cross* (c. 1708).

The stumbling attempts of his poetry, I thought, might help to inspire a musical articulation. The following quotation from the *Spiritual Canticle* indicates St John of the Cross' poetic attempt to talk about the experience of union with God:

> My Beloved, the mountains,
> and lonely wooded valleys,
> strange islands,
> and resounding rivers,
> the whistling of love-stirring breezes,
> the tranquil night
> at the time of the rising dawn,
> silent music
> sounding solitude.

In his commentary on this stanza, St John of the Cross makes one of his most significant references to Elijah. He begins by attempting to describe this experience in prose:

> Since this touch of God gives intense satisfaction and enjoyment to the substance of the soul and gently fulfills her desire for this union, she calls this union or these touches 'love-stirring breezes'. As we have said, the Beloved's attributes are lovingly and sweetly communicated in this breeze and from it the intellect receives the knowledge or whistling. She calls the knowledge a 'whistling' because just as the whistling of the breeze pierces deeply into the hearing organ, so this most subtle and delicate knowledge penetrates with wonderful savoriness into the innermost part of the substance of the soul, and the delight is greater than all others.[7]

---

7   St John of the Cross, *The Spiritual Canticle*, § 14.

This attempt at a prose description continues to rely heavily on poetic imagery. The attempt to talk of the metaphysical 'substance of the soul' and the reference to 'the intellect receiving knowledge' seem a little awkward beside the more fluent imagery of the 'wonderful savouriness', 'the communication in the breeze' and the 'whistling of the breeze'. Trying to penetrate and explain more clearly his meaning, St John of the Cross turns to the experience of Elijah on Horeb, emphasizing the direct experience, the 'substantial knowledge', received in his silent encounter:

> Since this whistling refers to the substantial knowledge mentioned, some theologians think our Father Elijah saw God in the whistling of the gentle breeze heard on the mount at the mouth of his cave (1 Kgs. 19:11-13 [10]). Scripture calls it 'the whistling of the gentle breeze' because knowledge was begotten in his intellect from the delicate spiritual communication. The soul calls this knowledge 'the whistling of love-stirring breezes' because it flows over into the intellect from the loving communication of the Beloved's attributes. As a result she calls the knowledge 'the whistling of the love-stirring breezes'.[8]

The ineffability of the experience of God is more than a linguistic limitation imposed on the author. The experience itself is a gift beyond human categories.

In one of his *Sayings*, St John of the Cross writes, 'The Father spoke one Word, which was his Son, and this Word he speaks always in eternal silence, and in silence must it be heard by the soul'. His words echo the opening of St John's Gospel:

> In the beginning was the Word: and the Word was with God. [...] All things were made by him: and without him was made nothing that was made [...] And the Word was made flesh and dwelt among us and we saw his glory, the glory as it were of the only begotten of the Father, full of grace and truth.

The Book of Wisdom, furthermore, recounts how 'when all was in quiet silence and the night was in the midst of her course, Thine Almighty Word, O Lord, leapt down from his royal throne'. Featured in Advent and Christmas liturgies, these passages may also be complemented with Isaiah 40.9: 'Get you up to a high mountain, O Zion, herald of good tidings; lift it up, do not fear; say to the cities of Judah, "Here is your God!"' Since a central theme in the Elijah episode is the command to go forth and proclaim God, I selected this text alongside John 1.1 and Wisdom 18.15 to serve as a paratext to 1 Kgs 19. Perhaps fittingly, the motto of the School of Divinity, St Mary's College — in which the TheoArtistry project was developed — is *In principio erat verbum* [In the beginning was the Word]. With these words, then, I opened a provisional set of lyrics which wove together 1 Kgs 19 with the paratext and St John of the Cross' *Spiritual Canticle*. The proposed lyrics, which were for Robertson to develop or disregard, were as follows:

---

8   Ibid., §14.

In principio erat verbum

The Word of the Lord came to Eliyahu[9]

> 'Eliyahu! Go, stand on the mountain before me'.
> Know the storm of earthquake,
> Know the storm of fire,
> Know the storm of wind.

> Eliyahu: 'My God is not in the earthquake.
> My God is not in the fire. My God is not in the wind'.

> When all was in quiet silence
> and the night was in the midst of her course,
> thine Almighty Word, Oh Elohim,
> leapt down from his royal throne.

> Eliyahu: 'Elohim! Elohim!
> My Beloved, the mountains,
> and lonely wooded valleys,
> strange islands,
> and resounding rivers,
> the whistling of love-stirring breezes,
> the tranquil night
> at the time of the rising dawn,
> silent music
> sounding solitude.'

The Word of the Lord came to Eliyahu

> 'Eliyahu! Go up to a high mountain
> Joyful messenger to Zion!
> Shout with a loud voice
> Joyful messenger to Jerusalem!
> Shout without fear,
> Say to the towns of Judah
> "Here is your God!"'.

In principio erat verbum

In the collaboration, my hope was to introduce Robertson to a theological perspective from within a particular Christian spiritual tradition. I tried to build on something with which she was deeply familiar — her own personal experience and love of the wild vastness of Scotland — to help her to explore new interior, theological territory. Her uptake of ideas, reconfiguring of juxtapositions, and skilled musical use of theological themes, was exciting and stimulating for me as a theologian and Christian. Her musical response showed them to me in a fresh light. This, presumably, is one of the key purposes of all artistic and theological collaboration.

---

9   Note: the Hebrew name for Elijah is Eliyahu which has a resonance with the name he uses here for God, Elohim.

List of Illustrations

11.1.1 Detail of Dorothea Reinecke, *Late Afternoon in South Sinai's Desert* (2016), Wikimedia, https://commons.wikimedia.org/wiki/File:Late_afternoon_in_South_Sinai%27s_desert.jpg, CCA-SA 4.0. Detail of Berthold Werner, Sinai Peninsula, *View from Mount Sinai* (2010), Wikimedia, https://commons.wikimedia.org/wiki/File:Mount_Sinai_BW_3.jpg, CCA-SA 3.0. Detail of Berthold Werner, Sinai Peninsula, *Way to Mount Sinai* (2010), Wikimedia, https://commons.wikimedia.org/wiki/File:Mount_Sinai_BW_6.jpg, CCA-SA 3.0   219

11.1.2 Details of: (18.9a) Unknown artist, *Fiery Ascent of the Prophet Elijah* (18th century), wood, gesso and tempera, Wikimedia, public domain; (18.9b) Unknown artist, *Holy Prophet Elijah with Selected Saints in the Fields* (1850), Wikimedia, public domain; (18.10) Juan de Valdés Leal, *Ascension of Elijah* (c. 1655–1645), oil on canvas, Church of the Nuestra Señora del Carmen, Córdoba, Spain, Wikimedia, https://commons.wikimedia.org/wiki/File:Ascensi%C3%B3n_de_El%C3%ADas,_de_Juan_de_Vald%C3%A9s_Leal_(Iglesia_de_Ntra._Sra._del_Carmen_de_C%C3%B3rdoba).jpg, public domain; (18.11a) Adolf von Meckel (attrib.), *Landschaft in Sinai* (c. 1893), watercolour on paper, Wikimedia, https://commons.wikimedia.org/wiki/File:Adolf_von_Meckel_(attr)_Landschaft_in_Sinai.jpg, public domain; (18.11b-g) Herbert Sanchez, *Lighting* (2010), oil on canvas, Wikimedia, https://commons.wikimedia.org/wiki/File:Iluminacion.jpg, CCA-SA 4.0; (18.13a) Unknown Artist, *Elijah the Prophet in the Desert* (15th century), Yaroslavl Art Museum, Yaroslavl, Russia, Wikimedia, https://commons.wikimedia.org/wiki/File:Elijah_(15_c.,_Yaroslavl_museum).jpg, public domain; (18.13b) Unknown Artist, *Fiery Ascension of the Holy Prophet Elijah* (c. 1800), tempora on wood, Wikimedia, public domain; (18.14) Photograph by Wikimedia User Léna of Marc Arcis, *Elijah, Prophet of the Carmelites,* 17th century, terracotta, Musée des Augustins, Toulouse, France, Wikimedia, https://commons.wikimedia.org/wiki/File:Le_Proph%C3%A8te_%C3%89lie.jpg, CCA 3.0; (18.15) Washington Allston, *Elijah in the Desert* (1818), oil on canvas, Museum of Fine Arts, Boston, USA, Wikimedia, https://commons.wikimedia.org/wiki/File:Washington_Allston_-_Elijah_in_the_Desert_-_Google_Art_Project.jpg, public domain.   222

11.1.3 Juan Rodrìguez Juárez, *The Virgin of the Carmen with Saint Theresa and Saint John of the Cross* (c. 1708), oil on canvas, Museo Nacional de Arts, Mexico City, Mexico, Wikimedia, https://commons.wikimedia.org/wiki/File:Juan_Rodr%C3%ADguez_Ju%C3%A1rez_-_The_Virgin_of_the_Carmen_with_Saint_Theresa_and_Saint_John_of_the_Cross_-_Google_Art_Project.jpg, public domain.   224

11.2. Composer's Reflections

Lisa Robertson

Of the texts suggested for the TheoArtistry project, I was immediately drawn to the passage from 1 Kgs 19.4-12. There were many aspects that sparked a creative interest for me, such as the dramatic 'wilderness' setting of Elijah's encounter with God. I believe that many of the emotions evoked through listening to music can also be brought about when one finds oneself alone, in awe, amongst dramatic scenes of nature. This text is dramatically heightened by its wild, mountaintop setting. Perhaps in this landscape, Elijah was perfectly disposed to receive the Word of God. I often turn to aspects of nature as sources of inspiration in compositions, so I was instantly drawn to creating a musical portrayal of the atmosphere, emotion and natural phenomena which are conveyed in Elijah's divine encounter. The main interest for me, which during the collaboration became the focal point of the piece, was the 'sound of sheer silence'. In isolation, this concept may seem to be the antithesis of both drama and of music, unless in reference to John Cage's famous work '4'33'. However, in the biblical episode, the boisterous earthly phenomena — the outbursts of the wind, the earthquake and the fire — that occur before the moment of silence arguably make this silence the most powerful, and even the most musically provocative, moment. I often use silence within my music as I feel that such pauses are necessary in order to provide contrast to louder musical sections and to allow for a moment of clarity for the music to be understood. The idea of heightening the importance of this silence was therefore inviting.

My preference for this text brought me happily into partnership with theologian, Mary Stevens. During our first meeting at the TheoArtistry Symposium in November 2016, we had very engaging conversations in which Stevens conveyed a great deal of information; she revealed certain aspects of the text that I had not been aware of, which opened up many possibilities for the piece. As Stevens has a musical background herself, she was aware of aspects which could be of interest and also of issues that might arise at different points during the process. Her hope was that we would be able to unravel the text using music. She explained that, in this passage, 'the sound of sheer silence' is really associated with an encounter with God; this suggests that 'knowing God' cannot be expressed through words alone. She hoped that music might convey a little of the emotion which cannot be described in words. In this text, silence may be a metaphor for an encounter with God and, in an extended sense, music could act as a further image to represent this silence. This was a compelling notion for me. The music which I write is often still and quiet in its nature. I wondered if using quiet music as a metaphor for silence might be, along with the possible juxtaposition of actual silence, a possibility for musical drama.

I was delighted to discover also that mountains are crucial symbols for annunciations or theophanies throughout the Bible. This confirmed my hope that taking inspiration from the vivid contrasts of a wild landscape might be important in portraying the meaning of the text. I took this as a cue to create a soundscape inspired by the vastness of mountains. Therefore, I adopted a sparse but widely spaced harmonic language in this piece. I also aimed to include large contrasts in the dynamics, texture and range. Stevens' experience within the Carmelite Order was also fascinating as she was able to demonstrate the influence of this episode, and of Elijah's life more generally, on Carmelite spirituality. She introduced me to the poetry of St John of the Cross, drawing particular attention to his phrases 'silent music' and 'sounding solitude'. These phrases bore a relevance to 1 Kgs 19.4-12; it also linked to the ideas which we had about using music as a metaphor for silence and juxtaposing actual silence with the music in order to draw attention to its importance.

Following the preliminary symposium, I left St Andrews with many creative sparks glimmering. My first step was to take Stevens' suggested lyrics and to judge which of the lines it would be possible to use within the three-minute time limit of the final piece. I was eager to use a great deal of the text as I felt that the interweaving of parallel texts would help to uncover the meaning of the passage. It also offered the possibility to add a sense of depth to the piece, which might be further appreciated by listeners who already have an understanding of the theological significance of these texts. We felt that it was important to frame the piece with God's calling to Elijah, as this also defines the structure of the text. As we discovered at the symposium, the story of Elijah's encounter differs from other annunciations because God calls him by name only once, rather than twice. However, in consultation with Stevens, I decided, in the music, to call Elijah by name twice in reference or homage to this formal trend of annunciations and because it felt musically appropriate. I also decided to use the names Elijahu and Elohim, for Elijah and God respectively. I felt that, as well as giving a sense of the context of the story, the words themselves had a pleasing natural timbre and rhythm.

In the opening, I wanted to create a feeling of confusion and mystery; the texture is therefore canonic, which masks the pulse. I then seek to introduce the picture of mountains where God calls Elijah, giving this music a sense of power and vastness by using a wide range and a unison texture. These 'calling' sections frame the piece. After initial conversations, it was clear that both Stevens and I hoped for the climax moment of the piece to be in the silence where Elijah appears to have an encounter with God. As this follows the three dramatic natural phenomena of the wind, the earthquake and the fire, it was possible to use these events as a means of intensifying the tension towards the climax point. I felt that the most successful means of achieving this would be to enhance the listener's musical expectations with four repetitions of musical material. The fourth repetition begins to conform to the listener's expectations, according to the pattern, but is then suddenly interrupted and, surprisingly, met with lengthy silence.

Instead of actually stating the phrase 'the sound of sheer silence', I decided to juxtapose several fragments of the text which Stevens had selected from the Christmas liturgy: 'when all was in quiet silence, the Almighty Word leapt down' from the Book of Wisdom and 'my beloved mountain, the tranquil night at the time of rising dawn […] silent music sounding solitude' from St John of the Cross' poetry. With these fragments, we hoped to describe not only the silence and stillness itself but also the significance of the silence in encounters with God. The piece returns from this exploration of silence to the story of Elijah with the phrase, 'Here is your God' which becomes something of a refrain for the remainder of the piece.

In our later discussions, Stevens found the phrase 'your God' to be significant as it implied a personal relationship with God. I wondered if, perhaps, we could also use the phrase 'my God', which would allow Elijah to speak and to acknowledge his search for this personal relationship. We also discussed the portrayal of different characters. We disliked the idea of separating the male and female voices specifically to enhance the difference between the voice of God, the voice of Elijah and the narration. A possibility would have been to use purely male voices for the voice of God. However, I thought that the choir singing *tutti* could portray the voice of God more powerfully, with an increased scope of range and louder dynamic. It may also make this important moment more inclusive, in keeping with the idea of portraying personal relationships with God.

After discussing the sections of the text where God is present and those where God is not, I was keen to find a way of distinguishing between them. It was at this point that I added percussive sounds to the sections where God is not present (for example, 'My God is not in the earthquake'). These also helped to intensify the tension towards the climactic moment of silence. In a way, the sections where God is present were harder to define musically. Stevens felt that the key point was that God was present from the moment of silence until the end of the section of text. However, it would not be possible to maintain the texture of silence for the rest of the piece. I sought to find, therefore, an audible means of representing silence. This was an idea which we had already considered due to various translations of the text. Other translations of 'the sound of sheer silence' include 'a still small voice', 'the sound of a gentle blowing' and 'a soft murmuring sound'. This made me think of using whispering sounds as an extended vocal technique. I felt that this contrast between whispering sounds and the regular timbre of singing might be a suitable replacement for the contrast between silence and sound. In previous compositions, I have used similar sounds to mimic the sound of wind and to enhance the aural portrayal of natural landscapes. On mentioning this to Stevens, she suggested that we could use the analogy of gentle wind to connect the whispering sound to other points in the Bible where God's presence is shown in wind, such as at the beginning of Genesis where the breath of God hovers over the waters.

A later addition to the piece was a series of performance indications. I took words from other translations of the passage and also other words which I thought might reflect the emotion of each point in the passage. I felt that this might help the performers to approach the music with the correct emotional intention. We also deliberated for a long time over the title, but eventually decided on 'The Silent Word Sounds' as it seemed to draw together several of the threads which we hoped to weave through the piece.

Being part of the TheoArtistry Composers' Scheme was a very interesting experience for me. It was a pleasure to approach a piece with Stevens. With her meticulously prepared research, I could begin to compose almost immediately as I had, already in place, an understanding of the text, ideas about structure, and a clear goal of what we hoped the final piece would become. Being able to consult with Stevens during the writing process was also useful. I was able to confirm with her whether ideas which I had during the process would be theologically appropriate and significant. This was creatively liberating, as I sought to unravel the text through musical portrayal.

 Lisa Robertson, 'The Silent Word Sounds', in *Annunciations: Sacred Music for the 21st Century*, St Salvator's Chapel Choir and Sean Heath, cond. by Tom Wilkinson (Sanctiandree, SAND0006, 2018), © 2017 University of St Andrews. Track 11. Duration: 3.41.
https://doi.org/10.11647/OBP.0172.35

'The Silent Word Sounds'

Lisa Robertson

The Silent Word Sounds

Lisa Robertson

'The Silent Word Sounds' © 2019 Lisa Robertson, CC BY 4.0

https://doi.org/10.11647/OBP.0172.21

*the large X indicates body percussion (tap leg with hand) This always occurse on the downbeat of the bars indicated.

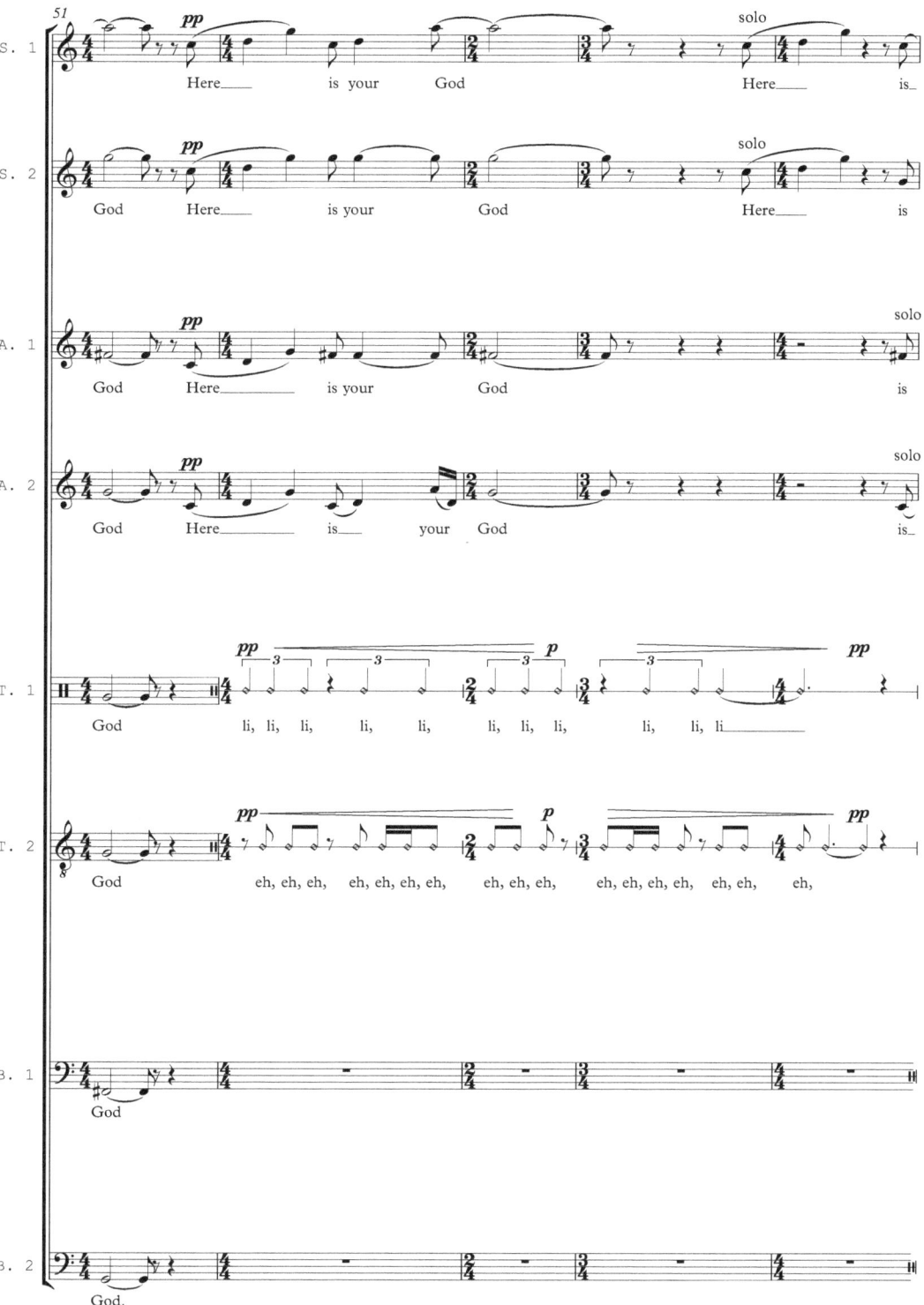

16

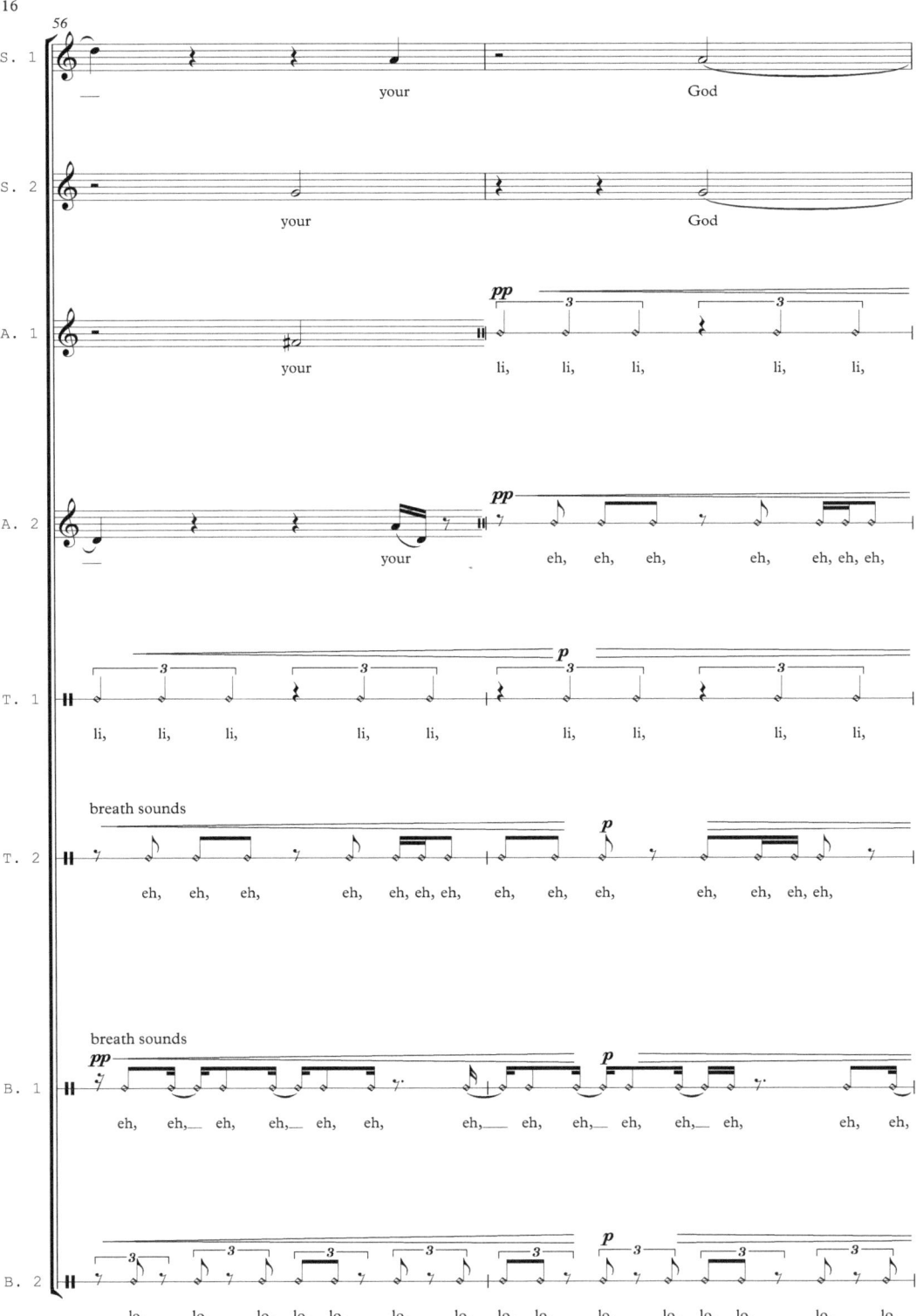

12.1. Musical Arguments and Gender Performance (Song of Songs 3.6-11)

Kimberley Jane Anderson

Oscar Wilde's tutor at Oxford was reported to have answered a suffragette student's question about the essential difference between men and women with an amusing double entendre: "Madam, I cannot conceive".[1] The idea of 'annunciation' as a metaphor for a human, holistic reception (and conception) of the divine in Christian meditation, should surely be applicable to all. Nevertheless, such an image contains an inherent biological incongruity for almost half of the human population. Mysticism is known to have opened remarkable spaces in which women, historically constricted in other spheres of life, were able freely to decipher, receive, and even dominate discourse (for instance, the formidable case of Teresa of Avila). However, the receptive, mystic posture ultimately represents a *retreat* from power. While there have been many examples of religious men honouring such an act of annunciation/renunciation, the traditional 'masculine' role, which has been projected across Western society for generations, demands a different pattern of behaviour. Compelled to present and perceive themselves as strong and independent, certain generations of men might understandably have trouble in finding a way for authentic religious self-expression. There is currently a documented disparity between the genders in religious commitment, and I have wondered for a while about the influence and function (or dysfunction) of projected role models in this situation.[2]

---

[1] Donald Christopher Nugent, 'There Was a Feminine Mysticism', *Mystics Quarterly*, 14 (1988), 135–42 (p. 135).

[2] See, for example, Callum G. Brown, 'Men Losing Faith: The Making of Modern No-Religionism in the UK, 1939–2010', in *Men, Masculinities and Religious Change in Twentieth Century Britain*, ed. by

Contributing to a piece of art seemed like an interesting method of exploring these gendered tensions further, especially in a project based on the theme of 'annunciation'. For my proposal, I tried to find an Old Testament passage which reflected this tension: an image of a man struggling against himself to accept (or reject) the overpowering embrace of the Almighty — whether that was God Himself or religion. Two possibilities sprang to mind: the story of Jacob wrestling with God in Genesis, and the approach of a mysterious bridegroom on his wedding day, in Song of Songs 3.6-11. I hoped that a culturally relevant, well-executed piece might contribute to general understandings of whichever biblical passage was used. The biblical content was intended to serve flexibly as a script — providing an immediate framework to our creation — but also required the capacity to be influenced, or even determined, by a much broader narrative. Thus, when provided with the chance to develop this proposal into a brief for one of the six composers, I resolved to prioritize understanding the cultural situation before turning to the question of staging the biblical passage. This chapter will cover those two issues respectively before discussing the profound effect of the collaborative process on the final product.

Exposition I: Religion in Culture and the Performance of Masculinity

In creating my proposal, I had a certain picture of masculinity in mind, which would create the aforementioned tensions about encountering God. Beginning my doctoral research into rock music, I thought of the persona projected in some Rolling Stones songs: enjoying (albeit, perhaps, with some irony) a sense of individual power in rebellion against all the social norms which represent God ('Sympathy for the Devil'), and only showing vulnerability on rare and specific occasions ('Angie').[3] This image tallies somewhat with what I observed during part-time work as a bartender in Scotland, seeing people at their extremes. Of course, the idea of gender is rightly being interrogated in mainstream culture today, and this role is not a particularly healthy one to inhabit.[4] And yet, for all its faults, I did have some sympathy for this type of character, especially with regards to religion.

It would have been easy (though not very original) to psychoanalyse and deconstruct 'fragile' masculinity when discussing its relationship to religion, but it seemed plausible that some religious institutions might also provide a problematic image of gender.

Lucy Delap and Sue Morgan (Basingstoke: Palgrave Macmillan, 2013), pp. 301–25; Thomas G. Long, 'Why Do Men Stay Away?', *The Christian Century* (20 October 2011), https://www.christiancentury.org/article/2011-10/why-do-men-stay-away

3   The Rolling Stones. These songs, and many others which provide a fuller picture of the persona discussed, can be found in *The Complete Collection 1971–2013* (iTunes, 2013).

4   The term 'gender performance' was coined by Judith Butler, in her influential work *Gender Trouble: Feminism and the Subversion of Identity* (New York: Routledge, 1999), first published in 1990. The documentary *The Mask You Live In*, directed by Jennifer Siebel Newsom (The Representation Project, 2015), covers a basic history of gender expectations, the harm this can do to men and ways of tackling it.

Certainly, accepting God as Almighty undercuts the idea of individual strength, as Christ's self-emptying (Philippians 2) exemplifies; this practice should be non-negotiable in the Christian faith. Yet some sociological studies suggest that traditional Christianity may accommodate, and even contribute toward, a 'strong' understanding of masculinity through modelling a superlatively dominating structure.[5] Reading the anecdotes of youth and childhood experiences in church — which were in different ways traumatic — the theme emerged that men renounced their faith not because it was not 'manly' enough, but because the masculinity modelled by preachers and role models was itself dysfunctional: 'postures of manipulation and control', bullying, non-egalitarianism and repression, and a strange combination of different, contradictory pressures.[6] By opposing feminism and radical politics, some churches alienated men as well as women in their old-fashioned authoritarian structures. As one participant describes in a particularly memorable anecdote, even young boys were motivated to defy this institution rather than emulate it:

> [The brethren] put up a tin hut, next to one of our out-farm properties, and they would preach. We were sent there and this guy would, you know, [talk about] hell, damnation, and we were determined we would not go up to the front you know, and be saved. And I remember sitting holding the seat so I wouldn't get up, and that was more out of embarrassment, shyness, but also [a] message that we didn't agree with this stuff.[7]

Perhaps this sympathetic portrayal of how, even from a young age, men (and women) can feel attacked and belittled by authoritarian religious figures would have provided enough cultural context for our piece. Yet, scandalized by these ills, I felt compelled to ask how this social pattern of domination could have developed. I therefore turned to explore whether these mishaps in Christian culture were doctrinally encouraged. Despite strong emphasis throughout the Bible that equality with God is not 'something to be grasped', there is evidence for a hierarchical gender structure which prioritizes male leadership in both Old and New Testaments.[8]

In Ephesians, women are told to be 'subject' to their husbands, as the Church is to Christ: 'the husband is the head of the wife' (Ephesians 5.23-4).[9] A similar relational model can also be perceived in the creation story, particularly as it is represented in John Milton's *Paradise Lost*. As the primal couple are introduced, Adam is said to have been made 'for God only'; Eve, 'for God in him'.[10] The natural spiritual leader is Adam, who is responsible for human communication with God. Angels converse, through sublime speculative reason, with Adam alone, and Eve prefers to wait for her husband to convey the information to her (VIII.39-57). Gender roles are defined in opposition to

---

5   Brown, 'Men Losing Faith', pp. 301–25.
6   *Ibid.*, p. 321.
7   Wilson Dillon, quoted in *ibid.*, pp. 307–08.
8   See Philippians 2.6; Matthew 16.23.
9   Throughout this chapter, the English Standard Version of the Bible (ESV) is used unless stated otherwise.
10 John Milton, *Paradise Lost*, ed. by John Leonard (London: Penguin Books, 2003), IV.299.

one another: Adam's masculine appearance 'declar'd/ Absolute rule' (IV.300), whereas Eve's 'wanton ringlets [...] impli'd/ Subjection' (IV.306-08).

Even within orthodox Christianity, there are indications that these gender prescriptions are not always helpful or practicable. Studying *Paradise Lost* — which adds psychological depth to the first man and woman described in Genesis — Kent R. Lehnhof argues that the imposition of Eve's 'hierarchical subordination' pushes her to take the fruit in a subversive act of female initiative.[11] Although this act is viewed negatively, the notion that less is expected of Eve than Adam might in fact be liberating for her. Her freedom from 'Adam's vexed maleness' makes her seem, as Adam himself remarks in the poem, 'in herself complete' (VIII.548).[12] By contrast, in order to truly be a man Adam is expected to perform a masculine role which is constantly in danger of being compromised. As Lehnhof suggests, he must never be overpowered, never subject to his wife, and never caught off guard or out of control; if any of these things happens, he is considered 'effeminate'. Such a role is, understandably, impossible to perform flawlessly. Being 'fondly overcome by Female charm' contributes towards him and his wife committing the first sin.[13] After this occasion, Adam expresses misogynistic sentiment for the first time in bitterness at his wife.[14] It is psychologically understandable that, after this immense failure to live up to the leadership role that he was given, Adam attempts to compensate for this 'effeminacy' by distancing himself from this sex. Perhaps it is also plausible that, due to this constant potential for failure, it becomes unthinkable for a man to let down his guard and show any vulnerability whatsoever, including in a religious context.

The foregoing description perhaps goes some way in illustrating the cultural pressure which has accompanied religious prescriptions of gender roles, at least since Early Modern times when Milton wrote *Paradise Lost*. However, further interrogation of the creation story in Genesis highlights that, even within this hierarchical social structure, there are small pockets where male vulnerability might surface, particularly in the context of marriage. Instances such as Adam being created first, and the referral to Eve as his 'helper' (Genesis [Gen] 2.20), might be taken to suggest that he is dominant and she is subject to his authority. Yet, when Adam is first brought to life, God says that 'It is not good that the man should be alone' (Gen 2.18); perhaps it is significant to note that 'aloneness' is never said to limit womankind. In a poetic phrase celebrating marriage as a rite of passage, it is *the man* who is said to 'leave his father and mother' in order to 'cleave unto his wife', and 'be one flesh' (Gen 2.24); in this figuration, it is never said that the female needs to find a partner in order to achieve independence from her parents. Furthermore, it is during Adam's passivity ('deep sleep', Gen 2.21) that Eve is created and 'brought unto' him (Gen 2.22), having been formed from Adam's rib (the very term 'Woman' *means* 'taken out of Man' (Gen 2.23)).

---

11 Kent R. Lehnhof, 'Performing Masculinity in *Paradise Lost*', *Milton Studies*, 50 (2009), 64–77 (p. 73).
12 Lehnhof, 71.
13 *Ibid.*, 66; quotes Milton, *Paradise Lost*, IX.999.
14 See Milton, *Paradise Lost*, X.867–908.

When Adam sees Eve, he calls her 'bone of my bones' (Gen 2.23). This phrase arguably signifies not only that Eve is derivative of Adam's substance, but that she is like a body part — a bone more core and intimate to him than his own (this use of the preposition 'of' understands it as a superlative, as in 'King of Kings').

Fig. 12.1.1 Michelangelo, *Creation of Eve* (1509–1510). God's creation of Adam first and the referral to Eve as his 'helper' (2.20) might seem to suggest that he is dominant and she is subject to his authority. Yet, when Adam is first brought to life, God says that 'It is not good that the man should be alone' (v.18). Indeed, Adam is more vulnerable than commonly appreciated in the creation narrative.

The image of Eve's creation is compelling. Physically, it could be seen as Adam giving birth: an 'annunciation', of sorts. If conception is generally seen as an act where the male 'adds to' the female and causes her in turn to bear fruit, here is a moment where the male is first 'added to', and a social and emotional reliance accompanies the physical image. This paradigmatic episode contravenes the suggestion that men must be invulnerable; thus, it counters the toxic, masculinist mindsets which might be allowed to exist in some Christian subcultures. The image seemed so strongly and intriguingly related to the image of 'annunciation' that I began to hope to include it in our musical setting. To do so entailed changing the ensemble of characters originally envisaged, making a woman take the place of God in the encounter. This would alter the dynamic of the piece substantially. In its duration of three minutes, some of the ideas from my initial proposal would have to be omitted. Nevertheless, since the passage was from Song of Songs — the Bible's famous marriage poem — it seemed right to give due emphasis to human love in the piece.

Exposition II: Staging the Encounter in Song of Songs 3.6-11

In the Christian tradition, the enigmatic yet sensual marriage poem *Song of Songs* has been understood as an allegory for Christ's love for the Church (wherein Christ is the bridegroom, and the Church the bride), or for God's love for the human soul. In these allegorical interpretations, gender is a contentious issue: readers have historically been instructed to imagine themselves (regardless of gender) as the bride, awaiting Christ, the (divine, almighty) bridegroom.[15] Certainly, the bride's emotional experience is prominent throughout the poem, making her the more obviously sympathetic character. The male character is more remote, but the passage in question, Song of Songs [Song] 3.6-11, is one of the few passages where he is described, alone, and psychological readings no longer seem implausible. Although "Solomon" is provided as a name for him in the text, and indeed included in the title of our piece, it is doubtful that the character is meant to be understood as a close representation of the famous biblical king. For our purposes he is more helpfully understood as an "everyman", with a focus on personal relationships: I therefore refer to him as the "bridegroom" throughout.

For this passage, parallels have been drawn between the bridegroom approaching his wedding and Christ going to fulfil His destiny in sacrificial death.[16] The wounding of Christ, typologically associated with the passage through the purple and red garments in which the bridegroom is dressed, has been iconized in homoerotic ways; his penetration places him in a potentially feminine role.[17] The passage therefore functioned fairly well as an example of masculine 'annunciation' (or 'anti-annunciation'): in submitting to the will of God, Christ showed Himself in a vulnerable, perhaps even emasculated, light, even to the point of death. My initial idea for staging the passage played on this Christological picture, but placed a more anxiously masculine character in his position. He would enter expecting conflict with this system that subjugates men, and the encounter with God might amount to his sense of self cracking under this majestic weight. This could be due to the fragility of his own (precarious) masculinity, but it is also believable that the system which is supposed to represent God is the real antagonist.

---

15 For a helpful, though sceptical introduction to the mystic, allegorical reading of the passage with emphasis on the 'gender-bending' implications of such an act, see Stephen D. Moore, 'The Song of Songs in the History of Sexuality', *Church History*, 69 (2000), 328–49.

16 These parallels were introduced to me in John Donne's sermon 'Denmark House, some few dayes before the body of King James removed to his Buriall, Apr, 26. 1625', in *The Sermons of John Donne*, ed. by George R. Potter and Evelyn M. Simpson, 10 vols. (Berkeley, CA: University of California Press, 1953–1962), VI, pp. 280–91. This sermon is also interesting because it attaches the Christ symbolism to the figure of King James — a human, although a king supposedly by divine right, also with rumoured homoerotic tendencies.

17 For a discussion of the (homo-)eroticisation of Christ's wounds, see Richard Rambuss, *Closet Devotions* (Durham, NC and London: Duke University Press, 1998).

Fig. 12.1.2 Gustave Surand, *Eve in Eden* (1932). The enigmatic yet sensual marriage poem Song of Songs has been understood as an allegory for Christ's love for the Church (wherein Christ is the Bridegroom and the Church is the Bride) or for God's love for the human soul. The bride's eager anticipation is prominent throughout the poem. The bridegroom is more elusive, but appears in 3.6–11.

With the idea of including a female lover in the piece, however, it became imaginable to turn to a more literal reading of *Song of Songs*, with a more positive outcome for the main character, falling in love as Adam does in Gen 2. In addition to this softer plot, this second structure was appealing for its attribution of power to women: it was unconventional to present the woman as being 'born' rather than giving birth, transforming the man rather than herself being transformed by him. Furthermore, if the woman might seem to take the place of God in this new version of the bridegroom's story, it may be appropriate to interpret this exuberant, vulnerable expression of human love as a representation — or 'sacrament' — of divine love. Ellen F. Davis suggests that *Song of Songs* represents a reconstitution of Adam and Eve's relationship, which was corrupted in the Fall, and a 'healing of the deepest wounds in the created order'.[18] In the context of considering masculinity, this marriage points not only towards the healing of his need to be invulnerable, but also towards reconciliation in his relationship with women and, ultimately, with God.

---

18 Ellen F. Davis, *Proverbs, Ecclesiastes and the Song of Songs* (Louisville, KY: Westminster/John Knox Press, 2000), p. 231.

Fig. 12.1.3 Egon Tschirch, *Cycle of Paintings, 'Song of Songs', no. 10* (1923).

I incorporated these potential associations into a brief for my composer, which challenged him to consider how such a bridegroom might feel on the day of his wedding. Perhaps the piece could display two contrasting sides to the bridegroom: one more exterior and the second more intimate. When he first appears, 'with pillars of smoke', surrounded by men bearing swords, dressed for battle, the character referred to as 'Solomon' is performing a ceremonious role. This powerful, almost hubristic description of the bridegroom's appearance, arguably conforming to a typical masculine persona, could be conveyed by a rhythmic ostinato, loud dynamics and raw timbres. In a second section of the piece, however, I suggested that we might try to give a voice to this man, reaching for his more hidden feelings as he discovers — and is overwhelmed by — love. For these purposes I tentatively proposed that Adam's speech about being disarmed at the sight of Eve, in Genesis or in *Paradise Lost*, might be incorporated into our libretto.

Development: Collaboration

The main reason for depicting the creation of Woman was because, ostensibly, in the context of a patriarchal tradition, it seemed to offer a challenge to the idea that men must always maintain an act of superiority and strength. Nevertheless, I became concerned that, in this scenario, the challenge to gender pressures was arguably too subtle. For this depiction to work, the bridegroom would most likely have to be heterosexual to fall in love with a woman. There was a risk that the heterosexual romance narrative, understood without sufficient nuance, might reduce the bridegroom's struggle in identity and spirituality to the anxieties of an inhibited, 'fragile' masculinity. In the context of *Song of Songs*, a book which accommodates queer readings well, this seemed particularly incongruous (the ornate description of the bridegroom in this passage is clearly ripe for an epicene portrayal). With such concerns in mind I emphasized my openness to alternative ideas when handing over to the composer.

Stuart Beatch's depiction of the bridegroom is, as he notes, a conscious 'misgendering' of the original text. The question 'Who is this' refers to a female voice in the Hebrew text. However, our final piece not only appropriates this question for a male character, but endows him with free, feminine traits. A climbing, shimmering melody seems to evoke the passage of the bridegroom through the hills 'with pillars of smoke'.[19] The kind of man depicted is not a violent or threatened one, but more undefined; he is young and aware of the gravity of this ceremonial situation, but certainly not feeling the need to act to a powerful, superior role. Rather than fleeing questions about identity, the implication is that the bridegroom asks them openly. With a shifting modality (Lydian and Mixolydian), and the absence of a fixed key, the first section is poised in a realm of potent ambiguity.

Alongside this 'misgendered' depiction, Beatch took up my suggestions for the second part of the piece, which introduces a woman as the bridegroom's love interest. The *Paradise Lost* text Beatch adopts explicitly gives 'Woman' as the 'name' of the beloved figure who shares such a rare emotional bond with Adam. Although the Genesis passage celebrates the creation of 'male' and 'female', and their difference is important to maintain, I felt somewhat uncomfortable presenting a heterosexual marriage as the solution for a character who was suggestively queer. In our first meeting, Beatch and I had discussed the potential for depicting conflict or encounter with Sonata form: a first theme is countered by a second in a kind of contest, with the victor shown to dominate in a final section. But was this heteronormative ending really something to be presented triumphantly? Discussing this with the other theologians and composers post-premiere, I was not the only person to notice the potential awkwardness of overwriting a queer character with a heteronormative narrative, and in a musical form which arguably has a history of gender violence.[20]

---

19   The text here is from the Authorised (King James) translation of the Bible, which is used in Stuart's final composition.
20   For an account of gender violence in Sonata form, see Susan McClary, *Feminine Endings: Music, Gender and Sexuality* (Minneapolis, MN: University of Minnesota Press, 2002).

Nevertheless, in Beatch's choral piece, the definiteness in Milton's words is softened. With a series of shifting, unpredictable cadences, the piece's second section conveys a quivering, innocent kind of excitement, alongside momentary self-consciousness. Perhaps, due to the presence of female voices as a prominent part of this harmonic mass, there is less of an impression that these words are direct speech, or even speech at all. Rather than being attached to a calculated character performance, Adam's words are painted as impulsive, immediate answers to timeless questions of being and identity through indefinite cadences, rising and falling in a way that imitates the unpredictability of human emotion. Whereas traditionally one side of the thematic dichotomy in a Sonata form is typically restated triumphantly, Beatch's ending conveys an air of mystery rather than closure: no possibility is eliminated and no rules are enforced. With gravity, but with none of the pomp that could have been imagined in the marriage of a king, a new key is reached in the last chord of the piece. Perhaps this modulation signifies that the character is more aligned with a liberated present/future than a repressive past in terms of gender identity.

Recapitulation

One of my main concerns with the collaboration was the over-interpretation and over-determination of the artistic interpretation of the passage. Having written some music myself, perhaps that experience caused me to overstep my role as theologian. Beatch might have had more freedom if I had been more circumspect, driving less towards an 'argument' or artistic vision (they seem to be much the same thing, interestingly) and providing more of a commentary and some open-ended suggestions. Yet, this has never been how I have started writing academic work, either. It is not, in any case, unprecedented to have a composition that bears traces of multiple parties with different ideas who each had shares in the creative process. Whimsically, it is possible to wonder whether the two voices in the Sonata — expressive of strong, yet sometimes mysterious male and female characters — may have reflected parts of the personalities of the two collaborators. Beatch's is a personality that I hope I can continue to get to know in an ongoing friendship which has grown from this partnership.

List of Illustrations

12.1.1	Michelangelo, *Creation of Eve* (1509–1510), fresco, Sistine Chapel, Vatican, Wikimedia, https://commons.wikimedia.org/w/index.php?curid=11420987, public domain.	257
12.1.2	Gustave Surand, *Eve in Eden* (1932), oil on canvas, Wikimedia, https://commons.wikimedia.org/w/index.php?curid=51546667, public domain.	259

12.1.3 Egon Tschirch, *Cycle of Paintings, 'Song of Songs', no. 10* (1923), tempora on cardboard, Rostock, Germany, Wikimedia, https://commons.wikimedia.org/wiki/File%3ADas_Hohelied_Salomos_-_Nr._10_(Egon_Tschirch%2C_1923).jpg, CCA-SA 3.0 Germany. 260

12.2. Composer's Reflections

Stuart Beatch

For the past three years, my experience as a composer has been almost exclusively in sacred choral music. I am hard-pressed to explain precisely why this has happened; religion has always been a part of my life, but my music for a long time had been secular, inward-looking, personal and self-referential. My fascination with sacred music was sparked in 2013, when I began my formal composition studies and simultaneously joined an Anglican cathedral choir. Submerging myself in the Anglican choral tradition, I realized that there is a direct emotional impact and harmoniousness in this music which is both unapologetic and inspiring. I soon found myself writing simple psalm settings for choir, lengthy collections of chants and hymns, and complex 'choral meditations' like *Pange Lingua* and *Resurrectio*. While postgraduate studies have put this passion on hold, I have continued to await eagerly the next chance to explore religiosity in music.

I have begun with this biographical sketch for two reasons: to offer a background as to why I participated in this project, and to affirm that contemporary music still has important things to say about religion. Fascinated by sacred music, my interest and skill have always been focused on religion as a medium for music, *not* vice versa. My principal concern as a composer is to write music, so one simply uses the text to serve those needs; in this way, I was treating the religious subject as just a singular trait of the text. This only reinforces the notion that I am not a theologian, and perhaps echoes the sentiments of other composers in this project. Thus, I was eager to collaborate with an expert as a way of challenging myself. It is not enough to use these texts on a literal level; one must understand the scholarly discourse, the context (both in *and* out of the Bible), and the deeper structure of a given sacred text in order to imbue a musical setting with a truly holistic meaning. To that end, I wanted to create more meaningful music that engages with religious themes in all their complexity.

The composers were welcomed to St Andrews in November 2016 for a preliminary conference, as well as an initial meeting with our theologian partners — in my case, Kimberley Jane Anderson. We were to investigate Song 3.6-11. However, prior to the conference, I had not been given guidance on how these collaborations would materialize, nor a hint as to how to interpret the scripture provided. This certainly coloured our first meeting, as we approached this excerpt from opposing sides. Naturally drawn to the salient textual elements — the beautiful language, the lush imagery, the formal elegance — I bypassed the chance to draw any deeper meaning. In contrast, Anderson was focused on the absence of male voice and agency in the excerpt, and the idea of 'masculine annunciations' (clearly the far more imaginative approach). We proceeded in engaging conversations on the context of this excerpt within the *Song of Songs*: how music has the potential to capture and represent masculine identity, and how this might be augmented through additional texts to expand the overall meaning of the work. A project like this requires careful contemplation and the slow digestion of varied thoughts, lest it run the risk of overloading with information and possible avenues. It was only after returning home that our collaboration, which would eventually become 'The Annunciation of Solomon', would truly start to take shape in my mind. I began plotting out the form of the piece, thinking of what the harmonic language would require, and getting my thoughts in order.

However, the most effective component of any collaboration — one which was used in this project — is a firm schedule of periodic meeting points. While composition is inherently an internal artistic act, it must be regularly informed by external dialogue if collaboration is to be effective; this proved crucial at several key points in my work with Anderson. Prior to writing the piece, we had been exploring the idea of incorporating additional text to provide a literal voice for the bridegroom, who is otherwise silent throughout our passage from the *Song of Songs*. It seemed, at first, an intriguing idea to highlight the potential connection of Solomon as a Christ figure, but through our discussions, we realized it was far more complex and interesting to call instead upon the voice of Adam.[1] This decision fundamentally altered the dialectic of the piece and how I approached the musical content. It was also through these discussions that we decided what sections of the original text would be used; six whole verses of scripture were simply too much to pack into a three-minute anthem. Anderson was sensitive to these matters, and we decided to pare the text down to its core essentials: the outer two verses.

A major difficulty that faces a collaborative effort like this is defining individual roles; however, I found our dialogue to be more beneficial when we broke down these barriers. Anderson, being trained in music, was attuned to issues of harmony, form, and text-setting. While she was apprehensive about commenting on musical issues at first, the feedback she gave *beyond* theological matters was useful. Indeed, even in a

---

1 See Genesis 3 and John Milton, *Paradise Lost*, ed. by John Leonard (London: Penguin Books, 2003), p. viii.

collaboration where there is no shared knowledge base, it would be advisable for both members to engage respectfully in both sides of the discussion. Some musical issues might be beyond the reach of a non-expert, but even simply listening to a computerized version of the music and commenting on how it sounds in relation to the theological goal has major potential to liberate new avenues of discussion.

The collaboration resulted in 'The Annunciation of Solomon', for SSATB choir and organ. The structure of the piece was defined in the end by our choice of text: a binary, or two-part, form. The first section is a lush and flowing (but strictly rhythmic) processional; in the excerpt from *Song of Songs*, this is the march of Solomon to his wedding. At the end of the section, the voices build to a fierce climax on the words, 'Behold, Solomon'[2] and are broken off by an opposing chord on the organ.[3] This leads directly into the second section: the voice of Solomon. The words call upon Adam in praise of Eve's beauty,[4] and provide the illusive male voice to this moment of marriage. This section sets the words through lush harmonies, seemingly breathless with the brevity of each phrase. The voices once again reach a climax — this time sparkling with joy — and they are again broken off by the organ, now completely in harmony with the voices. I decided to end the piece with a short coda adapted from the final verse of the excerpt: 'Go forth, O ye daughters of Zion'.[5] The music here is an Anglican chant, a musical form which not only carries deep personal significance, but which also represents a form of community, not unlike the chorales so important to the music of J. S. Bach.

By the end of our collaboration, I was pleased with the piece. It reflects a musical directness and simplicity for which I am always striving, and finds ways to address our original issues in unique ways. However, there are some issues. When I had initially shown the completed work to my husband (a musicologist), he disagreed strongly with our choice of text. Indeed, in considering the integration of Adam's voice into the dialogue of *Song of Songs*, it seems as if the male identity is beginning to subsume and subjugate the female. We were certainly aware of this dynamic at the outset. Even with our original plan in its most innocuous form — finding a way to give the bridegroom a voice — my music ran the danger of charging headstrong into subjugation, and this risk was only augmented by the addition of further masculine text. However, I do not believe my music has entirely buckled to this problem. Consider the opening phrase: 'Who is this that cometh out of the wilderness'.[6] We know, based on the original Hebrew, that it is referring to a woman; certain translations — such as the Douay-Rheims Bible — even render this verse with the female pronoun. By leaving the verse ambiguous (something already common to most translations), Solomon himself becomes 'perfumed with myrrh and frankincense, with all powders of the

---

2   Song of Songs 3.7.
3   A reference to John Tavener's *God is With Us* (1987).
4   Milton, *Paradise Lost*, viii, pp. 494–97, 499.
5   Song of Songs 3.11.
6   Song of Songs 3.6.

merchant'.[7] We chose to capitalize on this misgendering in the piece so that Solomon's masculinity would be purposefully feminized. Indeed, the female voice is given direct agency at the opening of the piece, since it is the sopranos and altos who first observe and define Solomon's identity.

Coupled with this issue, however, is the interpolation of masculine text. The choice to omit four whole verses of the original excerpt — thus omitting female voice and agency from a considerable portion of the music — is problematic, especially when it is replaced with such strongly masculine words as those of Adam. Although a seemingly minor decision, the implication is both heteronormative and arguably misogynistic, reinforcing the status of man as the sole origin and destiny of woman. There is truth in these arguments; the main flaw of the finished piece was due to an inability to identify the depth of the problem until long after our collaboration was finished. However, the matter was not entirely lost on me while I was composing. In this section of the music, I intentionally aimed to portray this masculine voice through stereotypically 'feminine' music: as mentioned earlier, the harmonies are lush, the phrases are short and breathless, and the rhythms are gentle. Moreover, the literal male voice — that is to say, the men of the choir — sing alone for only two brief moments. Otherwise, the 'male voice' of Adam is always sung by the entire (agender) choir as a method of weakening the otherwise-overt masculinity. This does not completely rectify the problem, but it sufficiently undermines it, in my view, to justify our creative decisions in this collaboration.

In any case, my work with Anderson was an incredibly formative and insightful experience for me as a composer. Perhaps I entered this experience with an illusory understanding of how to render religious texts in music. However, by collaborating directly with a theologian — especially one with shared musical interests — we created what I believe is a unique choral anthem which engages deeply, meaningfully, and respectfully with complex issues of voice and gender in a sacred context. I hope that this type of collaboration carries on and allows for the passionate interrogation of religious themes across all forms of contemporary art in the future.

 Stuart Beatch, 'The Annunciation of Solomon', in *Annunciations: Sacred Music for the 21st Century*, St Salvator's Chapel Choir and Sean Heath, cond. by Tom Wilkinson (Sanctiandree, SAND0006, 2018), © 2017 University of St Andrews. Track 12. Duration: 4.11.
https://doi.org/10.11647/OBP.0172.36

---

7   Ibid.

'The Annunciation of Solomon'

Stuart Beatch

*written in collaboration with the Institute for Theology, Imagination and the Arts
at the University of St Andrews, Scotland for the St Salvator's Chapel Choir (Tom Wilkinson, director)*

The Annunciation of Solomon
for SSATB choir and organ

Song of Solomon 3:6-7a, 11 (KJV)
and John Milton (1608-1674)

Stuart Beatch
(b. 1991)

'The Annunciation of Solomon'
© 2019 Stuart Beatch, CC BY 4.0
https://doi.org/10.11647/OBP.0172.24

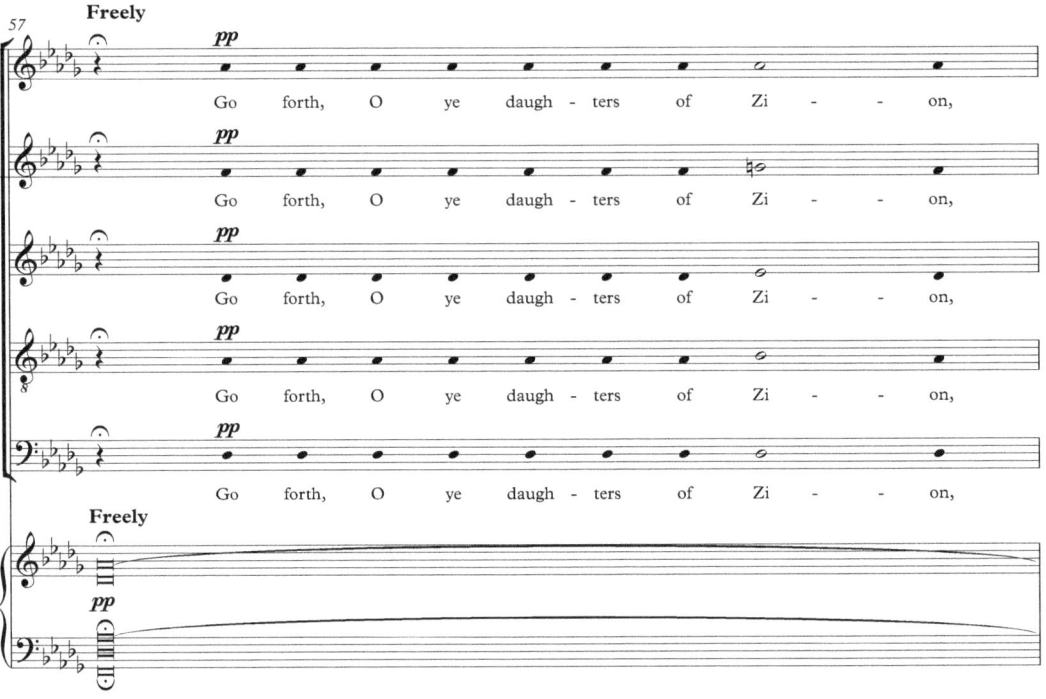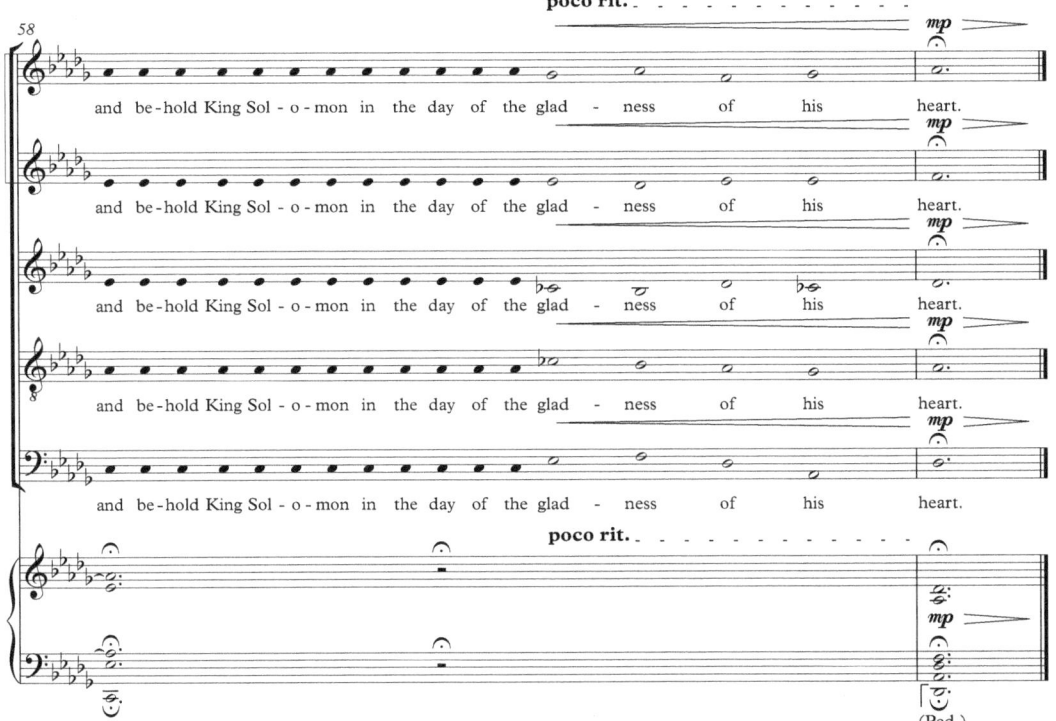

PART III:
PROGRAMMING AND PERFORMING SACRED MUSIC

# 13. Sacred Art Music in the Catholic Liturgy: Perspectives from the Roman Catholic Church in Scotland

Michael Ferguson

Scholars, theologians and artists continue to debate the relationship between theology and music. Central to this conversation are questions about the theological implications of music as theory versus music as praxis; the ability of music to embody inherent theological meanings versus those that are contingent on the listener; and, more generally, about how musical art can both inform and be informed by the work of theology.[1] Yet the notion of sacred music as *art*, and the composition and performance of this music as *artistry*, is largely taken for granted in these discussions. This chapter considers sacred music in the present-day Roman Catholic Church, where we will see that the idea of sacred music as art, and its legitimate role in Catholic worship, are not necessarily assured. To some extent there has always been an uneasy relationship between music and liturgy in Christian worship. In today's Roman Catholic Church, tensions around music have been shaped, in particular, by the outcomes of the Second Vatican Council (1962–1965). As a result, post-conciliar liturgical music is subject to functional demands that were hitherto unprecedented in the history of Catholic worship. We shall see that the expectation of music to facilitate congregational participation presents difficulties for Roman Catholics, who must somehow reconcile this function with music that also preserves and builds upon the Church's historical 'treasure' of sacred art music.

---

1   For a good insight into the scholarly debate about the contested relationship between theology and music, see George Corbett, 'TheoArtistry, and a Contemporary Perspective on Composing Sacred Choral Music', *Religions*, 9 (2017), 7, 1–18. For an additional account of the scholarly discourse, see Maeve Heaney, *Music as Theology: What Music Says About the Word* (Eugene, OR: Pickwick Publications, 2012), especially Chapter 5, 'Theological Aesthetics in Contemporary Theology', pp. 183–253.

Drawing upon the results of a national survey of Scottish parish music-making, this chapter considers liturgical music in the present-day Roman Catholic Church in Scotland. While scholarly discourses have tended to focus on defining 'good' liturgical music repertoire, and on outlining abstract principles of evaluation, the evidence suggests that those with the primary responsibility for shaping Catholic music-making in Scotland neither experience nor evaluate liturgical music in these purely abstract terms. These music-makers are less wedded to abstract notions of style than they are concerned with what liturgical music can do or achieve for them and for others in the liturgy. This runs counter to recent repertoire-focused attempts to critique and reform Catholic music. Arguably, any understanding of modern-day Catholic liturgical music — or attempts to shape its future — must first and foremost take into account those music-makers who actively shape, evaluate, and realize music in the Mass.

I. The Uneasy Relationship between Sacred Music and Roman Catholic Worship

Music and liturgy have been intimately connected throughout the history of Christian worship. Nevertheless, this relationship has often been complex, and the two elements have sometimes co-existed uneasily. Throughout the Church's history, Roman Catholics have voiced concerns about the potential of music to appeal to the senses and emotions, and, in doing so, to distract the listener from the worship of God.[2] Others have warned about the potential of secular influences to make their way into worship through music-making, or of the potential for new compositional practices to threaten existing ones.[3] The conduct of musicians has also come under scrutiny, with some complaining of unfit behaviour from music-makers during the Mass.[4] Nevertheless, in the midst of the complex relationship between music and liturgy, the notion of liturgical music as 'art' has generally been affirmed.

---

2   For example, see St Augustine's *Confessions*, where he describes his own struggles with sacred music. Here he describes being torn between 'the danger that lies in gratifying the senses and the benefits which…can accrue from singing' (St Augustine, *Confessions*, trans. R. S. Pine-Coffin (London: Penguin, 1961), Book X.33). Echoing Augustine in *Tra le Sollecitudini* (part of his 1903 *motu proprio*), Pope Pius X writes that 'the pleasure that music directly produces…is not always easily contained within the right limits' (Pope Pius X, *Tra le Sollecitudini* (promulgated 22 November 1903), http://www.sanctamissa.org/en/music/church-documents-on-liturgical-music/tra-le-sollecitudini.pdf, para. 1).

3   In *Docta Sanctorum Patrum* (1324–1325), Pope John XXII took steps to curb what he perceived to be the deformation of plainchant resulting from the fashionable *ars nova* polyphonic practices of the time (see Pope John XXII, 'Docta Sanctorum Patrum', in Robert F Hayburn, *Papal Legislation on Sacred Music: 95 A.D. to 1977 A.D.* (Collegeville, MN: Liturgical Press, 1979), p. 17).

4   The Council of Trent 'Decree Concerning the Things to Be Observed and Avoided in the Celebration of Mass' (1562), for example, sought to prohibit 'all worldly conduct, vain and profane conversations, wandering around, noise and clamour' from the liturgy, along with 'lascivious or impure' music-making. (See *The Canons and Decrees of the Council of Trent*, trans. H. Schroeder (St Louis, IL: Herder, 1941), p. 151). For an interesting overview of the musical implications of the Council, see Craig A. Monson, 'The Council of Trent Revisited', *Journal of the American Musicological Society*, 55 (Spring 2002), 1–37.

This was certainly the case at the dawn of the twentieth century. In his 1903 *motu proprio*, *Tra le Sollecitudini* ('Among the Concerns'), Pope Pius X upholds the importance of liturgical music as 'sacred art', setting out criteria by which it might be admitted into the Mass.[5] The pope draws a clear distinction between 'sacred art', and 'theatrical and profane art'. His intervention can be seen as an attempt to curb musical influences from the world of opera, which had been making their way into the Roman Catholic liturgy throughout the nineteenth century. Sacred art music, the pope warns, must be 'holy' (excluding 'all profanity' in content and performance, for example), must have 'goodness of form' (sometimes referred to as 'beauty'), and it must also be 'universal'. This universality does not necessarily refer simply to style; rather, the pope argues that true sacred art music is able to produce a universally good impression on the listener, irrespective of style, geographical location or culture.[6] Nevertheless, certain styles are held as more appropriate than others, with vocal music being 'proper' to the Roman Catholic liturgy, and Gregorian chant being the 'supreme model' of sacred art.[7]

Sacred art music faced new challenges in the wake of the Church's landmark Second Vatican Ecumenical Council (sometimes referred to as "Vatican II"). This global conference was convened during a period of great social and economic change in the Western world and, in many ways, it was the Catholic Church's response to these changing times. One of the Council's principal aims was to re-affirm the place of the Holy Mass at the centre of Roman Catholic spiritual life — over and above private devotions or prayers — and to embark upon a Church-wide 'reform and promotion' of the liturgy.[8] The drive towards liturgical reform stemmed from the Liturgical Movement, which had emerged during the second half of the nineteenth century, and had gained increasing momentum in the decades leading up to Vatican II. One of the movement's principal aims was to increase the participation of the faithful in the Mass. Initially, efforts to achieve this centred upon educating the laity about the Latin liturgy, but as the Liturgical Movement gained increasing momentum, attempts shifted towards reforming the Mass itself.[9]

Consequently, one of the cornerstones of the Second Vatican Council's reforms was to enable the 'full, conscious and active participation' of the faithful in the liturgy.[10] The Council Fathers recognized that this participation must firstly be internal — for example, that which results from coming to Mass with the appropriate disposition — but crucially, they also considered external participation, including

---

5   Pope Pius X, *Tra le Sollecitudini*, para. 1, §2.5.
6   *Ibid.*, arts. 1.2, 2.3.
7   *Ibid.*, art. 6.15.
8   See Second Vatican Council, *Sacrosanctum Concilium* ['Constitution on the Sacred Liturgy'], 4 December 1963, in *The Liturgy Documents: A Parish Resource*, ed. by David Lysik and others, 2 vols. (Chicago, IL: Liturgy Training Publications, 2004), I, art. 1, p. 3.
9   For a detailed account of the development of the Liturgical Movement leading up to the Second Vatican Council, see 'The Liturgical Movement', in Anthony Ruff, *Sacred Music and Liturgical Reform: Treasures and Transformations* (Chicago, IL: Hillenbrand, 2007), pp. 194–242.
10 Second Vatican Council, *Sacrosanctum Concilium*, art. 14, in Lysik, *The Liturgy Documents*, I, p. 6.

bodily gestures, speech, and singing to be fundamentally important.[11] This concern for 'active participation' underpins the bulk of the Vatican II reforms, not least those that deal with music.[12]

The Second Vatican Council devoted a whole chapter of *Sacrosanctum Concilium*, its new 'Constitution on the Sacred Liturgy', to its directives on liturgical music.[13] A range of areas are given careful consideration, including the training of musicians, musical instruments used, and styles of music permitted. However, the Council Fathers' instructions can be reduced to two overarching mandates on music.[14] First, the Council recognized music as a particularly effective means of facilitating congregational participation, especially in congregational singing, and urged that music should play this functional role in the Mass.[15] Alongside this recognition, though, the Council Fathers also urged that the Catholic Church's 'treasure of sacred music' — or in other words, the sacred art music traditions and repertoire that formed the basis of liturgical music-making before Vatican II — should be 'preserved and fostered with great care'.[16]

It is not difficult to see how the promulgation of these parallel mandates has presented Roman Catholics with difficulties since the Council. Those responsible for implementing the Council Fathers' reforms have somehow had to reconcile music's functional role in enabling musically untrained congregations to sing, with the requirement that it preserve and build upon repertoire that was originally intended to be performed by skilled church music specialists. In this way, the Council's directives potentially stand in direct tension with one another, and have presented particular difficulties when it comes to the evaluation of liturgical music. As Anthony Ruff observes in *Sacred Music and Liturgical Reform*, the side-by-side presentation of these opposing mandates is a compromise formulation by the Council Fathers between different priorities for music that existed at the Second Vatican Council.[17] Nevertheless, *Sacrosanctum Concilium* presents these two mandates in an unreconciled way, and, as a consequence, much of the debate about Catholic liturgical music since the Second Vatican Council has involved musicians, scholars and clergy trying to reconcile the inherent contradictions.

In practice, Catholics have tended to prioritize one of the central mandates at the expense of the other. These two paths are characterized by different liturgical-musical

---

11 See the Second Vatican Council's follow-up document to *Sacrosanctum Concilium*, which focuses specifically on music: Second Vatican Ecumenical Council, *Musicam Sacram* ['Instruction on Music in the Liturgy'] (Vatican.va, 5 March 1967), http://www.vatican.va/archive/hist_councils/ii_vatican_council/documents/vat-ii_instr_19670305_musicam-sacram_en.html, arts. 15a and 15b

12 For example, the loosening of restrictions on the use of vernacular languages in the liturgy was one of the reforms felt most keenly by Catholic congregations across the globe.

13 See 'Chapter VI: Sacred Music', in Second Vatican Council, *Sacrosanctum Concilium*, in Lysik, *The Liturgy Documents*, pp. 24–26.

14 Anthony Ruff makes this point in his *Sacred Music and Liturgical Reform*, where the second of the Council's two mandates forms the main focus of his study.

15 *Sacrosanctum Concilium* art. 114, in Lysik, *The Liturgy Documents*, 25.

16 *Ibid.*

17 See Ruff, *Sacred Music*, Chapters 12, 15 and 16.

'worldviews', each of which is informed by diverse values, priorities, and assumptions. In order to explore these, let us examine two different perspectives: that of Bernard Huijbers as outlined in *The Performing Audience* (1969),[18] and that of Pope Emeritus Benedict XVI (formerly Cardinal Joseph Ratzinger), as presented in his writings on liturgy published in the 1990s and 2000s.[19]

II. Two Opposing Worldviews in Post-Conciliar Music

Huijbers' *The Performing Audience* was published only a few years after the close of the Second Vatican Council. For some, it was a time of great optimism and idealism, and Huijbers' writing is infused with a strong sense of reformist zeal.[20] Principally, he understands 'active participation' to mean congregational singing, and considers the enabling of this singing to be the highest priority for post-conciliar music.[21]

For Huijbers, meeting the Council's call for 'active participation' requires a new kind of liturgical music, which must be composed by a new kind of liturgical music composer.[22] Consequently, the Church's repertoire of sacred art music, and its associated performance traditions, must be abandoned: in a practical sense, Huijbers argues that they can no longer bear the new functional role of music in the reformed liturgy. In an ideological sense, too, he regards sacred art music as no longer having a legitimate place. Here, Huijbers characterizes the pre-conciliar Latin liturgy and its music as a means by which Roman elites have historically exported and preserved their power in the global Church, in what he describes as a kind of 'musical colonialism'.[23] The liturgical reforms of the Second Vatican Council, therefore, offer the potential for the Catholic Church to restore its liturgical music-making to the people, which, as Huijbers perceives it, was the case in the early Christian Church. Borrowing the term 'elemental music' from German composer Carl Orff, he proposes a new style of liturgical music that is characterized by a minimalism of basic musical

---

18   Bernard Huijbers, *The Performing Audience: Six and a Half Essays on Music and Song in the Liturgy*, rev. edn. (Phoenix, AZ: North America Liturgy Resources, 1980). This work was originally published in Dutch as *Door Podium en Zaal Tegelijk* (Hilversum: Gooi en Sticht, 1969).
19   See especially Joseph Ratzinger, *The Feast of Faith: Approaches to a Theology of the Liturgy* (San Francisco, CA: Ignatius, 1986); *A New Song for the Lord: Faith in Christ and Liturgy Today* (New York: Crossroad, 1996); *The Spirit of the Liturgy* (San Francisco, CA: Ignatius Press, 2000).
20   See, for example, the work of *Universa Laus* ('Universal Praise'), an international study group for liturgical music that first met during the Council in 1962, and which was formally constituted in 1966, shortly after the end of the Council. The initial purpose of the group was to support those tasked with implementing the Council's reforms of liturgical music, and its work is primarily informed by a 'liturgist' approach to musical reform (in other words, prioritizing the functional potential of liturgical music to foster active participation in the Mass). For a history of *Universa Laus*, see the group's website: http://universalaus.org/history/. See also the group's two key documents on music for an insight into its core ideals and beliefs: *Music in Christian Celebration* (1980), and *Music in Christian Liturgies* (2002) (available: https://universalaus.org/documents/).
21   Huijbers, *Performing Audience*, pp. 9–12.
22   Ibid., pp. 75–76.
23   Ibid., pp. 8–12.

elements — melody, harmony, and rhythm — and which, at its core, is simple, repetitive, and formulaic.[24] While the 'elementary' nature of this music can only be determined relative to a particular congregation, Huijbers is clear that the Council's reforms must inevitably result in some loss of aesthetic quality in liturgical music, and that this loss is wholly acceptable.[25] Therefore, composers for the new Mass need no longer feel under pressure to be 'original', nor should they feel any need to maintain a connection with the world of contemporary secular art music, or with previous traditions of sacred art music — in spite of the Council Fathers' clear call to preserve and foster the sacred 'treasure'.[26]

Benedict XVI offers an entirely different worldview. Not only does he affirm the place of sacred art music in the reformed liturgy, but he also argues that the notion of 'art' is fundamental to an 'authentic' post-conciliar church music. For Benedict XVI, sacred music must be 'true art', which he distinguishes both from purely functional, 'utility music', and from the 'elitist aestheticism' he believes characterizes the secular art music world.[27] Fundamental to this concept of 'true art' is that it is not created by the human artist, but is rather a realization of God's divine art: intimately connected to, and revealing of the *logos*, the Word of God in a 'conversion of a vision into form'.[28] These ideas go back to the platonic notions of *Musica universalis*, where mathematical proportions in the universe, including the oscillations of the orbiting planets, are considered to be revealing of a God-given beauty and divine order.[29] For Benedict XVI, the sacred 'beauty' that is manifested in authentic sacred art music is an objective reality, rather than relative to a particular context or congregation. Like Pius X before him, Benedict XVI perceives plainchant and polyphony to be particularly 'effective models' which can provide good 'orientation' for composers, though post-conciliar music need not necessarily sound like these.[30]

These two positions reside at opposite ends of the spectrum. Each bears the hallmarks of two broader standpoints that have informed the debate about Catholic music since the Second Vatican Council: what have sometimes been dubbed 'liturgist' and 'traditionalist' positions.[31] Although it is a rather fundamentalist version,

---

24 *Ibid.*, pp. 19–25.
25 *Ibid.*, pp. 66–67.
26 *Ibid.*, p. 65. Huijbers clearly states, 'When the vernacular replaces Latin in the liturgy, the entire Latin repertoire disappears. […] The repertoire as a whole, as it has grown and functioned, will be lost'.
27 Ratzinger, *New Song*, chap. 6. See also Ratzinger, 'On the Theological Basis of Church Music', in Ratzinger, *Feast of Faith*, pp. 97–126.
28 Ratzinger, *New Song*, p. 129. See also 'Music and Liturgy' in Ratzinger, *Spirit of the Liturgy*, pp. 136–56.
29 See Wladyslaw Tatarkiewicz, 'The Great Theory of Beauty and its Decline', *The Journal of Aesthetics and Art Criticism*, 31 (Winter 1972), 165–80, for insight into the 'Great Theory' of beauty, and its decline, particularly in the twentieth century. See also 'Chapter 3. Music in a Christian Ecology', in Jeremy Begbie, *Resounding Truth: Christian Wisdom in the World of Music* (Grand Rapids, MI: Baker Academic, 2007), pp. 77–95.
30 Ratzinger, *New Song*, pp. 158–59.
31 Of course, one must exercise caution when applying broad categorization; nevertheless these two terms are in relatively common usage. Others like Edward Schaefer have opted for the term 'musician' rather than 'traditionalist', noting the growing debate between would-be reformers and music specialists leading up to the Second Vatican Council. In *Catholic Music Through the Ages*,

Huijbers' worldview resonates with the 'liturgist' perspective, which is characterized by a prioritization of music's functional role over aesthetic or artistic concerns. As mentioned above, 'active participation' is understood to mean congregational singing, while concepts such as beauty, holiness, and universality are understood to take their meanings relative to a particular liturgical context. Consequently, liturgists have been open to drawing upon musical styles from the secular world, particularly in their attempts to foster congregational singing; they have usually rejected the notion that any style of music is inherently superior due to its age or origin.

On the other hand, Benedict XVI's worldview resonates with what might be called a 'traditionalist' perspective.[32] Concepts such as beauty, holiness and universality are perceived to have objective meaning, rather than a relative one. Consequently, traditionalists have tended to attach more importance to the aesthetic quality of liturgical music, and have given more credence to the idea that congregational listening can be an equally valid means of fulfilling the Second Vatican Council's demand for active participation. Within this worldview, certain styles of music — especially plainchant and polyphony — are seen as inherently suited to the liturgy, whilst others — for example, those with strong secular associations — are seen as inherently unsuitable.

III. Mainstream liturgical music in the Catholic Anglosphere

Since Vatican II, in the Roman Catholic Anglosphere at least, the liturgist perspective has tended to dominate the mainstream of parish music-making. In the climate of reform immediately following the Second Vatican Council, some Catholic musicians and clergy — particularly in the United States — looked to folk styles that were popular at the time as the basis of liturgical music that could enable congregations to sing, that would be relevant to wider contemporary secular culture, and that would potentially appeal to a younger generation of Roman Catholics.[33] For the first time,

---

Schaefer presents some of the core differences between these groups (which he borrows from Ann Labounsky's study of Jean Langlais). The table itself is formulated from a largely traditionalist perspective; the liturgist view of Mass, for example, is described in negatively-loaded terms as 'informal, folksy worship [and a] spontaneous, human-centered meal'. See Edward Schaefer, *Catholic Music through the Ages: Balancing the Needs of a Worshipping Church* (Chicago, IL: Hillenbrand Books, 2008), p. 137.

32 In many ways, Benedict XVI's writings have directly informed this traditionalist perspective. See, for example, *Benedict XVI and Beauty in Sacred Music*, ed. by Janet Rutherford (Dublin: Four Courts Press, 2012). This book is the product of the Third Fota International Liturgy Conference. The Fota conferences are 'dedicated to the elucidation and promotion of Benedict XVI's vision of liturgical reform, emphasizing the importance of beauty in the celebration of the Church's rites, and the necessity to go forward as part of our inherited tradition' (p. 11).

33 Indeed, the Second Vatican Council coincided with a popular music revival in North America and the UK, which reached its peak in the second half of the 1960s. Ray Repp's *Mass for Young Americans: with Psalms and Refrains* (Chicago, IL: F.E.L Church Publications, 1966) was one of the first 'contemporary' folk-influenced Mass settings. Liturgical composers like the 'St Louis Jesuits' built upon these

instruments like flutes and guitars started making their way into Roman Catholic worship, alongside the more traditional pipe organs and choirs. In the decades that followed, folk-inspired repertoire became widespread throughout the Roman Catholic Anglosphere, due not least to the international dominance of the 'Big Three' American Catholic music publishers: GIA Publications, Oregon Catholic Press (OCP), and World Library Publications (WLP). In the United Kingdom, the global reach of these companies was supplemented by home-grown publishers such as Kevin Mayhew Limited., whose folk-infused hymnbook series, *Hymns Old and New*, became a staple for British Catholic parishes, and continues to be a primary source of folk-descended congregational repertoire today.[34]

While folk-inspired congregational music became the norm in English-speaking parishes, towards the end of the twentieth century some were becoming critical of the direction that mainstream liturgical music-making had taken. Thomas Day's controversial polemic *Why Catholic's Can't Sing: The Culture of Catholicism and the Triumph of Bad Taste* (1990) charts what he perceives to be the failure of the 'reformed-folk style' liturgical music to engage American Catholics in congregational singing.[35] Day portrays this repertoire as 'oozing with an indecent narcissism',[36] and argues that its prevalence in post-conciliar American Catholic worship represents a wider cultural shift after the Second Vatican Council which has seen individual performers — bolstered by microphones and amplified instruments — become the central focus of the liturgy.

While Day's polemic gives some insight into the criticisms levelled at mainstream Catholic music-making by the 1990s, more recently, others have taken a more scholarly approach to understanding the development of post-conciliar music, and to proposing solutions for its future. Benedict XVI's rise to the papacy in 2005 led to his writings gaining a greater Church-wide resonance, heightening the debate about Catholic music in the years that followed. Some Catholics perceived the arrival of the relatively

---

early experiments, and their congregational music achieved wide proliferation due to popular postconciliar hymn books like *Glory & Praise: Songs for the Worshipping Assembly* (Phoenix, AZ: North American Liturgy Resources, 1977). See Don Cusic, 'Catholics and Contemporary Christian Music', in *Encyclopedia of Contemporary Christian Music: Pop, Rock, and Worship*, ed. by Don Cusic (Santa Barbara, CA: Greenwood Press, 2010), pp. 45–47.

34 *Hymns Old and New* was the dominant Roman Catholic hymnbook in England and Wales at the turn of the twenty-first century. See Elizabeth Louise Theobald, 'Music in Roman Catholic Liturgies in England and Wales since Vatican II' (unpublished doctoral thesis, University of Southampton, 1997), p. 123. In the national postal survey of Scottish Catholic music-making undertaken by the present author in 2013/14, *Hymns Old and New* was also by far the most popular hymn book series amongst Scottish parishes, with 78.8% of respondent parishes reporting that they used some edition of the Kevin Mayhew Ltd publication. This compares, for example, to 17% using *Laudate* (published by Decani Music) and 10.8% using *Celebration Hymnal* (published by McCrimmon). See Michael Ferguson, 'Understanding the Tensions in Liturgical Music-Making in the Roman Catholic Church in Contemporary Scotland' (unpublished doctoral thesis, University of Edinburgh, 2015), pp. 230–32.

35 Thomas Day, *Why Catholics Can't Sing: The Culture of Catholicism and the Triumph of Bad Taste*, rev. edn. (New York: Crossroad, 2013).

36 *Ibid.*, p. 65.

conservative pope as an opportunity to reform Catholic music, and to foreground the Second Vatican Council's call for the sacred treasure to be preserved and fostered.[37] Others saw the arrival of Benedict XVI as a worrying sign of an increasingly traditionalist Roman Catholic Church, and as a potential threat to existing liturgical music-making practices and repertoire. Events such as the introduction of the new English translation of the Roman Missal throughout the Catholic Anglosphere in November 2011 — which required existing English-language settings of the Mass to be revised or abandoned — also prompted some Catholics to ask questions about the future direction of their liturgical music-making, and further heightened the debate.

In the midst of this debate, three major academic studies have sought to examine the state of Catholic music since Vatican II, and to recommend paths for its future. As previously mentioned, Ruff's *Sacred Music and Liturgical Reform* is an in-depth examination of the Second Vatican Council's core mandate that the treasure of sacred music should be preserved and fostered with great care. Ruff reaches the conclusion that in the midst of competing mandates, this 'treasure' cannot simply be taken to mean a fixed repertoire of historical works, but rather should be conceived of as a dynamic, living tradition. In light of the Council's call for active participation, not all of the Catholic Church's repertoire of sacred art music can survive intact. Newly-composed music, and repertoire from other Christian traditions, might also potentially form part of the Church's musical 'treasure'. Ultimately Ruff concludes that in light of the Council's inconsistencies on music, 'there is no absolute model of worship music in the Roman liturgy', where, 'too many ideals stand in creative tension with each other'.[38]

In the face of Ruff's assertion that there is no absolute model of Catholic music, others have proposed a theoretical basis for forming objective evaluations. In *Catholic Music Through the Ages: Balancing the Needs of a Worshipping Church* (2008), Edward Schaefer draws upon the familiar traditionalist totems to present the case for an ideal style of Catholic worship music. Schaefer argues that, throughout its long history, Catholic music has achieved a balance between 'formative' and 'expressive' dimensions. Nevertheless, he argues that since the Second Vatican Council, liturgical music's formative dimension has been greatly subordinated to its expressive one. Therefore, in a modern-day situation he sees as 'ripe for improvement', Schaefer suggests that the future of Catholic music depends upon a careful rebalancing of these expressive and formative dimensions.[39] He asserts that this rebalancing can be best achieved through the widespread re-introduction of Gregorian chant.[40]

---

37 This optimism may have been spurred on by Benedict XVI's interventions early on in his papacy, such as the promulgation of his 2007 *motu proprio* entitled *Summorum Pontificum*, which relaxed the restrictions on the celebration of the preconciliar Tridentine Mass. See Benedict XVI, *Summorum Pontificum: On the Use of the Roman Liturgy Prior to the Reform of 1970* (Vatican.va, 7 July 2007), https://w2.vatican.va/content/benedict-xvi/en/motu_proprio/documents/hf_ben-xvi_motu-proprio_20070707_summorum-pontificum.html

38 *Ibid.*, p. 610.

39 Schaefer, *Catholic Music*, p. 178.

40 *Ibid.*, esp. Chapter 10.

Most recently, Joseph Swain has sought to build an objective theory of evaluation in *Sacred Treasure: Understanding Catholic Liturgical Music* (2012). Criticizing the other major studies for their focus on liturgical and theological principles, Swain instead proposes a theory of post-conciliar music rooted in what he calls the 'hard facts of music'[41], or 'musical truths'.[42] In this way, he takes as a starting point the technical attributes of the music itself — melody, rhythm, and harmony — in order to show how the post-conciliar folk-derived styles are objectively unsuitable as the basis of a long-term, 'authentic' tradition.[43] While he accepts that no music can be intrinsically sacred, he argues that liturgical music can possess an objectively definable 'sacred semantic', which arises from it being both distinct from wider secular culture, and having developed long-time associations with the Roman Catholic liturgy. Like Schaefer, Swain believes that Gregorian chant best exhibits this sacred semantic, and therefore is best suited for the future of Roman Catholic worship.[44]

Each of these studies grapple with the inherent challenges of Catholic liturgical music thrown up by the Second Vatican Council. But, in doing so, they have generally focused on outlining model styles, or upon formulating abstract principles of evaluation which are underpinned by musical and theological concerns. In contrast to this, understandings of music in the wider field of musicology have moved away from an exclusive focus on decontextualized readings of musical text objects. Instead, there has been a movement towards approaches that recognize that music's meaning can only fully be known in the moment of realization (or to draw upon Christopher Small's now widely-used term, in the act of *musicking*).[45] This involves music-makers who create, shape and realize music. Similarly, the emerging field of Christian Congregational Music Studies has seen scholars take a conscious interdisciplinary approach to understanding Christian worship music, often drawing upon ethnomusicological research methodologies which recognize music-making as a living, human activity.[46]

With this in mind, let us now turn to examine liturgical music in the present-day Roman Catholic Church in Scotland. In contrast to the studies above, our understanding will be rooted primarily in the accounts of the clergy and music-makers who realize and experience music-making in Scottish Catholic parishes.

---

41   Joseph Swain, *Sacred Treasure: Understanding Catholic Liturgical Music* (Collegeville, MN: Liturgical Press, 2012), p. xiv.
42   Ibid., p. 17.
43   Swain presents a technical analysis of Robert J. Dufford's hymn 'You Shall Cross the Barren Desert (Be Not Afraid)' (Portland, OR: New Dawn Music, 1975), in an attempt to show how the periodic phrase structure inherent in the folk-descended style limits it to texts with highly regular poetic meter. He argues that such limitations make it 'nearly impossible' to set more irregular Mass texts like the Gloria and Credo (See Swain, *Sacred Treasure*, p. 49).
44   Ibid., p. 187.
45   Small uses his formulation to distinguish the *act* of music-making, from music as *text*. See Christopher Small, *Musicking: The Meanings of Performing and Listening* (Middletown, CT: Wesleyan University Press, 1998).
46   For a good introduction to this emerging interdisciplinary field of scholarship, see Mark Porter, 'The Developing Field of Christian Congregational Music Studies', *Ecclesial Practices*, 1 (2014), 149–66.

IV. Music in Present-Day Catholic Worship: Perspectives from the Roman Catholic Church in Scotland

Roman Catholics are a minority group in present-day Scotland, making up around 16 per cent of the Scottish population.[47] Scottish Catholicism has had a turbulent history, being effectively outlawed after the 1560 Scottish Reformation, with the Catholic hierarchy only officially restored in 1878.[48] Today, the majority of Scottish Catholics are descended from the Irish Catholic migrant workers who made their way to Scottish shores during the nineteenth and early twentieth centuries, settling primarily in Scotland's industrial heartlands of the West Central belt.[49] However, this population has been bolstered by migrants from Europe, and not least Roman Catholics from Poland who have settled in Scotland since Poland joined the European Union in 2005. In line with the rest of Western Europe, twenty-first-century Scottish society is becoming increasingly secularized, and the Catholic Church currently faces similar challenges to other Christian denominations, such as falling Mass attendance and a shortage of priests.[50] Nevertheless, the Roman Catholic population in Scotland is significantly younger than that of other denominations, and Scottish Catholics are more likely to regularly attend church services than their Church of Scotland counterparts.[51] Considering this, how do the challenges associated with music after

---

47 Results from the 2011 census of Scotland show that 841,053 people identified as Roman Catholic out of a total Scottish population of 5,295,403. See *Analysis of Equality Results from 2011 Census Part 2, Chapter 3: Religion* (National Records of Scotland, 2014), http://www.gov.scot/Publications/2014/10/8378

48 For insight into the revival of Catholic music-making in the decades leading up to the restoration of the Roman Catholic hierarchy in Scotland, see Shelagh Noden, 'The Revival of Music in the Worship of the Catholic Church in Scotland, 1789–1829' (unpublished doctoral thesis, University of Aberdeen, 2014).

49 See John McCaffrey, 'Roman Catholics in Scotland: Nineteenth and Twentieth Centuries', in *Scottish Life and Society: Volume 12 'Religion'*, ed. by Colin MacLean and Kenneth Veitch (Edinburgh: Birlinn, 2006), pp. 170–90. In fact, the distribution of the Roman Catholic population in twenty-first-century Scotland still bears the echoes of this pattern of settlement: in 2011 Roman Catholics were still at their highest concentrations in West Central council areas. See *Interactive Maps: Scotland's Census, 2011* (National Records of Scotland, 2011), http://www.scotlandscensus.gov.uk/ods-web/datavis.jsp?theme=Religion_v2_September_2013.

50 For example, in 2015 Archbishop Leo Cushley, Archbishop of St Andrews and Edinburgh, published his pastoral letter *We have found the Messiah: The Future of the Archdiocese of St Andrews & Edinburgh* (Archdiocese of St Andrews & Edinburgh, 2015), http://www.archdiocese-edinburgh.com/images/we_have_found_the_messiah_web.pdf. He summed up the problems facing his archdiocese: with 111 parishes in 2015, it was estimated that it would only have 33 priests to cover the area by 2020. Additionally, the Church's own statistics suggested that only 25% of the baptised population attended Mass regularly. To understand the challenges of secularization for Catholicism in modern Scotland, see Tom Gallagher, *Divided Scotland: Ethnic Friction and Christian Crisis* (Glendaruel: Argyll Publishing, 2013). Gallagher's argument is that while in the past it was militant Protestantism that represented the biggest threat to Catholicism in Scotland, now it is untrammelled secularization that presents the biggest challenge in twenty-first-century Scotland.

51 The Scottish Social Attitudes Survey 2014 suggests that 43% of Scottish Catholics attend a church service at least once per month, compared to 22% of those belonging to the Church of Scotland. See Stephen Hinchliffe and others, *Scottish Social Attitudes Survey 2014: Public Attitudes to Sectarianism in Scotland* (Scottish Government Social Research, 2015), http://www.scotcen.org.uk/media/830110/ssa2014_full-report-public-attitudes-to-sectarianism-in-scotland.pdf, p. 9, para. 2.8.

the Second Vatican Council play out in Scotland? And in the midst of tensions and ambiguities around the evaluation of liturgical music, how do those who create, shape and realize Catholic music in Scotland evaluate it?

There are two useful bodies of information that can help us to begin to answer these questions. First, a national postal survey of music-making in Scottish Catholic parishes was undertaken in late 2013 and early 2014.[52] As a result, data is available for 223 parishes out of the 447 parishes that existed at the time (49.9 per cent), from questionnaires that were completed by priests (67.5 per cent) and musicians (32.5 per cent). Second, in-depth interviews were undertaken with 21 music leaders from the 8 Roman Catholic dioceses in Scotland, including musicians, composers, and clergy.[53] This mixed-methods investigation had wide-ranging focus, and the data that was gathered in the study provides a detailed and multi-layered account of both Scottish Catholic music-making, and the people undertaking it. Nevertheless, for the purposes of our present enquiry, it is helpful to focus on survey questions that dealt specifically with the evaluation of liturgical music. Participants were invited to give open-ended, qualitative answers to the following questions:

1) In your opinion, what are the styles or types of music that make for particularly 'good' or 'appropriate' liturgical music? Why are these good or appropriate?

2) In your opinion, what are the styles or types of music that make for particularly 'bad' or 'inappropriate' liturgical music? Why are these bad or inappropriate?

While the respondents were asked to specify 'styles or types' of music, few of them mentioned specific styles. Indeed, the respondents seemed much less concerned with abstract notions of style, than with what liturgical music can *enable* or *achieve* for them and for others in the liturgy. Where specific styles were mentioned, the same styles were cited as both particularly good and particularly bad. For example, plainchant was cited in both positive and negative terms:

> Plainchant maintains tradition, simple melody in unison, easy for congregation, creates very spiritual ambience (Music leader, Diocese of Galloway).
>
> Plainchant — can be done without musicians, theologically and liturgically appropriate (Parish priest, Diocese of Paisley).
>
> Plainchant — culturally unfamiliar. Difficult for musicians and congregation. Not necessarily 'beautiful' — especially if done badly! (Organist, Diocese of Galloway).
>
> I have often found plainchant and complicated music does not go down well as people struggle to pick it up (Parish priest, Diocese of Motherwell).

---

52 For a detailed account of this survey, and full results, see Ferguson, 'Understanding the Tensions', pp. 183–260.

53 For methodological discussions relating to the national postal survey as well as focus interviews, see Ferguson, 'Understanding the Tensions', pp. 183–206 and pp. 261–68.

There was similar polarization in the few instances where folk and Renaissance polyphony styles were mentioned.[54] More commonly, though, participants mentioned that any style can be good or appropriate in the liturgy, provided that it does the right things, for example:

> All styles can be good if they are respectful, reflective, relevant to the readings of the day and involve the whole congregation (Organist, Diocese of Dunkeld).

> All styles have their place and a variety is important to help all people worship and pray. No style or type is superior to another (Parish priest, Diocese of Glasgow).

> All styles/types if quality and accessible (Parish priest, Archdiocese of St Andrews and Edinburgh).

Rather than hinging on abstract styles then, the evidence gathered suggests that music-makers' evaluations are principally shaped by two key factors: what liturgical music can enable for *the congregation* during the Mass, and what it can achieve as part of *the liturgy*.

The most common assertion by participants was that they evaluate liturgical music in relation to its ability to facilitate congregational singing. These respondents defined good or appropriate liturgical music as memorable (e.g. 'simple'[55] and 'uncomplicated', has a strong melody, is predictable, repetitive, is potentially already familiar to the congregation, or has 'big choruses and refrains'); as easy for the congregation to sing (e.g. has a comfortable pitch range, and no difficult leaps); as appealing to different age groups in the assembly (e.g. combines 'old' and 'new'); as enjoyable for the congregation (e.g. joyful and upbeat); and as generally 'inclusive'. On the other hand, they defined bad or inappropriate music as difficult to remember; as hard for the congregation to sing (e.g. having 'strange' or 'complex' melodies); as having overly elaborate or dominant accompaniments; as overly focused on soloists at the expense of the congregation; and as not appealing to what the congregation 'likes'. The term 'performance' was also specifically used by some to characterize liturgical music-making that excludes the congregation.

Participants were also concerned that liturgical music should connect or resonate with the congregation, for example:

> That which resonates with 'folk memory' or is inspiring in its quality (Parish priest, Diocese of Aberdeen).

> Easily learned and relevant to cultural setting. Style is secondary to relevance (Parish priest, Archdiocese of Glasgow).

---

54 It is interesting to note that similar polarization in evaluations was noted by Elizabeth Theobald in her survey of Roman Catholic music-making in in England and Wales in the late 1990s. Here, different members of the congregation evaluated the same pieces of music as 'most helpful' and 'least helpful' within the same worshipping community. See Theobald, 'Music in Roman Catholic Liturgies', esp. Chaps. 4 and 6.

55 Where quotation marks are used in this section, it indicates a direct quotation from at least one of the survey questionnaire responses.

For respondents that mentioned this, good or appropriate liturgical music was defined as strengthening the sense of community; resonating with 'folk memory'; having text and music that are 'meaningful' and 'relatable' for the congregation; as staying with the congregation after they leave the church; as appealing to different age groups; as appealing to different congregations within the same parish; as creating emotional resonance with the congregation; as fostering spirituality; as giving rise to 'sincere' worship; as being generally 'uplifting'; and as being 'liked' or 'enjoyed' by the congregation. On the other hand, participants defined bad or inappropriate liturgical music as overly 'highbrow', 'artistic', 'intricate' or 'long'; as culturally unfamiliar (for example, plainchant); as too familiar; as having an unintelligible text (e.g. being 'complicated' or in the Latin language); as creating 'resistance' in a congregation; as 'patronizing'; as being inappropriate for the age group of the assembly; as failing to 'lift hearts and minds' to God; and as being 'insincere'.

The liturgy itself formed the second most referenced criteria of evaluation, with participants mentioning music's ability to set the mood and tone of the liturgy. In this way, they defined good or appropriate liturgical music as that which creates an appropriate 'atmosphere' (e.g. is 'reflective', 'prayerful' or 'spiritual'); as fostering devotion; as in keeping with the 'mood' of the liturgy; as fostering a feeling of sacredness; as being dignified and not distracting from worship; as drawing attention to God, rather than the congregation; and as being 'beautiful'. Bad or inappropriate music, on the other hand, was defined as imbuing the liturgy with inappropriate meanings; as 'trite', 'dreary', 'tired' or 'banal'; as appealing overly to the emotions; as overly loud or distracting; as lacking a sense of the sacred; and as drawing attention towards the congregation, rather than to God.

Participants also evaluated music on the basis of its integration with the wider liturgical celebration. For example, some of the participants defined good or appropriate music as appropriate for the day, time, theme or readings of a particular Mass; as that which resonates with, or 'clarifies' the priest's homily; as having an appropriate text (for example, 'scans well' and is 'theologically sound'); as an effective accompaniment to a specific liturgical action or movement; as being at the 'service' of the liturgical whole, rather than being an 'end in itself'; as in a style 'proper' to the Roman liturgy — though as we have already seen, this was often not specifically defined; and as reflecting the history and tradition of the Roman Catholic Church. Likewise, bad or inappropriate liturgical music was characterized as inappropriate for the time, season, or theme of the liturgy; as disconnected from, or irrelevant to, the liturgy; as having theologically unsound texts; as harking back to a former era (e.g. 'music that takes us back to pre-Vatican II'); as disrupting the 'flow' or 'pace' of the liturgical action, and as being overly 'performance-led' (for example, too 'ornate' or 'showy').

V. Music-Makers in the Roman Catholic Church in Scotland

Alongside revealing how Scottish Catholic music leaders and clergy evaluate music for the Mass, the national survey also lends insight into who is responsible for realizing music in Scottish parishes. Strikingly, it suggests that music-making is an overwhelmingly volunteer activity. Those familiar with music in Scottish Catholic parishes may know this anecdotally, but the empirical data demonstrates that 90 per cent of the 223 respondent parishes have a volunteer musician, while only 12.3 per cent of parishes have a paid musician.

What is more difficult to know is the musical skill-set of this volunteer majority, and one should be careful about making any assumptions. In the face-to-face interviews, there were at least some volunteer musicians who had positions of significant musical responsibility, but spoke of having rather limited skill-sets, including low music literacy and low technical playing/singing ability. To some extent, the potential of at least some volunteers to have low skills-sets is summed up in the survey response of one music leader in the Diocese of Aberdeen:

> It is traditional in the Catholic Church that everyone is a volunteer, and this can be a great disadvantage in the context of liturgical music, since each parish depends so much on good will first, talent and expertise second. I have been involved in Church music for 50 years but have no qualifications other than from my teaching (teacher) education (in a Catholic Higher Education institute) and a lifetime of participation in the music liturgy.

One might speculate that what is practically viable for an untrained congregation to sing — which as we have seen, is often the primary lens through which parish music-makers and clergy evaluate liturgical music — is also viable for music leaders with low skill-sets to realize.

The face-to-face interviews also give some useful insight into the culture around music-making in Scottish Catholic parishes, and of the challenges and difficulties that can face volunteers. In particular, the interviewees mentioned four key challenges. First, the absence of standardized or formalized entry mechanisms. Interviewees explained that volunteer roles are rarely advertised formally, or opened up to a competitive application process. Rather, entry into liturgical music-making appears to often be down to personal contact with the priest, who they perceived to be the gatekeeper to involvement. Some participants were sought out by priests, while others approached priests in an attempt to gain entry. Others described being 'born into' music-making in their parish, describing liturgical music making as something that they had 'always done'. Secondly, few formal contracts of engagement. Both priests and volunteer musicians spoke of a lack of formal contracts of engagement, and described the challenges that this informality can raise. Each group mentioned a desire to better formalize obligations on both sides: priests spoke of difficulty managing volunteer musicians who were not fully accountable to them, while volunteer musicians often felt that their tenure was vulnerable, and subject to the personal discretion of an all-powerful priest. Thirdly, difficulty in transferring between roles. Volunteer musicians mentioned that once they had managed to gain entry into parish music-making, there was no guarantee that they could transfer their role in the event of moving to another parish. Participants spoke of a lack of means to demonstrate their prior responsibility, and a lack of formal 'qualifications' to attest to their experience. Fourthly, no standard measure of skill-set or competency. Linking closely with the point above, musicians and clergy complained that there are currently no standard measures of liturgical-musical skill-set in the Roman Catholic Church.

To conclude, we have seen that the Second Vatican Council clearly affirmed the place of sacred art music in the liturgy. Nevertheless, this music has also had to bear an important functional role after Vatican II: namely that of enabling the faithful to actively participate in the Mass by singing. In the midst of the ideological challenges thrown up by the Second Vatican Council's competing mandates, sacred art music has also faced challenges on a more practical level. In Scotland, we have seen that those responsible for choosing and realizing liturgical music have tended to evaluate it in reference to the congregation (and particularly in light of what they consider the congregation to be able to sing and understand). We have also seen that Catholic music-makers work within a volunteer culture in a Scottish Church that is characterized by precarious roles, a lack of standardization in training and qualifications, and a potentially wide variation in skill-sets. All of these factors impose potential limitations on parish music-making, and therefore also pose some real challenges to the viability of sacred art music in Scottish Catholic liturgies.

In light of the Vatican II mandates, it is clear that those who have sought to banish sacred art music from the liturgy are misguided, and their position cannot be supported by the Council documents. Nevertheless, considering what we have seen in Scotland, those who argue for the legitimate place of 'true art' in the liturgy are also mistaken in doing so in too abstract a fashion. Indeed, those who shape, evaluate and realize music in the Catholic liturgy do not necessarily experience, perceive or evaluate it in terms of abstract styles. Rather, this music must be realized in the liturgy. So, while Benedict XVI and others talk of the sacred musical work as a 'conversion of a vision into form', they would do well to consider that this music must somehow be realized in the liturgy by music-makers in order for it to have any form at all. Music-makers are an intrinsic and inseparable element of Catholic liturgical music, and are essential to its existence and meaning.

This has important implications for those wishing to shape the future of Catholic liturgical music. We have seen that attempts have often focused on recommending ideal musical styles or repertoire. However, drawing upon the metaphor of a seed, one might argue that works of sacred art music have the potential to play a role in the post-conciliar liturgy. However, these seeds must necessarily fall onto fertile soil — in this case, the music-makers, congregations, and clergy in a particular context — in order for their potential to be realized. Those approaches that simply promote ideal repertoire in the Mass — despite extolling the theological virtues of such repertoire — are akin to throwing seeds blindly onto potentially infertile soil, thereby rendering them unviable. What all this boils down to is that those wishing to shape the future of Roman Catholic liturgical music should aim to understand, before anything else, those clergy and music-makers who are essential to its viability.

14. Commissioning and Performing Sacred Music in the Anglican Church: A Perspective from Wells Cathedral

Matthew Owens

One of the questions central to the TheoArtistry Festival was: what does the future hold for sacred music?[1] Conceivably, this question would not have occurred to composers 800 hundred years ago. During the Mediaeval and Renaissance periods, the Church was the greatest supporter of the arts as well as being the main platform and disseminator for them. In music, if one thinks back to the great Renaissance composers such as William Byrd, Thomas Tallis, Giovanni Pierluigi da Palestrina, and Tomás Luis de Victoria, all of them benefited from ecclesiastical patronage during this time. Even in the later periods of the Baroque and Classical, composers including Johann Sebastian Bach, Henry Purcell, and Joseph Haydn had significant employment from the Church as composers, though not exclusively so.

The reality today is different. However, whilst the Church may no longer be a main patron for composers, its support for church music in general is still of paramount importance. The current standards of performance in England are agreed to be at an all-time high. Martin Thomas, in *English Cathedral Music and Liturgy in the Twentieth Century*, makes an interesting comparison with the Victorian era:

> Much of what is taken for granted in the musical life of the major English cathedrals in the late twentieth century was almost completely absent for most of the nineteenth century. Choirs then were ill-disciplined and musically unreliable. Lay clerks, who were paid less than domestic servants of the clergy, were often absent from weekday services and some aged and incompetent possessors of freehold. Choristers were poorly educated and surplices (if worn) were retrieved from beneath a seat or music stand. There was

---

1   The TheoArtistry Festival was held in St Andrews, 4–6 March, 2018.

no procession of clergy and choir at the start of the service, music was often chosen during the service and, of necessity, not advertised by way of a music list beforehand, repertoire was limited and repetitious, and psalms were sung to unpointed psalters with haphazard results.[2]

The contrasts today are striking. The forty-two Anglican Cathedrals in England now provide an invaluable infrastructure for sacred and liturgical music. They have their own choirs — the majority of which are professional — and attached to many of these foundations are choir schools for the education of choristers. Bodies such as the Royal School of Church Music, the Royal College of Organists, the Incorporated Society of Musicians, and the Guild of Church Musicians provide professional guidance and training, and there is a network of charitable support through national organizations such as Friends of Cathedral Music, and trusts such as The Ouseley Trust.

None of this should be taken for granted. The Church, on the whole (and for all kinds of reasons), does not and cannot support the commissioning of the arts in the way that it used to. Because it does not have the central place in the life of our nation that it once did, funding is more difficult to find for ecclesiastical foundations, especially in an age in which key external funders, such as The Arts Council, find it increasingly difficult to meet the fiscal demands of today's cultural organizations across the board. With this backdrop, one would perhaps be forgiven for being conservative in the commissioning of new music for our cathedral, collegiate, and church choirs. And, given that there is so much sacred/liturgical music already in existence, there might be a temptation to limit ourselves to what we know in performance; to the tried and the tested; to the familiar; to the works which we know will please congregations, choirs and clergies. Often, the promotion and performance of contemporary repertoire is met with criticism because it makes some people uncomfortable, particularly those who like what they know and know what they like.

As a cathedral director of music for nearly twenty years, I have spent a vast proportion of my life taking part in a daily choral tradition. For me, it is clear that contemporary music must form part of our living expression of worship in the Church; indeed, I feel we have a duty to create and perform new music in addition to singing the best music from the past 800 years. It is achievable, albeit with some required determination. At Wells Cathedral, where I have been Organist and Master of the Choristers since 2005, we have sought to make contemporary music an established part of worshipping and musical life in two ways. The first is our *Cathedral Commissions* scheme, which was established in 2006 in order to raise funds for new works from some of today's most exciting composers. The second is our annual festival, *new music wells* [sic], founded in 2008, which celebrates and raises awareness of new music through a week of services, concerts, and other events.[3] Furthermore, there is another major

---

2   Martin Thomas, *English Cathedral Music and Liturgy in the Twentieth Century* (Abingdon and New York: Routledge, 2016), p. 5.
3   For information about *new music wells,* see https://www.wellscathedral.org.uk/music-the-choir/new-music-wells/

commissioning project, *The Cranmer Anthem Book*, which involves the Cathedral Choir (but not exclusively), that I will touch on briefly at the end of the chapter.

Cathedral Commissions aims to share the excitement and thrill of commissioning with as many people as possible.[4] The scheme brings together a group of what James MacMillan once called 'the midwives to new music'.[5] The commissioners 'club together' to pay the commission fee for the composer. In return for their generosity, they are invited to the final rehearsal of their newly-commissioned work, to the first performance, to a special reception where they meet the composer; and they have their score signed (and the score has their name printed, with a dedication if they so choose). The commissioners are then kept informed of further performances, including broadcasts and recordings. They become involved in the ongoing life of the piece and have a feeling of ownership, which is important in engaging them with both contemporary music and sacred music.

Through this project the commissioners support living composers. They also support the continuation of the glorious 'English Choral Tradition' and, at Wells, they support the 1100-year-old Music Foundation.[6] *Cathedral Commissions* is based on the model of the Birmingham Contemporary Music Group's *Sound Investment* scheme,[7] and follows on from a similar project that I directed at St Mary's Episcopal Cathedral, Edinburgh, between 2001–2005, called *Capital Commissions*. With both schemes, one of the joys is the ever-growing community of committed commissioners. These commissioners have the opportunity to meet some of the great names of modern-day composition, question them about their music, and give feedback about their experience. The other beneficiaries are the cathedral choristers. For these boys and girls, aged between eight and fourteen, meeting the likes of Peter Maxwell Davies and Judith Weir is a formative experience, a memory to cherish, and perhaps a catalyst for a creative and/or spiritual spark in their young minds.

Still, it would be reasonable to ask why there is a need to commission anew for the Church when there is so much music from the past, and certainly more than one could realistically hope to perform in a lifetime. But our worshipping minds have always needed something new to challenge them, especially in the way in which we think about the texts encountered. The quest for the new was summed up perfectly by the late Maxwell Davies — the first president of *Cathedral Commissions* — who said of the scheme in Wells:

---

4   Since being launched in 2006, we have commissioned twenty-one major works from the following composers: Tarki O'Regan, Richard Allain, Peter Maxwell Davies, Gabriel Jackson, James MacMillan, Judith Bingham, Howard Skempton, Jonathan Dove, John Joubert, John Tavener, Michael Berkeley, Judith Weir, Philip Moore, Thea Musgrave, Diana Burrell, and Philip Wilby. For more information about the scheme, see Wells Cathedral Music Office, *Cathedral Commissions* (Wellscathedral.org, 2018), https://www.wellscathedral.org.uk/music-the-choir/cathedral-commissions/

5   James MacMillan made this remark at the launch of *Capital Commissions* (Edinburgh).

6   The Music Foundation at Wells Cathedral dates back to the year 909, when the first cathedral was consecrated. This predates the current Gothic one, begun in c.1185. Wells Cathedral School was founded for the education of the cathedral's choristers.

7   Birmingham Contemporary Music Group, *Sound Investment* (Bcmg.org.uk, 2018), https://www.bcmg.org.uk/Pages/Category/sound-investment/Tag/sound-investment

> The Church must always be abreast of developments in the cultural life of the society she serves. Her spiritual involvement in all aspects of this – philosophical, scientific, and artistic – is essential to ensure that, while steadfastly maintaining the eternal values for which she stands, she renews herself at the deepest levels, to make her meaning and relevance clear to each successive generation.
>
> A creative relationship with the musical thought of the time not only gives new and unexpected meaning to the words of religious texts, but also involves composers in a real living society – today, for obvious reasons, of supreme importance. It is for all these reasons that the Wells Cathedral initiative to commission composers is of such value.
>
> By being actively involved in a living Church, the composers commissioned have the opportunity to surpass themselves, irrespective of their personal belief or non-belief, and to make a contribution to our musical culture with very wide reference and resonance indeed.[8]

Maxwell Davies emphasizes the Church's need to connect with people in an ever-changing world: believers and non-believers, and those somewhere in the middle. Music has a transcendent power to do this. John Davies, the current Dean of Wells, often talks of music as being the conduit through which we may seek to connect earth with heaven. The Church should 'renew herself at the deepest levels' in theology, spirituality, liturgy, art, architecture, hymnody, music, and other areas as well. Consider how fresh, daring, challenging, and wonderfully unfamiliar those (now), well-loved works of Tallis and Byrd sounded when they were first performed. These composers broke new ground; they renewed the music of their generation.

As time has elapsed, however, the ideal of presenting music afresh has become increasingly challenging not just for composers, but also for performers. The regular or daily performance of 'Preces and Responses', from the Book of Common Prayer, is a good example. At Wells, we sing these prayers eight times a week. One of the best-known settings is that of the twentieth-century composer, Bernard Rose (1916–1996).[9] As the choir's conductor, it is important for me to remember that the music is familiar to most of the singers. Indeed, some of the Vicars Choral will have sung this setting literally hundreds of times.[10] I have to encourage them to perform it as if it were a new work and a total revelation, as it might have been when first performed in Oxford's Magdalen College Chapel back in 1961. I also encourage them to imagine the *text* afresh. The familiarity of the words can make us immune to their meaning. Choirs should be praying those responses every time that they sing them, but it is easy just to sing some beautiful and comfortingly familiar music.

Hopefully, John Tavener's 'Preces and Responses' — which were written for Wells Cathedral Choir shortly before his untimely death in November 2013 — and Howard

---

8   Extract from Peter Maxwell Davies's introduction to *Cathedral Commissions*, in a brochure published by Wells Cathedral in 2008.
9   This setting was written in 1961 for the choir of Magdalen College, Oxford, where Rose was Informator Choristarum (the chapel's Director of Music).
10 The Vicars Choral are the professional adult members of the choir, known as Lay Clerks or Songmen in other foundations.

Skempton's 'Preces and Responses', commissioned by *Cathedral Commissions* in 2017, help the members of the Wells congregation pray these sixteenth- and seventeenth-century prayers afresh. The contrast between the two settings could not be more marked: the Tavener setting is broad, sustained, majestic, slow in tempo; it is quite vulnerable at times and striking at others, with the use of double choir canon in some of the responses; and it possesses something of the prayerful, meditative Orthodox tradition still permeating the choral writing. Skempton's setting, on the other hand, is in his trademark style: simple, miniaturist, delicate, and subtle (too much so for some, perhaps); it is respectful to the liturgy; and it emphasizes the music serving the text, with the result that it is prayerful in a different but highly effective way. Through being unfamiliar, both settings may help members of the congregation become involved in the texts of these prayers, rather than simply letting the music (and the texts) wash over them. Many, who have been present for services where these settings have been sung, have commented on how moving they were. An added dimension to performing these two new settings is that it is then refreshing to revisit the more familiar settings by Tudor composers such as Byrd, Thomas Morley, William Smith, and Thomas Tomkins; and later settings by Richard Ayleward (1626–1669), the aforementioned Rose, Humphrey Clucas (b. 1941), Kenneth Leighton (1929–1988), and so on. The same can be said for anthems, mass settings, and canticle settings.

Another example of a challenge through music is a setting of the Mass by Jonathan Harvey (1939–2012), a composer who pushed the boundaries of liturgical choral and organ music. In 1995, Westminster Abbey commissioned a *Missa Brevis* from Harvey. This was the tercentenary year of the death of the Abbey's former Organist, Purcell (1659–1695), a revolutionary in his own day. Hearing this work for the first time, I was struck by its spiritual depth, and its ability to illuminate the familiar Latin texts of the Mass in a way that few other composers had done. It is not only the particular harmonic and melodic language of Harvey that is exhilarating and thought-provoking, but the almost visceral use of spoken word (some have written 'shouted'[11]) within the choral texture in the '*Gloria*'. At Wells, some people (in the choir and the congregation alike) still find this particular spoken use of the voice unnerving and strange in a choral and liturgical context, even though it has been performed since 2007. What is Harvey doing here? To my mind, he is expressing the earthbound nature of humanity praising God. There is something simple about speaking the text of the Mass. It has been celebrated this way for hundreds of years, yet the act of writing this into a sung setting makes some people uncomfortable. But this discomfort is surely a good thing: it is all too easy for liturgical music to be something warm, reassuring, and familiar, and — arguably — there are times when this is appropriate. Equally, a questioning, inquisitive, and alert faith — or, at least, the quest for it — needs challenge on its journey. Perhaps Harvey helps us with this challenge.

---

11 James O'Donnell, programme note accompanying the premiere recording of Jonathan Harvey's *Missa Brevis*, recorded on the album 'The Feast of St Edward, King and Confessor', Westminster Abbey Choir and Robert Quinney, cond. by James O'Donnell (Hyperion CDA 67586, 2006).

After first performing Harvey's *Missa Brevis*, a member of the congregation said that she did not care for the piece at all, and that the Sanctus had made her 'feel physically sick'. I was delighted to hear this — not because this elderly lady had 'felt sick' — but because the music and the performance of it elicited a strong reaction. She had engaged with it, and it had made her think; she had listened and had become involved. What could have engendered this reaction? The Sanctus starts in a mysterious way, especially in the context of following the Gloria, with a quiet and low-pitched chord of A-major in six parts. The stillness of the opening of the Sanctus is not dissimilar to some early Tudor masses: the *Missa Euge bone* of Christopher Tye (c. 1505–1573) springs to mind. These chords develop to encompass all twelve tones of the chromatic scale, perhaps — as Andrew Nethsingha suggests — representing all of God's creation.[12] The '*Pleni sunt caeli*' section ('Heaven and Earth are of full of Thy Glory'), again, represents God's creation through the quiet, microcosmic busyness of the texture, which is fascinating to see on the page of the score, as well as to hear performed. A spacious declamation of the '*Hosanna*' follows, which, through the bold use of silence, has something of the cosmic God about it. For some, the impact of this enforced stillness can be uncomfortable, even in a reverberant acoustic. Of his experience of silence whilst being a chorister at St Michael's College, Tenbury, Harvey wrote: 'The silence of the building was haunting… Music came out of it, dissolved back into it.'[13] Arguably, the effect of these 'composed silences' makes it one of the most thought-provoking settings that has ever been written. And this is what Maxwell Davies alluded to when he said 'a creative relationship with the musical thought of the time […] gives new and unexpected meaning to the words of religious texts'.[14] Harvey does make us think afresh about the God of the ever-expanding universe. The music is slightly incomprehensible; this strikes at the heart of our faith and worship: that which we call God, is — in so many ways — unfathomable.

On a Wells Cathedral Services and Music List, therefore, one will find plenty that is familiar, or — at least — plenty of composers who will be familiar. But one will also find commissioned works which are there to refresh the liturgy and the choir's role within the worshipping heart of the cathedral. In addition to the twenty-one works which Wells Cathedral Choir and I have premiered thanks to *Cathedral Commissions*, we have also given many first performances of works commissioned by other means (over 120, from January 2005 until July 2018): everything from works by student composers at Wells Cathedral School right through to a major new setting of the *St John Passion* by Bob Chilcott. Many of these new pieces have been broadcast and/or recorded, which is important in raising them to the attention of liturgical and concert choirs throughout the world. The most successful is probably Arvo Pärt's '*Nunc*

---

12 Andrew Nethsingha, 'Personal Reflections on the Music of Jonathan Harvey', *The Choir of St Johns Cambridge*, 6 May 2016, http://www.sjcchoir.co.uk/news/personal-reflections-music-jonathan-harvey-andrew-nethsingha
13 Quoted in Nethsingha, 'Personal Reflections', para. 1.
14 Maxwell Davies's introduction to *Cathedral Commissions*.

dimittis', which the Choir of St Mary's Episcopal Cathedral and I premiered in 2001. Taken up by choirs all over the world, it has been recorded over ten times, sung at the BBC Proms three times, and broadcast widely. This example, and many others, confirm the view of Skempton, that composing liturgical music — especially settings of the evening canticles, masses, and responses, but also anthems which are assigned to a particular feast day or season of the church's calendar — is rewarding because it will be performed so often.[15] Moreover, much of what has been written for Wells and the Anglican tradition would fit within the worship of other denominations.

The process of commissioning new works is always fascinating and stimulating. Three major works commissioned between 2012 and 2017 are examples of the different approaches to a similar project by three British composers: Chilcott's *St John Passion* (2013), John Joubert's *St Mark Passion* (2017), and Philip Moore's *St Luke Passion* (2018).[16] In his moving seventy-minute setting of the *St John Passion*, Chilcott provides specific instrumental colours for the three main roles: viola and cello for the Evangelist; two trumpets for Pilate; and horn, trombone, tuba and organ for Jesus. The organ and brass combine with timpani to accompany the choir in the crowd scenes and the hymns. The hymns punctuate the Gospel narrative, enabling the congregation to be involved in the same way as they would have been in a Bach Passion or in John Stainer's *Crucifixion*. Chilcott writes instantly memorable, original hymn tunes for well-known Passiontide hymn texts. He also intersperses several 'choral meditations' throughout the work. Chilcott commented:

> The larger role that the choir has to play is the singing of four meditations that punctuate various points of the drama. I have tried in these meditations to emulate the style of a strophic carol in the mould of a writer such as Thomas Ravenscroft, cast in a simple, melodic way. The texts they sing are English poems from the 13th to the early 17th centuries that express deeply human responses to death, to life and to man's relationship with the world and with God. Two of these meditations are sung by the choir with Soprano Solo, the last of which expresses most poignantly the human response to seeing Christ crucified on the Cross.[17]

The *St John Passion* is a stunning work, with rich yet economical orchestration, and well-written solo and choral parts.

Equally compelling, yet different, is Joubert's fifty-minute setting of the *St Mark Passion*. Joubert originally desired a large ensemble; however, in early discussions it was agreed that, for practical purposes — not least the financial considerations in engaging professional instrumentalists — the work would be more moderately

---

15 An opinion expressed during 'Composer Conversations with Michael Berkeley' (18 October 2017), *new music wells 77-17*, and on other occasions in personal communication with the author.

16 Bob Chilcott, *St. John Passion*, Wells Cathedral Choir, cond. by Matthew Owens (Signum Classics, SIGCD412, 2015); John Joubert, *St Mark Passion, Missa Wellensis and Locus iste*, Wells Cathedral Choir and David Bednall, cond. by Matthew Owens (Resonus Classics, RES10198, 2017); Philip Moore, *St Luke Passion*, Wells Cathedral Choir and Jeremy Cole, cond. by Matthew Owens.

17 Quoted from the composer's introduction in the 'Order of Service', Wells Cathedral, from Palm Sunday, 2013 (24 March 2013).

scaled than Chilcott's *St John*.[18] Thus, the cello accompanies the evangelist; the organ accompanies Christ and, of course, the chorus parts. Joubert chose to include hymns from *The English Hymnal*, sometimes keeping the original harmonies and adding his own compositional 'stamp'. It is an interesting selection: the plainsong version (*'Vexilla Regis'*) of 'The royal banners forward go' (with Joubert's own harmonization); 'Let all mortal flesh keep silence', with a re-harmonization of the French carol that traditionally accompanies these words, and what one might call 'vocal commentaries' from soprano and tenor soloists; 'Drop, drop, slow tears', using the beautifully plaintive 'Song 46' by Orlando Gibbons, with organ links between the verses in Joubert's complementary hand; the great Passiontide hymn, 'O sacred head, sore wounded', using well-known Bach harmonization of Hans Leo Hassler's melody (which, interestingly, Joubert does not touch); and — finally — 'When I survey the wondrous cross' to the glorious tune, 'Rockingham', once again with organ links provided by Joubert. Like Chilcott's *St John*, the soloist and choir parts are full of drama, with the parts of the Evangelist (marked 'Narrator' in the score) and Jesus being particularly demanding.

Moore's contribution to the (eventual) set of four gospel Passions is the longest of the settings, lasting approximately one hour and forty minutes.[19] It is scored for soloists, choir, and organ. Originally, Moore had proposed using saxophone in the work (an idea later dropped) and had also considered having Christ as a countertenor. This idea of varying the portrayers of the narrative from what might be called 'the traditional set-up', has found favour with, among others, MacMillan who, in his setting of the *St John Passion* (2007),[20] gave the role of the Evangelist to a 'narrator chorus', which the composer suggests should be sung by '8-24 singers of a professional standard'.[21] And, in MacMillan's *St Luke Passion* (2014),[22] he assigns *everything* to the main chorus (i.e. there are no soloists), and a children's choir portrays Christ. He explains his reasoning for the latter:

> Any Passion that casts Christ as a soloist immediately makes him take human form as an adult male, whereas I wanted to examine his otherness, sanctity and mystery. Employing a children's choir grants a measure of innocence to Christ as the sacrificial lamb, while the vocal line is either in unison or in three parts reflecting the oneness or Trinitarian implications of God.[23]

---

18   It should be noted that Chilcott also provided a version of the *St John Passion* with only two instruments: the organ and cello.
19   The final instalment of the Passion settings is by Philip Wilby (b. 1949), who is composing a *St Matthew Passion* for Palm Sunday 2019.
20   First performed in the Barbican Hall, London, by Christopher Maltman (baritone), the London Symphony Orchestra and Chorus, conducted by Colin Davies.
21   See scoring details: https://www.boosey.com/cr/music/James-MacMillan-St-John-Passion/49500
22   First performed on 15 March, 2014, in the Concertgebouw, Amsterdam, by Netherlands Radio Philharmonic and Choir, Vocaal Talent Nederland, National Jeugdkoor, conducted by Markus Stenz.
23   Boosey & Hawkes, 'James MacMillan: interview about *St Luke Passion*', *Boosey & Hawkes*, February 2014, https://www.boosey.com/cr/news/James-MacMillan-interview-about-St-Luke-Passion/100345&LangID=1, para. 5.

In the end, Moore settled for the traditional tenor for the Evangelist and bass-baritone for Christ. His approach to the hymnody is different again from Chilcott and Joubert. In recent years, Moore has spent a good deal of time in the United States and has become familiar with various American hymnbooks. This has led to an interesting selection of hymns for the choir and congregation to sing throughout this *St Luke*. For example, 'Of the glorious body telling' (normally sung to the plainsong *'Pange lingua'*) is set to 'Grafton' (a French *'Tantum ergo'* in *Chants Ordinaires de l'Office Divin*, Paris 1881); and there is an American folk hymn, 'What wondrous love is this', to the tune 'Wondrous Love' from the hymn book, *American Southern Harmony, 1835*. Perhaps most powerfully, there is a translation, by Francis Tucker, of the *'Solus ad victimam'* by the Mediaeval French theologian, Peter Abelard (1079–1142). The words are set to Tallis's haunting 'Third Mode Melody' — familiar to most, perhaps, as the main theme from Vaughan Williams's *Fantasia on a theme by Thomas Tallis*, which Vaughan Williams included in his 1906 edition of the English Hymnal. Moore sets *'Solus ad victimam'* as a piece for choir, and then — helpfully for the congregation — he subsequently uses the 'Third Mode Melody' in a hymn, with words by the great Methodist hymnodist, Fred Pratt Green (1903–2000). As well as the choral portrayal of the crowd scenes, there are some additional effective choral reflections which intersperse the gospel narrative: 'Meditation on "Wondrous Love"'; a setting of the Gradual for Maundy Thursday, *'Christus factus est'*; and 'A Litany', with words by Phineas Fletcher (1582–1650).

Another interesting comparison is between two settings of the *'Jubilate Deo'* (Psalm 100), which we commissioned for the 1100th anniversary of the Cathedral Choir. We chose two renowned composers — MacMillan and John Rutter — from different ends of the compositional spectrum, who we also knew would write engagingly for voices, organ, and instruments. The MacMillan setting has a difficult virtuoso organ part, opening with constantly moving semi-quavers darting between the pedal and the manuals in a menacing way. The choir writing — marked 'strepitoso' [noisily] — is boisterous and rhythmically punchy, at times in an almost jazzy way. It is an impressive, exciting, and challenging setting of these familiar words.[24] Rutter's setting is a wonderful contrast.[25] The commission came about through a request for a companion *'Jubilate Deo'* for the 'Winchester Te Deum', which was written in 2006.[26] The result is the 'Wells Jubilate', for brass quintet, percussion, timpani, organ, and

---

24 James MacMillan, *'Jubilate Deo'*, Track 1 in James MacMillan, *MacMillan: Choral Music*, Wells Cathedral Choir, cond. by Matthew Owens (Hyperion Records, CDA67867, 2011). An audio sample is available at Boosey & Hawkes, *Jubilate Deo* (2009): *James MacMillan* (Boosey.com, 2018), http://www.boosey.com/cr/sample_detail/MacMillan-Jubilate-Deo-2009/13154. The first page of the score may be viewed at Boosey & Hawkes, 'Jublate Deo SATB & Organ: James MacMillan' (Boosey.com, 2018), http://www.boosey.com/shop/prod/MacMillan-James-Jubilate-Deo-SATB-organ/2058559.

25 Sample pages are available at John Rutter, 'Wells Jubilate' (Oxford University Press Music Department, 2009), http://fdslive.oup.com/www.oup.com/academic/pdf/13/9780193366466.pdf. See also John Rutter, 'Wells Jubilate', Track 1 in John Rutter, *A Song in Season*, The Cambridge Singers and the Royal Philharmonic Orchestra, cond. by John Rutter (Hyperion Records, COLCD135, 2010).

26 The *'Te Deum'* and *'Jubilate Deo'* are the canticles which are often paired together in the Anglican service of Matins (the other canticles are the *'Benedicite Omnia opera'* and the *'Benedictus'*).

choir — the same scoring as the 'Winchester Te Deum'.[27] It bears all the hallmarks of Rutter: eminently singable and pleasing vocal lines, tonal, appropriately festive for the text, and fittingly joyful. Both settings of the '*Jubilate Deo*' are strong, original, and excellent additions to the canon already available to choirs and conductors, although the Rutter is more likely to be taken up widely owing to the fact that the MacMillan organ part is fearsomely difficult, and the choir parts are quite challenging.

Two other particularly challenging works that have been written for Wells Cathedral Choir are masses by Tavener and Joubert, both entitled *Missa Wellensis*.[28] They push the singers to the limits, especially vocally, but also musically. Both pieces are nevertheless rewarding to perform and fine additions to the repertoire. The Tavener setting has a lot of *divisi* in the vocal parts (the setting is for double choir and he splits all the parts within both choirs, giving SSAATTBB & SSAATTBB) meaning that one needs at least four singers per voice part, which a number of cathedrals in the UK and elsewhere do not have.

This question of the practicability of performance is, naturally, an important one. Whilst one should not be overly prescriptive in a commissioning brief, it is little use having an unperformable piece. From this point of view, I was especially pleased with Jonathan Dove's *Missa Brevis*, which we premiered in 2009. It was commissioned by the Cathedral Organists' Association (COA) and performed during its spring conference, held at Wells.[29] I was tasked by the COA to shape a brief for the commissioned setting, and to 'negotiate it' with Dove. I proposed the following:

- A Latin Missa Brevis ('Brevis' in the sense that there was to be no Creed).
- Accessible for the performers and congregations alike, but also stimulating and refreshing.
- No *divisi* in the choir parts.
- An organ part which should not be too difficult.
- Appropriate for the liturgy (i.e. which is not too long).

Dove fulfilled the commissioning brief so successfully that, immediately after the service in which it was premiered, around twenty-five cathedral directors of music said that they would add the work to their repertoire. Subsequently, it has been recorded at least twice for CD,[30] broadcast on television, webcast, and taken up by choirs all over

---

27 Rutter later published a version for organ only.
28 John Tavener, *Missa Wellensis*, Wells Cathedral Choir, cond. by Matthew Owens (Signum Records, SIGCD442, 2016); John Joubert, *Missa Wellensis*, Wells Cathedral Choir, cond. by Matthew Owens (Novello & Co., NOV293700, 2013).
29 For more information on the Cathedral Organists Association, see 'Association of English Cathedrals', *Cathedral Organistis Association* (Englishcathedrals.co.uk, 2018), https://www.englishcathedrals.co.uk/about-us/cathedral-networks/cathedral-organists-association/.
30 The only CD currently available of the *Missa Brevis* is the first recording by Wells Cathedral Choir. Jonathan Dove, *Choral Music by Jonathan Dove*, Wells Cathedral Choir, cond. by Matthew Owens (Hyperion Records, CDA67768, 2010).

the world, including many of the cathedral and collegiate choirs in the UK.[31] Dove's *Missa Brevis*, then, is a veritable lesson in itself for all composers and commissioners.

At Wells, Dove's *Missa Brevis* led to two further commissions: 'The Wells Service' ('*Magnificat*' and '*Nunc dimittis*') in 2012, and '*Te lucis ante terminum*' in 2014. For choirs, organists, and conductors, it is good to build relationships with composers, which in turn — and crucially — helps a congregation to build a relationship with the composers.[32] We have worked extensively over the years with many composers, immersing ourselves in their music and subsequently making single-composer discs of a number of composers, including David Bednall, Judith Bingham,[33] Geoffrey Burgon,[34] Chilcott,[35] Gary Davison,[36] Dove,[37] MacMillan,[38] and Joubert.[39] In addition, the choir has recorded single-composer discs by Leighton,[40] William Mathias,[41] and Tavener, once again becoming enriched by the individual language of these recent composers.[42]

In working with composers, it is always illuminating to know what has or has not influenced them. Chilcott talked of early musical influences:

> I was fortunate as a singer to sing the evangelist role in both the great Passions of Bach a number of times. I also remember as a boy chorister in King's College, Cambridge singing the simpler renaissance versions of the Passion chanted by the dean and chaplain of the chapel in holy week. It is the austerity, the agony and ultimately the grace of this story that has inspired me to write this piece, to be performed for the first time in a magnificent building where this same story has been commemorated for almost a thousand years.[43]

---

31 The *Missa Brevis* was broadcast live on Christmas Day 2009 from Chester Cathedral. Among other examples, the Choir of St John's College, Cambridge webcast the work in 2010. The Choir of St John's College, Cambridge, *Dove J – Missa Brevis* (Sjcchoir.co.uk, 2018), http://www.sjcchoir.co.uk/listen/sjc-live/dove-j-missa-brevis.

32 Sister foundations in which cultivating such relationships has worked well include Truro Cathedral where the choir (dir. by Christopher Gray) has worked extensively with Gabriel Jackson, Philip Stopford, and Dobrinka Tabakova, among others.

33 Judith Bingham, *Bingham: Choral Music*, Wells Cathedral Choir and Jonathan Vaughn, cond. by Matthew Owens (Hyperion Records, CDA67909, 2013).

34 Geoffrey Burgon, *Burgon Choral Music*, Wells Cathedral Choir, cond. by Matthew Owens (Hyperion Records, CDH55421, 2013).

35 Bob Chilcott, *Requiem & Other Choral Works*, Wells Cathedral Choir, cond. by Matthew Owens (Hyperion Records, CDA67650, 2012); Bob Chilcott, *St John Passion*, Wells Cathedral Choir, cond. by Matthew Owens (Signum Classics, SIGCD412, 2015).

36 Gary Davison, *The Armour of Light: The Choral Music of Gary Davison*, Wells Cathedral Choir and others, cond. by Matthew Owens (Regent Records, REGCD452, 2015).

37 Jonathan Dove, *Choral Music*, 2010.

38 James MacMillan, *MacMillan: Choral Music*, Wells Cathedral Choir, cond. by Matthew Owens (Hyperion Records, CDA67867, 2011).

39 John Joubert, *St Mark Passion*, 2013.

40 Kenneth Leighton, *The World's Desire & Other Choral Works*, Wells Cathedral Choir and David Bednall, cond. by Matthew Owens (Hyperion Records, CDA67641, 2008).

41 William Mathias, *Mathias: Choral Music*, Wells Cathedral Choir, cond. by Matthew Owens (Hyperion Records, CDA67740, 2009).

42 John Tavener, *Missa Wellensis & Other Sacred Music*, Wells Cathedral, cond. by Matthew Owens (Signum Classics, SIGCD442, 2016).

43 Bob Chilcott, 'Order of Service', 2013; reprinted as 'Introduction by Bob Chilcott', in Bob Chilcott, *St John Passion*, p. 3.

In relation to the *St John Passion*, Chilcott also recalls 'approaching the commission with a mixture of excitement and apprehension, daunted by the towering presence of Bach's *St John Passion* and mindful of more recent works by Arvo Pärt and James MacMillan'[44]:

> I had a similar feeling when I was asked to write a Requiem [...]. There are such incredible models to look up to, which of course made me nervous. With the St John Passion, you're taking on something deeply rooted in western music and also deeply rooted in Christian theology.[45]

Similarly, Joubert was initially reluctant to write a setting of '*Locus iste*' because of the 'shadow of Bruckner's setting'.[46] Thankfully, Joubert changed his mind and wrote a piece of almost symphonic proportions in the scale and demands of its choral writing. In contrast, having commissioned Skempton to write a setting of '*Beati quorum via*' and given the first performance of it, I discovered that he had never heard Stanford's well-known setting.[47]

Another way in which we seek, at Wells Cathedral, to bring new material to the liturgical and musical table, is through our festival, *new music wells* [sic], which started in 2008. The inspiration for the festival came from Norwich Cathedral, which, in conjunction with the University of East Anglia, used to host a Festival of Contemporary Church Music every two to three years between 1981 and 1997.[48] Further inspiration for *new music wells* was the London Festival of Contemporary Church Music, founded in 2002.[49] Based at St Pancras Parish Church, London, and founded by Christopher Batchelor, it is an important festival for new choral and organ music, even if it stretches 'contemporary' to include composers from the twentieth century, such as Herbert Howells, William Walton, Olivier Messiaen, and Mathias, within its programme.[50] It was, however, this element of *not* restricting our festival at Wells to living composers that helped the formation of a particular feature of the festival in Wells. Each year, *new music wells* is a retrospective of the previous forty years of music. Thus, when it

---

44 Andrew Stewart, 'St John Passion', in Bob Chilcott, *St John Passion*, pp. 4–9 (p. 5).
45 *Ibid.*
46 John Joubert, personal communication. For Joubert's setting of '*Locus iste*', see Joubert, Missa Wellensis, 2013.
47 Skempton wrote his setting of '*Beati quorum via*' for The Exon Singers for their 2008 Festival. The first performance was given during a BBC Radio 3 broadcast of Choral Evening from Buckfast Abbey. For the scores, see Howard Skempton, *Three Motets, New Horizons* (Oxford: Oxford University Press, 2008).
48 The festival took place in 1981, 1983, 1986, 1989, 1992, and 1997 and was the brainchild of Michael Nicholas (Norwich Cathedral, Organist and Master of the Choristers, 1971–1994) and Peter Aston (University of East Anglia, Professor of Music). They commissioned and programmed much adventurous repertoire. Sadly, the Norwich festival ceased, partly through lack of support by the authorities at the cathedral as Martin Thomas explains in Thomas, *English Cathedral Music*, p. 213.
49 For more information about the London Festival of Contemporary Church Music, see: The London Festival of Contemporary Music, About the Festival (LFCCM.com), http://www.lfccm.com.
50 For more information about composers included in the LFCCM programme, see 'The London Festival of Contemporary Music: 12–20 May 2018' (LFCCM.com, 2018), http://www.lfccm.com/wp-content/uploads/2018/03/LFCCM-2018-Brochure.pdf.

started, the music performed during *new music wells 68-08* dated back to 1968. Ten years later, the earliest work in our festival was from 1978. This annual change creates an interesting shifting focus and a constant programming challenge. Much of the music featured within the festival falls within the regular cathedral services of Evensong, Eucharist, and Matins. Consequently, all the canticles, anthems, responses, masses, and organ voluntaries must fall within the forty-year time span.[51] This constantly shifting time-frame is what makes *new music wells* unique: it is not a *contemporary* music festival (as that, arguably, should only include living composers), but a celebration of music from the last forty years.

In 2017, *new music wells 77-17* was the platform for the launch of *The Cranmer Anthem Book*. It is a major undertaking — over a period of ten to fifteen years — that will see all ninety-two Collects of the Book of Common Prayer, by Thomas Cranmer, set to music by some of the world's finest composers. The inspiration for this project is the well-known setting of 'Almighty and everlasting God' (the Collect for the Third Sunday after Epiphany) by the English composer, Orlando Gibbons (1583–1625). In my view, it is a most useful and versatile work for the following reasons:

- It is relatively straightforward, making it an ideal choice for choirs of all abilities.
- It is useful either as an introit or as an anthem because of its length (just under three minutes).
- It may be accompanied by the organ, or sung without accompaniment.
- It is simply scored for a four-part SATB choir, with no dividing parts.

Using this Gibbons anthem as a model, I am curating a collection of pieces entitled *The Cranmer Anthem Book*, commissioning composers to set these beautiful texts in order to provide attractive and useful works for choirs around the world from today's finest composers.

The first collect, the 'Collect for Saint Luke', was set by Francis Jackson, and premiered on the Eve of St Luke (17 October), just a couple of weeks after the composer's 100th birthday. Two days later, Skempton's 'Collect for the 18th Sunday after Trinity' was premiered. Other composers who have been commissioned for the project thus far are Richard Allain, Bingham, Diana Burrell, Davison, Joubert, Paul Mealor, Thea Musgrave, and Tarik O'Regan. I hope that *The Cranmer Anthem Book* will be a useful and inspirational resource for singers, choirs, and musicians in the church and the concert hall for centuries to come, in the same way that the Eton Choir Book has been since 1505.

The Eton Choir Book pushed the boundaries, and it is important that we all continue to do the same today: to deepen — through the transcendent power of music old and new — our understanding of what it is that we call 'God'. I am very optimistic

---

51 Currently, the only exceptions to the '40 year rule' are the hymn tunes and psalm chants.

about the place and future of sacred music in liturgical and concert settings.[52] Part of this optimism is borne from witnessing how people react to both established and new repertoire. With regard to the latter, nothing that we have done at Wells Cathedral is revolutionary, but I have been blessed with a committed Cathedral Chapter throughout my time, as well as with the supporters (i.e. commissioners, congregants, and concert attendees) of *Cathedral Commissions* and *new music wells* who have embraced what we are doing and who have been great evangelists for the cause. All that is needed is a 'grain of mustard seed' in order to continue to connect the church with the 'musical thought of our time'.

---

52 For a detailed discussion, see Jonathan Arnold, *Sacred Music in Secular Society* (London: Ashgate, 2014).

15. Music at the Borders of the Sacred: Handel, Elgar and Poulenc

Michael Downes

In the course of an interview with Jonathan Arnold, Rowan Williams discusses his reactions to a performance of Claudio Monteverdi's *Vespers* in the Sheldonian Theatre, Oxford:

> Both in Britain and on the Continent, from about 1590 onwards, liturgical music becomes something very different. It attracts a kind of theatrical surround to it, and Monteverdi's *Vespers* is one of the great examples of that. I'd say much the same of Purcell's proto-oratorios […] the writing is theatrical and virtuoso, in a way that for Palestrina and Byrd, would be unthinkable. These are show pieces and you may say that it is for the glory of God but it's not liturgical in the same way […] those are works that translate much more readily to the secular stage or the concert hall than Tallis and Byrd.[1]

Williams goes on to identify a series of works — the Masses of Wolfgang Amadeus Mozart and Joseph Haydn, and the Requiems of Johannes Brahms and Gabriel Fauré, among others — in which, although liturgical or scriptural texts may be set, 'the [musical] architecture dominates everything else and architecture of the liturgy disappears'.[2] But although such works 'don't really seem to work as liturgy', nor are they straightforwardly 'secular', they can evoke responses from the listener that are 'spiritual' and 'aesthetic'.[3] Whether such responses are produced on any given occasion will depend on the location and manner of the performance, as well as on the musical and religious proclivities of the individual listener. Nonetheless, by virtue of their ambivalent relationship to the category of 'sacred music', such works can tell us

---

1 Rowan Williams, interviewed by Jonathan Arnold in Jonathan Arnold, *Sacred Music in Secular Society* (Abingdon: Routledge, 2016), pp. 92–93.
2 *Ibid.*, p. 97.
3 *Ibid.*

much about music's capacity to evoke a spiritual response, however that is defined or understood.

The same is true, this chapter will argue, of a group of works that do *not* set liturgical texts and are *not* intended for performance in a religious building or during a religious ritual, but nonetheless engage with spiritual concerns in a way that goes beyond mere choice of text. By considering the lives of George Frideric Handel, Edward Elgar and Francis Poulenc — three composers with strong religious interests who were not primarily composers of sacred music — and by considering works in which they seem to explore religious concerns in a particularly personal way, this chapter will explore the peculiar interest of music that occupies a liminal position: music that we cannot, without qualification, define either as 'sacred' or 'not sacred'.

I. Handel: *Jephtha*

Although relatively little is known about Handel's intellectual or religious interests, his biographers concur that he was 'truly pious', particularly later in life.[4] William Coxe wrote that 'he frequently declared in conversation, the high gratification he enjoyed in setting the Scriptures to music'.[5] John Hawkins, who knew him well, recorded seeing him 'on his knees, expressing by his looks and gesticulations the utmost fervour and devotion'.[6] Hawkins adds, however, that although Handel was a Lutheran by birth:

> 'he was not such a bigot as to decline a general conformity with [the religion] of the country which he had chosen for his residence [...] he would often speak of it as one of the great felicities of his life that he was settled in a country where no man suffers any molestation or inconvenience on account of his religious principles.'[7]

This suggests an ability to empathize with a range of religious views rather than holding to a single doctrine, an ability that surely served him well in the oratorios that constitute his most important settings of scripture, notwithstanding the excellence of his liturgical music.

The genre of English oratorio was effectively invented by Handel: the first such work is generally considered to be *Esther*, which was composed for James Brydges (later Duke of Chandos) and premiered in about 1720 at Cannons, his country residence. At this time Handel was mainly concerned with Italian opera; he would dominate the London stage for the ensuing decade with works such as *Giulio Cesare*, *Tamerlano* (both 1724) and *Rodelinda* (1725). From the early 1830s, however, shifts

---

4   Charles Burney, *An Account of the Musical Performances in Westminster-Abbey, and the Pantheon, May 26th, 27th, 29th; and June the 3rd, and 5th, 1784. In Commemoration of Handel* (London: T. Payne and Son and G. Robinson, 1785), p. 34, https://archive.org/details/accountofmusical00burn/page/n8

5   William Coxe, quoted in Edward Blakeman, *The Faber Pocket Guide to Handel* (London: Faber & Faber, 2009), p. 24.

6   John Hawkins, *A General History of the Science and Practice of Music*, 5 vols. (London: T. Payne, 1776), V, p. 409.

7   *Ibid.*

in audience tastes; attacks on Italian opera by figures such as Alexander Pope, Jonathan Swift and John Gay; antagonisms within Handel's company; increasing competition from other promoters; and restrictions on theatrical performances during Lent, prompted Handel to investigate English oratorio as an alternative form of entertainment. His revival of *Esther* for the King's Theatre in 1732 — his first presentation of an English oratorio for public performance — sparked off a sequence of over twenty such works, though it was not until 1741, with *Deidamia*, that Handel completely abandoned Italian opera.

Handel's English oratorios were mostly premiered at either the King's Theatre or Covent Garden Theatre in London — with the famous exception of *Messiah*, first performed in Dublin in 1742. *Messiah* is also exceptional among the oratorios for not assigning its soloists named roles and not explicitly following a single continuous narrative. These are characteristics displayed by most (though not all) other oratorios, many of which drew their stories from the Old Testament. One of the most succinct definitions of the 'Old Testament oratorio' genre came from Newburgh Hamilton, librettist of *Samson* (1742), in his preface to the printed wordbook for that work: 'Mr Handel had so happily here introduc'd Oratorios, a musical drama, whose subject must be Scriptural, and in which the Solemnity of Church-Musick is agreeably united with the most pleasing Airs of the Stage'.[8] Hamilton points to the synthetic nature of the genre: forms of solo song, which Handel had brought to near-perfection in his operas — aria (particularly *da capo*) and recitative (both *secco* and *accompagnato*) — are juxtaposed with choruses that are far more extended and dramatically significant, as well as 'solemn', than anything found in Italian opera.

In most of the oratorios (again, *Messiah* is the exception rather than the rule), the chorus represents different bodies of people at different points in the drama. In *Samson*, for example, it represents Israelites, Philistines and Virgins. Although the choruses draw on 'the Solemnity of Church-Musick', they are often highly theatrical too. Paradoxically, the fact that the oratorios were not staged or costumed allowed Handel to give his choristers a bigger and more varied role in the action, characterizing them musically without any of the staging complexities that this would have involved in an opera. Although singers do not seem to have acted their roles, this does not mean that the visual presentation of the oratorios was neglected. The premiere of *Deborah*, in 1733, featured what David Vickers describes as 'an ambitious element of special decor and lighting especially for the occasion', and was praised by the *Daily Advertiser* as 'the most magnificent that has ever been exhibited on an English Theatre'.[9] However, the main stimulus to the audiences' imaginations came from the scene descriptions and stage directions published in the wordbooks and written out by Handel in his

---

[8] Quoted in Anthony Hicks, 'Handel and the Idea of an Oratorio', in Donald Burrows (ed.), *The Cambridge Companion to Handel* (Cambridge: Cambridge University Press, 1997), pp. 145–63 (p. 158).

[9] David Vickers, 'Staging Handel's Oratorios', in *2018 Glyndebourne Festival Programme Book* (Lewes: Glyndebourne, 2018), p. 107.

manuscripts. As Vickers notes, these descriptions allowed composer and audiences alike to construct 'an imaginary theatre of the mind'.[10]

Completed in August 1751 and first performed the following February, *Jephtha* was Handel's last oratorio (discounting the 1757 revision of *Triumph of Time and Truth*) and his last major work of any kind. The librettist was Thomas Morell, a classical scholar and Church of England minister who had also provided Handel with libretti for *Judas Maccabeus*, *Joshua*, *Alexander Balus* and *Theodora*; the last was notably unusual for being drawn from a religious novel rather than scripture. The story of *Jephtha* was taken from Judges 11, but — perhaps because of the sparseness of the biblical story and its problematic nature for a conventional Christian such as Morell — he supplemented it with elements from other sources. The most important of these works is *Jephthes, sive votum*, a Latin play written in the 1540s by the Scottish humanist, George Buchanan. Whereas in Judges Jephtha is the only named character in the story, in Buchanan there are several others, some of whom find their way into Morell's libretto: these include Storgè, Jephtha's wife (her name derived from a Greek word signifying affection between parents and children); and Iphis, the daughter whom Jephtha promises to sacrifice (her name clearly recalls that of Iphigenia, Euripides' similarly fated eponymous heroine). *Iphigenia in Aulis* itself, which Morell had recently translated for performance at Eton College, is another important source — as is the libretto for Giacomo Carissimi's 1640s oratorio *Jephthe*. In addition, Morell also drew on writers, including Milton, Pope and Joseph Addison, for seven specific lines that are marked as quotations in the printed libretto.

In the story in Judges, the central incident is the vow that Jephtha makes to God in order to secure victory in battle:

> And Jephthah vowed a vow unto the LORD, and said, If thou shalt without fail deliver the children of Ammon into mine hands, / Then it shall be, that whatsoever cometh forth of the doors of my house to meet me, when I return in peace from the children of Ammon, shall surely be the LORD'S, and I will offer it up for a burnt offering.[11]

The first thing that Jephtha sees when he returns from battle is his daughter, his only child, so he is forced to sacrifice her. She goes into the mountains for two months to 'bewail her virginity', but on her return, her father 'did with her *according* to his vow which he had vowed: and she knew no man'.[12] This causes a problem for Morell, since it presents the God of the Old Testament in a particularly harsh light: unlike in other comparable narratives (Abraham and Isaac, Saul and Jonathan), Jephtha's daughter is not spared. Of course, Morell was by no means the first writer to grapple with this issue. Several previous apologists for the Old Testament had argued that Jephtha's daughter was not sacrificed, including the influential medieval rabbinic commentator David Kimchi (1160–1235). In Deborah Rooke's words:

---
10 *Ibid.*
11 Judg 11.30-31. All biblical citations are taken from the King James Version, unless otherwise noted.
12 Judg 11.39.

> The Hebrew conjunction that is translated 'and' in the phrase '*and* I will offer it up as a burnt offering' can also be translated 'or'; so what Jephthah meant was, '… whatever comes out … shall surely be the Lord's, *or* I shall offer it up as a burnt offering' […] So Jephthah cannily hedges his bets, and says, 'If whatever comes out is not suitable for sacrifice, then it shall be dedicated to the Lord, but if it is suitable, then it shall be sacrificed.' Hence, when Jephthah's daughter comes out to meet him, because she is not suitable for sacrifice she is dedicated to the Lord in some other way, and this, according to Kimchi, meant that she became a celibate recluse.[13]

Although Morell followed Buchanan in many respects, including the naming of the characters, he departed from him by ensuring that *his* Iphis was saved from death. This interpretation was influenced not only by the apologists, whose work he knew well, but also by Euripides. Morell's dramatic turnaround is effected by an Angel who appears to explain to Jephtha that he has misunderstood his own vow. Jephtha had vowed in Act I Scene 4 that 'What, or whoe'er shall first salute mine eyes, / Shall be forever Thine, or fall a sacrifice.' 'Forever thine' seems quite clearly to offer an alternative to death, but Jephtha himself inexplicably either forgets this or fails to understand it until Act 3 Scene 1 when the Angel tells him:

> Rise, Jephtha, and ye rev'rend priests, withhold
> The slaught'rous hand. No vow can disannul
> The law of God, nor such was its intent
> When rightly scann'd; yet still shall be fulfill'd.
> Thy daughter, Jephtha, thou must dedicate
> To God, in pure and virgin state fore'er,
> As not an object meet for sacrifice,
> Else had she fall'n an holocaust to God.
> The Holy Sp'rit, that dictated thy vow,
> Bade thus explain it, and approves thy faith.

Although Morell's strategy is understandable as an attempt to exonerate the God in whom he believed — and whom he felt obliged to defend against what he felt to be the dangerous arguments of the Deist movement that was gaining influence at this time — it created a dramatic problem. If we, unlike Jephtha, interpret his vow logically, we are denied the dramatic tension of believing that Iphis will die; if we take Jephtha's anguish at his daughter's impending death at face value, then the intervention of the *angelus ex machina* risks retrospectively devaluing the heartfelt music that Handel gives him. This aspect of Morell's work attracted harsh criticism from earlier Handel scholars. Winton Dean wrote, in 1959, that he 'fails, and comes near to wrecking the oratorio […] his attempt to render the story palatable to Christian ears falsified it'. Paul Henry Lang wrote in 1967 that 'while the original story presented the librettist with a fundamentally simple and logical dramatic situation […] Morell sentimentalized it

---

13 Deborah Rooke, *Handel's Israelite Oratorio Libretti: Sacred Drama and Biblical Exegesis* (Oxford: Oxford University Press, 2012), p. 220.

[...] [he] was in a double dilemma, which he did try to solve in a Christian spirit — and he failed dismally'.[14]

Such criticisms, though understandable, perhaps underestimate the skill with which Handel translates his libretto into musical drama and disguises what would be fatal flaws in a spoken play. Jephtha's vow is set by Handel in a deliberately plain fashion, without musical rhetoric or elaborate accompaniment, allowing us to believe that he does not understand what he is saying; it is left to the Israelites in the following chorus ('O God, behold our sore distress') to express the fear that Jephtha fails to acknowledge. Another stark juxtaposition of contrasting musical idioms occurs in Act II Scene 3. The joyful, dance-like movement in which Iphis and the Virgins greet the victorious Jephtha is followed by his agonised recitative: 'Horror, confusion'. Handel also seems to have been aware of the danger that Morell was anachronistically 'Christianizing' the story. In a small but highly significant change to the chorus that ends Act II, Handel altered Morell's 'What God ordains is right' in order to quote Pope's *Essay on Man* with the words 'Whatever is, is right'. He then sets this in a highly emphatic fashion, suggesting mankind accepting an implacable Fate and also, perhaps, that he was more sympathetic to the Deist world-view than his doctrinally orthodox librettist. Finally, the sheer musical imagination with which he set Morell's text allows the drama to transcend the libretto's limitations. The quartet in Act II Scene 3, where the characters simultaneously express their contrasting reactions to Iphis' dilemma, is a particular highlight in this respect: it is the only such ensemble in any of Handel's biblical oratorios and anticipates the operas of Mozart.

As Susan Staves notes, some of Handel's contemporaries objected to the free-handed way in which he combined the 'Solemnity of Church-Musick' and 'Airs of the Stage'. Hamilton describes how:

> ... others resisted the oratorios as violating what they considered representational decorums appropriate for religious subject-matter. Not only did they object to representations of scripture in the theater, but they also invoked ideas of musical decorum according to which there ought to be firm distinctions between church, chamber, and theater music.[15]

But by deploying in this everything that he had learned as a composer of opera, instrumental and church music — as well as of oratorio — Handel opened up a space in which his audiences could think about the character and consequences of God's decrees in a way that would not have been possible at that time in any other genre.

---

14   Winton Dean, *Handel's Dramatic Oratorios and Masques* (London: Oxford University Press, 1959), p. 592. Paul Henry Lang, *George Frideric Handel* (London: Faber & Faber, 1967), p. 512.
15   Susan Staves, 'Jephtha's Vow Reconsidered', *Huntington Library Quarterly*, 71 (December 2008), 651–69 (p. 669).

II. Elgar: *The Apostles*

Although Elgar grew up in a household in which the Catholic Church played a significant role, his parents had very different views on religion, contributing to the conflicted attitude he displayed towards Catholicism throughout his life. In addition to keeping a music shop, Elgar's father William was organist of St George's Catholic Church, Worcester, from 1846 — eleven years before Edward's birth. His interest in Catholicism was purely professional, at least until his deathbed conversion: he routinely went to the pub during sermon, and wrote in 1852 of his dislike for the 'absurd superstition and playhouse mummery of the Papist'.[16] That same year, however, Elgar's mother, Ann, who had married William in 1848, converted to Catholicism, having initially attended services merely to keep her husband company. She remained a devout Catholic throughout her life and ensured that her children received a Catholic education; there was no Catholic boys' school in Worcester so Elgar joined his older sisters at the girls' school at the age of six. William undoubtedly resented Edward's Catholic education: there is a well-known anecdote about the anger he showed when, during the course of early attempts to write out music in the family music shop, his son produced a Gregorian stave with four lines.

Ann died in 1902, just before Elgar began *The Apostles*, but the pattern of female conversion and commitment to Catholicism repeated itself in Elgar's own marriage. Caroline Alice Roberts was born in India into a Protestant family distinguished for its military service. A published author eight years Elgar's senior, she became his pupil in 1886; in the early stages of their acquaintance, he lent her a copy of Newman's *Dream of Gerontius*. Despite the Roberts family's disapproval of both the Catholicism and the lower social status of the Elgars, they married in 1889 at Brompton Oratory and Alice converted to Catholicism three years later. She too remained devout for the rest of her life; Elgar, by contrast, experienced increasingly agonizing doubts, which he expressed much more strongly after Alice's death in 1920.

This event, and the almost complete creative block that it produced in Elgar, was only one among several severe challenges to his faith. From childhood he had resented that — due in part to his humble origins, but in particular to his Catholicism — he did not receive the professional opportunities that his talent warranted. Catholic emancipation had happened only in 1829, and Catholics were still not allowed to attend Oxford and Cambridge universities when Elgar was born in 1857; the general perception was that Catholics remained outside the British Establishment. Moreover, religious differences had prevented him from marrying the first woman with whom he fell in love, Helen Weaver, who came from a Unitarian family. As he entered middle age, various upheavals in his emotional life threatened both his faith and his mental stability: a love affair, probably unconsummated, with Alice Stuart Wortley, whom he called his 'Windflower' and may well have been the inspiration for his Violin Concerto; probably

---

16 Quoted in John Allison, *Edward Elgar: Sacred Music* (Bridgend: Seren, 1994), p. 10.

other love affairs too, one of which may have produced an illegitimate daughter. Ismene Brown speculates that Elgar's guilt over his abandonment of this daughter could have caused the depression and nervous breakdown that he experienced while working on *The Kingdom* between 1905 and 1907.[17] Finally, the First World War was a shattering experience for Elgar, one whose aftershock contributed to the absence of major works in the last fifteen years of his life, after the elegiac Cello Concerto of 1919.

Elgar's loss of faith was certainly apparent from the time of *The Kingdom*, originally planned as the centrepiece of a vast trilogy on religious themes. It was at this time that he stopped regularly attending Mass, and his disillusionment increased sharply following Alice's death. As he approached death, he said to his doctor, Arthur Thomson, that 'I believe there is nothing but complete oblivion'. He asked to be cremated, which was at that time prohibited by the Roman Catholic Church, although his wishes were ignored by his daughter Carice who also summoned a priest to administer the last rites. He suggested a few months before he died to his friend, Delius, a well-known atheist, that perceptions of him as a religious composer had skewed his reputation. He described the religious oratorios that Delius had criticized as the 'penalty of my English environment' and wrote that 'it has been a matter of no small amusement to me that, as my name somewhat unfortunately is indissolubly connected with "sacred" music, some of your friends and mine have tried to make me believe that I am ill-disposed to the trend and sympathy of your [*Mass of Life*]'.[18] By implication, by the time of his death Elgar was much closer to the Nietzschean world-view of Delius's cantata than to the Catholicism of his childhood.

Unsurprisingly, given his father's position as organist, and later his own (Elgar took over at St George's in 1883 following William's controversial dismissal), there is much church music among his early output. Elgar was strongly influenced by what he heard at St George's and by the possibilities the church offered. Unusually for that time, Viennese masses were often heard with orchestral accompaniment (nurturing Elgar's love for the European classical tradition), and visiting operatic soloists — most of whom were Catholic — were often invited to sing. Elgar was also strongly influenced by Gregorian chant, even — perhaps particularly — after he stopped writing for the church. John Butt points out the irony that Gregorian influence led him towards a modalism similar to that of Ralph Vaughan Williams and other contemporaries, but reached from an entirely different starting point: 'Perhaps, then, part of the very Englishness with which Elgar is so often yoked had its roots in that aspect of his background which was most "foreign" at the time, namely his loyalty to the Pope and the heritage of St Gregory.'[19] Much of his church music does not survive; there is no

---

17   Ismene Brown, 'Elgar's Enigma – A Love Child Named Pearl?', *The Arts Desk*, 26 January 2011, https://theartsdesk.com/classical-music/elgars-enigma-love-child-named-pearl

18   Quoted in John Butt, 'Roman Catholicism and Being Musically English: Elgar's Church and Organ Music', in *The Cambridge Companion to Elgar*, ed. by Daniel M. Grimley and Julian Rushton (Cambridge: Cambridge University Press, 2004), pp. 106–19 (p. 106).

19   *Ibid.*, p. 108.

complete mass setting, for example, though he probably wrote one at St George's. The Catholic church music that does survive — like the specifically Anglican pieces that he produced between 1897 (*Te Deum* and *Benedictus*) and 1914 — is well-crafted but not on the same level as the oratorios, which is where Elgar's true engagement with religious subject-matter is to be found.

The most significant musical influence on Elgar's mature choral works — *The Dream of Gerontius* (1900; strictly speaking not an oratorio), *The Apostles* (1903) and *The Kingdom* (1906) — is Wagnerian music drama. By the time Elgar composed those works, he had a deep knowledge of Wagner's work, which he heard in London in the 1880s and then in Munich and Bayreuth in the 1890s. Wagner's elevation of the status of opera to 'music drama' — from entertainment to something comparable to a religious ceremony — was highly controversial but also opened new possibilities for subsequent composers who wished to explore religious subject-matter outside the confines of the liturgy. The ambiguity of genre was most evident in the case of *Parsifal* (1882), which Wagner described as a *Bühnenweihfestspiel*, 'Stage Dedication Festival Play', and which includes a 'communion' scene; Elgar saw *Parsifal* twice in 1892 and it is a particularly strong influence on his music.

Despite subsequent recognition as a masterpiece, *The Dream of Gerontius* failed at its premiere in Birmingham Town Hall, in part due to woefully inadequate preparation of the chorus and the fact that the conductor, Hans Richter, received the score only the day before the first orchestral rehearsal. The choice of such a conspicuously Catholic text also proved controversial: changes to the text were demanded before the work was performed at Worcester Cathedral. However, the Birmingham Festival maintained its faith in Elgar and commissioned him to write a large choral work on a religious theme for the 1903 festival. He had nurtured the idea of writing a work on the subject of the Apostles since childhood, when a schoolmaster impressed him by describing Jesus's followers as 'poor men, young men, at the time of their calling; perhaps before the descent of the Holy Ghost not cleverer than some of you here'.[20] Under Wagner's inspiration, he now conceived the idea of a trilogy of oratorios, taking the story from the calling of the Apostles through the founding of the early Church before dealing in the final panel with the Last Judgement. In 1902, Elgar heard *Parsifal* again and the first three operas of the *Ring* in Bayreuth, where he had been invited by Hans Richter, who was sharing the conducting that year with Siegfried Wagner. In July he wrote to Ivor Atkins, organist of Worcester Cathedral, that 'I am now plotting GIGANTIC WORK'.[21]

Elgar decided to follow Wagner's example by creating his own libretto but, instead of writing it from scratch, he assembled it from the Bible, taking verses out of their original context to form a series of tableaux. Jesus himself became a relatively marginal figure, as Elgar focused on the 'flawed' characters of Peter, Judas and Mary Magdalene. The portrayal of Mary Magdalene, which includes an episode where she

---

20   R. J. Buckley, *Sir Edward Elgar* (London: The Bodley Head, 1905), p. 6.
21   E. Wulstan Atkins, *The Elgar–Atkins Friendship* (Newton Abbot: David and Charles, 1984), p. 76.

expresses shame about her former life using exclamations from the Old Testament and Apocrypha, is inspired in part by Henry Wadsworth Longfellow's 'The Divine Tragedy'. Mary's music, meanwhile, is influenced by Wagner's portrayals of the Venusberg in *Tannhäuser* and of Kundry and the Flower Maidens in *Parsifal*. Perhaps the most interestingly portrayed character, however, is Judas, to whom Elgar always had a particular attraction, as he revealed in 1904:

> I was always particularly impressed with Archbishop Whately's conception of Judas, who, as he wrote, 'had no design to betray his Master to death, but to have been as confident of the will of Jesus to deliver Himself from His enemies by a miracle as He must have been certain of His power to do so, and accordingly to have designed to force Him to make such a display of His superhuman powers as would have induced all the Jews — and, indeed, the Romans too — to acknowledge Him King'.[22]

Judas' flaw, according to the Richard Whately/Elgar view, lies in his limited and materialistic view of Jesus' mission, not in a desire to destroy Jesus. Elgar encapsulates this by attributing to Judas in Tableau IV, 'The Betrayal', words from the Wisdom of Solomon 2, which express a materialistic view of life and scepticism about the idea of an afterlife (in the Bible this text is preceded by the words 'And the ungodly said'): 'Our life is short and tedious, and in the death of a man there is no remedy; neither was there any man known to have returned from the grave. For we are born at all adventure, and we shall be hereafter as though we had never been'.[23]

This passage draws from Elgar some of his greatest and also most theatrical music: Judas' words are surrounded by wisps of string and woodwind sound, as if endorsing his view of the insubstantiality of human existence. Meanwhile choral groups successively represent worshippers singing a psalm within the temple and the baying crowd calling for Jesus to be crucified. The intensity (even sympathy) of Elgar's engagement with the most flawed figure in the story of the Apostles, combined with a dramatic sweep and an ability to convey multi-layered action — strengthened by his study of Wagner — allow him to create a structure in which both the desire for faith, and the challenges to it, are powerfully revealed.

III. Poulenc: *Dialogues des Carmélites*

Like Elgar, Poulenc received very different notions of religion from the two sides of his family. His father, Emile, director of the family pharmaceutical business that eventually became the giant Rhône-Poulenc, was from a devout Catholic family in Aveyron in southern France; his mother Jenny, née Royer, came from a Parisian family of artist-craftsmen of bohemian outlook who took little interest in organized religion. Poulenc regarded this dual heredity as the key to his musical personality: he associated

---

22   Rudolph de Cordova, 'Illustrated Interviews: LXXXI – Dr. Edward Elgar', *Strand Magazine*, 27 (May 1904), 542.
23   Wisdom of Solomon 2.1b-2.

his deep Catholic faith with his Aveyronais roots and attributed his artistic interests to his mother's family. It became a critical commonplace to speak of the co-existence of contradictory forces in his music, in an attempt to understand the wide divergences of style and character it revealed. This idea was most influentially formulated in Claude Rostand's July 1950 article for *Paris-Presse*, in which he wrote that there were 'two people [*deux personnes*] in Poulenc: the monk [*le moine*] and the ragamuffin or street-urchin [*le voyou*]'.[24]

As with Elgar, too, much in Poulenc's life challenged his faith. He was emotionally scarred from rejection by his childhood friend Raymonde Linossier — the only woman he ever wanted to marry — and then her death in 1930. He suffered depression from the late 1920s, and his behaviour exhibited a manic-depressive cyclical pattern thereafter. His emotional life was complex and closely bound up with his creativity, involving the birth of an illegitimate daughter in 1946 as well as several long-standing relationships with men. Though homosexual activity was not prohibited in France at this time as it was in the UK, the Catholic Church's official opposition to homosexuality meant that Poulenc's orientation was nonetheless a source of tension. As for Elgar, too, war was a devastating experience: he spent most of the Second World War at Noizay in the German zone of occupation and opposed the Nazis through his work with the Front National des Musiciens. Several of his friends either died in concentration camps or were executed for Resistance activities, and Poulenc experienced a further series of traumatic bereavements in the following years.

But unlike with Elgar, personal and professional difficulties led Poulenc back to a strong, if never straightforward, affirmation of his Catholic faith. The moment of reconversion was prompted by a terrible accident experienced by a fellow composer, as he later explained:

> The casual indifference of my mother's family led me, quite naturally, to a long period when I ignored religion. From 1920 to 1935 I was, I confess, very little concerned with matters of faith. In 1936, a crucial date in my life and in my career, I […] [asked Pierre] Bernac to drive me to Rocamadour, which I'd often heard my father talk about. This pilgrimage site is in fact quite near Aveyron. A few days earlier I'd just heard of the tragic death of my colleague Pierre-Octave Ferroud. The terrible decapitation of this composer who was so full of energy dumbfounded me. As I meditated on the fragility of our human frame, I was drawn once more to the life of the spirit. Rocamadour had the effect of restoring me to the faith of my childhood […] The same evening […] I began my *Litanies à la Vierge Noire* for female voices and organ.[25]

Having composed no religious music until that point, the *Litanies* opened the way for a steady flow of religious choral works in the remainder of Poulenc's life — including some of the most significant twentieth-century contributions to the religious choral

---

24 Quoted and translated in Richard D. E. Burton, *Outlines: Francis Poulenc* (Bath: Absolute Press, 2002), p. 15.
25 Francis Poulenc, *Francis Poulenc: Articles and Interviews*, ed. by Nicolas Southon, and trans. by Roger Nichols (Farnham: Ashgate, 2014), p. 233.

repertoire. Other important works comprised the *Mass in G* (1937), the *Stabat mater* (1950–1951) for soprano, mixed chorus and orchestra, the unsanctimonious and joyful *Gloria* (1959–1960) and the terse and musically advanced *Sept répons des ténèbres* (1961–1962).

But his most substantial and, in the estimation of many, greatest post-war work was the opera *Dialogues des Carmélites*. Both libretto and music had a complex genesis. The story of the Compiègne Carmelites, martyred in the aftermath of the French Revolution, was first told by Mother Marie of the Incarnation of God, who survived the Terror and lived until 1836. Publication of her *Relation* led to the beatification of the nuns in 1906. In 1931, the story was turned into a novella entitled *Die Letzte am Schafott* (*The Last to the Scaffold*) by the German Catholic convert Gertrude von Le Fort. The heroine Blanche de la Force, who joins the order to find refuge from her terror at the outbreak of the Revolution, was her invention — the similarity of the names suggests autobiographical identification. In 1947, the Austrian priest and French Resistance fighter, Father Brückberger devised a cinematic scenario based on Le Fort's novel and engaged the French novelist Georges Bernanos to write the dialogue. Just as Le Fort had written herself into her heroine, so Bernanos — then suffering from terminal cancer — concentrated on the dying Prioress' crisis of faith, giving her his precise age (fifty-nine) to underline the connection. Bernanos's work was deemed uncinematic and the film was never produced. However, when his friend Albert Béguin — literary executor and Swiss-born Catholic convert — found it in Bernanos's papers after his death, he assembled it for publication and gave it the title by which it (and the opera) is now known. Deemed, again, unsuitable for cinematic use, it was mounted as a stage play; first, in Zurich in 1951, in German, and then in its original language in Paris the following year, where it received three hundred consecutive performances. Poulenc saw it there on two occasions though did not immediately recognize its operatic potential.

Around this time, Guido Valcarenghi, director of the Milan-based publishing house Ricordi, invited Poulenc to compose a ballet for La Scala on the life of St Margaret of Cortona. Uninspired by this idea, Poulenc instead proposed an opera on a 'mystical' theme. Valcarenghi suggested adapting the Bernanos play as a source, an idea whose appeal grew on Poulenc as he reread the text:

> I had decided to consider the matter later, when I got back to Paris, but then, two days later, right in the middle of a bookseller's window in Rome, I saw *Les Dialogues* which seemed to be waiting for me [...] I bought the book and decided to read it again. So I sat down on the terrace of the café 'Tre scalini' on the Piazza Navone. It was ten o'clock in the morning. At midday I was still there [...] At half past midday I was drunk with enthusiasm, but there remained the acid test: could I find the music for such a text [...] At two o'clock I telegraphed to M. Valcarenghi, true psychic that he was, that I would write the *Dialogues*.[26]

---

26 *Ibid.*, pp. 56–57.

Composition proceeded quickly and the piece was completed in 1956, although the première was postponed until the following year because of legal wrangles over the rights to the text.

Work on *Dialogues* coincided with another period of personal turmoil for Poulenc. Alongside other attachments, he had been in a relationship since the late 1940s with a man ten years younger than himself, Lucien Roubert. In February 1955, Poulenc learned that Roubert was suffering from tuberculosis; he died in October, just as Poulenc was finishing the fair copy of the vocal score. In August Poulenc wrote a letter to his friend, the singer Pierre Bernac, which, if not strictly accurate about biographical details (the work was begun in Noizay, not Lyons, and it was not finished by this point), is revealing about his relationship to the theology underpinning the story:

> I have entrusted him to my sixteen blessed Carmelites: may they protect his final hours since he has been so closely involved with their story. Indeed I began the work at his side, in happiness, in Lyons in August 1953. After all the torment, which I need not describe to you, I have just finished the work, at his side, during the last days of his earthly life. As I wrote to you once before, I am haunted by Bernanos' phrase: 'We do not die for ourselves alone … but for, or instead of, each other.'[27]

This allusion to the Catholic doctrine of 'mystical substitution' is sung by Sister Constance. She makes a crucial intervention in Act III of the opera by claiming that it was her vote that prevented the sisters from accepting the acting Prioress' proposal that the nuns should martyr themselves: she says she has now reconsidered, and so the sacrifice can be made. In fact, the dissenting vote belonged to Blanche, with whom Poulenc seems to have strongly identified.

'Mystical substitution' refers to the idea — propounded from the start of the twentieth century by Catholic writers such as J. K. Huysmans, Léon Bloy and Jacques Maritain — that a saint, following the example of Christ, can 'substitute' him or herself for a sinner who would otherwise be damned. The sinner would then be vicariously redeemed, in Richard D. E. Burton's words, 'thanks to the mysterious "reversibility" of merits and to the solidarity of the saints working in communion with each other for the salvation of sinful humanity'.[28] Poulenc was acutely aware both of his own sinfulness, at least in relation to orthodox Catholic doctrine, and of the large numbers of friends and associates who had 'sacrificed' themselves — or so it seemed to him — so that he could live and compose. Uppermost in his mind at this time was not just Roubert but also Pierre-Octave Ferroud, whose death had led directly to his renewed embrace of the Catholic faith. It is telling that Poulenc changes the ending of Bernanos's text so that Sister Blanche voluntarily mounts the scaffold to be executed by the guillotine rather than dying at the hands of the mob. By making this change, Poulenc not only clarifies that she is sacrificing herself for the benefit of others, but also makes the manner of her

---

[27] Letter to Pierre Bernac, in *Francis Poulenc: Echo and Source, Selected Correspondence 1915–63*, ed. and trans. by Sidney Buckland (London: Victor Gollancz Ltd., 1991), p. 232 (August 1955).

[28] Burton, *Outlines*, p. 95.

death — decapitation — the same as that of Ferroud, whom he believed responsible for his own conversion.[29]

Jephtha, *The Apostles* and *Dialogues des Carmélites* are liminal in relation to the borders not only between 'sacred' and 'secular', but also between 'staged' and 'concert' music, and 'oratorio' and 'opera'. *Jephtha* and *The Apostles* are oratorios that come close to opera (particularly in the scenes highlighted above); *Dialogues des Carmélites* is an opera whose static, tableau-like quality sometimes brings it close to oratorio. All these pieces contain characters whose faith is tested or breaks; these musical portrayals are enlivened and deepened both by resonances with the personal struggles of the composers concerned and by the engagement of composers and librettists in the theological debates of their own time. The performance and reception of these works can only benefit from being 'theologically informed'; while the appreciation of the particular qualities of such liminal works, and the contribution they make to our understanding of religious experience, will in turn enrich our understanding of the broader relationship between music and the sacred.

---

29 *Ibid.*, p. 96: 'The life and, above all, the death of Blanche de la Force becomes a manifesto for the doctrine of mystical substitution [...] when set to music by Poulenc [it is given] its most moving, as well as its most coherent, expression.'

16. Sacred Music in Secular Spaces

Jonathan Arnold

When Giovanni Pierluigi da Palestrina wrote his Mass settings and motets, or J. S. Bach his cantatas and passions, they could not have imagined the ways in which their music would be heard today. We can now access sacred music in our living rooms, at work and on the commute: an hour-long compilation — entitled '*Agnus Dei*' — by the choir of New College, Oxford has nine and a half million views on YouTube, and five different versions of Bach's *St Matthew Passion* each have over a million.[1] This liberation of sacred music from its religious context and liturgical function has been recently complimented by a resurgence, in Britain at least, of interest in high quality sacred music performed *within* its ecclesiastical context, especially in cathedrals and chapels with choral institutions. But outside this setting, sacred music has been culturally re-appropriated into a multitude of private and public secular contexts, with the result that any theological resonances in the music have become diluted for the casual listener. But those who compose and perform sacred music today are not daunted by such a trend. Even Christian composers do not necessarily choose a liturgical service as the preferred context for their art, and some composers have abandoned institutional religion in favour of a more Universalist approach. Likewise, performers often find a secular setting a more powerful arena for the transmission of music's sacred message.

In this chapter, I shall explore the current interest in sacred music, both within and outside of its liturgical context. I will examine how sacred music has been freed from its ecclesiastical bonds and been re-appropriated into the globalized market of public and private consumerism; and I will investigate how composers, performers

---

1   This essay is an extended version of a lecture given at the TheoArtistry Festival, University of St Andrews, 5 March 2018. Parts of the essay have been published in J. Arnold, *Sacred Music in Secular Society* (Farnham: Ashgate, 2014); and in *idem*, 'Evensong', *The Spectator*, 24 March 2018, p. 52.

and listeners have responded to these developments. Arguably, the expansion of sacred music should not be a cause for alarm for confessional Christians. Rather, it is to be embraced, because sacred music reaches beyond the bounds of doctrinal and institutional propositional belief and reaches out to a world hungry for spiritual nourishment. Music that speaks deeply into the human condition, promotes human flourishing and evokes spiritual meaning, appeals to believers and non-believers alike, for it relates to the experience, encounter and relationality of an unknown reality that transcends both ourselves and the world around us. Beauty can help us to intuit a truth beyond the confines of our materialist existence and lead us to the source of all truth, which is ultimately love — a truth that some call 'God'. I will begin by exploring current trends in the performance of sacred music within its liturgical context.

I. Secular Listeners in Sacred Spaces

Spotify and smartphones have eliminated the need to visit a cathedral, church or chapel in order to hear sacred works of music, but yet visit we still do. While overall church attendance has fallen by two-thirds since the 1960s, attendance at traditional choral worship in England is on the rise, and has been for the last two decades in cathedrals, university college chapels and large parish churches with choral traditions.[2] Weekday choral services have contributed greatly to this resurgence in popularity in England's forty-two Anglican cathedrals: though the end of the twentieth century saw attendance at cathedral services falling by up to five per cent each year, figures are now up by a third in a decade — and that is excluding the tourists.[3] Evensong attendance at England's six most popular cathedrals rose by 34 per cent between 2008 and 2012 alone.[4] All this is in the face of a marked fall in biblical literacy in Britain through the generations, according to research released by the Bible Society.[5]

Evensong has barely changed since the publication of the Book of Common Prayer in 1662. It is perhaps not a coincidence that attendance at traditional choral services started to surge just as modern life began to seem most removed from their world of candles, canons and communal reflection: choral services offer an antidote to the modern age of instant digital gratification. As the working day ends, cathedral and chapel-goers can enter a beautiful space where they can be still, silent and receptive

---

2 John Bingham, 'Church of England Attendance Plunges to Record Low', *The Telegraph*, 12 January 2016, http://www.telegraph.co.uk/news/religion/12095251/Church-of-England-attendance-plunges-to-record-low.html; and *idem*, 'Looking for Britain's Future Leaders? Try Evensong', *The Telegraph*, 1 March 2016, http://www.telegraph.co.uk/news/religion/12176998/Looking-for-Britains-future-leaders-Try-evensong.html

3 Simon Jenkins, 'Why Cathedrals Are Soaring', *The Spectator*, 8 October 2016, https://www.spectator.co.uk/2016/10/why-cathedrals-are-soaring/

4 E. H. B., 'Sing and They Will Come', *The Economist*, 4 March 2014, https://www.economist.com/prospero/2014/03/04/sing-and-they-will-come

5 'Pass it on Report', *Bible Society*, February 2014, http://www.biblesociety.org.uk/press/uploads/final-copy-of-Pass-it-On-research-report_02070706.pdf, pp. 1–36 (p. 13).

to the gentle drama that unfolds. As the choir and clergy process in, and the scene is set with their flowing robes, worshippers can scrutinize their faces, see their folders of music and hear the blend of their distinct voices as they begin the 'Preces and Responses'. For many Christians, there exists an unwritten contract between priest, readers, musicians, listeners and the unseen divine. The music enhances the words of the service, giving beauty and character to the heartfelt words of the Psalms, to the joyful thanksgiving in Mary's song of praise and liberation (the '*Magnificat*'), to Simeon's grateful prayer for rest (the '*Nunc dimittis*') and to the prayers of the 'Collects'. The music of worship is interspersed with silence, in which our own thoughts and petitions creep in and become part of the tapestry of the liturgy.

Yet not all of those who attend these services are Christian. The cultural, ethnic, and religious diversity of those who attend Evensong is remarkable. Formal choral worship does not coerce the attendee into any particular doctrinal confession: even Richard Dawkins admits to having a 'certain love' for Evensong.[6] People are free to choose the extent to which they wish to engage with the worship, which is in many respects more passive than in Sunday services: at Evensong, the focus is on listening, and worshippers do not take communion. Quiet reflection is, indeed, hard to come by for a generation who struggle to sit in silence for mere minutes without taking out their phones. But peace and reflection are important, especially at a time when one in eight people suffers from an anxiety disorder.[7] So, too, is community: under 35s, who can trace their friends' every move through Facebook and WhatsApp, are nonetheless more likely than those over 55 to experience regular feelings of loneliness.[8] Attending a choral service offers a participation in something significantly other to ourselves. It takes the noise of our mental business and quietens us towards an inner silence. It points towards the transcendent and forges a bond between all in the sacred space by the shared experience of the liturgical rite.

The thirst for the sacred and spiritual remains a keen one. According to Brian Mountford, it is institutional Christianity's commitment to the 'search for truth through beauty' that has kept so many non-believers involved.[9] While theologians such as Hans Küng and Karl Barth suggest that the experience of transcendence can only be explained through the language of faith, Mountford argues that it can be accessed through religious art, architecture and music: within the Christian liturgy, sound

---

6　Douglas Murray, 'Richard Dawkins Interview: "I Have a Certain Love for the Anglican Tradition"', *The Spectator,* 14 September 2013, https://www.spectator.co.uk/2013/09/interview-richard-dawkins-on-what-hed-miss-if-christianity-vanished/

7　Louise Chunn, 'How Anxiety Became a Modern Epidemic Greater than Depression', *The Telegraph,* 11 June 2016, http://www.telegraph.co.uk/health-fitness/mind/how-anxiety-became-a-modern-epidemic-greater-than-depression/

8　Natalie Gil, 'Loneliness: A Silent Plague that is Hurting Young People Most', *The Guardian,* 20 July 2014, https://www.theguardian.com/lifeandstyle/2014/jul/20/loneliness-britains-silent-plague-hurts-young-people-most

9　Brian Mountford, *Christian Atheist*: *Belonging without Believing* (Winchester, UK and Washington D.C.: O Books, 2010), p. 20.

alone can 'enhance a sense of height, depth, sadness, joy, fear, loss or triumph'.[10] What some will hear through Christian ears is still beautiful when heard through secular ones. This is clear from the responses I have received from chapel-goers as part of my survey of attendee experiences of sacred music.[11] Listeners almost always describe choral music as profoundly moving: one recalled a sense of being transported 'out of the realm of everyday living. It was otherworldly and beautifully done'. However, sacred music not only attracts secular listeners into sacred spaces, it has been equally at home in secular spaces for many centuries.

II. The Sacred in Secular Spaces

Sacred music is accessed and consumed today in ways that would have been alien to past generations. We do not perform or listen to Bach today as those would have done in the eighteenth century, for instance. There have been major cultural, musical and liturgical shifts: 'The taste required for making and hearing music is culturally shaped and likewise evolves in relation to living traditions', as Frank Burch Brown has observed.[12] Since the eighteenth century, and the rise of the oratorio, sacred music has been liberated from the confines of the liturgy, and has been culturally assimilated into innumerable secular contexts. But even in the eighteenth century much sacred music was purposefully intended and written for newly-established concert halls: 'Although Handel appears to have been every bit as devout as Bach, his staging of oratorios in theatres for the paying public pointed the way to music's eventual emancipation from function'.[13]

Handel's *Messiah*, first performed in Dublin's New Music Hall in 1742, is still the most performed piece of classical music, year on year, in British concert venues.[14] This shift of sacred music from the church to the concert hall, gave rise to a re-imagining of music's function and a reconfiguration of the use of public and private space, as Philip Bohlman argues:

> With the new stage in modernity unleashed by the religious enlightenments at the end of the eighteenth century, worship and the music of worship moved from the sanctuary to the public square, sometimes in gradual stages, but often through the dramatic modulation of public soundscapes.[15]

---

10   *Ibid.*, p. 25.
11   For more information, see: Jonathan Arnold, *Experience of Music*, http://www.experienceofmusic.org.
12   Frank Burch Brown, *Good Taste, Bad Taste and Christian Taste: Aesthetics in Religion Life* (Oxford: Oxford University Press, 2000), p. 14.
13   Tim Blanning, *The Triumph of Music: Composers, Musicians and their Audiences, 1700 to the Present* (Harmondsworth: Penguin, 2008), pp. 82–85. For a discussion of the 'sacralisation' of music in society, see also *ibid.*, pp. 89–91, 122–46; Carl Dahlhuas, *The Idea of Absolute Music*, trans. by Roger Lustig (Chicago, IL: University of Chicago Press, 1990); Mark Evan Bonds, *Music as Thought: Listening to the Symphony in the Age of Beethoven* (Princeton, NJ: Princeton University Press, 2006).
14   Philip Bohlman, 'Music Inside Out: Sounding Public Religion in a Post-Secular Europe', in Georgina Born (ed.), *Music, Sound and Space: Transformations of Public and Private Experience* (Cambridge: Cambridge University Press, 2013), pp. 205–23.
15   *Ibid.*, p. 207.

Thus, sacred music had to 're-enter the modern history of public religion ... *as music*', i.e. not just as something sacred and secret but as music *per se*.[16] For an example, Bohlman cites the Turkish March from the final movement of Beethoven's *Ninth Symphony*, which 'bears witness to the pre-Enlightenment encounter between Christian Central Europe and the Muslim Ottoman Empire. In Herbert von Karajan's textless reworking of the Beethoven/Schiller 'Ode to Joy' as the 'European Anthem', however, the Turkish March is silent, the symbolic centre of the European Union purged of Turkish and Islamic history'.[17]

In addition to these political and ideological public expressions of sacred music, there is the more physical dimension of music's inherent existence within time and space, or musical motion.[18] Nicholas Cook has argued that music transforms space by giving it social meaning.[19] It retains its meaning even when reduced to a recording and connotes place well, but it can easily be extracted from its space and appropriated elsewhere.[20] For instance, on the macro level, the Polish people may identify, consciously or subconsciously, with the music of Frederick Chopin, or the Viennese may associate their cultural identity with the music of Mozart. However, if that music is transferred to a completely different context, such as an underground station in South Korea, although the cultural link with Poland or Austria might still resonate for a European listener, the music has been appropriated to the extent that, for a native South-Korean, '… it carries no connotations of European culture or cultural prestige; but rather embodies an apparently effortless or naturalised international modernism'.[21]

On the micro level, iPods and portable digital musical devices mean that we can create, even on public transport, a personal, private space. Such devices create a 'phenomenological space that is dissociated from physical space'.[22] Theodor W. Adorno's early work regarding audio recordings was remarkably prescient concerning the ability of this micro space (i.e., of one person listening to music on headphones) to convey transcendent, numinous, even divine truth. In this 'traffic with technology', as he called it, 'formulations capture the sounds of creation, the first and last sounds, judgement upon life and message about that which may come thereafter'.[23] Thus, the meaningfulness of sacred music can be translated into the secular space without any

---

16   *Ibid.*, p. 209.
17   *Ibid.*, p. 217, citing Caryl Clark, 'Forging Identity: Beethoven's "Ode" as European Anthem', *Critical Inquiry*, 23 (1997), 789–807.
18   Nicholas Cook, 'Classical Music and the Politics of Space', in Born (ed.), *Music, Sound and Space*, pp. 224–38 (p. 226). Cook cites Roger Scruton, *The Aesthetics of Music* (Oxford: Clarendon Press, 1997), p. 52.
19   Cook, 'Classical Music', p. 229.
20   *Ibid.*
21   *Ibid.*, pp. 229–30.
22   *Ibid.*, p. 230.
23   Theodor W. Adorno, 'The Form of the Phonographic Record (1928)', trans. by Thomas Y. Levin, in *Essays on Music*, ed. by Richard Leppert, and trans. by Susan Gillespie (Berkeley, CA: University of California Press, 2002), p. 277; quoted in Richard Middleton, 'Faith, Hope, and the Hope of Love: On the Fidelity of the Phonograph', in Born (ed.), *Music, Sound and Space*, pp. 292–310 (p. 298).

loss of power. Equally, however, sacred music can be appropriated to new cultural contexts and employed in ways unforeseen by the composer.

A recent example of this phenomenon is a recording of Thomas Tallis's forty-part choral motet *Spem in Alium*, one of the most popular pieces of sacred music in the repertoire today. When, in 2012, it reached number one in the classical charts, Peter Phillips, director of the *Tallis Scholars*, wrote:

> I am thrilled that *Spem in alium* has attracted such a large new audience. It is one of the most remarkable achievements of the human mind, an extra-ordinary and moving piece written for 40 individual singers … For me it ranks alongside the best works of Michelangelo and Leonardo da Vinci and confirms Tallis as England's greatest composer. It's on my iPod![24]

The recording may evoke a memory of a live performance, which may in turn help the listener to recall liturgical performances. Alternatively, there may be no association with the music's original historical, theological or cultural context. Neither Tallis nor Phillips could have predicted that the sacred piece would be used as the soundtrack to the erotic film *Fifty Shades of Grey*. It is doubtful whether many people watching that film would have associated the music with the Elizabethan Chapel Royal or the need to put their hope in the God of Israel! When sacred music is thus re-appropriated it is tempting to think that its theological significance becomes diluted, if not entirely obscured. But can the theological essence of sacred music be erased by its cultural context? Daniel Chua thinks not, because Western secular culture is shaped by its Christian heritage and, ironically, puts God centre stage by replicating old theological modes of thought; it 'acts as a kind of divine surrogate' and is heard as 'a mode of "secular theology" that exposes some of the major theological issues of our times'.[25] We cannot separate the sacred from the secular in our society because of the historical saturation of religious culture in the arts, as James Herbert has acknowledged. The sacred is simply part of the artistic language: 'Religious issues arise even in seemingly secular works [of art and music] where we might not expect them, because Christian mysticism and metaphysics thoroughly permeate the rhetoric and sensibility of western cultural production.'[26] Herbert is echoing the words of the Italian scholar Cianni Vattimo, in this respect: 'While our civilization no longer explicitly professes itself Christian but rather considers itself by and large a de-Christianized, post-Christian, lay civilization, it is nevertheless, profoundly shaped by that heritage at its source.'[27]

---

24 CMU Editorial, '50 Shades of Grey Propels Sixteenth Century Chant to Classical Number One', *Complete Music Update*, 17 July 2012, http://www.completemusicupdate.com/article/50-shades-of-grey-propels-sixteenth-century-chant-to-classical-number-one/
25 Daniel K. L. Chua, 'Music as the Mouthpiece of Theology', in Jeremy S. Begbie and Steven R. Guthrie (eds.), *Resonant Witness: Conversations between Music and Theology* (Grand Rapids, MI: Eerdmans, 2011), pp. 137–61 (p. 138).
26 James D. Herbert, *Our Distance from God: Studies of the Divine and the Mundane in Western Art and Music* (Berkeley, CA: University of California Press, 2008), p. 3.
27 Gianni Vattimo, *Belief*, trans. by Luca D'Isanto and David Webb (Stanford, CA: Stanford University Press, 1999), p. 43.

Robert Scholl also acknowledges a need in modern society for so-called spiritual music, which he defines as '… music that seems to gnaw at the wound of modernity as much as it desires the spear that might close the wounds and overcome human alienations from God'.[28] He suggests that there is a search for the absolute and for a reconfiguration of humanity which implies a kind of 'secular theology that, though it would like to transfigure the past, may, to varying degrees, question or simply remain open to an unknown outcome'.[29]

This 'secular theology' arises when the listener, regardless of the intentions of the composer or performer, imbues music that relates to the depth of the human condition with theological meaning. Conversely, Christian composers may intend their music, full of intentional theological resonance, to be performed in a secular space. Thus, I will now delve further into the relationship between composers, performers and listeners.

III. Composer, Performers and Listeners

Recent research has revealed that, for many contemporary composers of sacred Christian music, the religious liturgy is by no means the only intended destiny for their music, nor is it necessarily a significant motivation for composition.[30] For composers such as James MacMillan and Arvo Pärt, the concert hall is an equally valid, and perhaps an even more appropriate place, for sacred music to be encountered as a religious house of worship. Thus, in today's society, the sacred is no longer confined to the church-going few; it is now more available to the majority of people, through many different types of media, and in a more accessible way than ever before. A further erosion of the dividing wall between sacred and secular is evident in the abandonment of institutional religion by some twentieth-century Christian composers, in favour of a broader theological and humanitarian approach. Towards the end of his life John Tavener relinquished both institutional religion and secularism, seeing his music as a Universalist gift of healing to the world:

> The fact that I've been given this Universalist vision of the world makes it a possibility that I might be able to contribute, just fractionally, towards the healing of a planet that's torn to pieces at the moment, by strife, by war, by different religions warring with each other. But through the Universalist language of music perhaps there is a possibility to bring about a healing process and, after all, music originally was this function. If one listens or looks on the rituals of the American, Indian or African tribes one sees that all ritual ceremonies and all music was either addressed to the creator or it was music of healing in order to help heal. Music in the West has become so sophisticated […] that I think we've lost sight of this dimension in music.[31]

---

28 Robert Scholl, 'The Shock of the Positive: Olivier Messiaen, St. Francis, and Redemption through Modernity', in Begbie and Guthrie (eds.), *Resonant Witness*, pp. 162–89 (p. 187).
29 *Ibid.*
30 Arnold, *Sacred Music*, pp. 63–86.
31 John Tavener, interview by David McCleery, transcribed from 'John Tavener Reflects: A Recorded Interview' on the album *John Tavener: A Portrait* (Naxos, 8558152-53, 2004).

Similarly, Jonathan Harvey hoped that his music would lead people away from selfish and harmful individualism and towards a better community: 'I like to unify, not into an easy unity, but a unity which is rich and complex. I'd like music to speak of, to herald and to prophesy a better world, less entangled with personal egoistic emotions.'[32] At its best, therefore, music brings harmony and a shared experience broad enough to encompass everybody's individual experience, religious or otherwise, and thus bring them closer together.

Performers of sacred music also find the secular, concert-hall context a conducive setting for high-quality performance and musical interpretation.[33] For Phillips, sacred music is more powerfully communicated in a concert performance than in a liturgical one. If the performance quality is exceptionally good, moreover, the music's theological power is more effectively transmitted: 'I simply think the music is stronger theologically when it's being sung well, and that is more likely in a concert.'[34] For singer Francis Steele, musical interpretation is a crucial factor in communicating the sacred nature of music, regardless of context. This, he argues, is because sensitive interpretation can transform a relatively mundane text into one with authority and persuasiveness, bringing performer and listener alike closer to the mystery of God.[35] For both these performers music is able to transcend denominational and religious boundaries; their views are borne out by the opinions of respondents to a recent research survey.[36] For one respondent, there was a perceived community bond between the contemporary audience and those who had heard the same music in past generations:

> I enjoy the shared experience of making music and sharing it with the audience, and the communion between the contemporary audience and the craftsmen of past ages who built the parish church in Witney. I like to reflect on the similarities and differences between the modern audience's reaction to the music and that of past audiences.

For another respondent, the concert music inspired a spiritual experience:

> Sacred music always brings me back to the knowledge that I have a spiritual dimension. It enables me to be grounded in my prayer and meditation. For me sacred music, particularly Renaissance and Baroque, is a bridge between our worldly existence and the wonder, power and awesomeness of God.

Thus, some concert performances may not be easily categorized as either secular or sacred. Recent examples of concert series seeking to present a quasi-religious experience to concert performances have been those entitled 'Pilgrimage'. Harry Christophers' annual *Choral Pilgrimage*, with his choir *The Sixteen*; and John Eliot Gardener's *Bach Pilgrimage*, performed by *The Monteverdi Choir* and *English Baroque*

---

32 Daniel Jaffé, 'Jonathan Harvey: Interview', *Composition Today*, [n.d.], http://www.compositiontoday.com/ articles/jonathan_harvey_interview.asp
33 Arnold, *Sacred Music*, Chapter 3, pp. 63–83.
34 Ibid., p. 68.
35 Ibid., p. 54.
36 For survey results, see Arnold, 'Experience of Music', www.experienceofmusic.org

Soloists, both presented sacred music as concert programmes often performed within ecclesiastical settings, such as cathedrals, but without any liturgical or religious ritual. The result for the paying audience is a liminal experience which may be imbued with religious meaning or not, depending on the beliefs and intentions of the listener. But not all listeners are comfortable with this ambiguous arrangement. In a series of recent interviews with Anglican clergy, parish priest Nicholas Brown made a clear distinction between listening to sacred music within a worship context and listening in a concert context:

> Even where the music is performed as a concert in a sacred building, for instance a reconstruction of a Latin mass, for me that is still very different from if it is performed as part of a celebration of the Eucharist. The concert setting and the genuine liturgical settings could be visually and practically identical, but there's something about the intention of the musicians and clergy that affects the way I engage with it spiritually.[37]

This view is echoed by a comment made by an anonymous contributor to the recent research survey:

> I felt removed from daily worries and preoccupations to a greater awareness of the miracle of human life and creativity. That feeling would have been greatly enhanced had the performance taken place in a place of worship. Sacred music and churches usually give me a space where I can be other than my quotidian self.[38]

For some, religious liturgy is an important context for sacred music to be meaningful. For others, a sense of community (past and present), spirituality, prayer and meditation can be found by listening to sacred music in a secular setting. Indeed, even the terms 'religious' and 'secular', in the context of musical experience, encounter and relationship, can be misleading.

IV. Religion, Secularism and Faith — The Search for Truth through Beauty

One of the problems with these categories of 'religious' and 'secular' is the lack of recognition of the many people who do not neatly fall into either category; an experience of implicit faith is not the same as explicit propositional, ideological and doctrinal belief. A growing number of people want to label themselves as 'spiritual but not religious'. Nancy Ammerman has labelled such people as extra-theistic. Such people may be those who have never been to church; they might be those who have stopped attending church but who still seek meaning, joy, and the fulfilment of their humanity, in nature and beauty, whilst seeking somehow to explain the mystery of existence.[39] For this growing sector of society, institutional religion has less relevance

---

37 Interview with the Reverend Nicholas Brown (Team Rector, Louth Parish Churches), 2017.
38 See Arnold, www.experienceofmusic.org
39 Nancy Tatom Ammerman, *Sacred Stories Spiritual Tribes: Finding Religion in Everyday Life* (Oxford: Oxford University Press, 2013), quoted in Ian Mobsby, 'The Place of New Monasticism in a Post-Secular

than spiritual experience. For them, spiritual practice is a superior pursuit to doctrinal belief. As Bryan Turner has argued, 'philosophers tend [...] to concentrate on religious beliefs rather than on practice'.[40] In seeking spiritual nourishment through music, there emerges a sense of wonder that may have religious meaning, and may not. For some, 'spirituality becomes process, with notions of God replaced by notions of being-ness'.[41]

Thus, in order 'to understand the more general relevance of religion as a public cultural resource',[42] we might need to focus not so much on belief as on practice.[43] It is into this realm of practice, or praxis, that culture and the arts fit so well. Between the theist viewpoint of transcendence as an experience that leads one to the divine and the rationalist approach which explains it as a heightened level of feeling, there is a sense that truth can be found through the experience of beauty rather than doctrine alone.[44] This non-theistic standpoint elevates art and nature as access points to a better moral life, as Iris Murdoch has written: 'The appreciation of beauty in art or nature is not only [...] the easiest available spiritual exercise; it is also a completely adequate entry into [...] the good life, since it *is* the checking of selfishness in the interest of seeing the real.'[45]

Those who attend concert performances of sacred music, whether in a secular space or a de-sacralized religious space, may be confessional Christian believers seeking religious meaning in the sacred words. Alternatively, they may have a less definite sense of the divine or spirituality in the numinous mystery of the music. No art form is arguably better for 'spiritual expression and religious resonance' despite, or rather because of, its non-verbal essence.[46] Nothing better conveys meaning and 'communicates to our senses and to our reflection what little we can grasp of the naked wonder of life'.[47]

Culture'; Nancy Tatom Ammerman, 'Spiritual But Not Religious? Beyond Binary Choices in the Study of Religion', *Journal for the Scientific Study of Religion*, 52 (2013), 258–78 (p. 258 and *passim*).

40 Bryan S. Turner, 'Religion in a Post-Secular Society', in Bryan S. Turner (ed.), *The New Blackwell Companion to the Sociology of Religion* (Chichester: Wiley Blackwell, 2010), pp. 649–67 (p. 650); quoted in Marcus Moberg, Kennet Granholm, and Peter Nynäs, 'Trajectories of Post-Secular Complexity: An Introduction', in Peter Nynäs, Mika Lassander and Terhi Utriainen (eds.), *Post-Secular Society* (New Brunswick, NJ: Transactions, 2015), pp. 1–26 (p. 6).

41 June Boyce-Tillman, *Experiencing Music — Restoring the Spiritual: Music as Well Being* (Oxford: Oxford University Press, 2016), p. 49.

42 Michele M. Dillon, 'Can Post-Secular Society Tolerate Religious Differences?', *Sociology of Religion*, 71 (2010), 139–56 (p. 142); quoted in Marcus Moberg, Kennet Granholm, and Peter Nynäs, 'Trajectories', in Nynäs, Lassander, and Utriainen, *Post-Secular Society*, p. 7.

43 Turner, 'Religion in a Post-Secular Society', p. 658.

44 Mountford, *Christian Atheist*, p. 22.

45 Iris Murdoch, *The Sovereignty of Good* (London: Routledge, 1970), pp. 64–65, quoted in Mountford, *Christian Atheist*, p. 23.

46 *Ibid*.

47 George Steiner, *Real Presences* (London: Faber, 1989), pp. 216–17; Philip Bohlman, 'Is All Music Religious?' in Jon Michael Spencer (ed.), *Theomusicology — A Special Issue of Black Sacred Music: A Journal of Theomusicology* (Durham, NC: Duke University Press, 1994), pp. 3–12 (p. 9); Jeremy Begbie, *Resounding Truth: Christian Wisdom in the World of Music* (Grand Rapids, MI: Baker Academic, 2007), pp. 16–17.

Conclusion: Encounter, Experience and Relationship

In the twenty-first century, music that speaks deeply to the most fundamental aspects of human flourishing inevitably concerns encounter, experience and relationship. For this reason, sacred music continues to appeal to a secular audience, because, as George Steiner has put it: 'Music means. It is brimful of meanings which will not translate into logical structures or verbal expression.'[48] Moreover, 'Music has long been, and continues to be, the unwritten theology of those who lack or reject any formal creed.'[49] The reason, therefore, that so many atheists hang on to the 'coat tails' of religion is that 'art, music and literature provide their closest access to religious experience.'[50]

The search for truth through beauty is one that can be undertaken by the believer, the agnostic and the atheist alike. For people of faith, they might discern traces of an unknown reality that transcends the world.[51] While for others, the experience of transcendence through music need not point towards a supernatural reality but, rather, is firmly of this world.[52] Either way, whatever our faith stance, through sacred music we often encounter a transformative relational experience. In relationships we may perceive a spark of divinity, or spirit; in art we might take that experience one stage further and intuit a deep knowledge of the spiritual life that cannot be found by reasoned argument or deductive thinking. It is in this context that community becomes so important. It is through experience, encounter, and relationship — encompassing music and the arts, nature and the world around us, and relationships with people — that knowledge of a deeper reality of self and other emerges. The arts, and music in particular, offer an important path that can take our experience of the world beyond ourselves and help us to perceive the reality and mystical truth of something greater.

---

48 *Ibid.*, pp. 18–19.
49 Steiner, *Real Presences*, p. 218; quoted in Maeve Louise Heaney, *Music as Theology: What Music Says about the Word* (Eugene, OR: Wipf and Stock Publishers, 2012), p. 6.
50 Mountford, *Christian Atheist*, p. 20.
51 John Cottingham, *The Spiritual Dimension: Religion, Philosophy and Human Value* (Cambridge: Cambridge University Press, 2005), p. 136; Hans Küng, *Mozart — Traces of Transcendence* (London: SCM, 1992), p. 35; Mountford, *Christian Atheist*, pp. 20–21.
52 *Ibid.*, p. 20.

17. Music and Theology: Some Reflections on 'the Listener's Share'

Gavin Hopps

In an essay exploring the spiritual dimensions of human creativity, James MacMillan invokes Luke's account of the Annunciation and, in particular, Mary's posture of receptivity as a way of thinking about artistry and the role of divine inspiration. As MacMillan observes: 'In St Luke's account of the Annunciation, it is not just Mary's fecundity that is inspiring to a creative person. A more powerful and more pertinent metaphor for the religious artist is the balance between, on the one hand, Mary's independent free will and, on the other, her openness to the power of the Holy Spirit'.[1] Similarly, as MacMillan explains, 'an artist or composer who thinks in real and meaningful terms of a divine inspiration' should at the same time recognize 'the full and active participation of all one's human faculties', for it is 'through the interaction of all that makes us human — our intellect, our intelligence, our emotion and our physicality, our universal experience of joy and despair, our flesh and blood — with the breath of God which brings forth creative fruit (for an artist new work, new art, new music)'.[2]

In this chapter, I want to draw on this model of receptivity as a matter of openness and active participation. However, instead of focusing on the artist or composer, I wish to consider the role of the listener and the ways in which musical meanings are also interactively constituted. Whilst in general this is a relatively uncontentious argument, which broadly accords with widespread developments within the field of musicology, to argue for such an interactive approach in relation to *religious* meanings is to diverge from dominant interpretive models within that discipline and, perhaps more surprisingly, within the sub-field of music and theology. Before setting out

---

1   James MacMillan, 'God, Theology and Music', *New Blackfriars*, 81 (2000), 16–26 (p. 23).
2   *Ibid.*

the positive case for a conception of music-listening as a matter of active receptivity, therefore, I shall outline the influential approaches to music that keep this interactive model from view. The first of these argues for the importance of 'social' and 'subjective' meanings but seeks to exclude certain religious possibilities; the second argues for music's religious significance but neglects the role of the listener in co-producing this. In arguing for a third way between these extremes, my conclusion thus owes something to the wisdom of 'Goldilocks and the Three Bears'.

I. Closed-World Musicology

Perhaps the most prominent development within musicology over the last thirty years has been a widening of the predominantly 'formalist' focus away from a concentration on 'the music itself' to encompass, on the one hand, the ways in which music's meanings are socially and culturally constituted in the subjective experience of music listening, but also, on the other hand, how music is chiastically involved in the formation and enhancement of listeners' identities. One of the most articulate and pioneering advocates of this development — which is associated with 'new', 'postmodern' or 'critical' musicology[3] — is Lawrence Kramer.

Kramer's work has been influential in ways that can only be briefly acknowledged here. To begin with, it has been instrumental in dismantling the institutionalized segregation of music and language, which shored up the sense of music's radical autonomy, which, in turn, he believes, shuffled classical music 'out of the public sphere' to 'an honorific place on the margins of high culture'.[4] Kramer's subversion of the music-language divide — by means of which he sought to deconstruct the dualistic categories of the 'music itself' and the 'extra-musical', as well as 'the subjective musical response and objective musical knowledge'[5] — has also played a vital role in opening up the discipline of musicology to an array of critical discourses and interpretive practices that have foregrounded the 'worldly' character of music (which was often occluded in readings that privileged its aesthetic autonomy) and have helped us to recognize the ways in which music contributes to the construction of social realities. In addition, Kramer's conception of music as 'cultural practice' — the underlying rationale of which is 'simply a demand for human interest'[6] — has brought increased legitimacy not only to the idea of 'performative listening' and the 'subjective' meanings that ordinary

---

3 Although manifestly differing in their connotations, these three terms have all been used to describe the work of Lawrence Kramer, Richard Leppert, Susan McClary, Rose Subotnik and others, whose once intensely controversial approaches to music have now been largely absorbed into common practice. See *Musicology: The Key Concepts*, ed. by David Beard and Kenneth Gloag (London: Routledge, 2005), p. 122.
4 Lawrence Kramer, *Classical Music and Postmodern Knowledge* (Berkeley, CA: University of California Press, 1995), pp. 5–6.
5 *Ibid.*, p. 3.
6 *Ibid.*, p. 1.

listeners bring to music,[7] but also to informally evocative acts of interpretation — that is, 'unsystematic, freely metaphorical or epithetical [...] semantic improvisations'.[8] All of which has formed part of an immensely productive effort to release music from what Theodor Adorno described as a condition of 'inane isolation',[9] which, according to Kramer, is fostered by 'a hard epistemology that admonishes us not to impose our merely subjective interpretations on the semantic indefiniteness of music'.[10] It is this sort of active participation by the listener in the co-constitution of music's meanings that I am referring to as 'the listener's share' and that along with Kramer I wish to affirm.[11]

There are, however, some problems with Kramer's attack on the idea of musical autonomy, which have significant ramifications for a theological approach to music. Most obviously, whilst Kramer's interdisciplinary model of cultural practice purports to defend the value of 'situated' subjective responses to music and 'context-related meanings',[12] it seems that certain listening experiences have more 'human interest' than others. For in arguing against the 'ineffable' autonomy of music, Kramer disparages another kind of ineffability too — namely, the sense of transcendence that may be evoked by music, which he derides as a 'fable' and the 'relic of a certain nineteenth-century vogue for sentimental metaphysics'.[13] Indeed, ideas about the autonomy and ineffability of music are deemed to be so pernicious that they are classed as 'destructive irrationalisms' by Kramer and portentously associated with those who 'justify unspeakable things'.[14] Even more bizarrely, just as formalist musicological activities are positioned outside the sphere of human interest — in contrast to the practices of those across the corridor who favour socio-political approaches — acts of

---

7   By 'subjective' Kramer is not referring to 'the condition of the self-regarded as a private monad', but to 'lived positions' or 'the process whereby a person occupies a series of socially defined positions from which certain forms of action, desire, speech, and understanding become possible' (Lawrence Kramer, 'Musicology and Meaning', *The Musical Times*, 144 (Summer 2003), 6–12 (p. 6)). Kramer thus advocates a highly reflexive model of musical meaning, in which the listening subject has a constructive role and music can serve as a form of 'world-making' (ibid., p. 7).
8   Ibid., p. 7.
9   Theodor W. Adorno, *Introduction to the Sociology of Music*, trans. by E. B. Ashton (New York: Continuum, 1989 [1st edn 1962]), p. 62.
10 Kramer, *Classical Music and Postmodern Knowledge*, p. 2.
11 In speaking of 'the listener's share', I am drawing on the work of the art historian E. H. Gombrich, who spoke analogously of 'the beholder's share' — that is, the psychological and emotional involvement of the viewer that an artwork invites and by means of which it is 'completed'. See Chapter 6 of E. H. Gombrich, *Art and Illusion: A Study in the Psychology of Pictorial Representation*, 6th edn (New York: Phaidon Press, 2002).
12 Lawrence Kramer, 'Introduction: Sounding Out', in idem, *Musical Meaning: Toward a Critical History* (Berkeley, CA: University of California Press, 2002), pp. 1–9.
13 Lawrence Kramer, *The Thought of Music* (Oakland, CA: University of California Press, 2016), pp. 46–47. Kramer describes the 'paradigm of autonomy' in listening as 'the rapture of being wholly absorbed or deeply moved or touched by musical experience, revealed to oneself in the ineffability of music' (Kramer, *Musical Meaning*, p. 4). This 'double ideal of autonomy' is the *bête noire* of critical musicology, whose practitioners have a rather un-critical tendency to assign all faults to the idea of autonomy and all merits to 'social meanings'.
14 Kramer, *Musical Meaning*, 5.

listening that involve a sense of transcendence are set over against 'the realities of the social world',[15] as though such experiences and the effects they have on the listener took place somewhere *outside* the real.[16]

Yet surely it is possible for a listener to have 'situated' *religious* experiences — even if these are experiences of transcendence — and for music's 'context-related meanings' to be inflected by faith or *theistic* concerns? Part of the problem with Kramer's account is that he seems to think of experiences of transcendence in purely negative terms, as a kind of aesthetically induced concussion or a condition of vacancy that lacks any positive lure of its own and so is only significant as a 'turning away'. For those more open to religious possibilities though, the experience of transcendence tends to be conceived as a positively motivated 'turning towards' — that is, as a 'freedom to' at least as much as it is a 'freedom from' — which is typically associated with a movement into I-Thou relation or a realization of divine presence that entails an expansion or intensification of being.[17] As such, for the believer, rather than constituting a withdrawal from the real, the experience of transcendence is an opening of the self to an *ultimate* reality.

Yet even if one is uninterested in religious possibilities, one might also wonder if contemplative rapture in listening — even when it is an enchanted tarrying with aesthetic forms — is really so reprehensible.[18] Are not such experiences, like going

---

15 Richard Leppert and Susan McClary, 'Introduction', in *Music and Society: The Politics of Composition, Performance and Reception*, ed. by Richard Leppert and Susan McClary (Cambridge: Cambridge University Press, 1987), pp. xi–xix (p. xix).

16 Like Kramer, Leppert and McClary bring together under the heading of 'the ideology of autonomy' both the ostensible self-sufficiency of the musical work and the 'conventional musical reception of the "music lover" who listens to music precisely in order to withdraw from the real world' (*ibid.*, xiii). The idea that imaginative engagement with transcendent worlds is something that is set against the real has been vigorously challenged by Graham Ward, who argues that such acts of imagination are not ephemeral cognitive events that pass without footprints in a virtual sphere, but are instead acts that involve the body and can have real-life, extra-aesthetic effects that survive the experience and bear 'ontological weight' (see Graham Ward, *Unbelievable: Why We Believe and Why We Don't* (London: I. B. Tauris, 2014), Chapter 6, pp. 133–60).

17 This is not to suggest that the divine can be magically conjured by works of art, after the manner of Aladdin rubbing his lamp, but that art may serve as an affective trigger, which can radically transfigure our vision and open up new possibilities for being in the world. In this sense, what is transcended in such experience is an obstacle in us — namely, our customary alienated perception of the world — and what is revealed is the depth of the reality in which we *always already* stand. This conception of transcendence does not therefore entail an instrumentalization of the divine or usurp God's free and prevenient agency (even though something radically changes or needs to 'realized' by the perceiver), and yet it remains a form of revelation, in which something ordinarily unapprehended is disclosed to us.

18 Thankfully, this somewhat puritanical critique of escapism has recently been challenged by a number of thinkers in various fields who have defended such modes of aesthetic absorption. See, for example, Elaine Scarry, *On Beauty and Being Just* (Princeton, NJ: Princeton University, 1999); Jane Bennett, *The Enchantment of Modern Life: Attachments, Crossings, and Ethics* (Princeton, NJ: Princeton University Press, 2001); Rita Felski, *The Uses of Literature* (Oxford: Blackwell, 2008); and Marie-Laure Ryan, *Narrative as Virtual Reality 2: Revisiting Immersion and Interactivity in Literature and Electronic Media* (Baltimore, MD: Johns Hopkins University Press, 2015). However, it might in any case make sense to adopt a more nuanced model of contemplative experience, which recognizes an interplay between engrossment and detached reflection, thus involving an epistemological balancing of credulity and scepticism. For a consideration of this 'twofold' model of aesthetic absorption, see Sarah Tindal Kareem, *Eighteenth-Century Fiction and the Reinvention of Wonder* (Oxford: Oxford University Press, 2014).

to the cinema or watching sport, a sort of healthy 'holiday' from one's quotidian concerns? Moreover, as the practices of music therapy have shown, surely there are all sorts of psychological, emotional and social benefits to be gained from experiences of musical transcendence.[19] Nevertheless, like Richard Leppert and Susan McClary,[20] Kramer positions experiences of 'rapture' and 'sublime transcendence' on the same side of the fence as aesthetic autonomy, which is set over against '"real-world" concerns' and the 'actual' conditions of 'life and thought.'[21] In other words, what we find in Kramer's reading of music is an ideological privileging of *certain kinds* of 'social utility' and contextual meanings along with an un-argued-for suppression of others, which is based on a refusal of religious possibilities.[22]

Of course, Kramer is entitled to hold whatever views he wishes about religion.[23] However, the problem is that he seeks to delegitimate certain possibilities on the basis of unaired presuppositions, and in doing so performs something of a vanishing trick on music's transcendental significance.[24] Against such taken-for-granted assumptions, I want to suggest that, although they may have been marginalized by the dominance of a secular construction of the real, these possibilities were never entirely effaced and music may *still* serve as 'a venue for transcendence'.[25]

---

19 For a theologically informed discussion of 'musical healing' and the ways in which the art-form offers us the possibility of transformation and strengthened living, see June Boyce-Tillman, *Constructing Musical Healing: The Wounds that Sing* (London: Jessica Kingsley, 2000), and *Experiencing Music — Restoring the Spiritual: Music as Well-Being* (Bern: Peter Lang, 2016).

20 See Leppert and McClary, 'Introduction', pp. xi–xix.

21 Kramer, *Musical Meaning*, pp. 4–5, 12.

22 Kramer's narrow conception of 'the social', as a matter of interpersonal relations, is called into question by Bruno Latour's actor-network theory, which brings to light the 'heterogeneous nature of the ingredients making up social ties' and accordingly reconceives the social as an imbroglio of 'actants', which may be human, non-human, this-worldly or transcendent. See Bruno Latour, *Reassembling the Social: An Introduction to Actor-Network-Theory* (Oxford: Oxford University Press, 2005).

23 Kramer makes no secret of his allegiance to a form of 'closed-world' materialism, which may explain his allergy to the idea of transcendence. See, for instance, Lawrence Kramer, *Expression and Truth: On the Music of Knowledge* (Berkeley, CA: University of California Press, 2012), p. 155.

24 See, for example, the opening chapter of *Classical Music and Postmodern Knowledge*, in which Kramer notes that once upon a time music was experienced as 'a venue for transcendence', and agrees with Carl Dahlhaus that during the nineteenth century 'autonomous music capable of conveying the "inexpressible" became a replacement form of religion'; however, he goes on to claim that 'Gradually […] the religious truth signified by autonomous music is effaced by the very autonomy that is, or had once been, its signifier. Where "strict concentration on the work as self-contained musical process" once meant the apprehension of the work in its unworldliness, the same concentration now means the apprehension of the innate character, the complex unity-in-diversity, of the musical process itself' (ibid., p. 16). Quite a lot is asserted — and erased — in Kramer's 'now means'. Perhaps most conspicuously, it absolutizes the already sweeping assertion about the gradual effacement of music's transcendental significance into a universal truth, which not only assumes that no one now listens to music in this way but also quietly seems to deprive music of the very possibility of such significance. This broad-brush narrative, in which the transcendental significance of music becomes a purely formal transcendence — in the sense of a cordoned off aesthetic sphere — such that music loses its potential metaphysical import, is repeated elsewhere in Kramer's work. See, for instance, Kramer, *Musical Meaning*, Chapter 1, pp. 11–28.

25 For evidence that troubles Kramer's assumptions, see, for example, Alf Gabrielsson's *Strong Experiences with Music: Music Is Much More than Music* (Oxford: Oxford University Press, 2011), which offers a snapshot of the multiplicity of things that music 'now means' — in the socially mediated and

Whilst methodologically this might appear to be advocating a retrograde step, this sort of interpretation of music can be maintained not only in light of, but even in terms of, Kramer's critical musicological agenda. For, in its staging of a modality 'at ontological odds' with 'the spatio-temporal object world',[26] music can serve an 'iconic' function, offering the listener intimations of the infinite or an analogical experience of transcendence. (As all the eschatological data are not yet in, it would seem premature either to take the validity of such intimations for granted or to rule them out in advance.) In this sense, then, the purported ineffability of music is not necessarily a matter of aesthetic autonomy sequestered from extra-musical meanings, as Kramer's critique appears to assume. Rather, its ineffability and the sense of transcendence it evokes may paradoxically be a referential matter — even if its referent is *in itself* ineffable. To put this another way, what tends to get lost in the 'either-or-ism' of debates about music's aesthetic autonomy, and deconstructions of its apparently transcendent self-sufficiency, is the possibility that music's distance from quotidian reality may itself have a mimetic dimension.

Since it is often assumed to the contrary, it should be emphasized that although such experiences of transcendence are performative effects artfully induced by worldly constructs, this does not in any way prevent them from having an 'iconic' function. What matters from a devotional perspective is what takes place *in front of* the work — which is to say, how the possibilities it opens up are appropriated and 'realized' in the life of the listener. Whether a particular cultural product serves an ideological or revelatory function — and these are not mutually exclusive options — is only to be determined after the fact by the work's effects.[27] Neither does an affirmation of music's productive aesthetic significance entail a denial of its 'social meanings'. On the contrary, it is possible to acknowledge the constructedness of musical works and their embeddedness within 'the densely compacted, concretely situated worlds of those who compose, perform and listen'[28] whilst simultaneously recognizing their ability to serve as a technology of enchantment, which can augment our vision of the real and offer us intimations of transcendence.[29]

Although for many in the latter decades of the previous century, 'transcendence' was something of a dirty word — which smacked of escapism or mystification and an

---

        subjective sense that is espoused by Kramer — and which includes a range of spiritual, ecstatic and transcendental experiences.

26 Ronald W. Hepburn, *'Wonder' and Other Essays: Eight Studies in Aesthetics and Neighboring Fields* (Edinburgh: Edinburgh University Press, 1984), p. 150.

27 See Paul Ricoeur, 'Imagination in Discourse and in Action', in *From Text to Action*, trans. by Kathleen Blamey and John Thompson (London: Continuum, 2008).

28 Kramer, 'The Musicology of the Future', *Repercussions*, 1 (Spring 1992), 5–18 (p. 10).

29 In advancing this argument I am diverging from the views of Susan McClary, who sees 'metaphysical' readings of music as 'irreconcilable' with approaches that recognise it as a 'socially grounded, socially alterable construct' ('The Blasphemy of Talking Politics during Bach Year', in Leppert and McClary (eds.), *Music and Society*, pp. 13–62 (p. 15)). Against this assumption, I want to contend that it is possible for a 'worldly' phenomenon such as music to be concretely situated and socially constructed *and yet still* evoke something beyond itself.

occlusion of socio-political concerns — such notions have, it seems, become more widely thinkable again, at once encouraging and encouraged by the so-called 're-enchantment' of the West.[30] Indeed, one of the most surprising features of postmodernity is the way its radical epistemological scepticism appears to have precipitated an openness to mystery and a questioning of secularism's confident exclusions.[31] In such a context, the 'demystifying' gestures of critical musicology — which purport to 'unmask' the metaphysical pretensions of music as social constructs (in the sense of claiming that 'X is *really* Y') — start to seem as ideological as the stance they reject.

Drawing together the strands of this section: it seems possible to hold, against Kramer's critique, that music may serve as a technology of transcendence without banishing it to a sequestered autonomy; without denying its social construction; and without suppressing its 'human interest'. Indeed, perhaps the most important thing that is brought into view by the foregoing discussion of Kramer's work is the possibility of a *religious* form of critical musicology; for although in Kramer's anti-metaphysical account moments of rapture and transcendence in listening are set over against 'real-world' experiences, one might to the contrary affirm that the ability to mediate intimations of the infinite — that is, to engender a sense of transcendence or a radiant 'more' at the heart of being — is one of the 'social utilities' of music.

II. Theological Imperialism

If Kramer's work helps to open the way for a constructive theological account of music, even as it refuses religious possibilities, the work of Jeremy Begbie demonstrates how music can illustrate theological ideas, though it does so in a way that leaves little or no room for the kind of active receptivity that for Kramer — and most contemporary musicologists — is a vital part of the listening experience.[32] In order to explain this

---

30 For a consideration of these changes, see Christopher Partridge, *The Re-Enchantment of the West: Alternative Spiritualities, Sacralization, Popular Culture, and Occulture*, 2 vols. (London: T&T Clark, 2004 and 2005).

31 For an account of this paradoxical development — by someone who has no desire to promote it — see Quentin Meillassoux, *After Finitude: An Essay on the Necessity of Contingency*, trans. by Ray Brassier (New York: Continuum, 2008). Kramer's stance is somewhat ambivalent in this respect, since on the one hand he prefaces his discussion of transcendence in *The Thought of Music* with an exposition of Derrida's reflections on the modality of the 'perhaps' and the 'as if' structure of humanistic knowledge (pp. xii–xiii) — which would seem to announce a radical openness to the nature of the real — and yet, on the other hand, when it comes to determining the legitimacy of religious intuitions, this Derridean reserve disappears and there is little evidence of any real openness to different possibilities.

32 Another nagging problem with Begbie's project, which there is not space to elaborate here, is his apparent antipathy towards *popular* music, which aside from a few tokenistic references is all but excluded from serious consideration. This rather illiberal exclusion zone, which seems to me theoretically and theologically very hard to justify, is especially glaring as his work purports to be concerned with music in general, and focuses on extremely widespread features, such as tension and resolution or the simultaneous sounding of different notes within the same musical space. Thus, his consistent disinclination to give any sustained attention to popular music, along with his fervent denunciation of 'light' and 'sentimental' forms gives the distinct impression that he considers it to be an inferior art-form of little or no religious significance. For a consideration of this problem, see David Brown and Gavin Hopps, *The Extravagance of Music* (London: Bloomsbury, 2018), Chapter 5, pp. 187ff.

omission and why it is a problem, we need to consider the methodology that Begbie espouses and has defended in the face of recent criticism by David Brown and others.[33] Before doing so, however, it should again be acknowledged that there is not space here to do justice to the importance of Begbie's work more generally, which has done so much to invigorate the theological study of music, in particular by highlighting how it can serve a catechetical purpose in providing us with new and fruitful ways of modelling Christian doctrine.[34] Nevertheless, in spite of his sustained and fertile defence of music's theological value, Begbie's approach involves what amounts to a 'listener-free' model of musical meaning — which is to say, it presents us with an account of music in which its meanings are predetermined by the theologian and imposed upon rather than co-produced by the listener. What is the rationale behind this?

In Begbie's view, theological engagements with music need to begin *not* with particular pieces of music, whose religious significance might then be considered, but rather with what he calls 'the controlling truth criteria',[35] which are to be determined by the theologian and only thereafter applied to specific works. A clear exposition of this methodology is provided by Begbie in the opening essay of *The Beauty of God: Theology and the Arts*, which begins by abstracting from the New Testament a list of Christological criteria (although the criteria according to which these criteria are determined are not themselves presented for inspection), which are then 'translated' into musical equivalents.[36] In this way, Begbie sets up a sort of theological algorithm by means of which it is supposed to be possible to measure the 'Christian-ness' of particular pieces of music, according to the degree to which they conform to his list of metaphorical criteria.[37]

Furthermore, in an attempt to exclude all secular influence and to establish a 'purely' theological model of aesthetics, Begbie insists upon a conception of beauty

---

33   See, for example, David Brown, *God and Grace of Body: Sacrament in Ordinary* (Oxford: Oxford University Press, 2007), p. 245ff.; William Dyrness, *Poetic Theology: God and the Poetics of Everyday Life* (Grand Rapids, MI: Eerdmans, 2011); pp. 149–51; Heidi Epstein, *Melting the Venusberg: A Feminist Theology of Music* (New York: Continuum, 2004), pp. 84–87; and Philip Stoltzfus, *Theology as Performance: Music, Aesthetics and God in Western Thought* (New York: Continuum, 2006), pp. 14–16.

34   See, for instance, Jeremy Begbie, *Theology, Music, and Time* (Cambridge: Cambridge University Press, 2000).

35   Jeremy Begbie, 'Created Beauty: The Witness of J. S. Bach,' in *The Beauty of God: Theology and the Arts*, ed. by Daniel J. Treier, Mark Husbands and Roger Lundin (Downers Grove, IL: InterVarsity Press, 2007), pp. 19–44 (p. 32).

36   Begbie passes briskly over the process of translation upon which his methodology rests; though it seems to me that the equivalences he attempts to secure — between the specifics of salvation history and the polysemic openness of sonorous forms — are much more precarious and problematical than his account acknowledges.

37   This kind of theological approach has been helpfully characterized by Gordon Lynch as an 'applicationist' methodology, which he defines as follows: 'In this approach [...] culture is subjected to a critique on the basis of certain fixed theological beliefs and values. A basic assumption of this approach is that it is possible to identify core theological truths from a particular source (e.g., the Bible or Church tradition) and then apply these critically to the beliefs and values of [...] culture. Having identified these religious beliefs and values, [...] culture is then evaluated positively or negatively to the extent that it fits with this particular religious view of the world' (Gordon Lynch, *Understanding Theology and Popular Culture* (Oxford: Blackwell, 2005), p. 101).

that rejects traditional understandings of that notion and instead seeks to mirror, in an 'emblematic' fashion, the content of revealed theology. (Thus, such things as 'broken beauty' are elevated in his hierarchy of forms and presented as *intrinsically* more 'Christian' than such things as 'closed harmonies'.) In this way, his 'controlling truth criteria' are tethered to specific aesthetic forms in advance of any consideration of particular works or experiences of listening.[38]

Whilst Begbie's defence of an applicationist method appears to be motivated by understandable concerns about the demotion of theological criteria in the process of evaluation, his attempt to safeguard the authority of this interpretive vantage is puzzling in a number of respects — not least of which is the suggestion that this pre-emptive approach is the *only* valid theological method, and that all the alternatives are unwittingly beholden to secular criteria and are therefore insufficiently Christian. As George Corbett has noted, Begbie at times gestures towards a sort of '*via media* between what he perceives as the "double hazard" of "theological instrumentalization" (where "music is treated as essentially, or no more than, a vehicle, a mere tool at the behest of theology") and "theological aestheticism" (where an overriding concern with the "autonomy of music" leads people to give music "a semi-independent role in relation to theology", and to attribute to it a "veridical access to the divine")'.[39] Yet there is little sign of this middle ground in practice; for whilst it is clear that Begbie keeps his distance from the latter, it is hard to see how an approach that insists upon the pre-emptive assertion of 'controlling truth criteria', and evaluates works of music on the basis of their conformity to this theological checklist, can avoid the first of these hazards.[40] As I have highlighted the hermeneutical problems with this approach

---

38 This promulgation of a normative model of 'Christian' beauty, based on a checklist of privileged aesthetic features (Christian beauty will involve A, B, C, and Christian beauty will avoid X, Y, Z), inevitably consigns a vast amount of art and human experience to the category of the 'not beautiful' or 'not Christian'. The obvious question that is raised by this is: does 'Christian' necessarily have to mean 'formal correspondence to a gospel-shaped pattern'? Can it not be a matter of moral or spiritual effects, doing as Christ did, or work performed for the greater glory of God *irrespective* of the particular forms?

39 George Corbett, 'TheoArtistry, and a Contemporary Perspective on Composing Sacred Choral Music', *Religions*, 9.1 (2018), 1–18 (p. 10), and Chapter 3 in this volume, pp. 31–43.

40 Begbie's hardline stance on this matter has come to the fore in a spate of recent essays that take issue with the flourishing of approaches that appeal to notions of sacramentality and natural theology. See for example 'Natural Theology and Music', in *The Oxford Handbook of Natural Theology*, ed. by Russell Re Manning (Oxford: Oxford University Press, 2013), pp. 566–80; 'The Future of Theology amid the Arts: Some Reformed Reflections', in *Christ across the Disciplines: Past, Present, Future*, ed. by Roger Lundin (Grand Rapids, MI: Eerdmans, 2013), pp. 152–82; and 'Openness and Specificity: A Conversation with David Brown on Theology and Classical Music', in *Theology, Aesthetics and Culture: Responses to the Work of David Brown*, ed. by Robert MacSwain and Taylor Worley (Oxford: Oxford University Press, 2012), pp. 145–56. In these essays, which have been gathered together and republished in *A Peculiar Orthodoxy: Reflections on Theology and the Arts* (Grand Rapids: Baker Academic, 2018), Begbie adopts a more combative posture, describing his own riposte as the firing of 'warning shots across the bow of this fashionable steamer' ('The Future of Theology amid the Arts: Some Reformed Reflections', pp. 181–209 (p. 156)), and appears to insist that his applicationist approach is the only legitimate theological method. This rather exclusivist stance is also reinforced by a series of delegitimizing evaluations of alternative approaches, such as those espoused by Albert Blackwell, David Brown, William Dyrness, Anthony Monti, Philip Stoltzfus and Richard Viladesau, all of which are summarily deemed to be unconvincing.

elsewhere, I shall concentrate here on its sidelining of the listener and its troubling neglect of difference, which seems to be an inevitable consequence of the pre-emptive determination of musical meaning.[41] In what sense is this so?

In contrast to Kramer's interactive model — which makes room for differences in gender, race, social circumstances and disposition etc., in allowing meanings to be subjectively co-constituted in the act of reception — Begbie's approach seeks to establish the meaning of music's constituent features, in a prevenient and essentialized fashion, aside from the particular context of reception.[42] What this means in practice, in spite of Begbie's theoretical disapproval of 'theological imperialism', is that the theologian dictates to the listener what the meaning of the music will be. Gone, it seems, is the possibility of more subjective responses to music. Gone is the polysemous openness of a-semantic sonorous forms. And gone is the dependence of meaning upon context, which Jacques Derrida among others so persuasively established.[43] As Frank Burch Brown reminds us, 'people of different genders and of varying social classes, educational backgrounds, personal dispositions, and aptitudes often respond differently to different aesthetic styles'.[44] Yet what room is there for such differences of response in an approach that dogmatically lays down in advance what the theological meaning of musical forms will be?

There is, however, a further opportunity cost, as Begbie's theologizing 'through' the arts — which gives us the answers ahead of the questions — is a very rationalistic affair, which shows how music can provide helpful analogies of doctrinal loci, like illustrations in a theological handbook, but which has little to say about the devotional uses or affectivity of music.[45] This tendency to restrict music's religious significance

---

41 Begbie is of course aware of and claims to disapprove of such 'theological imperialism' (see, for example, Jeremy Begbie, *Resounding Truth: Christian Wisdom in the World of Music* (London: SPCK, 2008), p. 21). Indeed, he frequently begins his works with an anticipatory caricature of precisely such a posture, presumably in an attempt to put some distance between it and his own practice. However, I do not think the problem can be taken care of with disclaimers, since it appears to be an *in-built tendency* of his pre-emptive approach.

42 For a scathing critique of Begbie's work from a feminist perspective, see Heidi Epstein, *Melting the Venusberg*, pp. 84–87.

43 As Derrida argued, signs — including, and perhaps especially, musical signs — can always signify 'more, less, or something other than what [the author] would mean' (Jacques Derrida, *Of Grammatology*, trans. by Gayatri Chakravorty Spivak (Baltimore, MD: Johns Hopkins University Press, 1976), p. 158). This is because every sign can be performed, cited or 're-sited' in a context that altogether alters its meaning. The upshot of which is that the meaning of musical forms cannot be fixed in advance according to a system of formal correspondences, for signs cannot be forcibly stabilized to an 'essence', neither can they be tethered to any one context nor 'ideally' established *outside of* all context. Instead, their meaning is provisionally and pragmatically determined by particular contexts of reception and performance, whose meanings are always open to supplementary re-contextualizations, which neither the context of origin nor the author's intentions are able to control. In light of these widely accepted conclusions, Begbie's attempt to foreordain the meaning of musical forms and establish a system of context-transcending correspondences would seem to be hermeneutically somewhat naïve.

44 Frank Burch Brown, *Religious Aesthetics: A Theological Study of Meaning Making* (Princeton, NJ: Princeton University Press, 1989), p. 182.

45 This aspect of Begbie's work has been severely criticized by William Dyrness, who writes as follows: whilst Begbie offers us 'a helpful discussion of music as providing the conceptual tools to explore the temporal and interpenetrating dynamics of God's creation', on Begbie's view, 'music is still only

to an illustrative ideational function appears to be tied up with Begbie's aversion to natural theology, which is itself a metonymy of a wider pessimism that shapes his approach.[46]

Of course, it will at first seem odd to describe Begbie's project as pessimistic, given that he has, across a series of scholarly studies, championed the religious significance of music and promoted its ability to clarify theological insights. And yet, when it comes to music's effects, its epiphanic potential or the 'subjective' uses that Kramer and other musicologists celebrate — indeed, when it comes to anything beyond the ability of music to provide us with analogues of Christian doctrine (which I suspect is not the primary reason most people listen to music) — he is extremely reluctant to grant it any airtime and prefers instead to dwell on the dangers at the expense of a more constructive reading that explores the *possibilities* of music.

In summing up, therefore, we might say that Begbie's approach to music discourages that daring but discerning hospitality to mystery that John Keats referred to as 'negative capability' — that is, the willingness to dwell in openness with indeterminacy and to hold oneself in 'uncertainties, Mysteries, doubts', content for the present with 'half-knowledge', without any 'irritable reaching after fact and reason'.[47] Begbie's approach, in contrast to this, encourages a distrust of any intimations of divine presence that lack explicit Trinitarian form.[48] Indeed, it seems what is wrong with natural theology for Begbie is that it is not revealed theology. What I mean by this is that instead of considering natural theology and revealed theology as compatible but different things, based on different kinds of data and involving different modes of knowing,

---

metaphor; it is a giver of insight' (William A. Dyrness, *Poetic Theology: God and the Poetics of Everyday Life*, p. 151). Along with a number of others, Dyrness wonders if this is *all* that music can do. Suggesting that it can perhaps do or be something more, he asks: 'Can it perhaps be a kind of icon, transparent to its eternal ground? Can it perhaps stop us in our tracks and make us aware of a Presence before which we may be transformed?' (*ibid*.). See also the work of Philip Stoltzfus, who complains that Begbie's approach is not 'a constructive one', since it serves only 'to reinforce or reconceptualize the already existing, unexamined "*cantus firmus*" of "the triune God, definitively disclosed in Jesus Christ"'. Stoltzfus worries that such an approach 'merely assist[s] us in providing apologetic décor to previously articulated doctrinal positions' (Philip Stoltzfus, *Theology as Performance*, p. 16).

46 See, for example, the conclusion to *Theology, Music and Time*, which ends with a rather pessimistic coda, emphasizing 'the effects of human corruption' and distancing his project from natural theology (p. 247ff.). See also Jeremy Begbie, *Music, Modernity, and God: Essays in Listening* (Oxford: Oxford University Press, 2013), in which Begbie provides an informative historical discussion of the relationship between music and natural theology in the eighteenth century, which opens up all sorts of fruitful possibilities that are then summarily closed down in the chapter's pessimistic reflections on the value of natural theology in contemporary culture (pp. 90–94).

47 John Keats, letter to his brothers, George and Thomas, 21 December 1817 (*Keats's Poetry and Prose*, ed. by Jeffrey Cox (New York: Norton, 2009), p. 109).

48 Begbie's most extensive treatment of this issue is contained in his latest monograph, Jeremy Begbie, *Redeeming Transcendence in the Arts: Bearing Witness to the Triune God* (Grand Rapids, MI: Eerdmans, 2018), which patiently summarizes and then proceeds to unpick an array of theological approaches to the arts that affirm the value of vesperal intimations of the divine and art's ability to engender a sense of transcendence. For a more positive consideration of natural theology, which includes a helpful account of how the theological quest for 'disciplinary purity' and 'the single-minded security of an essentialist approach' led to the denigration and eventual eclipse of the 'inherently "impure" enterprise of natural theology', see Russell Re Manning, 'Natural Theology Reconsidered (Again)', *Theology and Science*, 15 (2017), 289–301 (pp. 289, 297).

each with their own distinct uses and value, Begbie has a tendency to treat the former as a faulty or inadequate version of the latter, which taints our perception of natural theology and encourages the impression that it is more trouble than it is worth. The problem with this, as Conor Sweeney has observed in another context, is that Begbie is 'so concerned to avoid idolatry that he ends up short-changing the full experience of created being'.[49] Moreover, this reticence towards natural theology — which leads Begbie to leave aside in his approach to music the less certain, more open and more mysterious experiences of listening — also leads to a neglect of the ways in which subjectively inflected meanings emerge in the interaction *between* the music and the listener. This neglect, I have suggested, is an inevitable consequence of his pre-emptive methodology, according to which theology lays down criteria in advance that prescribe and control the meanings of music, which leaves little or no room for the active receptivity of the listener.

III. A Hospitality to Possibilities

So where does this leave us? Having considered the problems with the approaches espoused by Kramer and Begbie, how might we more constructively fashion a 'third way' that draws on the insights of both approaches whilst taking account of their reciprocal critique?

What in general I wish to propose is what might be described either as a theological variant of Kramer's model of 'critical' musicology or a 'post-hoc' alternative to Begbie's applicationist approach. In contrast to Kramer's 'closed-world' model, such an approach would not rule out religious possibilities and would not, or not necessarily, construe the 'escapist' experience of absorbed listening or the evocation of an enchanted 'elsewhere' as a negative activity. Rather, I suggest, this sense of transcendence in music listening, which is obviously an aesthetic construct, can nonetheless serve a devotional purpose — as an icon or analogical foretaste of what, for a believer, may be a reality to come. And in contrast to Begbie's pre-emptive approach, which encourages an essentialization of musical meanings, I think the criteria of evaluation should be introduced at the other end of the interpretive process, after, rather than before, the listening experience, so that it is possible to take account of what the music does and how it is used by individual listeners. Since the value, from a theological point of view, of widening Kramer's model of listening to encompass the possibility of religious experience should be readily apparent, I shall concentrate in this final section on the advantages of adopting a more hospitable 'post-hoc' alternative to Begbie's predetermining approach.[50] But first though, what might such an alternative look like in practice?

---

49 Conor Sweeney, *Sacramental Presence after Heidegger: Onto-Theology, Sacraments, and the Mother's Smile* (Eugene, OR: Cascade Books, 2015), p. 200.

50 In developing this more optimistic theological approach to music, I have been influenced by the example of David Brown, whose ground-breaking work on theology and culture focuses attention on the ways in which works of art — including ostensibly secular art — may be capable of eliciting religious experience (see, for example, David Brown, *God and Grace of Body*).

In contrast to the 'theological imperialism' of an applicationist approach, which seeks to assign religious meanings (and hence also values) to musical forms in advance of the event of music listening, a 'post-hoc' approach would encourage us more courteously first of all to attend with 'a maximum of openness' to the particular work,[51] along with the context of its performance and reception, and only afterwards to reflect on its religious value, in light of its effects on the individual listener (which may be positive, negative or theologically neutral).[52] Thus, the difference between the approaches pertains not only to the point at which theological criteria are introduced but also the *kind* of criteria employed.[53] For whilst, according to Begbie's applicationist model, theological significance is a matter of formal correspondence with what John Shepherd somewhat facetiously calls 'a shopping list of meanings',[54] according to the alternative I am proposing, the criteria of evaluation would be more practical or experiential, in that they would be related to the moral or spiritual fruits of the experience in the life of the individual listener. In the view of John Hick, this moral or spiritual 'fruits' criterion — which would allow us to make judgments about religious experiences more ecumenically in terms of their congruence with the teachings of any particular tradition — is 'the universal criterion of the authenticity of religious experience', common to all of the major world religions.[55] It also accords with the

---

51 Robert Johnston, *Reel Spirituality: Theology and Film in Dialogue* (Grand Rapids, MI: Baker Academic, 2006), p. 65. Johnston makes this point with reference to film; however, I think his argument can be generalized to other forms of art, including music. As Johnston avers: 'to first look at a movie on its own terms and let the images themselves suggest meaning and direction — is not to make theology of secondary importance. Religious faith is primary. […] But such theologizing should follow, not precede, the aesthetic experience' (p. 64).

52 In his study of the role of music in contemporary worship, Frank Burch Brown recommends a parallel model of 'aesthetic hospitality'. Very briefly, according to Burch Brown, the process of responding 'hospitably' to an artwork should entail three discrete elements: first of all, it involves apperception (that is, taking in 'everything relevant to whatever makes the work of art the thing it is'), followed by appreciation (registering our personal likes or dislikes about the work), and finally appraisal, which, he argues, we must learn to postpone until we are sufficiently familiar with the particular style or form of art under consideration (Frank Burch Brown, *Inclusive yet Discerning: Navigating Worship Artfully* (Grand Rapids, MI: Eerdmans, 2009), pp. 20–21). See also Trevor Hart's essay 'Conversation after Pentecost? Theological Musings on the Hermeneutical Motion', *Literature and Theology*, 28 (2014), 164–78, in which he argues to the contrary of Begbie that it is the 'kenotic' suspension of pre-emptive criteria in the 'conversation' with aesthetic phenomena that constitutes a distinctly *Christian* model of hermeneutics.

53 For some reason Begbie appears to assume that hermeneutic priority is determined by sequence alone, as if beginning the act of interpretation with works of art rather than Christological criteria necessarily entails ceding authority to the former. Yet surely it is possible to engage in criticism from a Christian perspective without first of all seeking to fix the meaning of aesthetic forms, according to a checklist of metaphorical correspondences? And surely the act of suspending judgment — or refraining from *pre*-judging the religious significance of tonally moving forms — is not the same as renouncing a Christian standpoint? Can one not turn to theology or scripture *after* allowing music its say, without this relativizing our religious orientation? Surely one can listen to others without ceasing to be a Christian?

54 John Shepherd, 'How Music Works — Beyond the Immanent and the Arbitrary: An Essay Review of *Music in Everyday Life*', *Action, Criticism, and Theory for Music Education*, 1 (2002), 1–18 (p. 14).

55 John Hick, *The New Frontier of Religion and Science: Religious Experience, Neuroscience and the Transcendent* (Basingstoke: Palgrave, 2006), Chapter 4, pp. 39–51.

traditional Augustinian principle of charity, which exhibits what we might refer to as an 'adverbial' logic.[56] Very briefly, this might be explained as follows.

Since, for the present, according to Augustine, the earthly and the heavenly cities 'are entangled together [...] until the last judgment effects their separation',[57] the city to which we ultimately belong is determined not according to *what* we love but according to the *kind* of love we exhibit (whether our love ends in the thing itself or whether the object mediates and entices our love beyond itself). Therefore, whilst Augustine can be severely critical of pagan culture, and worries about even as he delights in the allure of this-worldly beauty, there is a more fundamental principle of charity consistently running through his work, according to which the value of this-worldly phenomena is not to be determined in an 'essentialist' manner by things 'in themselves'. Instead — to employ an anachronistic idiom — it is performatively constituted according to the good it does or to which it leads. In short, for Augustine, if it serves the good, it *is* good.[58] (Jean-Luc Marion's well-known distinction between the icon and the idol also evinces an 'adverbial' logic that parallels Augustine's principle of charity, in that icons and idols are not defined for Marion on the basis of their intrinsic properties; rather, they are constituted by the kind of gaze or comportment they engender. Hence, any phenomenon can function as an idol — irrespective of its content — if the gaze it elicits terminates in, and is exhausted by, its object, just as any phenomenon can function as an icon — again, irrespective of its content — if it orients the gaze beyond itself towards the unenvisageable divine.[59]) The criteria that I would therefore propose, as an alternative to Begbie's pre-emptive approach, pertain to the charitable *effects* of a work, and not simply its formal constituents. In Augustine's terms, if a thing leads to an increase in our love of God and love of our neighbour, then we may call it good.[60]

There are, I suggest, several interrelated advantages to this sort of 'post-hoc' theological method, which may be clustered into two key points — to do with openness and diversity — by way of conclusion. In the first place, this kind of approach to music — which is broadly indebted to the 'turn to affect' — is important because we can never securely determine in advance what stimuli will elicit what effects, so that

---

[56] I am alluding to Joseph Hall's theological adage: 'God loveth adverbs; and cares not how good, but how well' ('Holy Observations', in *The Works of Right Reverend Father in God, Joseph Hall, D. D. Successively Bishop of Exter and Norwich*, ed. by Josiah Pratt, 10 vols. (London: Williams and Smith, 1808), Vol. 6, p. 85).

[57] Augustine, *The City of God*, I.35, trans. by Marcos Dods (New York: The Modern Library, 1950), p. 38.

[58] Augustine discusses the hermeneutical implications of his 'principle of charity' in *De doctrina christiana*, where he argues that the ultimate criterion of evaluation is whether or not an interpretation inspires a 'double love' — that is, 'love of God and love of [our] neighbour' (Augustine, *On Christian Teaching*, trans. by R. P. H. Green (Oxford: Oxford University Press, 2008), I, p. 86 and II, p. 11).

[59] See Jean-Luc Marion, *God without Being: Hors-Texte*, trans. by Thomas A. Carlson, 2nd edn (Chicago, IL: University of Chicago, 2012), especially Chapter 1.

[60] Gordon Lynch advocates a more detailed but less explicitly theistic variant of this pragmatic approach in Lynch, *Understanding Theology and Popular Culture*, pp. 190–91. His criteria are intended to help us form aesthetic judgments 'on the basis of their effects for human experience, relationships and communities'; however, one of his criteria is 'Does [the particular cultural work] make possible a sense of encounter with "God", the transcendent, or the numinous?' (ibid.).

we cannot with any certainty say what sacred artefact might become an idol or what ostensibly profane work of art might serve as an icon and kindle within us a sense of the divine. After all, who could have predicted the effect that reading *Phantastes* would have on C. S. Lewis?[61] Of course, this means — as Plato and Augustine amongst others recognized — that music can be dangerous, which is why discernment in relation to its effects is necessary. Yet this openness is also an affordance structure and a source of hope, as it is this that allows music to be coupled to an incorrigible plurality of things, in ways that can radically transfigure our environment, extend or enhance our natural capacities and open up new modes of being in the world.[62] Music, in other words, has a transformative potential — which is dependent upon even as it reciprocally elicits the active participation of the listener — and can serve a variety of devotional purposes, such as clearing a space for contemplation, scaffolding acts of domestic piety or evoking intimations of transcendence. In contrast to applicationist approaches — which seek to constrain or set aside the generative openness of music's affects by tethering its forms to readymade meanings — a more capacious post-hoc approach leaves room for us to evaluate these often unforeseeable affordances and their effects on the listener (as well as the ways in which music is able to illustrate doctrine). Thus, without losing sight of the dangers or letting go of theological criteria, a post-hoc approach encourages a more hopeful posture of openness and a hospitality to possibilities in the midst of 'uncertainties, Mysteries, doubts'.

In the second place, this sort of approach is much more attuned to human diversity. This is because in beginning with a 'one-size-fits-all' template of pre-evaluated musical meanings, prescriptive theological approaches like Begbie's evince a troubling disregard of the ways in which differences in gender, ethnicity or sexual orientation may condition the subjective reception of music. (In presenting his theological criteria as a neutral précis of the scriptural witness that is supposed to be normative for all Christians, Begbie displays a parallel disregard for denominational differences and a failure to recognize that his distillation of scripture is an *interpretation* of

---

61   Lewis famously ascribed a vital role to the experience of reading George MacDonald's *Phantastes* in his conversion to Christianity. 'What it actually did to me', he wrote some years later, 'was to convert, even to baptize […] my imagination' (Introduction to *George MacDonald: An Anthology* (London: Geoffrey Bles, 1946)). This experience prompted him to observe wryly: 'A young man who wishes to remain a sound Atheist cannot be too careful of his reading. There are traps everywhere — "Bibles laid open, millions of surprises", as Herbert says, "fine nets and stratagems". God is, if I may say it, very unscrupulous' (C. S. Lewis, *Surprised by Joy* (London: Collins, 2012), pp. 221–22).

62   The notion of affordance, as developed by the psychologist J. J. Gibson, allows us to recognize both the specific properties of music and the openness of its potential effects, and so enables us to steer a pragmatic middle course between 'immanent' and 'attributed' models of meaning. For a good discussion of this kind of balancing of affordance and affect, see Tia DeNora, *Music in Everyday Life* (Cambridge: Cambridge University Press, 2000). For a more critical account of how music can be used to transfigure our surroundings, see Michael Bull, *Sound Moves: iPod Culture and Urban Experience* (New York: Routledge, 2007), which offers a socio-political analysis of auditory 'technologies of separation' that highlights in particular their 'dystopian' aspects. However, his account also brings into view the possibility of a more positive reading of the ways in which such listening practices offer an escape from or transformation of the blankness and 'repelling nature' of urban life (p. 31).

scripture, which is shaped by the preferences of a particular tradition.[63]) Moreover, in presuming to determine in advance what constitutes 'good' and 'bad' Christian music for all listeners, such approaches fail to leave room for pragmatic pastoral considerations — about what aspects of the Christian narrative it might, in particular times of need, be appropriate to foreground; for surely what is damaging and what is conducive to a person's spiritual and psychological wellbeing will vary widely according to their experiences and existential circumstances. Thus, the other principal advantage of a post-hoc theological approach is that it takes cognizance of human diversity and allows us to recognize the role of context, cultural conditioning and individual difference in the constitution of musical meaning (which thereby ceases to be something that is imposed from on high and becomes, instead, reflexively determined by the listener's active reception of the music). Adopting this sort of approach to music also means that the criteria of evaluation — which encompass the music's effects on the listener — can be tailored to the individual's own particular conception of the good, be it religious or secular. As I have argued, postponing the act of evaluation in this way need not entail an elevation of aesthetic over theological judgments; though it does involve making room for diversity in determining the *sort* of theological perspective to which one appeals, and it does endorse a pluralistic vision that honours the inflections of lived experience.

---

63 This is especially problematical in his evaluation of composers whose music is criticized from the perspective of traditions other than their own. For example, what it seems Begbie is criticizing in the music of the Catholic Messiaen and the Orthodox Tavener is that it doesn't sufficiently reflect the emphases of the Reformed tradition (see Begbie, *Theology, Music and Time*, p. 145; and Begbie, *Resounding Truth*, p. 175).

Index

Abelard, Peter 305
Abigail 63
Abimelech 51
Abraham 47, 50, 53, 61–62, 67, 103, 129, 131, 162, 314
absolute music 287
Adam 3, 32–33, 53, 75, 97–98, 100–01, 103–04, 106–08, 112–14, 255–57, 259–62, 266–68
Addison, Joseph 314
Adorno, Theodor W. 329, 339
Advent 78, 225
Aeschylus 205
aesthetics 35, 39, 165–66, 168–71, 174–75, 284–85, 311, 338, 340–42, 344–46, 348, 352
Agamemnon 205
agnosticism 10, 141, 335
Ahaz 52
Allain, Richard 309
Alter, Robert 48
Ambrose, St 62
America, American 286, 305, 331
Ammerman, Nancy 333
Angel Gabriel 4, 45–50
Anglican 1, 6, 17, 19–20, 265, 267, 298, 303, 319, 326, 333. *See also* Church of England
annunciation, annunciations 3–5, 32–35, 38, 43, 45–54, 57, 63–64, 67, 78, 89, 113–14, 174, 202, 218, 220, 230, 253–54, 257–58, 266–68, 337
  type-scene 46–50
Apocrypha 320
Apostles 317, 319–20
Aquinas, Thomas, St 33, 42
Arnold, Jonathan 1, 6, 113, 311

art music 6, 279, 281–84, 287, 294
atheism 10–11, 16, 318, 335
attendance (church) 1, 289, 317–18, 326–28, 333
Auden, W. H. 11, 91
Augustine, St 350–51
Augustinian 100, 350
Ayleward, Richard 301

Babylonians 24
Bach, J. S. 20, 141, 267, 297, 303–04, 307–08, 325, 328
  St Matthew Passion 325
Baroque 202, 205–06
Baroque music 22, 202, 205–06, 297, 332
Barth, Karl 327
Batchelor, Christopher 308
Bayreuth 319
BBC Proms 303
beauty 15, 19–20, 35, 60, 75, 141, 266–67, 281, 284–85, 290, 292, 300, 304, 309, 326–28, 333–35, 344–45, 350
Bede, St 62
Bednall, David 307
Beethoven, Ludwig 329
Begbie, Jeremy 4, 37–41, 168, 343–51
Béguin, Albert 322
Benedictus, the 57, 61, 63, 319
Benedict XVI, Pope 1, 283–87, 294. *See also* Ratzinger, Joseph
Benjamin 132
Bernac, Pierre 321, 323
Bernanos, Georges 322–23
Bernard of Clairvaux, St 63

Bernard Shaw, George 98
Bethel 129, 132
Bingham, Judith 307, 309
Birtwistle, Harrison 111
Blake, William 10–14, 16
Blond, Phillip 11
Bloy, Léon 323
Bohlman, Philip 328–29
Bonaventure, St 57, 59–66
Book of Common Prayer 300, 309, 326
Bosco, Mark 15
Bothy singing 22
Boulez, Pierre 15
Brahms, Johannes 311
Brancacci Chapel 98
Brenner, Athalya 48
Britain, British 1, 5, 13–14, 16, 111, 137, 286, 303, 311, 317, 325–26, 328
Britten, Benjamin 5, 16, 69–71, 73, 75, 80, 82
  'A Hymn to the Virgin' 70, 80, 82, 92
  'Rejoice in the Lamb' 69–70, 73, 75
Brown, David 41, 344
Brown, Ismene 318
Brueggemann, Walter 189, 196
Brueghel the Elder, Jan 98
Brydges, James 312
Buchanan, George 314–15
Burch Brown, Frank 41, 328, 346
Burgon, Geoffrey 307
Burrell, Diana 309
Burton, Richard D. E. 323
Butt, John 13, 318
Byrd, William 297, 300–01, 311

Cage, John 15, 229
Calvary 26
Caravaggio 114
Carissimi, Giacomo 314
Carmelite 15, 220, 223, 230, 322–23
Catholic, Catholicism 1, 6, 13–16, 26, 32, 58, 279–90, 292–95, 317–23
Celtic 21–22, 86
Chesterton, G. K. 10, 16
Chilcott, Bob 302–05, 307–08
Chopin, Frederick 329
choral music 1–2, 5–6, 19, 70, 75, 77, 85–86, 91, 164, 265, 328
choral service 326
choral tradition 265, 298, 326
choristers 19, 297–99, 302, 307, 313

Christian, Christianity 1–2, 5–6, 11, 15, 17, 19–20, 25–26, 28, 32–34, 37–43, 46, 49, 57–59, 61, 65, 67, 114, 138, 173, 223, 226, 253, 255–58, 279–80, 283, 287–89, 308, 314–16, 325–31, 334, 344–45, 347, 351–52
Christmas 78, 225, 231
Christological 41, 258, 344
Christophers, Harry 332
Chua, Daniel 330
Church of England 314. *See also* Anglican
classical music 3, 5, 17–18, 31, 85, 328, 338
  history of 5, 31
Clucas, Humphrey 301
Clytemnestra 205
Cohen, Leonard 141
collaboration 3–5, 11, 36–43, 111–12, 114, 127, 141, 161, 164–65, 168–70, 173–75, 190, 197–98, 201, 206, 217, 226, 229, 254, 262, 265–68
commissioning music 5–6, 21, 38, 75, 220, 298–03, 305–10, 319
Compline 62, 64
concert hall (performance) 3, 309, 311, 328, 331
congregation 6, 132, 279, 282–86, 290–94, 298, 301–03, 305–07, 310
congregational participation 6, 279, 282
Cook, Nicholas 329
Corbett, George 345
Council Fathers 281–82, 284
Covenant, the 58, 218
Coxe, William 312
Cranach the Elder, Lucas 100
Cranmer, Thomas 299, 309
Creation 32, 60
creativity, artistic 1–2, 4–5, 12, 16, 29, 32–34, 36–37, 39, 43, 59, 66–67, 127, 161, 164–65, 169–70, 174, 198, 206, 229–30, 262, 268, 287, 299–300, 302, 317, 321, 333, 337
Cross, Crucifixion 21–22, 25–27, 59, 108–09, 113, 220, 223–25, 230–31, 303–04
culture 1–3, 10–17, 26, 28–29, 31, 41–42, 97–98, 100, 103–04, 106–07, 142, 190, 205, 254–56, 281, 285–86, 288, 291, 293–94, 298, 300, 327–30, 334, 338–39, 342, 350, 352

Daily Office 24
Damascus 221
Daniel 51
Danielson, Denis 98
Dante Alighieri 13

David 45–46, 51, 53, 62
Davies, John 299–300, 302
Da Vinci, Leonardo 330
Davis, Ellen F. 259
Davison, Gary 307, 309
Day, John 60, 100
Day of Judgment 60
Day, Thomas 286
D'Costa, Gavin 42
Dean, Winton 315
Deist movement 315–16
Derrida, Jacques 346
devotion 62, 282, 292, 312
diabolus in musica 25, 206
Dickinson, Emily 135, 138, 142
divine, divinity 2–6, 18–20, 23–24, 29, 31–33, 35–36, 40, 42, 46–47, 49–54, 57–59, 61, 63, 66–67, 100–01, 104, 106–08, 113, 129, 131–32, 137, 162, 166–71, 174, 192–93, 202, 229, 253, 258–59, 284, 320, 327, 329–30, 334–35, 337, 340, 345, 347, 350–51
Divine Office 57, 61
Donne, John 11
Doré, Gustave 98, 137
Douay-Rheims Bible 267
Dove, Jonathan 306–07
Dun, Tan 85
Dürer, Albrecht 98
Dylan, Bob 141

Easter 4, 59
Edwards, Katie B. 100
Egypt, Egyptian 51, 162, 174, 192–93, 218
Elgar, Edward 6, 10, 13–14, 16, 312, 317–21
 The Dream of Gerontius 13–14, 16, 319
Eli 189–98, 201–06, 221
Elijah 3, 77, 217–18, 220–21, 223–26, 229–31
Eliot, T. S. 10–14, 16
Elisha 47–48
Elizabeth 45–46, 48, 50, 61
emotion 13, 17, 23, 26, 29, 107, 113, 134, 162, 166, 168–71, 173, 175, 190, 198, 229–30, 232, 257–58, 261–62, 265, 280, 292, 317, 321, 332, 337, 341
England, English 11, 13–14, 21, 25, 101, 142, 286–87, 297–99, 303–05, 309, 312–14, 318, 326, 330
Englishness 318
Epiphany 309
Esau 48, 128

Esther 63, 312–13
Eucharist 59, 309, 333
Euripides 314–15
Europe, European 15, 202, 223, 289, 318, 329
Eve 3, 33, 97–98, 100–01, 103–04, 106–08, 112–14, 255–57, 259–60, 267
Evensong 309, 326–27
experience 173, 175, 265, 268
experience, religious 6, 20, 324, 332, 335, 348–49
Ezekiel 50

faith 1–2, 5–6, 10, 12–15, 18–20, 25, 28, 32, 34–35, 40, 43, 57, 132, 168, 173, 255, 301–02, 315, 317–24, 327, 333, 335, 340
Fall, the 5, 98, 259
Fauré, Gabriel 141, 311
festival, of music 9, 297–98, 308–09, 319
fire 161–62, 164–67, 169–70, 173, 218, 221, 226, 229, 231
Fletcher, Phineas 305
Flynn, William 66
France, French 15, 304–05, 320–22
Franciscan 57, 59–60
freedom, creative 12, 14, 70
French Revolution 15, 322
function of music 280, 282–83, 285

Galilee 45
Ganeri, Martin 42
Gardener, John Eliot 332
Garden of Eden 97–98, 100, 104, 107–08, 113
Gay, John 313
gender 6, 97, 169, 254–56, 258, 261–62, 268, 346, 351
Germany, German 15, 283, 321–22
Gibbons, Orlando 19, 304, 309
Gideon 50
Glocker, Johann Friedrich 137
Gloucester Cathedral 14
God 3–5, 18, 20–21, 23–27, 29, 31–35, 40–43, 45–55, 58–67, 73, 75, 77–80, 82, 84, 97, 100–01, 103–04, 106–09, 112–14, 128–29, 131–32, 134–35, 137–38, 141, 161–64, 166–71, 173–74, 189–98, 201–07, 209, 217–18, 220–21, 223–26, 229–32, 254–59, 267, 280, 284, 292, 301–04, 309, 311, 314–16, 322, 326, 330–32, 334, 337, 344, 350
 experience of 137–38, 170–71, 190, 223–25, 324, 326–27, 332, 334–35
 revelation of 3, 18, 51, 135, 161, 168, 191–92

silence of 3, 6, 190, 192, 220–21, 225, 229–31
speech of 24, 162, 167, 193, 225
Golgotha 108, 113
Good Samaritan 66
Gorecki, Henryk 16
Gospels, the 57, 59
Gounod, Charles 141
grace 33, 60, 63–65, 104, 106, 108, 112–14, 225, 307
Greek 46, 50, 58, 205, 314
Gregorian 86, 281, 287–88, 317–18
Gubaidulina, Sofia 12, 16

Hagar 47–50, 58
Hamilton, Newburgh 313, 316
Hamilton, Victor 101, 103
Handel, George Frideric 6, 312–16, 328
   Jephtha 314–16, 324
Hannah 47–48, 50, 59
harmony 20, 60, 69–71, 75, 84–85, 89, 91, 174, 204–05, 266–67, 284, 288, 332
Harvey, Jonathan 9, 16, 301–02, 332
Hassler, Hans Leo 304
Hawkins, John 312
Haydn, Joseph 297, 311
Heaney, Maeve Louise 35
Heaney, Seamus 11
Heaven 26, 302
Hebrew 3–5, 24–25, 46–47, 49–50, 54–55, 58–59, 62–63, 101, 108, 112–14, 129, 131, 137, 142, 162, 174, 198, 202, 205, 220, 261, 267, 315
Herbert, George 11, 330
Herbert, James 330
Hezekiah 52
Hick, John 349
Hildesheim Cathedral 66
Historically Informed Performance (HIP) 3
Holy City 24
Holy Innocents 65
Holy Spirit 23, 33, 40, 45, 49, 51–52, 63–65, 174, 319, 337
Holy Trinity 174
Hopkins, Gerard Manley 18, 134–35
Hopps, Gavin 6, 40
Hough, Stephen 13
Howells, Herbert 308
Huijbers, Bernard 283–85
humanity 25, 32, 35, 170–71, 301, 323, 331, 333

Huysmans, J. K. 323

Ignatius of Loyola, St 106
imagination 5, 11, 15, 18, 34, 57–58, 67, 71, 97–98, 104, 106–07, 111, 143, 161, 164, 166, 168, 193–94, 197, 258, 300, 316
Incarnate 19, 34
Incarnation, the 34, 58, 62–64, 107–08, 322
Infancy Narratives 57, 59, 61, 63–64
inspiration, artistic 2, 12, 21, 29, 32–33, 66–67, 111–12, 132, 142, 171, 198, 224, 229–30, 307, 309, 317, 319
intention of the composer 63, 112, 114, 143, 331
Iphigenia 314
iPod 329–30
Isaac 47–48, 50–51, 129, 131, 162, 314
Isaiah 50, 52
Ishmael 48
Islam, Islamic 11, 49, 329
Israel, Israelite 46, 53, 57–58, 61–62, 64, 67, 128, 132, 138, 163, 169, 174, 191–92, 202, 204–05, 218, 221, 313, 316, 330
Italian 312–13, 330
ITIA, the Institute for Theology, Imagination and the Arts 2–3, 37–38, 40–41, 114, 161

Jabbok 127–29
Jackson, Francis 309
Jacob 3, 45–46, 48, 50–51, 53, 127–29, 131–32, 134–35, 137–38, 142–43, 145, 147, 162, 254
Jael 63
Jeremiah 50
Jerome, St 62
Jerusalem 24, 226
Jesuit 106
Jesus Christ 19, 21, 23, 25–27, 33–35, 40, 45–46, 49–51, 53–54, 57–66, 87, 107–09, 114, 223, 225, 255, 258, 303–05, 319–20, 323
Jew, Jewish 15, 46, 49–50, 141, 220, 320
John the Baptist, St 45, 48, 57, 61
Jonah 58
Jonathan 314
Jones, David 5, 11–12, 14
Jordan 135, 142
Joseph, St 45–46, 48, 50–52
Joubert, John 303–309
Judah 53, 225–26
Judaism 15, 218
Judas 314, 319–20
Judith 63

Jung, Carl G. 10

Kancheli, Giya 16
Karajan, Herbert von 329
Karris, Robert 60
Keats, John 347
Kimchi, David 314–15
Knoblauch, Abby 166
Kramer, Lawrence 338–43, 346–48
Kuhn, Bruce 106
Küng, Hans 327

Lang, Paul Henry 315
Larrivé, Jean 137
La Scala 322
Last Judgement 319
Lauds 62–63
Lauridsen, Morten 85
lectio divina 104
Lehnhof, Kent R. 256
Leighton, Kenneth 5, 80, 301, 307
Leloir, Alexander Louis 137
Lent 313
Leppert, Richard 341
Lewis, C. S. 24, 351
Linossier, Raymonde 321
listening, listeners 3–4, 6, 15, 18–19, 23–26, 28, 35–36, 39, 61, 71, 76–77, 80, 85, 87–89, 91, 104, 108, 113–14, 138, 141, 143, 167–68, 189, 193, 196, 198, 229–31, 279–81, 285, 302, 311, 325–33, 337–40, 342–49, 351–52
Liturgical Movement 281
liturgical reform 281
liturgy 5, 17, 19, 33, 39, 57, 59, 61–62, 65–67, 127, 132, 138, 231, 279–81, 283–88, 290–94, 300–02, 306, 311, 319, 327–28, 331, 333
Lonergan, Bernard 35
Longfellow, Henry Wadsworth 320
Lutheran 312
Luther, Martin 17, 20, 23, 28
Lydian 261

MacLeish, Archibald 100
MacMillan, James 2, 4–5, 9–16, 31–39, 43, 69, 78–80, 82, 85–86, 88–89, 91, 114, 299, 304–08, 331 337
  'And lo, the Angel of the Lord Came upon Them' 78, 80
Magdalene, Mary, St 319–20
Magi 65
Malachi 64–65

Manoah's wife 47–48
Marion, Jean-Luc 350
Maritain, Jacques 323
Mary, the Virgin 4, 26, 33–35, 43, 45–55, 59, 61–63, 65–67, 223, 327, 337
  Ave Maria 62–63, 69, 86, 88–89, 91–93
  Magnificat 57, 59, 61–63, 67, 80, 92, 307, 327
  Stabat Mater 18, 20, 25–26, 28–29, 322
Masaccio 98
Mass 15, 65, 280–82, 284, 287, 289, 291–95, 301, 318, 322, 325
Mathias, William 20, 307–08
Maundy Thursday 305
Maxwell Davies, Peter 299–300, 302
McClary, Susan 341
McGregor, Richard 88
McGuire, Charles 13
Mealor, Paul 5, 17–29, 309
media 1, 38–40, 109, 168, 331, 345
medieval 26, 57, 59, 66–67, 297, 305, 314
Melchizedek 59
melody 143, 261, 284, 288, 290–91, 304
Messiaen, Olivier 10, 12, 15–16, 308
Messiah, Messianic 4, 46, 51, 62, 67, 218, 313, 328
metre 70
Michelangelo 98, 100, 330
Milton, John 11, 255–56, 262, 266–67, 314
  Paradise Lost 255–56, 260–61, 266–67
Minimalism 89
Mixolydian 261
Moberly, Walter 193
modern 10–11, 15–16, 58, 63, 98, 100, 135, 280, 287, 299, 326, 329, 331–32
modernism 5, 10, 14–16, 329
Monteverdi, Claudio 311
Moore, Jerrold 11, 13, 304–05
Moore, Philip 303
Morell, Thomas 314–16
Morley, Thomas 301
Moses 3, 50, 53, 103, 113, 128, 161–64, 168–70, 173–74, 218, 220
Mount Carmel 221, 223
Mountford, Brian 327
Mount Horeb 218, 220–21, 225
Mozart, Wolfgang Amadeus 141, 311, 316, 329
Murdoch, Iris 334
Musgrave, Thea 309
musical formation 2, 31, 326

musicology 288, 337–38, 343, 348
mystery 10–11, 18, 63, 65, 67, 71, 127, 131, 138, 230, 254, 262, 302, 304, 323, 332–34, 343, 347–48
mysticism 10–11, 15, 23, 75, 220, 223, 253, 322–23, 330, 335

naming 127–29, 315
Nazareth 45, 50
Nethsingha, Andrew 302
Nevader, Madhavi 5, 113
New Age 16
Newman, John Henry 13, 16, 35, 317
Nietzschean 318
Nietzsche, Friedrich 190
Norwich Cathedral 308
Nunc dimittis 57, 62, 80, 302, 307, 327

opera 4, 15, 281, 312–13, 316, 318–19, 322–24
oratorio 6, 311–16, 318–19, 324, 328
O'Regan, Tarik 309
Orff, Carl 283
organ 14, 70, 73, 80, 87, 166–67, 224, 301, 303–06, 308–09, 317–19, 321
Orthodox 15, 301

Palestrina, Giovanni Pierluigi da 297, 325
Pärt, Arvo 9, 16, 85, 89, 302, 308, 331
participation 6, 26, 28, 161, 279, 281–83, 285, 287, 293–94, 327, 337, 339, 351
Passiontide 20, 303–04
Passover 218
Paul, St 33, 53, 58, 98, 114
Paul VI, Pope 67
Penderecki, Krzysztof 12
performance of music 2–3, 5, 32, 34–35, 43, 66, 71, 77, 279, 281, 283, 291–92, 297–300, 302, 306, 308, 311–14, 322, 324, 326, 330, 332–33, 349
Peter, St 319
Pharaoh 51, 162
Phillips, Peter 330, 332
philosophy, philosophers 12–13, 18, 21, 42, 300, 334
Pilate, Pontius 303
Pius X, Pope 281, 284
Plato 351
polyphony 1, 78, 80, 112, 142, 284–85, 291
Pope, Alexander 313–14, 316
Poulenc, Francis 6, 12, 15–16, 312, 320–23
  Dialogues des Carmélites 15, 322–24

Pratt Green, Fred 305
prayer 15, 18–21, 24–26, 39, 47–48, 57, 59, 63–64, 67, 70, 104, 132, 196, 199, 223, 281, 291–292, 300–01, 309, 326–27, 332–33
preaching 59, 64–66, 255
priest 20, 59, 190, 192, 194, 197, 289–94, 315, 318, 322, 327, 333
prophecy 3, 18, 46, 48, 51, 54, 58, 62, 65, 67, 218, 221, 332
Protestant 317
Provan, Iain 100
Purcell, Henry 297, 301, 311
Purgatory 16

Rachel 47–48, 132
Rahab 54
Ratzinger, Joseph 6, 283. *See also* Benedict XVI, Pope
Ravenscroft, Thomas 303
Rebekah 47–48, 51
recording of music 3–4, 6, 141, 299, 329–30
Reich, Steve 89
Rembrandt 137
Renaissance 1, 100, 114, 206, 291, 297, 332
Reno, R. R. 100
Resistance 321
Revelation 58, 64
Reynolds, Joshua 196
rhythm 70, 80, 108, 166, 230, 260, 284, 288
Richter, Hans 319
Riley, Terry 89
Rilke, Rainer Maria 134
Roberts, Caroline Alice 317
Rolling Stones 254
Roman liturgy 287, 292
Rome, Roman 53, 283, 322
Rooke, Deborah 314
Rose, Bernard 300–01
Rostand, Claude 321
Ruff, Anthony 282, 287
Ruth 54, 63
Rutter, John 305–06

Sabbath 218
sacred 1–2, 5–6, 9–10, 15–16, 19–20, 31, 33, 36, 60, 69–70, 91, 220, 279, 281–84, 287–88, 292, 294, 297–99, 304, 310–12, 318, 324–35, 351
  music 1–6, 19, 31, 69–70, 91, 279–80, 282, 284, 287, 297, 299, 310–12, 325–26, 328–35
Salvation 62

salvation history 4, 60, 63, 67
Samson 47–48, 50, 131, 313
Samson's mother 47, 50
Samuel 3, 6, 48, 50, 84, 103, 189–90, 192–98, 201–04, 206–07, 209
Sant, James 196
Sarah 47–48, 50, 58
Saul 314
Savran, George 49
Schaefer, Edward 287–88
Schiller, Friedrich 329
Schnittke, Alfred 10, 12, 16
Schoenberg, Arnold 12, 15, 113
Scholl, Robert 331
Schubert, Franz 25
Scotland, Scottish 6, 22, 226, 254, 280, 288–90, 293–94, 314
Scottish Reformation 289
Scripture 40, 60, 225
Scruton, Roger 9, 89
Second Vatican Ecumenical Council 1, 6, 279, 281–88, 290, 292, 294
secular 1–2, 6, 11, 14–17, 20, 31, 36, 41, 97, 280, 284–85, 288, 311, 324–25, 328–35, 341, 344–45, 352
sensation 170, 205
Shepherd, John 349
Shiloh 189, 191, 201
Shostakovich, Dmitri 16
Shunammite Woman 47–48
Sibelius, Jean 21, 113
silence 3, 6, 15, 33, 66, 114, 167, 190, 192, 220–21, 223–26, 229–32, 302, 304, 326–27, 329
Silvestrov, Valentyn 16
Simeon 4, 62, 64–66, 327
Simon, Paul 141
sin 98, 100–01, 103–04, 106–09, 112–14, 256, 323
Sinai 218
singing 19, 21–23, 29, 34, 69–71, 73, 75, 84–85, 141, 231–32, 282–83, 285–86, 291, 293–94, 298, 300, 303–04, 306–07, 309, 313, 320, 323, 330, 332
Sistine Chapel 98, 100
Sixteen, The 332
Skempton, Howard 301, 303, 308–09
Small, Christopher 288
Smith, William 301
Solomon 51, 89, 258, 260, 266–69, 271, 320

Sonata 261–62
Song of Hannah 63
spirituality 2–3, 9–10, 15–16, 19, 26, 31, 34, 61, 98, 132, 134, 166, 168–71, 192, 223, 225–26, 230, 255, 261, 281, 290, 292, 299–301, 311–12, 326–27, 331–35, 337, 349, 352
Stainer, John 303
St Andrews, University of 2, 9, 37–38, 76, 78–80, 82, 84, 86, 88–89, 114, 141, 143, 175, 206, 230, 232, 266, 268, 291
St Asaph's Cathedral 19
Staves, Susan 316
Steele, Francis 332
Steiner, George 35, 335
St John of the Cross 220, 223–25, 230–31
  Spiritual Canticle, The 220, 224–25
St Mary's Episcopal Cathedral 299, 303
Stockhausen, Karlheinz 15
Stravinsky, Igor 10, 12, 14
Strimple, Nick 85–86
style of music 280–83, 285, 287–88, 290–92, 294
Swain, Joseph 288
Sweeney, Conor 348
Swift, Jonathan 313
Symmons Roberts, Michael 4, 11–12, 14, 36–37, 317

Tallis, Thomas 297, 300, 305, 311, 330
Tavener, John 9, 16, 84, 89, 267, 300–01, 306–07, 331
Teresa of Avila, St 220, 223, 253
text 13, 23–26, 36, 46–48, 54–55, 59–61, 64–66, 70–71, 77, 80, 89, 91, 97, 104, 106–07, 112–13, 127, 132, 134–35, 137–38, 142–43, 161–64, 166, 168–70, 198, 217, 220, 223, 225, 229–32, 258, 261, 288, 292, 299–303, 306, 309, 311–312, 316, 319–20, 322–23, 332
texture 70–71, 73, 75, 77, 80, 91, 143, 197, 230–31, 301–02
TheoArtistry scheme 2–5, 9, 32, 34, 36–38, 40–41, 43, 69, 75, 89, 91, 107, 112, 141, 143, 161, 173, 175, 190, 201, 204, 225, 229, 232, 297
Theologically Informed Programming and Performance (TIPP) 3, 324
theology and music, the interdiscipline 2, 29, 38, 40–42, 111, 279, 288, 339
Theology Through the Arts (TTA) 4, 37, 40
theophany 46, 49–50, 166
Thomas, Martin 297

Thomist 42
Tintoretto, Jacopo 100
Todi, Jacopone da 26
Tomkins, Thomas 301
tonality 29, 85–89, 91, 114, 306
transcendence 6, 10, 16, 18, 31, 169–70, 193, 218, 300, 309, 326–27, 329, 334–35, 339–43, 348, 351
Tucker, Francis 305
Tudor 301–02
Turner, Bryan 334
twentieth century 3, 11, 15, 20, 85, 281, 286, 297, 300, 308, 321, 323, 326, 331
twenty-first century 5–6, 9, 17, 28, 42, 91, 289, 335
Tye, Christopher 302
typology 57–59, 61, 66–67, 113, 163

Universalist 325, 331
Uriah 54
Ustvolskaya, Galina 16

Valcarenghi, Guido 322
Vattimo, Cianni 330
Vaughan Williams, Ralph 5, 75, 77, 305, 318
Very, Jones 134–35, 350
Vespers 61–63, 311
Vickers, David 313–14
Victorian 297
Victoria, Tomás Luis de 297
Viennese 318, 329
vocation 5, 12, 17–18, 20, 29, 32, 53

voice, human 34, 73, 75, 84, 87, 112, 138, 143, 168–70, 192–93, 231, 260–62, 301, 305–06, 321, 327
voice-leading 70, 86
voice, of God 84, 168–69, 190, 192–94, 217, 220–21, 223, 231

Wagner, Richard 9, 319–20
Wales, Welsh 17–18, 20–22
Waltke, Bruce 101
Walton, William 308
Weir, Judith 299
Wells Cathedral 6, 298–303, 306–08, 310
Westminster Abbey 301
Whately, Richard 320
Wilde, Oscar 253
Williams, James G. 48
Williams, Manon 21–23, 311
Williams, Rowan 37–38, 311
Worcester Cathedral 14, 319
worship 1–2, 6, 279–80, 286–88, 291–92, 298–99, 302–03, 326–28, 331, 333
Wyeth, Newell 196

Yeats, W. B. 112

Zakovtich, Yair 54
Zechariah 4, 48, 61–64
Zion 89, 225–26, 267

Index of Scriptures

Genesis [Gen]
  2 97, 101, 104, 107, 112, 256–57, 259
  3 3, 97–98, 100–01, 103–04, 106–08, 111–13
  4 100
  16 47
  17 129
  18 47
  20 51
  22 50, 103
  25 47, 51
  28 51, 131
  29 47
  31 50, 131
  32 3, 53, 127, 129, 131–32, 137–38
  33 129
  34 129
  35 129, 132
  46 50, 131
  48 131

Exodus [Exod]
  3 3, 50, 53, 103, 113, 161–62, 164, 166, 168, 170, 173, 218
  24 218
  33 128
  34 103

Deuteronomy [Deut]
  5 218

Judges [Judg]
  11 314
  13 47, 131

1 Samuel [1 Sam]
  1 47
  2 47, 63, 191, 202
  3 3, 50, 103, 190, 192–96, 198, 201–04

1 Kings [1 Kgs]
  3 51
  19 3, 218, 220, 225, 229–30

2 Kings [2 Kgs]
  4 47

Nehemiah [Neh]
  4 65

Job
  1 129

Psalms [Pss]
  8 65
  17 132
  133 25

The Song of Songs [Song]
  3 3, 65, 254, 258, 266–67
  8 65

The Book of Wisdom [Wis]
  2 320
  18 225

Isaiah [Isa]
  6 50
  7 50, 52
  40 225

Lamentations [Lam]
  1 24

Habakkuk [Hab]
  2 64

Malachi [Mal]
  3 64–65

Matthew [Mt]
  1 50–54
  2 65
  12 58

Luke [Lk]
  1 45–46, 48–50, 61–63, 337
  2 62, 65
  3 53–54
  18 132
  19 66

John [Jn]
  1 53, 225
  8 67
  15 21, 23

Romans [Rom]
  5 64, 98

1 Corinthians [1 Cor]
  10 58

Galatians [Gal]
  4 33, 58

Ephesians [Eph]
  2 114
  5 255

Philippians [Phil]
  2 255

Hebrews [Heb]
  7 59

Revelation [Rev]
  21 26
  22 113

Bibliography

For the editions and translations of the Bible, see individual chapters.

Adorno, Theodor W., *Introduction to the Sociology of Music*, trans. by E. B. Ashton (New York: Continuum, 1989).

Allison, John, *Edward Elgar: Sacred Music* (Bridgend: Seren, 1994).

Alter, Robert, 'How Convention Helps Us Read: The Case of the Bible's Annunciation Type-Scene', *Prooftexts* 3 (1983), 115–30.

Ammerman, Nancy Tatom, *Sacred Stories Spiritual Tribes: Finding Religion in Everyday Life* (Oxford: Oxford University Press, 2013).

—, 'Spiritual but Not Religious? Beyond Binary Choices in the Study of Religion', *Journal for the Scientific Study of Religion,* 52 (2013), 258–78.

Aquinas, Thomas, *Summa Theologica,* trans. by the English Dominican Province, 5 vols. (Notre Dame, IN: Ave Maria Press, 1981).

Arnold, Jonathan, *Sacred Music in Secular Society* (Farnham: Ashgate, 2014).

Ashmon, Scott A., *Birth Annunciations in the Hebrew Bible and Ancient Near East: A Literary Analysis of the Forms and Functions of the Heavenly Foretelling of the Destiny of a Special Child* (Lewiston, NY: Edwin Mellen Press, 2012).

Atkins, E. Wulstan, *The Elgar–Atkins Friendship* (Newton Abbot: David and Charles, 1984).

Auden, W. H., 'Yeats as an Example', *Kenyon Review,* 10 (1948), 187–95.

Augustine, *The City of God*, trans. by Marcos Dods (New York: The Modern Library, 1950).

—, *Confessions*, trans. by R. S. Pine-Coffin (London: Penguin, 1961).

—, *On Christian Teaching*, trans. by R. P. H. Green (Oxford: Oxford University Press, 2008).

Beal, Gregory K., *Handbook on the New Testament Use of the Old Testament: Exegesis and Interpretation* (Grand Rapids, MI: Baker Academic, 2012).

Beard, David, and Kenneth Gloag (eds.), *Musicology: The Key Concepts* (London: Routledge, 2005).

Begbie, Jeremy, 'Created Beauty: The Witness of J.S. Bach', in *The Beauty of God: Theology and the Arts*, ed. by Daniel J. Treier, Mark Husbands and Roger Lundin (Downers Grove, IL: InterVarsity Press, 2007), pp. 19–44.

—, *Music, Modernity and God: Essays in Listening* (Oxford: Oxford University Press, 2013).

—, 'Openness and Specificity: A Conversation with David Brown on Theology and Classical Music', in *Theology, Aesthetics and Culture: Responses to the Work of David Brown*, ed. by Robert MacSwain and Taylor Worley (Oxford: Oxford University Press, 2012), pp. 145–56.

—, *A Peculiar Orthodoxy: Reflections on Theology and the Arts* (Grand Rapids, MI: Baker Academic, 2018).

—, *Redeeming Transcendence in the Arts: Bearing Witness to the Triune God* (Grand Rapids, MI: Eerdmans, 2018).

—, and Steven R. Guthrie (eds.), *Resonant Witness: Conversations between Music and Theology* (Grand Rapids, MI: Eerdmans, 2011).

—, *Resounding Truth: Christian Wisdom in the World of Music* (Grand Rapids, MI: Baker Academic, 2007).

—, (ed.), *Sounding the Depths: Theology Through the Arts* (London: SCM Press, 2002).

—, *Theology, Music and Time* (Cambridge: Cambridge University Press, 2000)

Benedict XVI, Pope, *Summorum Pontificum: On the Use of the Roman Liturgy Prior to the Reform of 1970* (7 July, 2007), https://w2.vatican.va/content/benedict-xvi/en/motu_proprio/documents/hf_ben-xvi_motu-proprio_20070707_summorum-pontificum.html

Bennett, Jane, *The Enchantment of Modern Life: Attachments, Crossings, and Ethics* (Princeton, NJ: Princeton University Press, 2001).

Blakeman, Edward, *The Faber Pocket Guide to Handel* (London: Faber & Faber, 2009).

Blanning, Tim, *The Triumph of Music: Composers, Musicians and their Audiences, 1700 to the Present* (Harmondsworth: Penguin, 2008).

Blond, Philip, *Post-Secular Philosophy: Between Philosophy and Theology* (London: Routledge, 1998).

Boden, Anthony, *Three Choirs: A History of the Festival – Gloucester, Hereford, Worcester* (Stroud: Alan Sutton, 1992).

Bohlman, Philip, 'Is All Music Religious?' in *Theomusicology — A Special Issue of Black Sacred Music: A Journal of Theomusicology*, ed. by Jon Michael Spencer (Durham, NC: Duke University Press, 1994), pp. 3–12.

—, 'Music Inside Out: Sounding Public Religion in a Post-Secular Europe', in *Music, Sound and Space: Transformations of Public and Private Experience*, ed. by Georgina Born (Cambridge: Cambridge University Press, 2013), pp. 205–23.

Bonaventure, *Breviloquium*, trans. with notes by Dominic V. Monti (St Bonaventure, NY: Franciscan Institute Publications, 2005).

—, *Commentary on the Gospel of Luke*, trans. and ed. by Robert J. Karris (St Bonaventure, NY: Franciscan Institute Publications, 2001–2004).

—, *Doctoris Seraphici S. Bonaventurae Opera Omnia*, 10 vols. (Quarrachi: Collegium S. Bonaventurae, 1882–1902).

Bonds, Mark Evan, *Music as Thought: Listening to the Symphony in the Age of Beethoven* (Princeton, NJ: Princeton University Press, 2006).

Bosco, Mark, 'Georges Bernanos and Francis Poulenc: Catholic Convergences in *Dialogues of the Carmelites*', *Logos*, 12 (Spring 2009), 17–39.

Bougerol, Jacques Guy, 'Bonaventure as Exegete', in *A Companion to Bonaventure*, ed. by Jay M. Hammon and others (Leiden and Boston: Brill, 2014), pp. 168–74.

Boyce-Tillman, June, *Constructing Musical Healing: The Wounds that Sing* (London: Jessica Kingsley, 2000).

—, *Experiencing Music – Restoring the Spiritual: Music as Well Being* (Oxford: Oxford University Press, 2016).

Brenner, Athalya, 'Female Social Behaviour: Two Descriptive Patterns within the "Birth of the Hebrew" Paradigm', *Vetus Testamentum*, 36 (1986), 257–73.

Brown, Callum G., 'Men Losing Faith: The Making of Modern No-Religionism in the UK, 1939–2010', in *Men, Masculinities and Religious Change in Twentieth Century Britain*, ed. by Lucy Delap and Sue Morgan (Basingstoke: Palgrave Macmillan, 2013), pp. 301–25.

Brown, David, *Divine Generosity and Human Creativity: Theology through Symbol, Art and Architecture*, ed. by Christopher R. Brewer and Robert MacSwain (London: Routledge, 2017).

—, and Gavin Hopps (eds.), *The Extravagance of Music* (London: Bloomsbury, 2018).

—, *God and Enchantment of Place: Reclaiming Human Experience* (Oxford: Oxford University Press, 2004).

—, *God and Grace of Body: Sacrament in Ordinary* (Oxford: Oxford University Press, 2007).

—, *God and Mystery in Words: Experience through Metaphor and Drama* (Oxford: Oxford University Press, 2008).

Brown, Raymond E., *The Birth of the Messiah: A Commentary on the Infancy Narratives in the Gospels of Matthew and Luke*, AB Reference Library (New York: Doubleday, 1993).

Brueggemann, Walter, *First and Second Samuel* (Louisville, KY: Westminster John Knox Press, 2012).

Buckley, R. J., *Sir Edward Elgar* (London: The Bodley Head, 1905).

Bull, Michael, *Sound Moves: iPod Culture and Urban Experience* (New York: Routledge, 2007).

Burch Brown, Frank, *Good Taste, Bad Taste and Christian Taste: Aesthetics in Religion Life* (Oxford: Oxford University Press, 2000).

—, *Inclusive yet Discerning: Navigating Worship Artfully* (Grand Rapids, MI: Eerdmans, 2009).

—, 'Preface', in Brown and Hopps (eds.), *The Extravagance of Music*, pp. v-xvii.

—, *Religious Aesthetics: A Theological Study of Making and Meaning* (Princeton: Princeton University Press, 1989).

Burney, Charles, *An Account of the Musical Performances in Westminster-Abbey, and the Pantheon, May 26th, 27th, 29th; and June the 3rd, and 5th, 1784. In Commemoration of Handel* (London: T. Payne and Son and G. Robinson, 1785), https://archive.org/details/accountofmusical00burn/page/n8

Burton, Richard D. E., *Outlines: Francis Poulenc* (Bath: Absolute Press, 2002).

Butler, Christopher, 'Innovation and the avant-garde, 1900–1920', in *The Cambridge History of Twentieth-Century Music*, ed. by Nicholas Cook and Anthony Pople (Cambridge: Cambridge University Press, 2004), pp. 69–80.

Butler, Judith, *Gender Trouble: Feminism and the Subversion of Identity* (New York: Routledge, 1999).

Butt, John, 'Roman Catholicism and Being Musically English: Elgar's Church and Organ Music', in *The Cambridge Companion to Elgar*, ed. by Daniel M. Grimley and Julian Rushton (Cambridge: Cambridge University Press, 2004), pp. 106–19.

Butzkamm, Aloys, *Ein Tor zum Paradies. Kunst und Theologie auf der Bronzetür des Hildesheimer Doms* (Paderborn: Bonifatius, 2004).

Cameron, Jasmin, *The Crucifixion in Music: An Analytical Survey of Settings of the Crucifixus between 1680 and 1800* (Lanham, MD: Scarecrow Press, 2006).

The Canons and Decrees of the Council of Trent, trans. H. Schroeder (St Louis, IL: Herder, 1941).

Catechism of the Catholic Church (Rome: Urbi et Orbi Communications, 1994).

Chapman, Stephen B., *1 Samuel as Christian Scripture: A Theological Commentary* (Grand Rapids, MI: Eerdmans, 2016).

Chesterton, G. K., *William Blake* (New York: Cosimo Classics, 2005).

Chua, Daniel K. L., 'Music as the Mouthpiece of Theology', in Begbie and Guthrie (eds.), *Resonant Witness*, pp. 137–61.

Clark, Caryl, 'Forging Identity: Beethoven's "Ode" as European Anthem', *Critical Inquiry*, 23 (1997), 789–807.

Clines, David J. A. (ed.), *The Dictionary of Classical Hebrew* (Sheffield: Sheffield Academic Press, 1993).

Cogan, Mordechai, *I Kings: A New Translation with Introduction and Commentary* (New Haven, CT and London: Yale University Press, 2008).

Cole, Bruce, and Adelheid Gehalt, with an introduction by Michael Wood, *Art of the Western World: From Ancient Greece to Post-Modernism* (London: Simon & Schuster Paperbacks, 1989).

Cook, Nicholas, 'Classical Music and the Politics of Space', in *Music, Sound and Space: Transformations of Public and Private Experience*, ed. by Georgina Born (Cambridge: Cambridge University Press, 2013), pp. 224–38.

Corbett, George, 'TheoArtistry, and a Contemporary Perspective on Composing Sacred Choral Music', *Religions*, 9.1 (2018), 7, 1-18 (Special Issue: Music: Its Theologies and Spiritualities – A Global Perspective). https://doi.org/10.3390/rel9010007

Cottingham, John, *The Spiritual Dimension: Religion, Philosophy and Human Value* (Cambridge: Cambridge University Press, 2005).

Cullen, Christopher, *Bonaventure* (Oxford: Oxford University Press, 2006).

Cusic, Don, 'Catholics and Contemporary Christian Music', in *Encyclopedia of Contemporary Christian Music: Pop, Rock, and Worship*, ed. by Don Cusic (Santa Barbara, CA: Greenwood Press, 2010), pp. 45–47.

Dahlhaus, Carl, *The Idea of Absolute Music*, trans. by Roger Lustig (Chicago, IL: University of Chicago Press, 1990).

Danielson, Denis, 'Fall', in *A Dictionary of Biblical Tradition in English Literature*, ed. by David Lyle Jeffrey (Grand Rapids, MI: Eerdmans, 1992), pp. 271–73.

Davis, Ellen F., *Proverbs, Ecclesiastes and the Song of Songs* (Louisville, KY: Westminster John Knox Press, 2000).

Day, John, *From Creation to Babel: Studies in Genesis 1-11* (London: Bloomsbury T&T Clark, 2013).

Day, Thomas, *Why Catholics Can't Sing: The Culture of Catholicism and the Triumph of Bad Taste* (New York: Crossroad, 2013).

D'Costa, Gavin, *Theology in the Public Square: Church, Academy and Nation* (Oxford: Blackwell Publishing, 2005).

Dean, Winton, *Handel's Dramatic Oratorios and Masques* (London: Oxford University Press, 1959).

—, '3.iv: Early 20th Century', in Richard Cohn, Brian Hyer, Carl Dahlhaus, Julian Anderson and Charles Wilson, 'Harmony', *New Grove Online*, http://doi.org/10.1093/gmo/9781561592630.article.50818

De Lubac, Henri, *Medieval Exegesis: Volume I: The Four Senses of Scripture*, trans. by Marc Sebanc (Grand Rapids, MI: Eerdmans Publishing Co., 1998).

DeNora, Tia, *Music in Everyday Life* (Cambridge: Cambridge University Press, 2000).

De Roos, Simone A., Jurjen Iedema and Siebren Miedema, 'Influence of Maternal Denomination, God Concepts, and Child-Rearing Practices on Young Children's God Concepts', *Journal for the Scientific Study of Religion*, 43 (2004), 519–35.

Derrida, Jacques, *Of Grammatology*, trans. by Gayatri Chakravorty Spivak (Baltimore, MD: Johns Hopkins University Press, 1976).

Dickie, Jane R., Lindsey V. Ajega, Joy R. Kobylak, and Kathryn M. Nixon, 'Mother, Father, and Self: Sources of Young Adults' God Concepts', *Journal for the Scientific Study of Religion*, 45 (2006), 57–71.

Dillon, Michele M., 'Can Post-Secular Society Tolerate Religious Differences?', *Sociology of Religion*, 71 (2010), 139–56.

Donne, John, 'Denmark House, some few dayes before the body of King James removed to his Buriall, Apr, 26. 1625', in *The Sermons of John Donne*, ed. by George R. Potter and Evelyn M. Simpson, 10 vols. (Berkeley, CA: University of California Press, 1953–1962), VI, pp. 280–91.

Dorsey, David A., *The Literary Structure of the Old Testament: A Commentary on Genesis — Malachi* (Grand Rapids, MI: Baker, 1999).

Dyer, Rebekah M., 'Multivalence, Liminality, and the Theological Imagination: Contextualising the Image of Fire for Contemporary Christian Practice' (unpublished doctoral thesis, University of St Andrews, 2018). http://hdl.handle.net/10023/16452

Dyrness, William A., *Poetic Theology: God and the Poetics of Everyday Life* (Grand Rapids, MI: Eerdmans, 2011).

Edwards, Katie B., *Admen and Eve: The Bible in Contemporary Advertising* (Sheffield: Sheffield Phoenix Press, 2012).

Eliot, T. S., 'Blake', in *idem*, *The Sacred Wood: Essays on Poetry and Criticism* (New York: Alrfred A. Knopf, 1921), pp. 137–43.

Epp-Tiessen, Dan, '1 Kings 19: The Renewal of Elijah', *Direction, A Mennonite Brethren Forum*, 35 (Spring 2006), 33–43.

Epstein, Heidi, *Melting the Venusberg: A Feminist Theology of Music* (New York: Continuum, 2004).

Eslinger, Lyle M., *Kingship of God in Crisis: A Close Reading of 1 Samuel 1-12* (Sheffield: JSOT Press, 1985).

Felski, Rita, *The Uses of Literature* (Oxford: Blackwell, 2008).

Ferguson, Michael, 'Understanding the Tensions in Liturgical Music-Making in the Roman Catholic Church in Contemporary Scotland' (unpublished doctoral thesis, University of Edinburgh, 2015).

Finlay, Timothy D., *The Birth Report Genre in the Hebrew Bible*, FATII 12 (Tübingen: Mohr Siebeck, 2005).

Fleming, David L., *What is Ignatian Spirituality?* (Chicago, IL: Loyola Press, 2008).

Flynn, William T., *Medieval Music as Medieval Exegesis* (London: The Scarecrow Press, 1999).

Fuchs, Esther, *Sexual Politics in the Biblical Narrative: Reading the Hebrew Bible as a Woman*, JSOTSupp 310 (London: Sheffield Academic Press, 2000).

Fuller, Michael, 'Liturgy, Scripture and Resonance in the Operas of James MacMillan', *New Blackfriars*, 96.1064 (July 2015), 381–90.

Gabrielsson, Alf, *Strong Experiences with Music: Music Is Much More than Music* (Oxford: Oxford University Press, 2011).

Gallagher, Tom, *Divided Scotland: Ethnic Friction and Christian Crisis* (Glendaruel: Argyll Publishing, 2013).

Ganeri, Martin, 'Tradition with a New Identity: Thomist Engagement with Non-Christian Thought as a Model for the New Comparative Theology in Europe', *Religions* 3 (2012), 1054–74.

Gant, Andrew, *O Sing Unto the Lord: A History of English Church Music* (London: Profile Books, 2015).

Glory & Praise: Songs for the Worshipping Assembly (Phoenix, AZ: North American Liturgy Resources, 1977).

Gnuse, Robert Karl, *The Dream Theophany of Samuel: Its Structure in Relation to Ancient Near Eastern Dreams and Its Theological Significance* (Lanham, CT: University Press of America, 1984).

Goehr, Lydia, *The Imaginary Museum of Musical Works* (Oxford: Oxford University Press, 1994).

Gombrich, E. H., *Art and Illusion: A Study in the Psychology of Pictorial Representation* (New York: Phaidon Press, 2002).

Gordon, Robert P., *I & II Samuel: A Commentary* (Grand Rapids, MI: Zondervan, 1999).

Gowan, Donald E., *From Eden to Babel: A Commentary on the Book of Genesis 1-11* (Grand Rapids, MI: Eerdmans, 1988).

Gregg, Robert C., *Shared Stories, Rival Tellings: Early Encounters of Jews, Christians, and Muslims* (New York: Oxford University Press, 2015).

Griffiths, Paul, *The Penguin Companion to Classical Music* (London: Penguin Group, 2005).

Hall, Joseph, *The Works of Right Reverend Father in God, Joseph Hall, D. D. Successively Bishop of Exeter and Norwich*, ed. by Josiah Pratt, 10 vols. (London: Williams and Smith, 1808).

Hallo, W. W., and K. Lawson Younger (eds.), *Context of Scripture. Volume 1: Canonical Compositions from the Biblical World* (Leiden and New York: E. J. Brill, 1996).

Hamilton, Victor, *The Book of Genesis: Chapters 1-17*, New International Commentary on the Old Testament (Grand Rapids, MI: Eerdmans, 1990).

Hamori, Esther, *'When Gods Were Men': The Embodied God in Biblical and Near Eastern Literature*, Beihefte Zur Zeitschrift Für Die Alttestamentliche Wissenschaft, Bd. 384 (Berlin: Walter De Gruyter, 2008).

Hart, Trevor, 'Conversation after Pentecost? Theological Musings on the Hermeneutical Motion', *Literature and Theology*, 28 (2014), 164–78.

Hawkins, John, *A General History of the Science and Practice of Music*, 5 vols. (London: T. Payne, 1776).

Hayburn, Robert F., *Papal Legislation on Sacred Music: 95 A.D. to 1977 A.D.* (Collegeville, MN: Liturgical Press, 1979).

Hays, Richard B., *Echoes of Scripture in the Letters of Paul* (New Haven: Yale University Press, 1993).

Heaney, Maeve Louise, *Music as Theology: What Music Says About the Word* (Eugene, OR: Wipf and Stock Publishers, 2012).

Hens-Piazza, Gina, *1-2 Kings* (Nashville, TN: Abingdon, 2006).

Hepburn, Ronald W., *'Wonder' and Other Essays: Eight Studies in Aesthetics and Neighbouring Fields* (Edinburgh: Edinburgh University Press, 1984).

Herbert, James D., *Our Distance from God: Studies of the Divine and the Mundane in Western Art and Music* (Berkeley, CA: University of California Press, 2008).

Hick, John, *The New Frontier of Religion and Science: Religious Experience, Neuroscience and the Transcendent* (Basingstoke: Palgrave, 2006).

Hicks, Anthony, 'Handel and the Idea of an Oratorio', in Donald Burrows (ed.), *The Cambridge Companion to Handel* (Cambridge: Cambridge University Press, 1997), pp. 145–63.

Hinchliffe, Stephen, and others, *Scottish Social Attitudes Survey 2014: Public Attitudes to Sectarianism in Scotland* (Scottish Government Social Research, 2015).

Hopkins, Gerard Manley, *The Poems of Gerard Manley Hopkins*, ed. by William Henry Gardner and N. H. MacKenzie (Oxford: Oxford University Press, 1967).

Howells, Edward, *John of the Cross and Teresa of Avila: Mystical Knowing and Selfhood* (New York: Crossroad, 2002).

Hughes, Christopher G., 'Art and Exegesis', in *A Companion to Medieval Art*, ed. by Conrad Rudolph (Oxford: Blackwell, 2006), pp. 173–92.

Huijbers, Bernard, *The Performing Audience: Six and a Half Essays on Music and Song in the Liturgy* (Phoenix, AZ: North America Liturgy Resources, 1980).

John of the Cross, *The Collected Works of Saint John of the Cross*, trans. by David Lewis, 3 vols. (New York: Cosimo, 2007).

Jones, David, *The Anathemata* (London: Faber & Faber, 1972).

—, 'Art and Sacrament', in *Every Man an Artist: Readings in the Traditional Philosophy of Art*, ed. by Brian Keeble (Bloomington, IN: World Wisdom, 2005), pp. 141–69.

Johnston, Robert, *Reel Spirituality: Theology and Film in Dialogue* (Grand Rapids, MI: Baker Academic, 2006).

Jung, Carl Gustav, *Letters of C. G. Jung: Volume 1 of 2, 1906–1950*, ed. by Gerhard Adler and Aniela Jaffé, trans. by R. F. C. Hull (London: Routledge, 1992).

Kareem, Sarah Tindal, *Eighteenth-Century Fiction and the Reinvention of Wonder* (Oxford: Oxford University Press, 2014).

Karris, Robert J., 'St Bonaventure as Biblical Interpreter: His Methods, Wit, and Wisdom', *Franciscan Studies*, 60 (2002), 159–208.

Keats, John, *Keats's Poetry and Prose*, ed. by Jeffrey Cox (New York: Norton, 2009).

Kim, Koowon, *Incubation as a Type-Scene in the Aqhatu, Kirta, and Hannah Stories: A Form-Critical and Narratological Study of KTU 1.14 I-1.15 III, 1.17 I-II, and 1 Samuel 1:1-2:11, VTSupp 145* (Leiden: Brill, 2011).

Kingsbury, Stephen A., 'The Influence of Scottish Nationalism on James MacMillan's "A New Song"', *The Choral Journal*, 47 (August 2006), 30–37.

Klein, Ralph W., *1 Samuel* (Nashville, TN: Thomas Nelson, 2008).

Knight, George, *Theology in Pictures: A Commentary on Genesis Chapters One to Eleven* (Edinburgh: Handsel, 1981).

Knoblauch, A. Abby, 'Bodies of Knowledge', *Composition Studies*, 40.2 (2012), 50–65.

Kramer, Lawrence, *Classical Music and Postmodern Knowledge* (Berkeley, CA: University of California Press, 1995).

—, *Expression and Truth: On the Music of Knowledge* (Berkeley, CA: University of California Press, 2012).

—, *Musical Meaning: Toward a Critical History* (Berkeley, CA: University of California Press, 2002).

—, 'Musicology and Meaning', *The Musical Times*, 144 (Summer 2003), 6–12.

—, 'The Musicology of the Future', *Repercussions*, 1 (Spring 1992), 5–18.

—, *The Thought of Music* (Oakland, CA: University of California Press, 2016).

Kreider, Alan, 'Introduction', in *Composing Music for Worship*, ed. by Stephen Darlington and Alan Kreider (Norwich: Canterbury Press, 2003), pp. 1–14.

Kuipers, Joel C., 'Ululations from the Weyewa Highlands (Sumba): Simultaneity, Audience Response, and Models of Cooperation', *Ethnomusicology*, 43 (1999), 490–507.

Küng, Hans, *Mozart – Traces of Transcendence* (London: SCM, 1992).

Lang, Paul Henry, *George Frideric Handel* (London: Faber & Faber, 1967).

Latour, Bruno, *Reassembling the Social: An Introduction to Actor-Network-Theory* (Oxford: Oxford University Press, 2005).

Lehnhof, Kent R., 'Performing Masculinity in *Paradise Lost*', *Milton Studies*, 50 (2009), 64–77.

Leppert, Richard, and Susan McClary (eds.), *Music and Society: The Politics of Composition, Performance and Reception* (Cambridge: Cambridge University Press, 1987).

Leuchter, Mark A., and David T. Lamb, *The Historical Writings: Introducing Israel's Historical Literature* (Minneapolis, MN: Fortress Press, 2016).

Lewis, C.S., *The Problem of Pain* (San Francisco: HarperSanFrancisco, 2001).

—, *Surprised by Joy* (London: Collins, 2012).

Licht, Jacob, *Storytelling in the Bible* (Jerusalem: Magnes Press, 1986).

Luther, Martin, *The Life of Luther Written by Himself: Collected and Arranged by M. Michelet* (London: George Bell & Sons, 1904).

—, *Luther's Works, Vol. 53: Liturgy and Hymns*, ed. by Ulrich S. Leupold (Philadelphia, PA: Fortress Press, 1965).

Lynch, Gordon, *Understanding Theology and Popular Culture* (Oxford: Blackwell, 2005).

Lysik, David (ed.), *The Liturgy Documents: A Parish Resource*, 2 vols. (Chicago, IL: Liturgy Training Publications, 2004), Vol. 2.

MacMillan, James, 'God, Theology and Music', *New Blackfriars*, 81.947 (January 2000), 16–26.

—, and Richard McGregor, 'James MacMillan: A Conversation and Commentary', *Musical Times*, 151.1912 (Autumn 2010), 69–100.

—, 'Parthenogenesis', in Begbie (ed.), *Sounding the Depths*, pp. 33–38.

Marion, Jean-Luc, *God without Being: Hors-Texte*, trans. by Thomas A. Carlson (Chicago, IL: University of Chicago, 2012).

Matthew, Iain, *The Impact of God: Soundings from St. John of the Cross* (London: Hodder & Stoughton, 1995).

McCaffrey, John, 'Roman Catholics in Scotland: Nineteenth and Twentieth Centuries', in *Scottish Life and Society: Volume 12 'Religion'*, ed. by Colin MacLean and Kenneth Veitch (Edinburgh: Birlinn, 2006), pp. 170–90.

McCarter, P. Kyle, *I Samuel* (New Haven, CT: Doubleday Religious Publishing Group, 1995).

McClary, Susan, *Feminine Endings: Music, Gender and Sexuality* (Minneapolis, MN: University of Minnesota Press, 2002).

McGrath, Alister, *Christian Theology: An Introduction* (Chichester: John Wiley & Sons, 2017).

McGregor, Richard, '"A Metaphor for the Deeper Wintriness": Exploring James MacMillan's Musical Identity', *Tempo*, 65 (July 2011), 22–39.

McGuire, Charles Edward, 'Measure of a Man: Catechizing Elgar's Catholic Avatars', in *Edward Elgar and His World*, ed. by Byron Adams (Princeton, NJ: Princeton University Press, 2007), pp. 3–38.

—, and Steven E. Plank, *Historical Dictionary of English Music: ca. 1400–1958* (Plymouth, UK: Scarecrow Press, 2011).

Meillassoux, Quentin, *After Finitude: An Essay on the Necessity of Contingency*, trans. by Ray Brassier (New York: Continuum, 2008).

The Methodist Hymnal (New York and Cincinnati, OH: The Methodist Book Concern, 1905).

Middleton, Richard, 'Faith, Hope, and the Hope of Love: On the Fidelity of the Phonograph', in *Music, Sound and Space: Transformations of Public and Private Experience*, ed. by Georgina Born (Cambridge: Cambridge University Press, 2013), pp. 292–310.

Millgram, Hillel I., *The Invention of Monotheist Ethics: Exploring the First Book of Samuel* (Lanham: University Press of America, 2009).

Milton, John, *Paradise Lost*, ed. by John Leonard (London: Penguin Books, 2003).

Moberg, Marcus, Kennet Granholm, and Peter Nynäs, 'Trajectories of Post-Secular Complexity: An Introduction', in *Post-Secular Society*, ed. by Peter Nynäs, Mika Lassander and Terhi Utriainen (New Brunswick, NJ: Transactions, 2015), pp. 1–26.

Moberly, Walter, 'To Hear the Master's Voice: Revelation and Spiritual Discernment in the Call of Samuel', *Scottish Journal of Theology*, 48 (1995), 443–68.

Monson, Craig A., 'The Council of Trent Revisited', *Journal of the American Musicological Society*, 55 (Spring 2002), 1–37.

Moore, Stephen D., 'The Song of Songs in the History of Sexuality', *Church History*, 69 (2000), 328–49.

Mountford, Brian, *Christian Atheist: Belonging without Believing* (Winchester, UK and Washington D.C.: O Books, 2010).

Murdoch, Iris, *The Sovereignty of Good* (London: Routledge, 1970).

Nagy, Gregory, *The Ancient Greek Hero in 24 Hours* (Cambridge, MA: Harvard University Press, 2013).

Noden, Shelagh, 'The Revival of Music in the Worship of the Catholic Church in Scotland, 1789–1829' (unpublished doctoral thesis, University of Aberdeen, 2014).

Nugent, Donald Christopher, 'There Was a Feminine Mysticism', *Mystics Quarterly*, 14 (1988), 135–42.

Ocker, Christopher, and Kevin Madigan, 'After Beryl Smalley: Thirty Years of Medieval Exegesis, 1984–2013', *Journal of the Bible and its Reception*, 2 (2015), 87–130.

Osborne, Charles, *The Opera Lover's Companion* (New Haven, CT: Yale University Press, 2004).

Paintner, Christine Valters, and Lucy Wynkoop, *Lectio Divina: Contemplative Awakening and Awareness* (New York: Paulist Press, 2008).

Panufnik, Roxanna, 'Beyond a Mass for Westminster', in *Composing Music for Worship*, ed. by Stephen Darlington and Alan Kreider (Norwich: Canterbury Press, 2003), pp. 76–85.

Partridge, Christopher, *The Re-Enchantment of the West: Alternative Spiritualities, Sacralization, Popular Culture, and Occulture*, 2 vols. (London: T&T Clark, 2004 and 2005).

Patterson, Dorothy Kelley, and Rhonda Harrington Kelley, *Women's Evangelical Commentary: Old Testament* (Nashville: B&H Publishing Group, 2011).

Paul VI, Pope, *Marialis Cultus* (1974), http://w2.vatican.va/content/paul-vi/en/apost_exhortations/documents/hf_p-vi_exh_19740202_marialis-cultus.html

Pius X, Pope, *Tra le Sollecitudini* (22 November 1903). http://www.sanctamissa.org/en/music/church-documents-on-liturgical-music/tra-le-sollecitudini.pdf

Polzin, Robert, *Samuel and the Deuteronomist: A Literary Study of the Deuteronomic History Part Two: 1 Samuel* (Bloomington, IN: Indiana University Press, 1993).

Porter, Mark, 'The Developing Field of Christian Congregational Music Studies', *Ecclesial Practices*, 1 (2014), 149–66.

Poulenc, Francis, *Francis Poulenc: Articles and Interviews*, ed. by Nicolas Southon, and trans. by Roger Nichols (Farnham: Ashgate, 2014).

—, *Francis Poulenc: Echo and Source, Selected Correspondence 1915–63*, ed. and trans. by Sidney Buckland (London: Victor Gollancz Ltd., 1991).

Pratt Jr., R. L., *He Gave us Stories* (Brentwood, TN: Wolgemuth & Hyatt, 1990).

Pritchett, James, *The Music of John Cage* (Cambridge: Cambridge University Press, 1993).

Provan, Iain, *Discovering Genesis: Content, Interpretation, Reception* (Grand Rapids, MI: Eerdmans, 2015).

Rambuss, Richard, *Closet Devotions* (Durham, NC and London: Duke University Press, 1998).

Ramsey, George W., 'Is Name-Giving an Act of Domination in Genesis 2:23 and Elsewhere?', *The Catholic Biblical Quarterly*, 50 (1988), 24–35.

Ratcliffe, Shirley, 'MacMillan', *Choir and Organ*, 8 (1999), 39–42.

Ratzinger, Joseph, *The Feast of Faith: Approaches to a Theology of the Liturgy* (San Francisco, CA: Ignatius, 1986).

—, *A New Song for the Lord: Faith in Christ and Liturgy Today* (New York: Crossroad, 1996).

—, *The Spirit of the Liturgy* (San Francisco, CA: Ignatius Press, 2000).

—, 'That Music, for Me, Is a Demonstration of the Truth of Christianity', trans. by Matthew Sherry (Chiesa.espresso.repubblica.it, 2015), http://chiesa.espresso.repubblica.it/articolo/1351089bdc4.html?eng=y

Re Manning, Russell, 'Natural Theology Reconsidered (Again)', *Theology and Science*, 15 (2017), 289–301.

Reno, R. R., *Genesis*, Brazos Theological Commentary on the Bible (Grand Rapids, MI: BrazosPress, 2010).

Repp, Ray, *Mass for Young Americans: with Psalms and Refrains* (Chicago, IL: F.E.L Church Publications, 1966).

Ricoeur, Paul, *From Text to Action*, trans. by Kathleen Blamey and John Thompson (London: Continuum, 2008).

Rilke, Rainer Maria, 'Der Schauende', in *Das Buch der Bilder* (Berlin: Axel Junker Verlag, 1906), pp. 151–54.

Rooke, Deborah, *Handel's Israelite Oratorio Libretti: Sacred Drama and Biblical Exegesis* (Oxford: Oxford University Press, 2012).

Ruff, Anthony, *Sacred Music and Liturgical Reform: Treasures and Transformations* (Chicago, IL: Hillenbrand, 2007).

Russell, Charles Taze, *Expanded Biblical Comments - Commentary of the Old and New Testament* (Chicago: Chicago Bible Students, 2014).

Rutherford, Janet (ed.), *Benedict XVI and Beauty in Sacred Music* (Dublin: Four Courts Press, 2012).

Ryan, Marie-Laure, *Narrative as Virtual Reality 2: Revisiting Immersion and Interactivity in Literature and Electronic Media* (Baltimore, MD: Johns Hopkins University Press, 2015).

Samson, Jim, *Music in Transition: A Study of Tonal Expansion and Atonality, 1900–1920* (New York and Oxford: Oxford University Press, 1977).

Savran, George W., *Encountering the Divine: Theophany in Biblical Narrative* (London: T&T Clark, 2005).

—, 'Theophany as Type Scene', *Prooftexts*, 23 (2003), 119–49.

Scarry, Elaine, *On Beauty and Being Just* (Princeton, NJ: Princeton University, 1999).

Schaefer, Edward, *Catholic Music through the Ages: Balancing the Needs of a Worshipping Church* (Chicago, IL: Hillenbrand Books, 2008).

Schlosser, Marianne, 'Bonaventure: Life and Works', in *A Companion to Bonaventure*, ed. by Jay M. Hammon and others (Leiden and Boston: Brill, 2014), pp. 7–59.

Scholl, Robert, 'The Shock of the Positive: Olivier Messiaen, St. Francis, and Redemption through Modernity', in Begbie and Guthrie (eds.), *Resonant Witness*, pp. 162–89.

Scruton, Roger, *Death Devoted Heart: Sex and the Sacred in Wagner's Tristan and Isolde* (Oxford: Oxford University Press, 2004).

Shepherd, John, 'How Music Works — Beyond the Immanent and the Arbitrary: An Essay Review of *Music in Everyday Life*', *Action, Criticism, and Theory for Music Education*, 1 (2002), 1–18.

Slivniak, Dmitri M., 'Our God(s) is One: Biblical and the Indeterminacy of Meaning', *Scandinavian Journal of the Old Testament*, 19.1 (2005), 3–23 https://doi.org/10.1080/09018320510032411

Small, Christopher, *Musicking: The Meanings of Performing and Listening* (Middletown, CT: Wesleyan University Press, 1998).

Smalley, Beryl, *The Study of the Bible in the Middle Ages* (Oxford: Blackwell, 1952).

Snyder, Kerala J., *The Organ as a Mirror of Its Time: North European Reflections, 1610–2000* (Oxford: Oxford University Press, 2002).

Staves, Susan, 'Jephtha's Vow Reconsidered', *Huntington Library Quarterly*, 71 (December 2008), 651–69.

Steiner, George, *Real Presences* (London: Faber & Faber, 1989).

Stoltzfus, Philip, *Theology as Performance: Music, Aesthetics and God in Western Thought* (New York: Continuum, 2006).

Strimple, Nick, 'Choral Music in the Twentieth and Early Twenty-first Centuries', in *The Cambridge Companion to Choral Music*, ed. by André de Quadros (Cambridge: Cambridge University Press, 2012), pp. 43–60.

Strong, James, *Strong's Exhaustive Concordance of the Bible: Updated and Expanded Edition* (Peabody, MA: Hendrickson Publishers, 2007).

Stuart, Douglas K., *Exodus*, New American Commentary (Nashville: B&H Publishing Group, 2006).

Sutherland, Ian, and Sophia Krzys Acord, 'Thinking with Art: From Situated Knowledge to Experiential Knowing', *Journal of Visual Art Practice*, 6 (2007), 125–40.

Swain, Joseph, *Sacred Treasure: Understanding Catholic Liturgical Music* (Collegeville, MN: Liturgical Press, 2012).

Sweeney, Conor, *Sacramental Presence after Heidegger: Onto-Theology, Sacraments, and the Mother's Smile* (Eugene, OR: Cascade Books, 2015).

Sweeney, Marvin A., *I & II Kings: A Commentary* (Louisville, Ken.: Westminster John Knox Press, 2013).

Symmons Roberts, Michael, 'Author's Note' and 'Study for the World's Body', in Begbie (ed.), *Sounding the Depths*, pp. 39–40.

—, 'Contemporary Poetry and Belief', in *The Oxford Handbook of Contemporary British and Irish Poetry*, ed. by Peter Robinson (Oxford: Oxford University Press, 2013), pp. 694–706.

—, 'Freeing the Waters: Poetry in a Parched Culture', in *Necessary Steps: Poetry, Elegy, Walking, Spirit*, ed. by David Kennedy (Exeter: Shearsman Books, 2007), pp. 124–31.

Taruskin, Richard, *The Oxford History of Western Music*, 5 vols. (Oxford: Oxford University Press, 2010).

Tatarkiewicz, Wladyslaw, 'The Great Theory of Beauty and its Decline', *The Journal of Aesthetics and Art Criticism*, 31 (Winter 1972), 165–80.

Tavener, John, and Mother Thelka, *Ikons: Meditations in Words and Music* (London: HarperCollins, 1994).

Theobald, Elizabeth Louise, 'Music in Roman Catholic Liturgies in England and Wales since Vatican II' (unpublished doctoral thesis, University of Southampton, 1997).

Thomas, Martin, *English Cathedral Music and Liturgy in the Twentieth Century* (Abingdon and New York: Routledge, 2016).

Torff, Bruce, and Howard Gardner, 'Conceptual and Experiential Cognition in Music', *The Journal of Aesthetic Education*, 33.4 (1999), 93–106.

Turner, Bryan S., 'Religion in a Post-Secular Society', in *The New Blackwell Companion to the Sociology of Religion*, ed. by Bryan S. Turner (Chichester: Wiley Blackwell, 2010), pp. 649–67.

Turner, Steve, *Imagine: A Vision for Christians in the Arts* (Downers Grove, IL: Intervarsity Press, 2001).

Vattimo, Gianni, *Belief*, trans. by Luca D'Isanto and David Webb (Stanford, CA: Stanford University Press, 1999).

Very, Jones, 'Jacob Wrestling with the Angel', in *Chapters into Verse: Poetry in English Inspired by the Bible*, ed. by Robert Atwan and Laurance Wieder, 2 vols. (Oxford: Oxford University Press, 1993).

Von Heijne, Camilla Hélena, *The Messenger of the Lord in Early Jewish Interpretations of Genesis*, Beihefte Zur Zeitschrift Für Die Alttestamentliche Wissenschaft, Bd. 412 (Berlin: Walter De Gruyter, 2010).

Von Rad, Gerhard, *Genesis: A Commentary* (London: SCM, 1972).

Walsh, Jerome. T., 'Genesis 2:4b-3:23: A Synchronic Approach', *Journal of Biblical Literature*, 96 (1977), 161–77.

—, and Christopher T. Begg, '1-2 Kings', in *The Jerome Biblical Commentary*, ed. by Raymond Edward Brown et al. (Dallas, TX: CDWord Library, 1989).

—, and David W. Cotter, *1 Kings* (Collegeville, Minn.: Liturgical Press, 1996).

Waltke, Bruce K., *The Book of Proverbs, Chapters 1-15* (Grand Rapids, MI: Eerdmans, 2004).

—, with Cathi J. Fredricks, *Genesis: A Commentary* (Grand Rapids, MI: Zondervan, 2001).

—, with Charles Yu, *An Old Testament Theology: An Exegetical, Canonical, and Thematic Approach* (Grand Rapids, MI: Zondervan, 2007).

Ward, Graham, *Unbelievable: Why We Believe and Why We Don't* (London: I.B. Tauris, 2014).

Webster, James, *Haydn's 'Farewell' Symphony and the Idea of Classical Style: Through Composition and Cyclic Introduction in His Instrumental Music* (Cambridge: Cambridge University Press, 1991).

Wenham, Gordon J., *Genesis 16-50*, Word Biblical Commentary (Waco, TX: Word Books, 1994).

Wilcox, Hui Niu, 'Embodied Ways of Knowing, Pedagogies, and Social Justice: Inclusive Science and Beyond', *NWSA Journal*, 21 (2009), 104–20.

Williams, James G., 'The Beautiful and the Barren: Conventions in Biblical Type-Scenes', *JSOT*, 17 (1980), 107–19.

Williams, Rowan, 'Making it Strange: Theology in Other(s') Words', in Begbie (ed.), *Sounding the Depths*, pp. 19–32.

Wood, Irving, 'Folk-Tales in Old Testament Narrative', *Journal of Biblical Literature*, 28 (1909), 34–41.

Zakovitch, Yair, 'Inner-Biblical Interpretation', in *Reading Genesis: Ten Methods,* ed. by Ronald Hendel (Cambridge: Cambridge University Press, 2011), pp. 92–118.

Video and CD Recording

Boos, David, 'TheoArtistry: Theologians and Composers in Creative Collaboration', 20.53, https://www.youtube.com/watch?v=U2NoaJHcp2E

—, 'The Power of the Arts to Communicate the Divine: TheoArtistry at St Andrews', 3.49, https://www.youtube.com/watch?v=Ow5sumd_DrI

St Salvator's Chapel Choir, *Annunciations: Sacred Music for the 21st Century,* St Salvator's Chapel Choir and Sean Heath, cond. by Tom Wilkinson (Sanctiandree, SAND0006, 2018), http://stsalvatorschapelchoir.wp.st-andrews.ac.uk/recordings/

This book need not end here...

Share

All our books—including the one you have just read—are free to access online so that students, researchers and members of the public who can't afford a printed edition will have access to the same ideas. This title will be accessed online by hundreds of readers each month across the globe: why not share the link so that someone you know is one of them?

This book and additional content is available at:
https://doi.org/10.11647/OBP.0172

Customise

Personalise your copy of this book or design new books using OBP and third-party material. Take chapters or whole books from our published list and make a special edition, a new anthology or an illuminating coursepack. Each customised edition will be produced as a paperback and a downloadable PDF.

Find out more at:
https://www.openbookpublishers.com/section/59/1

Like Open Book Publishers

Follow @OpenBookPublish

Read more at the Open Book Publishers BLOG

You may also be interested in:

The Sword of Judith
Judith Studies Across the Disciplines
*Edited by Kevin R. Brine, Elena Ciletti
and Henrike Lähnemann*

https://doi.org/10.11647/OBP.0009

Beyond Holy Russia
The Life and Times of Stephen Graham
Edited by Michael Hughes

https://doi.org/10.11647/OBP.0040

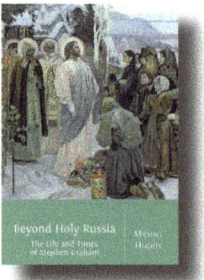

Tellings and Texts
Music, Literature and Performance in North India
Edited by Francesca Orsini and Katherine Butler Schofield

https://doi.org/10.11647/OBP.0062

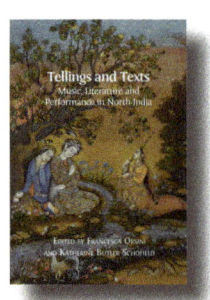

God's Babies
Natalism and Bible Interpretation in Modern America
John McKeown

https://doi.org/10.11647/OBP.0048

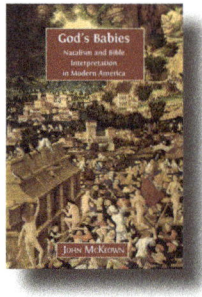

Lightning Source UK Ltd.
Milton Keynes UK
UKHW052200300419
341873UK00001B/1/P